DRESSING RENAISSANCE FLORENCE

CAROLE COLLIER FRICK

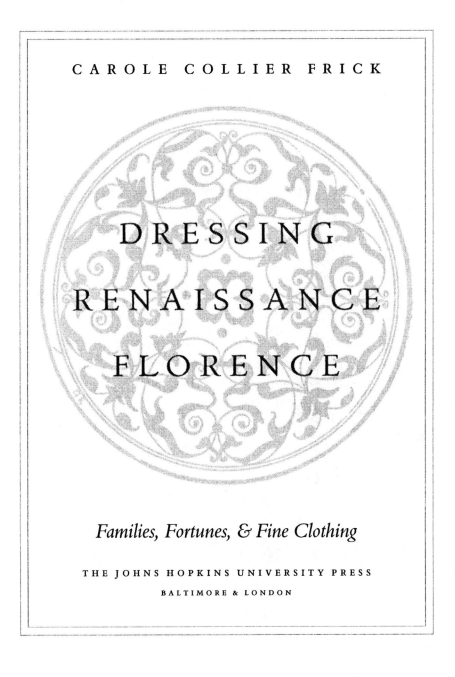

DRESSING RENAISSANCE FLORENCE

Families, Fortunes, & Fine Clothing

THE JOHNS HOPKINS UNIVERSITY PRESS

BALTIMORE & LONDON

© 2002 The Johns Hopkins University Press

All rights reserved. Published 2002

Printed in the United States of America on acid-free paper

Johns Hopkins Paperbacks edition, 2005

2 4 6 8 9 7 5 3 1

The Johns Hopkins University Press

2715 North Charles Street

Baltimore, Maryland 21218–4363

www.press.jhu.edu

Frontispiece: Giovanna degli Albizzi, in pink and gold dress.

Detail from Ghirlandaio, *Birth of John the Baptist* (1486–90).

Tornabuoni Chapel, Santa Maria Novella, Florence.

The Library of Congress has cataloged the hardcover edition of this book as follows:

Frick, Carole Collier.

Dressing Renaissance Florence : families, fortunes, and fine clothing / Carole Collier Frick.

p.　　cm. — (The Johns Hopkins studies in historical and political science; ser. 120, no. 3)

Includes bibliographical references and index.

ISBN 0-8018-6939-0 (hardcover: alk. paper)

1. Clothing trade—Italy—Florence—History—To 1500. 2. Tailoring—Italy—

Florence—History—To 1500. 3. Costume—Italy—Florence—History—15th century.

4. Florence (Italy)—Social life and customs. I. Title.

TT496.182 F574 2002

391′.02′09455109024—dc21

2001006217

ISBN 0-8018-8264-8 (pbk.: alk.paper)

A catalog record for this book is available from the British Library.

To Ann and Bob

Contents

Illustrations and Tables

xi

TABLES

Acknowledgments

IT IS MY PLEASURE to acknowledge and thank all those who have contributed to the research and writing of this book, and without whom it would not have come to fruition. Lauro Martines first suggested the topic of clothing to me in a seminar at the University of California–Los Angeles and has always been encouraging, helpful, and unfailingly supportive of my endeavors. His enthusiasm and energy for writing and historical inquiry continues to be inspirational. I am also indebted to Betsy Perry, for her kindness and understanding at an early juncture. Gene Brucker, David Herlihy, and Judith Brown all generously shared their knowledge of the possibilities and pitfalls of such a potentially vast project at the outset.

In Florence, Anthony Molho and Christiane Klapisch-Zuber kindly pointed me to promising sources in the archives and manuscript libraries there, and the staffs of the Archivio di Stato di Firenze, Biblioteca Laurenziana, Kunsthistorische, Biblioteca Nazionale, the library of the Villa I Tatti, and the Archivio Datini in Prato were always most professional and helpful. Without the expertise and friendship of fiorentino Gino Corti, the erudition and joie de vivre of fellow researcher Rebecca Emigh, and the hospitality of the Budini-Gattai family and Joyce Treble during the early stages of this project, my time in Florence would not have been as rich or interesting as it was.

I would also like to express my gratitude to Joanna Woods-Marsden, Christiane Klapisch-Zuber, and Lauro Martines, for their specific comments and editorial advice on portions of the manuscript, as well as to the anonymous readers for the Johns Hopkins University Press, for their opinions and expertise. Dale Kent, Patricia Simons and Jean Cadogan were also all very generous with their attention and resources. To my editor Henry Tom and to Peter Dreyer my copyeditor, I thank you for your enthusiasm for this project, as well as for your attention to form and to detail.

At Southern Illinois University, I have had assistance from many. Fiorentina Patrizia Bittini lent her language expertise to this endeavor, and to her, as well as to Shannon Waters and Laura Million, who worked on the illustrations, and Rick Bunch and Wendy Shaw, who helped create the map, I am indebted. To my wonderful colleagues and students in the Department of Historical Studies, mille grazie for your enthusiastic camaraderie.

I also want to recognize the valuable support that I have received for this project from both the Edward A. Dickson Foundation and the Ahmanson Foundation. In addition, the Graduate School and College of Arts and Sciences at SIUE have provided me with the sustenance necessary to be able to complete this sustained historical project.

Finally, to my husband Arthur, thank you for your love and astute critical judgement, and to Fay and my sisters Robbi and Cynthia, my gratitude for your feminine spirit and strength. Arthur Andrew and Lucien, you should know that without your patience and an understanding of what your mother does, this book would have been impossible. You are both my continual inspiration.

DRESSING RENAISSANCE FLORENCE

INTRODUCTION

Strip us totally nude and you would see us as equal; reclothe us in your dress
and you in ours, and we would, without a doubt, seem noble and you base;
because only poverty or riches makes us unequal.
—The Ciompi, quoted in Niccolò Machiavelli, *Le istorie fiorentine*

. . . and in the presence of his entire company and all others present, he had her stripped
naked and the garments he had had prepared for her brought forward; then he immediately had her dress and put on her shoes, and upon her hair—as disheveled as it was—
he had a crown placed. . . . The young bride seemed to have changed her soul and ways
along with her garments: . . . so that she seemed to be not the shepherdess daughter
of Giannucolo but rather the daughter of some noble lord.
—The story of the Patient Griselda, in Boccaccio, *The Decameron*

Clothing as a metaphor for the dream (or nightmare) of transforma-
tion was central to the society of Renaissance Florence from Boccaccio to Machiavelli. Its citizens wrestled daily with self-identity,
appearance, and display, and it is in this combative arena that my study lies.
Florentine clothing, its meaning, its making, and its wearing, has occupied
me for the past few years, as I have rummaged through *ricordanze* and *statuti*
from the fifteenth century looking at records of people's personal wardrobes
and trying to figure out, not only what people wore, but also why they wore
it, who the people were that made it for them, and what it all meant.

When the rich Florentine widower Francesco di Matteo Castellani decided to marry Lena, the daughter of Francesco Alamanni, on November 13,
1448, a beautiful new gown for his bride was in order. She was to be his
second wife, in a marriage shepherded into being by Cosimo de' Medici,
pater patriae of Florence, fourteen years after he regained power in the city.

Her dowry had been negotiated by Francesco de Ventura, a relative of the Castellani house.[1] Ginevra Strozzi, his first wife and daughter of Palla Strozzi, had died a few years earlier, but even for his second marriage, Francesco spared no expense in commissioning a crimson cut-velvet overgown, "una cioppa d'alto e basso chermisi."[2] This gown formed part of his wedding gift to his bride, the so-called "counter-trousseau," and many family members, friends, and associates were involved in its creation.

The process was complex. First of all, after the materials were assembled (overseen undoubtedly by Francesco himself), the crimson cioppa was fashioned of the finest quality cut-and-figured silk velvet cloth by the tailor, Andrea da Bibbiena, who also worked for other families of the Florentine ruling class. What was *usual* about the making of this cioppa is that it was a project of great concern and interest to the family, as were all pieces of clothing for which there was a public occasion, especially a wedding. Typically, in fifteenth-century Florence, many family members were involved and avidly interested in the making of an important garment. With Lena Alamanni's cioppa, included in its making were, not only Francesco's kinsmen, but also a relative from Lena's natal family. By the time the story had come to a close (some eight years after it first began), members of both the Castellani and Alamanni houses had been party to this family undertaking, family friends had been consulted, and the tailor, three embroiderers, a dyer, and the esteemed poet Luigi Pulci had all given their advice—a total of at least a dozen men concerned with one dress. Members of rich families were preoccupied with creating a magnificent outfit for a specific bridal display, and there were many choices to be made regarding these clothes. The complicated, laborious process by which garments were commissioned and made required the direct involvement of the paterfamilias to make the final decisions. What was *unusual* about the making of this particular gown is that it is doubtful whether Lena ever saw her dress, much less wore it as a bride

In spite of Anne Hollander's cautionary observation that clothing may, in fact, be "mentally indigestible" as a serious human phenomenon, I wanted to make sense of all this.[3] I have been curious about the specifics. How many clothes did people actually own? How much did this all cost? Why were clothes so important to these people, so elaborate, and why did they keep such fastidious records of everything? How did it all work in republican

Florence, with an economy founded on fortunes in cloth, a city where ascent into the ruling circles was possible for a "new man" with the right marriage, a little *fortuna*, and the right clothes? Florence had no court, no prince; rather, it was a city full of rich textile merchants and bankers, who exported their most exotic cut-and-figured silk velvets and brocades to the harems of Turkey—silks with names like "pink sapphire" (*rosa di zaffrone*), "Apollo's hair" (*capel d'Apollo*), "throat of the dove" (*gorgia di piccione*), and "peach blossom" (*fior di pesco*). Paradoxically, Florence was a place where the wearing of its own finest garments was prohibited, because the Commune continually passed sumptuary legislation that restricted vestimentary display.[4]

Florentine men attempted to be visually frank, eschewing foppish ornament for plain, classical-looking garments of luxurious fabric, which was eloquent testimony to the fact that everyone, from *sottoposti* (laborer) to magnate, knew cloth and could easily evaluate the worth of its wearer. As they said, "Cloth and color makes an honorable man."[5] This belief undoubtedly motivated Cosimo de' Medici to provide the famously scruffy Donatello with crimson clothing suitable to such an illustrious artist, and explained why he was upset when Donatello eschewed his offering.[6] Humanists toyed with the most radical of notions. "Strip us totally nude and you would see us as equal," the lowest-tier laborers of the wool industry (the Ciompi) say in Machiavelli's *Florentine Histories*.[7] Given upper-class unease about the Florentine populace and the transformational power of clothing, it is no surprise that clear codes were deemed important.[8]

The rich attempted to make the rules very clear. Florentine artists like Domenico Ghirlandaio, who worked for wealthy patrons producing portraits in religious frescoes for private family chapels, represented the women of the city's elite in brocades and voided velvets embroidered over with pearls, with silver tinsel and gilded ornaments, richly ribboned and padded sleeves, and often luxurious trains, lined and bordered with fur. The frontispiece shows Giovanna degli Albizzi in formal dress in a detail from Ghirlandaio's *Birth of John the Baptist* (1486–90) in the Tornabuoni Chapel, Santa Maria Novella, Florence. This woman looks out at the viewer from within a painted religious scene, self-consciously posed and composed in her most elaborate public gown. She is the visual embodiment of familial honor, dressed to the nines. Diane Owen Hughes has written that expensive clothing had lost its meaning as a mark of concupiscence in the fifteenth century, and that such clothing became a mark of virtue, respectability, and honor, denied to Jews, prostitutes, and people of the lower classes.[9] The Patient Griselda in Boccaccio's *Decameron* is transformed by her new clothes.

Certain scholars of the period have recently located the advent of consumerism and conspicuous consumption, along with the development of material culture, in Renaissance Florence. Richard Goldthwaite opened this line of study with his work on the growth in the construction trade in fourteenth- and fifteenth-century Florence, spurred by the tastes and ambitions of the rich for private palatial homes.[10] He then broadened his approach with a study on the consumer demand for artwork and its impact on the art itself, serving to elucidate the socioeconomic milieu in which Botticelli, Brunelleschi, and Masaccio worked and the Medici ruled; where rich customers publicly demonstrated their social prestige by patronizing recognized artists.[11] Anthony Molho's work on the unique institution of the Monte delle doti has shown the struggle of the city to bolster communal finances by simultaneously regulating display and providing ever-increasing dowry sums to accommodate what he terms the increasing "aristocratization" of Florentine society.[12] While these studies have contributed to our understanding of escalating demands for display among the elite, as well as the "world of goods" that were now being produced and made available, no one has as yet looked at how much money these people spent on their clothes. If, in fact, the clothing industry was as thriving an economic sector as the artwork from the period would indicate, there would surely be evidence of the motives at work in the commissioning and wearing of these most personal statements of one's social standing.

By concentrating this study on clothes (the buying and commissioning of clothing, its fabrication, purpose, use, portrayal in art, resale, auctioning, and pawning), I hope to shed light on the nature of this commercial marketplace, the motivations of the elite who patronized it, and the relationship between the craftspeople and their customers. This book attempts to better understand the society of this fifteenth-century city, not by focusing on a particular event or group of people, but instead by investigating a node of common concern among them, that is, their clothes. I am interested in the irony that the *making* of clothing functioned to unite people across class lines, while at the same time the clothes themselves were manipulated to amplify the distinction between those classes.

Perhaps as an instinctive corrective to Burckhardt's nineteenth-century vision of Renaissance society that left out entire segments of the population (in fact, the majority), historians of Renaissance Florence have studied the Revolt of the Ciompi for a hundred years now.[13] The revolt of the sottoposti of the wool guild in 1378 provided scholars with a defined rip in the social fabric; an opening by which to investigate a cohesive group and their relationship to the *classe dirigente*.[14] This opportunity included an inherent problem. The majority of the sottoposti that it shed light on were at one end of the socioeconomic spectrum, while the merchant elite for whom they worked were at the other. By looking at the poles of fifteenth-century Florentine society, we primarily saw polarization. These investigations began in Florentine studies just fifty years after Marx and excluded women almost entirely.[15]

What of those in the middle, in between these two extremes? Was there, in fact, any "middle," or were there simply two distinct "cities" of people within the rings of walls in Florence, with the rich in the center and poor at the margins?[16] Christiane Klapisch-Zuber has written that the workers of the Ciompi did not so much "choose" work as simply take a job, any job, out of desperate need.[17] But between the sottoposti who labored in the cloth industry, on the one hand, and the very rich magnates, international bankers, and the merchants of wool and silk, on the other, were there artisans who lived their lives and practiced their occupations under different circumstances? What of those occupations that produced a finished personal product, such as the artisans in the needle trades and ancillary crafts: tailors, doublet makers, furriers, goldsmiths, designers, belt makers, shoemakers, purse makers, hatmakers, embroiderers; those whose crafts provided the goods bought by the Florentines themselves for their own personal display? Could this be part of a "new middling class" that one historian has noted?[18]

In this book, I highlight one key group of these artisans in the clothing process, the tailors, who have not as yet been the focus of study. I would argue that the tailors were typical of those artisans who provided a kind of link between rich and poor, who, by necessity, had intimate dealings with their social "betters." In a letter between two notaries in the employ of the Medici, one, acting as family ambassador to Siena, refers to a tailor as "your friend and mine."[19] Picture, if you will, a fifteenth-century scenario. It is decided that the nubile daughter of an elite family needs a dress for an important public occasion. A tailor is called in. To where does he come? Who else is there? Who *is* he? Is it a *she?* Measurements need to be taken. The tailor needs to touch the body of the young woman. His (or her) person (and hands) would need a certain level of propriety. How did this all work in a society that has been characterized as increasingly polarized? How was this organized, and was the tailor simply "in the pocket" of the rich for whom he worked?

This book, then, examines this process through written description and artistic representation. My goal here has been to slice vertically through the rich layers of Florentine society to better understand issues of class relations, identity, and the honorable self-representation of the elite by studying the complexity of just getting dressed.[20]

THE APPROACH

By necessity, I have brought together areas of inquiry that encompass widely disparate historical traditions. My base has been the richness of contemporary scholarship on Renaissance Florence, which not only includes social and economic studies but has been refigured to address questions of gender and class relations, sumptuary legislation, women and work, and the nature and place of the laboring classes. This study owes much to the pioneering work of Klapisch-Zuber, above all.[21] A new melding of socioeconomic concerns with cultural issues such as Renaissance art has given the historian of clothes a rich palette with which to work. In the 1990s, expanded investigations of the role of clothing manufacture in the early modern economy have resulted in a better understanding of the importance of clothing in a broad cultural context.[22]

History of Costume | In addition to historical studies of Florence, the work of historians of dress and costume has been central to this project. This field of inquiry has been built to a large extent on a necessarily uncertain visual foundation, using Renaissance paintings and fashion books as transparent texts; seeing historical images as clothing "illustrations."[23] The difficulty is the inability to lay hands on any real Renaissance clothes, the actual garments not having survived to the present day (for the most part). Historians have therefore looked to ancillary sources, either images of the clothes or written sources about them. Here, they confronted the challenge of matching the garment type and color named in one document or shown in one artifact, with that of another. This line of scholarship is perhaps best illustrated for Italian costume studies by Egidia Polidori-Calamandrei's early *Le vesti delle donne fiorentine nel Quattrocento,* followed by many others in the same vein, until the first breakthrough in costume studies, Elizabeth Birbari's *Dress in Italian Painting, 1460–1500,* which attempted to make a direct connection between the clothing depicted in paintings and the clothes themselves; using painted clothes to date paintings and recreate costumes.[24] A generation ago, history of costume began making systematic use of primary evidence. Jacqueline Herald's valuable *Renaissance Dress in Italy, 1400–1500* used not only visual images but written sources such as clothing inventories, which further elucidated the range of clothing in the Renaissance wardrobe.[25]

Clothes and Human Society | And finally, I have looked at the literary theme of clothes and human society, which is as old as *Cinderella,* and includes Thomas Carlyle's satire *Sartor Resartus* (1833–34), Hans Christian Anderson's *The Emperor's New Clothes* (1837), and Mark Twain's *The Prince and the Pauper* (1881), each which examined the notion of the transformational possibilities of clothes. Whether fairy tale or novel, they all struggled with what it meant to be clothed or unclothed, what clothing indicated about the wearer and the society that created it, and what constituted "fashion." Caroline Walker Bynum, speaking on metamorphosis in the Western tradition, has identified clothing as "the mark of civilization," that which shows us to be civilized human beings.[26] For the twentieth century, new studies of dress emerged, with Georg Simmel's early *Philosophie der Mode,* Frank Alvah Parsons's *The Psychology of Dress,* Quentin Bell's *On Human Finery,* and James Laver's many contributions, ranging from the 1930s through the 1960s.[27] Others have studied the meanings of shape, volume, color, and gendered differences in clothing.[28]

In the mid 1960s, building on the new field of semiology, pioneered by Ferdinand de Saussure, Roland Barthes tackled the challenges of interpreting the tangible objects of material culture as represented in language and pictures.[29] His work in semiotics attempted to develop a structure for understanding this "mentally indigestible" subject of clothes. Applying Saussure's earlier work on the elements of *langue et parole* to the garment system, Barthes saw the realm of clothing as a contained sign system of its own; as a vocabulary with which one could sartorially "speak." For Barthes, the *langue*, or language, of clothing was the way a garment is made; its construction, fabric, color, and surface decoration. The *parole*, or speech, of clothing was either the way one wore one's clothing—the choices made in putting elements together—or the garment chosen for a particular circumstance or event.[30]

Barthes tailored Saussure's structural model specifically to the twentieth-century world of contemporary fashion, further dividing the "fashion system" into three elements: the "technologic," or actual garment; the "iconic," or image of the garment; and the "verbal," or written description of the garment accompanying the photograph.[31] But we can read these three elements for the clothes of the Renaissance as well. The overarching realm for Barthes was the verbal, or written, realm of clothes. He argued that in the modern world, *writing* about clothes creates the imagined space in which fashion resides ("a slim linen dress for morning," "a broad-brimmed hat for an afternoon garden party"); further, that the medium of writing makes the connection between individuals participating and communicating visually with each other in the fashion "game." This written medium creates an associative mental realm of fashionable clothes, which then are purchased and worn by the readers of fashion magazines to manifest these associations. Their audience, of course, becomes *other* readers of the same magazines and runway shows who are able to conjure up this common referential construct. All others are left out of the esoteric world of fashion, at least as defined by the corporate and moneyed participants in the fashion world.[32] In addition to Barthes's basic contributions to the analysis of material culture, the work of Veblen, Hollander, and Alison Lurie has certainly illuminated the complexity of this most culturally embedded of subjects.[33]

PREVIEW OF THE CHAPTERS

Part I | It is in the midst of these many disparate and yet related discourses that this book lies. Chapter 1 attempts to establish the place of the primary makers of clothing, the tailors (*sarti*), in a discussion of the economic structure of the Florentine guild system over time. Their place in the world of work and their problematic changing guild associations are taken up in the first chapter, as are the physical locations of the guild headquarters and *botteghe* in the neighborhood streets of the old city districts. Chapter 2 shifts to the specialty craftspeople who worked alongside the tailors, and whose shops comprised the bulk of the Quattrocento marketplace. These artisans were part of the fifteenth-century "rag trade" who worked under the jurisdiction of the guilds—the doublet makers, hatters, slipper and shoemakers, furriers, jewelers, and hosiers—and also the craftspeople who worked outside of the formal structure; those who contributed the making of undergarments, personal linens, and embroidery from the family home or behind convent walls. The marginals are treated too, looking at the place of used-clothes dealers, peripatetic vendors, and workers who barely made their living "day to day like little birds."[34] Chapter 3 then refocuses on tailors in the fifteenth century and investigates questions of class relationships and linkages of patronage between artisans and their clientele—the merchant guildsmen and patricians for whom they worked. Some contemporaries feared the tailors were in league with their wealthy patrons, making "silk purses out of sows' ears" and getting rich themselves in the process. Did they?

Part II | Chapter 4 moves to the other side, taking up the rich families who purchased and wore the clothes made by the artisan tailors and craftspeople. What were their motives in creating ever-increasing luxury; why this obsession with clothes? Who commissioned and controlled clothing choices? The notions of "honor" and societal place are examined by looking at occasions that called for the hiring of tailors, the involvement of family members in clothing projects, and the eventual disposition of the clothes when the occasion for which they had been made had passed. Chapter 5 then confronts the issue of costs, prices, and family fortunes, looking at exactly how much was expended by rich families in florins and soldi on their own display. Here I also examine how many clothes people owned, and what percentage of their total wealth was locked up in clothes closets and chests. Chapter 6 gives specific instances of this conspicuous consumption as it related to marriage alliances and dowries, tracing the coming into being of three wedding outfits to record the concerns and tensions involved in making a dress, a cloak, a headdress. Continuing with consumption, chapter 7 takes up the fashioning of two sisters' very different trousseaux. The multiple meanings and implications of the first, for a public wedding, and the second, for entering the private realm of a convent, are both included here.

Part III | Finally, beginning with chapter 8, we move from artisans and customers, to the products themselves and how the Commune dealt with them. Chapter 8 details the clothing; what pieces made up an outfit, how outfits differed for men, women, and children and from class to class. I also examine what Renaissance Florentines themselves called various garments and what colors, fabrics and design elements were popular. Further, and perhaps more basically, I ask how we think we *know* any of this. Here, I investigate the difficulties of interpreting not only the written but also the visual evidence. Chapter 9 then looks at the issue of the policing of these clothes, the sumptuary legislation. Having created and fully articulated glorious outfits, *could* anyone, *did* anyone, actually *wear* them in Florence? What was the relationship between sumptuary restrictions and the advent of fashion; between controls on "honorable" women's dress and those considered less than honorable? The way in which this Commune gingerly policed its own cultural practices of sumptuous dress and conspicuous consumption is explored. And, finally, chapter 10 concludes with an interpretive essay on the depiction of contemporary clothing in Florentine art, using the work of Domenico Ghirlandaio. In his family chapel portraits, each member of the citizenry portrayed served to reinforce a particular vision of the Florentine republican utopia, dressed to the hilt. In this last chapter, I argue that there is no visual source from the Renaissance that can be thought of as a mere clothing "illustration" through which we are able to clearly "see" the dress of the past. We *see* just what the Florentines wanted us to see. What we are able to *read,* however, does help inform us about their societal obsession with clothes.

Why is Florentine Renaissance clothing important as a topic for serious historical inquiry? I would argue that we have imbibed the "look" of an increasingly elite Florence, not only the architecture, urban planning, philosophy, music, and literature, but, above all, the citizens' depictions of *themselves.* The visual legacy of this particular city has been one of the most influential aspects of Renaissance culture for subsequent generations, up until our own day. I believe that examining the process of clothing this Renaissance city enables us better to understand what drove its traditional society, in which historians have often been disappointed not to find our twentieth-century values of republicanism and modernism.[35]

I

GUILDS AND LABOR

TAILORS AND
THE GUILD SYSTEM

W ho were the craftspeople who made the clothes for the elite of Renaissance Florence and what do we know about them? Were they part of the popolo minuto, the "fluid and amorphous" poor that formed the mass of the Florentine population, the so-called "men who were born yesterday," or were they competent and respected guildsmen, part of those whom Villani identified as "great men of good works and reputation, who worked in manufacturing and trade"?[1] The physical setting in which the tailors had their spartan botteghe and practiced their expertise, their assistants at work sitting on the floor of the shop on a piece of carpet, legs folded "tailor-style" and hunched over a lapful of fabric and thread, was complex and diverse.

Formally, the tailors of Florence worked within and around the guild system in which rich merchants and bankers topped a socioeconomic hierarchy structured by twenty-one guilds. The height of guild republicanism, with an estimated 7,000 to 8,000 matriculated members participating in government, had passed by the end of the fourteenth century.[2] In the fifteenth century, the duties, rights, and privileges of major and minor guildsmen, not to mention those left out of the guilds altogether, ranged widely from full power to complete exclusion.[3] The earliest mention specifically of a tailor in Florence comes from the year 1032, noting the physical location of a shop, "Casa

Florentii Sarti."[4] Within the reality of the guild structure of the city, however, the location and status of a tailor were much more ephemeral. Not actually producing a product from scratch, not simply providing a service, and by physical necessity, not being an anonymous artisan to his or her client, a tailor combined product with attentive intimacy, thus occupying a unique and somewhat problematic position in the Renaissance world of work.

In Florence, real fortunes were made not necessarily in manufacturing fabric but in the selling of locally finished and dyed foreign cloth on the international luxury market. There was a strict hierarchy among occupations, professions, and trades based upon the guild affiliation or lack thereof, such affiliation reflecting the importance of that sector within the city's export market. From at least the tenth century on, Florence had been a cloth town. The Arte della lana, or wool guild, had organized that growing Florentine industry, active at least as early as the eleventh century, into a corporate trade association. In this city, every successful cloth merchant certainly had available to him an inventory of cloth, of perhaps excellent or even exceptional quality.[5] This would have been a valuable part of the goods of the family business, and its owner undoubtedly would want control over its use as garments for himself and his family, in terms of style and cut.[6] And so, who did these men hire to cut their cloth into garments, and how much was this *cucitore* paid?[7] Herein lay the difficulty for tailors in a textile town. Authority over products made with that cloth, especially garments produced for the personal use of the merchant elite, was not relinquished lightly. So as not to lose control over the precious commodity that had made so many families rich, strict regulations were imposed on cutters of cloth and stitchers of garments. In Florence, male cutters and stitchers quickly gained precedence over female cutters and stitchers in work with expensive cloth, but those same male cutters were subjected to close scrutiny by the men who had hired them, men who were their social betters and whose own companies often supplied the very cloth the tailors were to use in fashioning their all-important clothes.[8]

GUILD LOCATIONS

The means of regulating those who made the clothing for the elite lay in the guild system of Florence.[9] Wedged in between the shops were the headquarters of the various guilds, which located themselves in *palazzi* on main thoroughfares or narrow side streets, off tiny *piazze,* and not uncommonly up above the retail or wholesale shops that dealt in the products under their control. The major guilds, or *arti maggiori*, were in the center of the medieval city. The Arte della lana was the oldest in the city and had positioned itself at the very commercial hub, directly across from the old grain market of Orsan-michele. It was located at the site of the ancient Palazzo de' Compiobbesi. Mixing cloth processing with marketing, numerous wool-fulling mills and six large stretching grounds and sheds were flung across the city center.[10] The chronicler Benedetto Dei wrote that wool botteghe themselves, some 270 strong, could be found literally all over Florence (see map).[11]

Another of the oldest guilds, the Arte dei vaiai e pellicciai (guild of furriers and skinners), mentioned in documents from 1197, was located near the Mercato Vecchio and the Via Lambertesca, in the environs of great Ghibelline families such as the Lamberti, Toschi, Cipriani, Palermini, Cosi, Erri, Pilli, and others. The grand shops, *i negozi bellissimi,* of the furriers, fronted the street bearing their name, the Via Pellicceria, where the post office is now, from the Piazza della Parte Guelfa to the Mercato Vecchio.[12] A few blocks away, branching off Via Lambertesca, on the narrow Chiasso Baroncelli and ending in the Piazza della Signoria, was the headquarters of the shoemakers, the Arte dei calzolai, one of the minor guilds. Shoe shops were found throughout the central district.[13] The tower of the powerful silk guild, the Arte della seta, housed the consuls of the guild on Via di Capaccio, next door to the Church of Santa Maria sopra la Porta.[14] Silk shops strung themselves out along the Via Vacchereccia, Por Santa Maria, and Via Porta Rossa.[15] The residence of the merchants of the Calimala, the guild that controlled the finishing and marketing of all *panni franchesi*, that is, luxury foreign cloth, was situated on Calimala, which opened onto the Mercato Vecchio (now the Piazza Repubblica), from Via Porta Rossa. The major houses dealing in foreign cloth were also on Calimala.[16]

The guild halls of the other *arti* involved in the "rag trade" were also in the historic center. The Arte dei rigattieri e linaiuoli (guild of used-cloth/clothing and linen merchants) was based at the Piazza di Sant' Andrea near the Mercato Vecchio. Having acquired their residence in 1387, twenty-four years later, in 1411, they would be the first guild to commission Donatello to

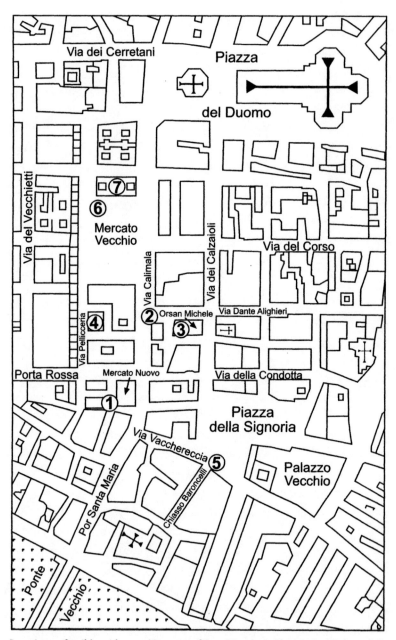

Locations of guild residences (Quarter of San Giovanni, Florence): (1) Arte della seta, (2) Calimala, (3) Arte della lana, (4) Arte dei vaiai e pellicciai, (5) Arte dei calzolai, (6) Arte dei rigattieri e linaiuoli, (7) Arte dei medici, speziali e merciai. *Source:* Adapted from Walther Limburger, *Die Gebäude von Florenz* (Leipzig, 1910).

sculpt a statue of St. Mark, their patron saint, for an exterior niche of Orsan-michele.[17] The botteghe of this second most numerous of clothiers (shoe-makers having first place) were further toward the Duomo, for the most part fronting on Piazza de' Brunelleschi, and along the Via Brunelleschi, orig-inally known as the Via dei Rigattieri, and within what Robert Davidsohn called that "tangle of little streets" near the Mercato Vecchio.[18] Of the 160 heads of household who declared their trade as *rigattieri* in 1427 (including 8 women), 76, that is, almost half of the city's dealers in used clothing and fabric industry remnants, filed their tax declarations (*portate*) from the quarter of San Giovanni.[19] Lastly, the Arte dei medici, speziali e merciai (guild of doc-tors, spice merchants, apothecaries, and shopkeepers) was based in the an-cient tower of the Caponsacchi, also located near S. Andrea across from the Mercato Vecchio, and next door to the Arte del cambio (guild of bankers and money changers).

CHANGING GUILD AFFILIATIONS

The challenge of locating tailors within this system has to do with the gradual evolution of the guilds over time, which charts a struggle for economic and political control of the city. What it does not elucidate in a clear diachronic narrative, however, is the social and economic status of those who were excluded from guild representation, including most tailors and other clothing and accessories makers. Tailors in Florence, unlike tailors in other cities, never had a guild of their own. In Milan, a *corporazione* of weavers, tailors, and dyers existed as early as 1102, and in northern Europe, the first corporate charter for *Schneidern* is noted in Germany in 1152.[20] In thirteenth-century France, *tailleurs de robes* stood at the head of a well-defined hierarchy of clothier guilds, each with its own statutes governing the specific metier.[21] Florentine tailors instead, despite appearing by occupational designation early on in the official records of the city (a tailor among the "good men" recorded in documents between 1089–1141), were only minor members of other guilds.[22] In fact, Davidsohn wrote that among the craftspeople who worked in attire, tailors enjoyed little credit.[23] They were among the unorganized marginal workers of Florence until 1225, individual artisans with no corpo-rate political identity. Even when they did become attached to a guild, tailors were always subordinated to another, more dominant craft and remained in the shadows of those whose occupations were considered primary to the Florentine economy.[24]

The Arte di Por Santa Maria | Tailors' first and only alliance with a guild that was to become one of the major guilds was with the Arte di Por Santa Maria, which organized the retailers of luxury items. The tailors who matriculated into this powerful guild of exotic goods were master sarti who worked primarily in silk-based cloth (brocade, velvet, taffeta, and silks with a metallic wound weft of gold or silver).[25] In the first matriculation list for the guild in 1225, seven tailors are listed by profession, along with nine retailers (ritagliatori), three belt makers (cintolarii), two merchants (mercatanti), and one smith (fabbro). Tailors only constituted some 18 percent of the total initial matriculees.[26] Between 1225 and 1299, some twenty-seven more tailors matriculated, along with two doublet makers (farsettai). From a perusal of the names listed, none of these sarti necessarily indicates a family relation; early families of tailors in the Por Santa Maria cannot be discerned.

After 1299, tailors' matriculation declined precipitously, and for the next 130 years, only seven more tailors are listed. The silk-tailoring art that did remain in the silk guild was doublet making. Doublets were the major upper-body fitted garment for men in the Renaissance, often of a silk-based fabric such as brocade.[27] For the same time period, 1299 to 1430, some 300 doublet makers matriculated, with seven combination sarti/farsettai listed. In addition to the doublet makers, the most common occupational designations noted in the membership lists of the early Por Santa Maria are the aforementioned retailers, along with goldsmiths (orafi), a few embroiderers (ricamatori), used-clothing merchants, and bedcover makers (copertorai).[28]

From the 1290s on, there were certain criteria one had to meet in order to formally matriculate into a guild. For full membership, besides paying the highest entrance fee, an artisan had to operate a retail shop (bottega), without which one was considered a mere laborer; having one's own bottega indicated what Alfred Doren calls "civic independence and full efficiency."[29] The master tailors in this category who had their own shop and had become part of the body, or corpo, of this guild, would never have been more than a small minority of the total population of tailors in Florence at any one time. Many tailors instead worked in other tailors' shops, or even as casual laborers who found only occasional employment.[30] For some seventy years, the few tailors who fashioned primarily silk clothing were enrolled in the Por Santa Maria.

This initial alliance with the retailers guild, which in the Dugento and Trecento was for the most part a guild of luxury-item retailers and associated craftsmen, would indicate that the art of tailoring, especially tailoring of silk clothing, was at that time associated strongly with sumptuous consumer goods only for the most wealthy. Florentines may not routinely have hired a tailor to make their garments but might rather have engaged a humble seamster or seamstress to cut out the piece of clothing under the customer's supervision, which would then be stitched, lined, and trimmed by the women of the family.[31] A *sarto* (identified as a "master tailor" by Florence Edler de Roover) would only have been hired to cut out and stitch the most important formal pieces of clothing. While business documents of the time are for the most part silent on female tailors (*sarte*), we do know there were women tailoring garments, because guild statutes occasionally refer to regulations for both male and female tailors.[32] Alessandro Stella's figures from the *Estimi* (tax declarations) show a precipitous drop-off in female practitioners of this art. Thirteen sarte are noted in 1352, only one in 1378, and two in 1404.[33] By 1427, there are no female tailors listed as heads of households.[34] However marginalized this occupation became for women in the fifteenth century, we do know that they still carried on this traditionally female work.[35] One fifteenth-century example of an independent female tailor (*sarta*) undoubtedly representative of many more, does appear in the records of a Florentine foundling hospital. A Monna Nanna di Pucieri, of Santo Ambrogio, was employed by the Spedale di Santa Maria degli Innocenti in 1455 as an individual woman working outside the guild system to make little shifts for the small children in residence. For eleven *guarnelli*, she received the small sum of 6 lire 10 soldi, or about 12 soldi per garment.[36] It appears that the male tailors captured the lucrative portion of the garment-making business, while female tailors were relegated to more humble but still essential aspects of the art. The number of male tailors in Florence almost doubled between 1352 and 1404, increasing from 60 to 111.[37]

The Arte della seta | As the production of silk increased in Florence throughout the Trecento and into the Quattrocento, however, producers rather than merchants came to dominate the Por Santa Maria guild, to which the elite tailors belonged. After 1350, reflecting an influx of exiled Lucchese silk workers, silk workers became a separate category within the guild. Some eighty years later, the revised statutes of the guild in 1429 show that manufacturers had come to dominate it, the membership hierarchy showing *setaiuoli grossi* (big silk merchants) at the top. As a result, by the first decades of the fifteenth century, the Por Santa Maria was commonly referred to as the "Arte della seta."[38] In addition to silk dealers, drapers, goldsmiths, and bankers associated with the guild, its ranks included both big silk merchants, such as Buonaccorso Pitti, and more modest ones, such as Andrea Banchi. In the fourteenth century, the tailors who remained in the Por Santa Maria, or Arte della seta, which had been led by priors, or consuls, since 1283, were gradually relegated to a separate secondary tier of the guild and included among the so-called *setaiuoli minuti,* who enjoyed only limited rights.[39] Although minor members in general were subject to the policing power and judgments of the guilds, they were not considered true guildsmen (*veri artifices*) per se. That is, they could not participate in the administration of the guild, were not written into the matriculation lists, or had separate lists, and did not pay the full admission fee that would have qualified them for all guild privileges.[40]

The membership tier of the setaiuoli minuti in the Arte della seta in the later Trecento grew to encompass a dozen or so subsidiary occupations within the guild. These workers were all involved in the silk-making process, from loom warpers (*orditori*), weavers (*tessitori di drappi*), dyers (*tintori*), silk designers (*disegnatori*), and printers (*stampatori*) to those who crafted garments and other items from the finished silken cloth, including doublet makers, embroiderers, belt makers, liturgical vestment makers, and bedcover makers.[41] As Stella has noted for the Arte della lana, these so-called sottoposti subordinated within the guild formed a strict hierarchy of their own and earned from little to even less.[42]

Attachment to the Por Santa Maria did not, however, attract the majority of the tailors of Florence, few of whom could have made a living working in silk fabrics (brocade, damask, velvet, or taffeta) for the rich. Edler de Roover notes that the silk merchant Andrea Banchi had difficulty selling brocades and brocaded velvets in Florence. Demand was small, due to two factors; first, these fabrics were very expensive, and secondly, communal sumptuary legislation, as we shall see below, severely restricted their wearing to specific

TABLE I.I

The Changing Affiliations of Tailors in Renaissance Florence

YEAR	AFFILIATION
1032	independent
1225	Por Santa Maria, after 1429 referred to as the Arte della seta (tailors of silk only)
1296	Arte dei rigattieri (tailors of wool and other non-silk-based fabrics)
1378	Arte dei farsettai (22d revolutionary guild)
1382	Arte dei rigattieri e linaiuoli
1387	Arte dei rigattieri e linaiuoli e sarti
1534	Università dei rigattieri, linaiuoli, sarti, vinattieri e albergatori

events.[43] Between 1292 and 1330, the Florentine guild system entered a period of transition, in which the Commune set in place general guidelines for all to follow. In 1293, tailors, along with the other artisans of the city, were legally required to be under the dicta of one of the twenty-one officially recognized guilds in order to come under the statutes of the Commune.[44] Those tailors who were not among the relatively few among the setaiuoli minuti of the Por Santa Maria established a new alliance, beginning in 1295, with the Arte minore of the Rigattieri; that is, the retailers of used clothing and fabric industry remnants. (See Table 1.1 for the changing guild alliances of the tailors.)

Tailors in the Arte dei rigattieri | The Arte dei rigattieri (called the "Arte dei Baldrigari" by Giovanni Villani) had been first formed in 1266 as the retail guild of dealers in second-hand clothing, cloth, household linens, and related items, which organized the first Florentine ready-to-wear marketplace. In 1295, the Rigattieri were at the bottom of the list of the *arti mediani,* or "middling guilds," which would all be demoted six years later to lesser-guild status. The Rigattieri not only bought and sold clothing, furs, brocades, and remnants of silk tissue, wool, and linen from the cloth-industry workshops but also traded in cushions, rugs, mattresses, and bed linens, as well as trunks, chests, and coffers, horse covers and used campaign awnings, old glass, and even discarded ecclesiastical cowls and cassocks. They acquired the clothing of deceased persons (first appraised by brokers, called *sensali*), buying it either direct from their heirs or from the churches to which the items had been willed; bid at public auctions; purchased woven and knitted handwork from independent female home-laborers; and bought up the remnants generated by the city's cloth industry.[45] These dealers were allowed to sell the cheaper foreign cloth (*panni milanese e bresciano, bigelli romagniuoli*) from their shops, as well as yardage of thin wool (*saia*) and linen (*rensa*) used by women for the making of washable undergarments (*camicie*) for their families. They also dealt in fabric used for making coverlets, curtains, bed canopies and chair backs, as well as already made-up soled and lined hose, socks, trousers, berets, and caps.[46]

In 1296, thirty years after it was first organized, the Rigattieri opened its membership to unaligned tailors and to ambulatory vendors of cloth, fur, rags, and used clothing, many of whom were women, in an attempt to bring these previously unrepresented elements under control.[47] From the outset, the Rigattieri had had an association with the Arte dei linaiuoli (linen producers' guild), but the latter continued to have their own separate statutes until 1340, when the name of the guild changed to include them.[48] While in the Rigattieri, tailors were under its dictates, but as in the Por Santa Maria, they were not given full rights of membership. Instead, they were confined strictly to the business of tailoring clothing and were prohibited from expanding their activities to include selling cloth or anything else from their shops.[49] Tailors remained in this ancillary position in the Rigattieri for over fifty years, the guild only providing them with surety, not full rights.[50] Even though tailors were not allowed by the Arte to participate in guild elections, the guild nevertheless demanded unconditional obedience to its statutes. It also required occasional unpaid labor to staff its guild offices and the shouldering of honorific burdens, even if these duties were time-consuming and against the artisan's own interests.[51]

Finally, in 1350, some fifty-four years after first being placed under the dictates of the guild, tailors obtained the right to elect consuls. In 1367, a matriculation specifically for tailors was introduced for those who wished to matriculate ("qui sponte in ipsa . . . immatriculari volunt"), but they were still not equal members with the used-clothing dealers or the linen merchants.[52] Five years later, tailors won the right to become officials of the guild, but, as an ordinance of 1376 indicates, this only applied to tailors who were residents of the city and had their own bottega ("sartores a bottega residentes").[53]

Figures compiled by Stella confirm the constriction of overall opportunities in the tailoring profession (and others) over time. While the numbers of sarti almost doubled between 1352 and 1404, as we have seen, the numbers of those who described their occupations more humbly as "ista a sarto" and "lavoratore di sarto" (that is, as just working *for* a tailor), grew much more dramatically (from none to about sixteen). The opportunity to become an independent master craftsman with a shop of one's own seems to have diminished in the course of the fourteenth century for tailors, as it did for other Florentine clothiers and accessory makers in this same time frame.[54] The solitary sewing associated with tailoring (which usually employed just a few hired *lavoranti*) kept tailors isolated and outside the organized world of work, which conferred political voice, but at the same time they had access to their rich clientele, which many of them presumed upon to better their social place through their networks of association.[55]

TAILORS' CHANGING SOCIAL PLACE

Their extended tenure in the Arte dei rigattieri indicates much about the way in which tailors were viewed by the commune of Florence. For one thing, this guild controlled the general retail marketplace in cloth and clothing items for the city, excluding the luxury crafts, which were regulated by the silk guild. While the makers of men's doublets stayed within that exclusive collective, most tailors moved to the less rarefied milieu of the used-clothing dealers. One must ask why this occurred. First of all, as we have seen above, the majority of tailors did not work primarily in silk. Secondly, even if a tailor could make brocade and velvet clothing for wealthy local clients, the export market, which represented the bulk of the silk guild's business, offered little scope for personal tailoring. Ready-made silk hats, purses, belts, gloves, and ecclesiastical cloth could be easily sold in this market, and in fact, Florence became famous for such items. These trades were therefore of continuing interest to the major merchant guilds and stayed within these guilds, which sought to profit from the foreign marketing of these items by controlling them within their own jurisdiction.[56] If goods were created primarily for local consumption, however (products such as clothing, shoes, candles, wine, and foodstuffs), the wealthy international merchandising guilds were not interested in exercising control over them within their own guilds. In marked contrast to locally finished and dyed foreign cloth, locally tailored clothing (especially as fashions became more fitted throughout the Trecento and into the Quattrocento) had no large international market. Clothes needed too much individual attention and too many personal adjustments by tailors to be profitable to the silk guild.

Thirdly, as the making of clothes became professionalized, the use of tailors became more common in the urban milieu and lost the exoticism associated with the silk guild. The clothing made by tailors was more properly included with the hats, hosiery, and bed linens handled by the used-clothing dealers and linen merchants than with the embroidered chasubles and lengths of voided velvet fabric offered by the silk guild and marked for the export trade. Eventually many doublet makers, too, would leave the silk guild and join with tailors in a new guild during the revolt of the Ciompi in 1378, examined below.

After 1296, even though the majority of the tailors were allied not with the prestigious silk guild but with the minor guild of the Rigattieri, their rights within that guild rose, as we have seen. Along with increased guild rights came a relatively higher social standing for some tailors after the mid Trecento. As Samuel Kline Cohn Jr. has noted, in the fourteenth century, notaries did not often identify their clients who were sottoposti by occupation. Among them only *sartores* were designated by their trade, perhaps indicating a certain cachet. Further, there was a correspondingly higher economic level among sarti than they had previously held. In the second half of the fourteenth century, there were tailors who could give their daughters dowries or themselves receive dowries that, Cohn writes, "could match those of certain branches of the degli Serragli or members of other old Florentine lineages." In fact, among three different families of tailors, he found what he called "striking upward mobility" among tailors' daughters. Two young women married up to husbands who were guildsmen in the arti maggiori.[57]

EXTRAGUILD CONTROLS ON TAILORS

Given a degree of upward mobility and professional pride, it must have been onerous to be subjected to repeated communal regulation. For in addition to subordination within the economic and political milieu of guild corporatism in the Trecento, tailors were also subject to the control of various magistracies in the city of Florence. Most obvious were the communal sumptuary laws that not only regulated the wearer of the offending garment but fined its creator.[58] Beginning in the late thirteenth century and stretching through the Quattrocento, these laws were revised at least eighty times in Florence.[59] Added to sumptuary controls, independent tailors with no guild affiliation were under the jurisdiction of the Ufficiali della grascia. This included all ambulatory workers and the vast majority of female tailors, as well as what Doren calls all "disorganized elements" outside guild control.[60] The Ufficio della grascia carried out the communal policy of provision from Orsan-michele, policing the grain market, fixing maximum prices for foodstuffs, keeping track of supplies, and also regulating guildless artisans and laborers.[61] It is not surprising, then, that one of the demands of the Ciompi in 1378 was the abolition of this office.[62]

The magistrate of the Podestà also set general ordinances that regulated the marketplace of Florence. By the Statuto del Podestà of 1325, tailors were prohibited from pawning leftover cloth, wool, linen, or mixed wool and flax, whether cut or uncut, from their shops. In addition, they were not to pawn garments, finished or unfinished. Fines for noncompliance were set at 25 lire and were levied both on the sarto and the person to whom the item had been pawned.[63] Further, in November 1348, after the demographic decline and resulting social chaos of the Black Plague, in which Florence lost more than half of its population and labor demands increased, the Commune reduced the number of minor guilds to seven in a desperate attempt to regain control of the marketplace. It also gave the Ufficio della grascia the authority to fix the prices of goods and services furnished by merchants and the seven re-maining arti minori. A year later, in November 1349, and lasting to October 1350, the arti minori were subjected to what were termed "antimonopolis-tic" price controls. With the authority of a *balia* (emergency ruling commit-tee) passed on October 20, 1349, in the wake of the social chaos of the Black Plague of 1348, all the lesser guilds were now to answer to a foreign notary, and the consuls of these guilds lost any authority in questions of monopoly.[64]

Seven years later, the same lesser guildsmen, including tailors, were sub-mitted to further minute controls. In 1355, by guild-sponsored communal ordinance, tailors' shops were inspected by the Quattro ufficiali della biada, a four-man tribunal that modified the Ufficio della grascia after the plague. The ufficiali della biada, having had more authority under the *balie* of 1349, were now to have complete jurisdiction over not only the "disorganized elements" but also an increasingly resentful group of minor guildsmen.[65] These officials held authority over a wide range of market activities. They were to fix prices for items produced by the lesser guilds, monitor the selling of meat, fish, and other foodstuffs, adjudicate disputes between litigants of minor guilds, prevent the assembly of their membership, and, among other controls, oversee those artisans who provided personal services, including the inspection of the materials and construction of their products. Tailors, shoe-makers (*calzolari* or *zoccolai*), slipper makers (*pianellai*), hosiers (*calzaioli*), and many other trades, came under this newly expanded authority and were now all obliged to pay a deposit to the Commune to do business.[66] These controls over the sottoposti and the arti minori were finally swept away twenty-three years later in the 1378 revolt of the Ciompi.

THE WORKERS' REVOLT OF 1378

The guild system, especially the large cloth guilds of the Lana and Seta, had been organized for the benefit of the lanaiuoli and setaiuoli, not for the large numbers of workers that were required as the textile business became more complex and highly refined. With complexity came worker stratification, various levels of members having more or less rights within the guild.[67] The lowest ranks of workers, the so-called sottoposti in both industries, were subject to guild rules and regulation by the Commune but had no representa-tion or real place in its politics. Florentine communal policy and guild policy developed into the late Trecento with one thing in mind: to keep workers from organizing their own collectives, which could have carried concomitant political voice.[68] However, the revolt of the Ciompi, in which three new revolutionary guilds were formed, "may reasonably be viewed as a guild revolution and as the last serious attempt by Florentines to construct a policy on corporate principles," as John Najemy has written.[69]

Demands for Representation | By the 1340s, certain sottoposti in the Arte della lana (especially the dyers) had begun to agitate to form a guild of their own, and the Florentine War with the Papacy of 1375–78 gave these dis-

gruntled skilled artisans an opportunity to shake off the control of the la-
naiuoli. The two dominant factions in Florence during the war were the
oligarchic Parte Guelfa and the populist republican government. The Parte
Guelfa wanted a peaceful settlement and to get rid of the "new men" of
Florence: advocates of popular government and enemies of the conservative
Church. This stance provoked a reaction from the prowar faction led by
Salvestro de' Medici—champion of the "new men" who had risen from the
lower ranks—who himself then moved to restrict the power of the Parte.

In June 1378, prowar factions burned the houses of Parte members, and
anti-Parte legislation was passed by the communal government. Following
that, in mid July, a second wave of proletarian agitation exploded in violence,
which toppled the government and established a new "democratic" regime.
At this time, three new guilds were formed: a doublet makers' Arte dei farsettai, which included tailors, a dyers' Arte dei tintori, and an arte composed
of the lowest stratum of sottoposti workers in the wool industry, the so-called
Ciompi, represented for the first time in government.[70] Those included in
the emergency ruling committee, or balìa, of this truly revolutionary government of Florence were guildsmen from the twenty-one established guilds
(many of whom were shopkeepers, but who also included the silk merchant
Michele di Ser Parente), plus the members of the three newly formed guilds,
about 13,000 men in all.[71]

The Ciompi guild of the lowest rung of workers lasted for only six weeks,
however, until late August 1378. By then, a second wave of labor unrest had
erupted, motivated at least in part by the perception that the new leaders of
the Ciompi had used the tumult for their own personal benefit, creating a
secret closed *consorteria,* which gave salaries to themselves.[72] A coalition of
merchants and artisan guildsmen who had gained control that summer turned
against them, and the Ciompi were crushed. The other two revolutionary
guilds lasted for four years, until January 1382, when conservative forces
composed of employers and oligarchs reasserted themselves and the original
twenty-one arti were reestablished to take charge of the economic and political life of the Commune.[73]

Tailors in the Revolutionary Guilds | It is not so much the complaints and
demands of the day-laborer sottoposti, or Ciompi, in the twenty-fourth guild
that are of interest here, but rather those of the members of the twenty-

second and twenty-third guilds, the Arte dei farsettai and the Arte dei tintori, which together represented about 4,000 workers.[74] The dyers had been lobbying for independent recognition for some thirty-eight years prior to 1378. However, the doublet makers, who had been among the *membri minori* of the Por Santa Maria since at least the first quarter of the thirteenth century, won the first revolutionary guild to be created out of the foment of the summer's revolt. What motivated this guild, which was presented in a petition to the priors and approved by the councils on September 22, 1378, is perhaps unknowable. Historians of the events that transpired that summer are still remarkably divided about the composition of this guild, and even how it was referred to by number.[75]

As to the composition of these guilds, again historians are divided. Gino Scaramella saw simply an "irrational division of workers into the three revolutionary guilds," but Najemy notes that the three new guilds included "two for the skilled artisans of the textile industries and one for the unskilled Ciompi."[76] As for the Arte dei farsettai specifically, Raymond de Roover wrote that it "grouped together a miscellaneous crowd of doublet-makers, tailors, shearmen, hatters, banner-makers, and barbers," while Richard Trexler says that "the 23rd guild was mainly composed of small merchants unrelated to the textile industries, though it did contain the wool shearers."[77] Our clearest source on the composition of the Arte dei farsettai comes from Doren, who wrote that it consisted of *membra supposita*, that is, the second-tier minor members of various guilds, including doublet and vestment makers, who would have been from the Por Santa Maria, the tailors, the great majority of whom had been in the Rigattieri, with a few still in the Por Santa Maria, the barbers (*barbieri*), who were in the Arte dei medici e degli speziali, the retailers, who could have been from the Por Santa Maria or the Rigattieri, and, lastly, the hatmakers (*cappellai*) and shearers (*cimatori*), who already possessed a bit more status, from the Arte della lana.[78]

We have then a new guild made up of artisans from at least four different guilds, divided into four membership groups, (1) the doublet makers, (2) the tailors, (3) the shearers, and (4) the barbers. This guild had six consuls, one or two alternately from each group.[79] Trexler is careful to note, however, that only certain established guildsmen actually joined a revolutionary guild, therefore the tailors included in the twenty-second guild would not have necessarily been all the tailors of Florence, who by 1427 would have numbered roughly 100 men.[80] The rationale behind the particular composition of workers brought together in these two guilds may have been as straightforward as the fact that the Arte dei farsettai joined together "cutters," that is, those trades that cut things, from tailors to barbers to shearers. The Arte dei tintori, on the other hand, grouped different wet processes involved in the cloth-making business (dyers, soap makers, wool washers, and combers).

For four years (between 1378 and 1382), these guilds were part of the political process in Florence, with consular representation in the government. In 1378, the 4,000 guildsmen of the twenty-second and twenty-third guilds initially had combined with the 9,000 of the twenty-fourth to total some 13,000 men, a large enough number to threaten any easy oligarchic hegemony.[81] Finally, in 1382, with the 9,000 members of the Ciompi defeated within months, the patriciate engineered the disbanding of the last 4,000 members of the other two guilds, which had survived four years. The tailors again rejoined the Rigattieri, which five years later was headquartered in the Casa d'Anzio at the corner of the Mercato Vecchio.[82] Their position within this guild remained subordinate into the fifteenth century.[83]

CONTINUING CONTROL OVER TAILORS

By the late Trecento, then, some tailors had achieved a measure of recognition within the organized guild structure and a modicum of financial success, enabling them to give their daughters adequate dowries. In the Quattrocento, in spite of a general codification of statutes in 1415 that limited what a tailor could charge for a wide variety of garments, more than a few made modest personal fortunes. The statutes of 1415 had fixed prices for the making up of seventy-two different articles of clothing for both men and women, and even for the stitching up of mourning clothes for funerals. The prices were set relatively low, at from 1 lira 2 soldi up to 1 florin 1 lira 15 soldi.[84] The penalty for charging amounts in excess of those set by communal statute was 25 lire.[85]

Price ceilings of this type, covering essentially every item an artisan would have made, did not exist for any other occupation. In fact, the statutes of 1415 had set out such a detailed pricing structure that Robert Davidsohn, for one, felt that this legislation represented a general suspicion of tailors as a group.[86]

Fig. 1.1. A tailor. G. B. Moroni, *Il Sarto* (ca. 1560). National Gallery, London.

Even though other historians may seem to concur with Davidsohn's assessment that tailors were kept down by communal micromanagement, Gene
Brucker, who located the profession of tailoring "among the inferior trades in
Florence," points out that Lorenzo Ghiberti's tailor, to whom he owed the
rather large sum of 15 florins, was called "Antonio, El Maestro."[87] Neither the
amount of Ghiberti's debt nor the tailor's title indicates a particularly inferior

status. In the mid Cinquecento, G. B. Moroni would paint a portrait of an Italian tailor (Fig. 1.1) looking up from carefully cutting a piece of cloth, shears in hand. The shrewd, level gaze with which he takes the viewer's measure is consistent with the craftsman best known as "ottimo Geometra" (excellent geometrician) at least 100 years earlier.

Due to the nature of the art of making clothes, which required training, experience, and skill (and even rewarded talent), those who worked *as* tailors, or even *for* tailors as stitchers or cutters, did not experience the same degree of loss of independence that befell workers in less-skilled jobs, workers who were increasingly collected into larger companies with more structured and stratified workforces. In fact, the tailors who served the ruling elite became craftsmen of some repute, and their services were in demand. By the mid 1400s, price restrictions were not preventing some tailors from charging more money for making apparel. While the communal statutes of 1415 had limited the amount a tailor could charge for making one garment to a little over a florin, by 1640, we have a record of a tailor from Naples receiving 500 ducats for fashioning two lavish overgowns of heavy watered silk of gold decorated with fine lacework for the king and queen of Poland.[88]

Tailors were not the only craftspeople involved in the dressing of Renaissance Florence, however. In the Quattrocento, well over half of the cost of a woman's public ensemble went for ornamentation and trims, jewelry, belts, shoes, and headpieces.[89] Not only did cloth need to be purchased and a tailor commissioned, but also all the sewing notions, jewelry, and ornaments for gown and hair had to be acquired from the tradespeople who sold them and delivered to the specialty craftspeople who did the embroidery work, gem setting, and garment decoration. Increasingly, men of the classe dirigente needed the services of the accessorizers to present the women of their families with the most magnificent embellishment possible. Aside from the tailor, the physical process involved in getting an outfit together necessarily came to include those who created and dealt in those accessories, from the most intimate item of personal linens to the most eloquent public headdress. Florentine crafts involved an entire spectrum of providers, from the masters of the guilds to the most humble peripatetic sottoposti working outside formal guild control. It is to the myriad other clothiers that we turn our attention next.

THE CRAFTSPEOPLE

The manufacturing and marketing of the luxury items in apparel that were produced in the city of Florence was organized, regulated, and policed by the guilds of Florence. Goods had been sold in the various fixed marketplaces established from the earliest history of the Commune.[1] Robert Davidsohn tallied over 1,500 shoemakers in the large Trecento population of the city, who practiced their craft along with other artisans, from hosiers and belt and purse makers, to velveteers and embroiderers.[2] By the 1470s, Benedetto Dei, boasting of his "Florentie bella," counted some 353 wholesale wool and silk concerns, forty-four jewelers, thirty-three gold and silver shops, and some thirty-two drapers' establishments "that cut and sell cloth of crimson and scarlet and blue violet and black and dark brown and tan and purple and blue black and azure and green."

MARKETPLACES

Dating back to 1225, the most important market was the central marketplace (*foro*), which came to be known as the Mercato Vecchio, including the area of the "Kalimala" (later the Calimala), from Via Porta Rossa to the Piazza Repubblica, in the direction of Via Por Santa Maria. Many of the shops under the aegis of the silk guild were located here. In the fifteenth century, the

Fig. 2.1. *La strada dei commercianti de stoffe e arredi* (1470). Bologna, Museo civico,
Matricula Societatis Draperiorum, MS 931.

prominent markets were found at the Mercato Vecchio, the Mercato Nuovo, and around Orsanmichele. There were also large groupings of botteghe in the Via Porta Rossa and Via Por Santa Maria, as well as along Calimala, in the Piazza Brunelleschi, and the Piazza della Parte Guelfa.[3] In Florence, whole-sale shops and retail outlets for cloth and cloth products operated side by side, along with shops for gold and jewelry (*gioiellerie*), notions (*merciai*), a large sector of used clothing, bed linen, remnant, and old clothes dealers (*riven-ditori*).[4] Figure 2.1 conveys the bustle of such a street.

David Herlihy and Christiane Klapisch-Zuber counted 866 clothiers in Florence who identified themselves by occupation in 1427. Franco Fran-ceschi has shown the distribution of 909 households headed by sottoposti working within the Arte della lana, throughout the *gonfaloni* (neighbor-hoods) of the city.[5] From this same survey, we can ascertain which quarters had concentrations of specific artisans.[6] San Giovanni had the most used-clothing dealers and shoemakers, about one-third of the goldsmiths were in Santo Spirito; and Santa Croce had many leather workers, including not only shoemakers but also purse makers and leather-furnishings dealers.[7] Santa Maria Novella was home to the highest percentage of embroiderers and menders. This complex commercial center also included more elusive par-ticipants: ambulatory female vendors (*venditrice*) of veils, caps, and head-scarves; roaming seamsters, seamstresses, and shoemakers; and pieceworkers making items such as embroidery, lace, and personal linens either at home or in convents.[8]

GUILD-AFFILIATED OCCUPATIONS

The Major Guilds | The vast majority of the people in the clothing and accessories crafts and trades had come under the control of the guild system of Florence by the early fourteenth century (see Table 2.1 for Florentine clothiers and the guilds that controlled them). Luxury-trade wholesalers, retail shopkeepers, and individual craftspeople (for example, tailors, doublet makers, embroiderers who worked in silk, and goldsmiths) were all regulated by the silk guild (Arte della seta). Three other major guilds regulated the makers of clothing accessories and their sale: the wool guild (Arte della lana); the guild of furriers (Arte dei vaiai e pellicciai); and the guild of doctors,

TABLE 2.1

Florentine Clothiers and the Seven Guilds That Controlled Them (ca. 1415)

MAJOR GUILDS

1. *Arte della lana*
   a. *berrettai* (wool beret makers)
   b. *cappellai* (wool hatmakers)
   c. *cerbolattai* (goat-hair manufacturers)
2. *Arte della seta (originally the Por Santa Maria); oversaw the luxury marketplace*
   a. *armaiuoli* (button, stud, and metal-ornament makers)
   b. *berrettai e cappellai* (merchants of berets and hats of imported fabric)
   c. *calzaiuoli* (hosiers)
   d. *calzettai* (sock makers)
   e. *cinturai* (silk belt makers)
   f. *farsettai* (silk doublet makers)
   g. *orafi* (goldsmiths)
   h. *ricamatori* (embroiderers)
   i. *sarti* (tailors of silk clothing)
3. *Arte dei medici, speziali e merciai; oversaw the accessories and notions marketplace*
   a. *borsai* (fabric purse makers)
   b. *cappellai di paglia e feltro* (straw and felt hat makers)
   c. *cuffai o fabbricanti di cappucci* (cap, cowl, and bonnet makers)
   d. *fibbiai* (clasp, buckle, and brooch makers)
   e. *guantai* (glove makers)
   f. *merciai* (notions dealers)
4. *Arte dei pellicciai e vaiai*
   a. *pellicciai* (fur-pelt dealers)
   b. *vaiai* (furriers)

MINOR GUILDS

5. *Arte dei calzolai*
   a. *calzolai* (shoemakers)
   b. *ciabattini* (cobblers)
   c. *pianellai* (slipper makers)
   d. *zoccolai* (clog makers)

TABLE 2.1 (continued)

Florentine Clothiers and the Seven Guilds That Controlled Them (ca. 1415)

6. *Arte dei rigattieri e linaiuoli e sarti; oversaw the retail clothing and linens market*
   a. *farsettai* (doublet-makers)
   b. *rigattieri* (used-clothing and retail linens dealers)
   c. *sarti* (tailors)
7. *Arte dei correggiai*
   a. *borsai* (leather purse makers)
   b. *cinturai* (leather belt makers)
   c. *fabbricanti delle scarselle* (leather pouch makers)
   d. *pezzai* (retailers of leather uppers for shoes, sold to shoemakers)
   e. *suolai* (shoe sole makers)

apothecaries, and mercers (Arte dei medici, speziali e merciai), under which were grouped a diverse collection of occupations, from doctors, apothecaries, drapers, and painters (including, among other well-known painters, Andrea del Sarto), to hairdressers, veil and purse makers, booksellers and stationers, mask and lantern makers, and even perfumers.[9]

The Minor Guilds | Three minor guilds also played a large role in the accessories and clothing business: the guild of used-clothing and linen merchants (Arte dei rigattieri e linaiuoli), which included most tailors as sottoposti, as we have seen, the guild of shoemakers (Arte dei calzolai), which also encompassed sandal, slipper, and clog makers, cobblers, and the guild of leather dealers (Arte dei correggiai), under which were grouped shoe-leather cutters, the belt and strap makers, and pouch and purse makers.[10] A total of seven guilds, then, four from the major guilds and three from the minor guilds, regulated the clothing accessories market in Florence.

CONTROL OVER MARKETS AND WORKERS

The Arte della lana and Arte dei rigattieri e linaiuoli | The local marketing of clothing, shoes, accessories, and all types of linens was overseen by four of the twenty-one guilds in Florence. Statistics compiled in 1442 show that the Arte della lana, specializing in woolen cloth, limited its ready-made items to purses (*borselle*) and soled stockings and caps (*calze e chapelline*), which it sold by the dozen. Secondly, the Arte dei rigattieri e linaiuoli sold imported and domestically made doublets (*farsetti d'ogni ragione*), bed linens (*choltre e chopertojo*), and towels and tablecloths (*sciugatoi e tovaglie da tavola*).[11]

The Arte della seta | The third market was larger, stocking luxury goods and overseen by the silk merchant's guild. It carried a more extensive inventory of imported accessories and controlled the sale of silk items from doublets and hosiery to hats and silk embroidery. Silver and gold thread from Venice and Lucca was offered there (*ariento e oro filato Lucchese e Viniziano*), all types of silk purses (*borse di seta, di drappo soriano, di ciambellotto, di filugiello, di stame*), silk buttons, imported berets by the dozen (*barrette d'oltramonti d'ogni Terra, di lana di Pescie, treccie di bambagia*), gold-embroidered decorations (*fregi d'oro ricamati*), many types of fringe and ribbon by the pound (*frangia di filugiello, di seta, di chatarzo, nastri di refe*), and flowers to sew on head garlands by the dozen (*fiore da filare ghirlande, la dozina*). This marketplace also carried six types of pearls, veils, headscarves, face veils, and flowered and cotton headcaps (*veli, bende, orali, chuffie di fiore, e di bambagia*).[12]

The Arte dei medici, speziali e merciai | Lastly, the doctors, apothecaries and drapers guild controlled the marketplace for purses, clasps and buckles, gloves, and caps, and similar furnishings.[13] Drapers' shops carried bolts of fabric and caps of wool and leather, caps lined with silk, fabric shoes, and gloves of wool or chamois. They had everything metallic for military wear; swords, lances, spurs, helmets, breastplates, and horse covers. It was also the venue for much of the bric-a-brac of accessorizing, including glass pearls (*perle di vetro*), three types of coral, crystal by the pound (*christallo la libbra*), copper and iron wire, feathers (*da impennare*), paternostri of coral or amber, and wooden clogs (*zoccoli*).[14]

Independent Workers | The physical setting for the ancient marketplaces of Florence was complex in its juxtaposition of layers of urban society. Full guildsman worked in close proximity to sottoposti craftspeople and extra-guild vendors. (See Appendix 2 for categories of clothiers and accessorists.) Many formerly independent craftspeople who made accessory items were by the early fourteenth century under the dictates of one of the composite guilds in a lesser tier of minor members. The Por Santa Maria (later the Arte della seta) controlled the goldsmiths, jewelers, and *armaiuoli* (who fashioned buttons, studs, and other metal gown and hat ornaments).[15] In addition to the tailors and linen manufacturers, the Rigattieri attempted periodically to control the roving vendors. If a male craftsperson held guild membership, he retained control over his product from its creation to sale. However, the vast majority of craftswomen, being denied guild entrance, either worked as *lavoratore* for a guildsman on a piecework basis or sold their output, whether it be veils, headscarves, purses, socks, or hose, to retail shopkeepers, who were themselves under guild control.

WOMEN IN THE MARKETPLACE

Vendors: The *Venditrici* and *Rigattiere* | Down on the narrow back lanes of the city, a certain number of the active participants in the cloth and clothing business lacked any guild control and were a constant source of irritation to the guild community at large because of that and for their perceived entrepreneurial zeal. Women in this category were considered a special problem; some were thought too brash and pushy, and they were generally thorns in the side of the guild system. Peripatetic female vendors who sold various merchandise alongside the fixed botteghe of the guildsmen were called *rigattiere* or *venditrici*. One of the characters in Matteo Bandello's *Novelle* takes a fancy to such a *bella giovane*: "He was strongly enamored by a young beauty who sold caps, headdresses, cords, gorgets, and other accessories for women."[16] The account books of one Miliadusso Baldiccione of nearby Pisa also refer to female vendors. His *ricordi* note that he purchased a large veil and bird-catching nets (among other things), from a "mona Giana venditrice" on June 5, 1359. On November 2 of the same year, he bought a new headscarf for a woman named "Tedda" from the same woman, and later that day, he bought a bordered face veil from a "monna Chola venditrice."[17]

The problem of controlling such ambulatory female vendors occupied many rubrics of the continually revised statutes of the used-clothing and linen dealers guild. In 1318, a venditrice had to post surety of 20 lire per year to be able to vend her wares.[18] But by 1371, the guild temporarily prohibited women from selling goods house-to-house, saying that many female vendors of cloth and notions made a practice of insinuating themselves into dwellings and enticing women with their wares to the damage of their husbands ("et seducunt mulieres. . . . ad dampnum virorum").[19] Both Alfred Doren and Judith Brown have interpreted this as signifying gender bias against women, that is, an inherent suspicion of female garrulousness seducing weak-willed female customers. "Surely, the guild took a different view of the male members of the trade who displayed similar skills," Brown writes.[20] Aggressive behavior was applauded in men, but considered anathema in females, hence this bias against female vendors. The supposedly passive housewives were seen as displaying understandable female behavior, while the female vendors displayed behavior acceptable only in males. Prohibiting women from freely vending door-to-door was consistent with other controls the patriarchy attempted to exert over women in late Trecento and Quattrocento Florence.[21]

Klapisch-Zuber has noted such an enterprising female, a widow by the name of "Monna Bernarda," who in 1354 married a Lippo del Sega as his second wife. She was the sister of a pawnbroker and brought with her as her dowry three houses, some land, and eighty weaving combs (*pettini da tessitore*), worth 80 florins. Lippo and Bernarda stayed together for four years, then separated. He took one of her houses, she kept the combs. In his *ricordanza*, Lippo accused Bernarda of being a "niggardly, pub-crawling, lousy rigattiera who thieved from her first husband." He also noted that she went out "every day . . . all over Florence, earning money with her combs."[22] Whether *rigattiera* here was simply a pejorative term used by a husband defeated by an energetic peripatetic wife is unimportant. What is important is that he characterized Bernarda as such, using *rigattiera* as a commonplace to indicate a wife who engaged in inappropriate female behavior of the type castigated by the guilds.

FEMALE CRAFTSPEOPLE

The *Camiciai* | Other craftswomen ubiquitous in the Florentine needle trades were the *camiciai*, who fashioned the most basic items of clothing, the family linens (*panni lini* and *camicie*), working on an informal basis.[23] By dealing in a category of clothing for the most part outside guild regulation, the marketplace for personal linens kept itself cheaply stocked. Just as these camiciai were invisible in the structured world of professionally organized work, the garments they made were invisible in the art of the period, because the *camicia* showed only at the neckline and wrists of overgarments, although it was sometimes provocatively pulled through decorative slashes in sleeves. This intimate "woman's work" provided the clothing layer next to one's skin, while the professional (male) tailor was increasingly called upon to make the public layer of formal, decorated attire.

The *camiciaia* worked for individual clients from her own home or convent. In the wardrobe accounts of Duke Lorenzo de' Medici, one such craftswoman appears, with the curious appellation of "Signora di Madonna," to whom are consigned "four pieces of unbleached linen . . . to make camicie for il Signore." It is unfortunately not recorded how much this woman was paid to fashion the duke's undershirts, but the four pieces of cloth (which would have amounted to about forty-five braccia, or yards), cost 75 ducats. At about three and a half yards per camicia, she would have been able to make roughly thirteen undershirts for "Il Signore," bringing his cost per shirt to a pricey 5¾ ducats (florins).[24] The Medici duke was certainly an exceptional case, however, both in financial and social terms. Lorenzo did business with at least forty-seven different persons or companies to supply his wardrobe in the space of one year alone.[25]

Even the women of very rich families oversaw the making of personal linens, which could have been crafted by a camiciaia. However, with only 4.42 people in the average Florentine home in 1427, a certain percentage of families would have lacked a woman to see to these basic garments. In fact, widowers, bachelors, frérèches, orphaned children, or "seemingly unrelated" individuals accounted for one out of six households in Quattrocento Florence. Many of these unusual groupings may have relied on seamstresses outside the family to do this most intimate work.[26]

Traditionally, wives and mothers dealt informally with other woman, either servants and slaves employed in the home or young unmarried women (*zitelle*) or nuns working from convents, to supply the family linens, which included towels, sheets, pillowslips, and other washable items. This was one of the only areas of the Renaissance cloth and clothing trade that remained, for the most part, unprofessionalized, that is, not guild-related, and women on all levels of society participated. The letters of three women of wealthy families—the widowed Alessandra Strozzi, Margherita Datini, and Clarice Orsini, wife of Lorenzo "Il Magnifico"—serve to illustrate this responsibility. From the correspondence of Margherita Datini, a consistent picture emerges of a *donna governa* who sees to the undergarments of her husband Francesco and also those of the servants, retainers, and staff in her childless household. Visiting in Florence for the summer, Margherita writes to remind her husband Francesco that a certain Lapa had made a length of linen cloth four years ago, from which Margherita had had eight undershirts made for herself and twelve for him. She further recounts that a large part of the sewing was done by "Fensi's wife," but because she was too slow, Margherita had given the remainder to "Mona Chita" at the monastery of Santo Nicholaio.[27]

Writing to her exiled sons Filippo and Lorenzo some forty-five years later, Alessandra Strozzi likewise alludes to undershirts. In spite of the fact that the sons are grown and have been away from their mother for years in Naples, Alessandra still sees to their intimate apparel. In 1450, she says, "First, I am sending you four undershirts, six handkerchiefs. . . . the shirts styled and cut in our family manner [*a modo nostro*], . . . I have not made more shirts, because I do not know if you will like these."[28] Alessandra Strozzi skillfully negotiated marriage alliances, bought and sold property, and prudently managed her own and deceased husband's estates, but she nonetheless still personally provided her sons' linens, made *a modo nostro*. This same letter continues with Alessandra promising her son Filippo that when his sister Lesandra leaves home to be married, she (his mother) will have much more time to devote to his and his brother's things. "I shall furnish you such linens that you will be well off," she writes. "When she leaves, I shall not have to attend to anything except everything for the three of you . . . and I shall be a little better at household affairs."[29]

In a third letter, from one woman to another, both married into the Medici family, Clarice Orsini writes to her mother-in-law Lucrezia Tornabuoni complaining that there was "nothing but the walls" in the family house in Gagliano, where her husband had installed her and the children to escape a wave of plague. "I would like you to send me various things from Florence, for I have nothing for the use of the family," she pleads, listing forks, sheets, tablecloths, and "twenty braccia of linen cloth so that I can make camicie for these children."[30]

Beside undershirts, personal head coverings also fell into the category of homemade linens, including caps (*cuffioni*) worn under cowls or hoods, helmets, and at night to bed. Headscarves (*benducci*) were worn by both men and women to ward off a chill. In a letter dated May 8, 1394, from Prato to Florence, Margherita sends her husband Francesco "two new cuffioni for you," and also "a little cuffiolina to put under your hood, and two benducci."[31] It seems clear from these women's letters that they were not simply directing household servants or seamstresses to sew for the family but were personally picking up needle and thread. Alessandra Strozzi, Margherita Datini, and even Lorenzo de' Medici's wife Clarice herself had ultimate responsibility for the family linens. In another letter from Florence to her husband, Margherita asks him to send her some things she needs, explaining that more garments would be forthcoming but that "we have not had a needle to sew with."[32] About three months later, Margherita asks Francesco to send her some fabric, with which she would undoubtedly begin yet another sewing task.[33]

Sarte in the Convents | But not all women had families for which they were obliged to sew. In fact, as dowry amounts soared in the Quattrocento, many girls of elite lineage never married, instead being housed by their families in one of the increasingly numerous convents in Florence. As Molho has noted, some of the fathers of the young women living in these institutions had taken advantage of the option of not having to expend perhaps personally ruinous amounts to dower a daughter who had a spiritual calling or little chance of making a marriage for one reason or another. A family head could arrange to settle a daughter in a convent with a small monastic dowry and make subsequent payments over time for her support.[34] This allowed elite families to avoid the social embarrassment of being unable to afford the dowries necessary to contract honorable marriages for multiple daughters and, at the same time, provided the only "honorable" alternative for young women of noble lineage, that is, to become virginal nuns, praying for their city.[35] (The issue of convents is examined more closely in Chapter 7.)

But besides praying, such young women from upper-class families, with perhaps no spiritual or scholarly inclinations, could devote their energies to the hypnotic involvement of daily needlework within the confines of conventual life, making a wide range of decorated cloth items, from embroidered vestments for the Church to lace handkerchiefs for themselves and their families.[36] Some of these women in convents actually manufactured items for sale. By the Cinquecento, some convents in Italy accepted young girls of impoverished families between the ages of six and twelve, even daughters of prostitutes.[37] Maria Elena Vasaio notes that these girls were taught to read, write, weave, sew, and embroider by the *figliole perpetue della casa,* that is, by female superiors. Unlike their more privileged counterparts, these unfortunates needed to learn a skill in order to accumulate dowry funds if they were ever to marry and leave convent life, an option ironically not usually open to their social betters. Their female superiors taught them to weave both linen and woolen cloth, from which they made their own plain, unadorned clothes. In winter, they wore gray wool smocks of *berettino,* and in the summer, coarse linen cloth of the same color, also woven there.[38]

But these girls, who were allowed no personal ornamentation for themselves, did often sew and embroider for others. After they had finished their day's work for the convent, they were allowed to embroider items such as fancy handkerchiefs (*bellissimi fazoletti*) and striped shawls (*scialle rigati*) for outside customers, notwithstanding rules restricting the activities of cloistered women.[39] Early religious institutions for women were often desperate for cash and took to supporting themselves by lacemaking, silk embroidery, or fashioning purses. After the Gregorian reforms of the late eleventh century had cloistered the convents, however, the Church hierarchy forbade these economic connections with the secular world. Nuns were no longer to make "alms-bags, frill-collars, needle cases, and such things; nor should they do any work in silk except to make things pertaining to the Divine Service."[40] In other words, nuns were to use their time only to embroider ecclesiastical cloth and liturgical vestments for use by priests at Mass, but not to develop a potentially threatening independent economic base of their own.

As time went on however, the role of the convents as places of residences or temporary shelter for single young women forced the Church to accommodate the secular nature of their stay. Extra needlework jobs (convent residents are also recorded as thread makers) helped to establish a dowry, which less-fortunate girls would need if they hoped to attract the attention of a male visitor and someday marry.[41] At Santa Caterina della Rosa in Rome, residents who had not yet taken vows were allowed to participate in a procession outside the convent every year, on November 25, the feast day of their patron saint, to give the young women an opportunity to be seen safely by the unmarried men of the community. They were also allowed a limited amount of talking to visitors at a convent window, where they not only could establish a reputation for personal modesty and attractiveness but could show off their talents by casually displaying a sample of their needlework to impress an interested man. Vasaio recounts the case of a poor custodian, one Alessio Laurentani, who became infatuated with a young woman there, a Lucrezia Casasanta, after he saw a sample of her needlework in the form of an embroidered handkerchief.[42] Another couple were also introduced at St. Catherine's. An impoverished tailor, one Oratio Cavallo Bresciano, married Laora Fontana, a resident there. He was so poor that the Order had to provide her with the 100 scudi dowry for a white wedding gown, then considered essential to establish her reputation as an honorable bride.[43]

Once married, Laora Fontana and other women like her, having been convent-educated in weaving, sewing, and embroidery, could work as seamstresses to augment their husbands' earnings.[44] Earlier, Margherita Datini had dealt with women in convents in the environs of Florence. On March 6, 1395, she writes to her husband Francesco: "I had thirty towels that Mona Vivola made for me and twenty-four big ones from Mona Chita. . . . and I had twelve tablecloths made. . . . and five pairs of large sheets, that Mona Chita at the monastery of Santo Nicholaio [made]."[45] Cloistered women of a modest social level, then, provided a percentage of the sewing of personal and household linens. Their more elite warehoused sisters, however, whose options were limited by their elevated social status, for the most part languished within the walls with only a casual needle and thread to pass the time, being considered too "honorable" to work as seamstresses.

FEMALE ACCESSORISTS

In general, women not only crafted the personal linens of the wardrobe but also participated in making products worn and used by women, which can be divided roughly into two categories: belts, bags, and hosiery, and hats and headwear.[46]

The *Borsai, Calzaiuoli,* and *Cinturai* | The first category comprises purse, hosiery, and silk belt making. These seem to have been women's specialties, even though both men and women could carry a bag (*borsa*) and wear a belt or hose. The latter were primarily worn by men in the Quattrocento with their doublets. Purse makers (*borsai*) who made bags for women, however, were most likely women themselves. Silk purses were also one commonly convent-made object. Herlihy cites Francesco da Barberino's poem about a lovely young uncloistered religious woman (*pinzochera*) who made "fine and beautiful" purses of silk to support her family.[47] While there were male purse makers, who were in a lesser tier of the Arte dei medici, speziali, e merciai and may have had their own shops, female purse makers either sold their wares informally or to a mercer. In 1427, eighteen male purse or pouch makers identified themselves as carrying on this craft in Florence, over half of them (some 60 percent) residing in the quarter of Santa Croce. These guildsman probably crafted bags and pouches of leather, as this quarter was also densely populated with slipper makers and furnishings dealers (*guarnai*), who carried leather merchandise among a range of clothing accessories for sale.[48]

Secondly, hosiers produced the soled leg wear that had been a specialty of Florence since at least 1132. They had first organized themselves into an association with drapers (*pannaioli*) around 1282. This early association was then incorporated into the Por Santa Maria, where they constituted a tier of minor members of the guild. Female hosiers also worked outside the guild, and Davidsohn tells us that in the early fourteenth century, these women owned their own tools.[49] Hosiery itself was made of perpignan cloth (*perpignano*), a washable and stretchy woolen jersey fabric, originally developed by weavers in Perpignan, France. Hidetoshi Hoshino has shown, however, that by the Quattrocento, Florentine production of perpignano increased to accommodate the growing market.[50] Family logbooks detail the purchase of this cloth in scarlet, rose, blue, "dark," and specifically, dyed with *grana*, one of the most prized dyestuffs for the color red.[51]

Last in this group of clothiers were the belt makers. The craft of belt maker initially appeared in Florence on the first matriculation list of the Por Santa Maria in 1225, where three belt makers are listed.[52] Women were involved in this craft from the beginning; in 1294, a female *cinturaia* matriculated into the "Arte e Universitas Zonariorum," another early guild of belt makers. One Donna Santa, wife of Palmerio, paid a three-lire entrance fee and swore to observe the statutes and regulations of the guild. The document was signed by a rector of the guild and witnessed by another rector from the guild of strap makers.[53] This early *societas* then also became a *membra minora* of the Por Santa Maria.

In the Trecento, a woman's belt (the wide *cintola* or *cintura,* or the thinner *cordone*) was her most important accessory and was usually the only ornament she owned. Women of humble families living in the Florentine *contado* (countryside) often had as their most valuable possessions a silver-embroidered silk belt, *una cintura di seta ricamata d'argento,* and a few silver buttons.[54] Belts in upper-class family wardrobes could be more elaborate, even dazzling, however, as we shall see below.

The *Mazzocchiai, Ghirlandai,* and *Cuffai* | The second category of female occupations comprised the making of headwear. Women were employed in this sector making bulbous-shaped foundations of willow or wire that became turbanlike hats (*balze*), circular hat forms of cork (*mazzocchi*) that, when covered with fabric and decorated, became *ghirlande* (literally, garlands), and *cappucci* (constructed headgear). These women lacked formal guild association.[55] Marco Parenti dutifully recorded his dealings with a "Sandra mazzocchiaia" in 1447, to whom he paid the rather large sum of 2 florins 18 soldi to fashion a headdress for his bride. Sandra was hired to sew two strands of braided pearls to the garland-shaped hat form of what would become an elaborate headpiece.[56] Twelve years later, in 1461, a craftswoman with the same name appears in the records of the Rinuccini family, making a net for another woman's mazzocchia.[57] Clients supplied the various elements of a headdress, consisting of a willow foundation, silk brocade or velvet, and pearls, gilded tinsel, spangles, and even peacock feathers, to a mazzocchiaia or ghirlandaia, who then custom-crafted the piece to go with a specific ensemble. Although many of their wares may have been sold by guildsmen, the actual making of the headwear item was not under guild control.

The construction of close-fitting caps or bonnets (*cuffie*) began as an independent female occupation, to meet the need for light, washable, linen hair coverings. In time, cuffie came to be worn by both genders, either alone or under other head coverings such as hoods and helmets, for warmth or protection. Male practitioners of this craft, known as *cuffai,* along with makers of cappucci, were recorded as sottoposti to the Por Santa Maria as early as 1225, and in 1255, a *cuffiaio* was a member of the Consiglio of the Commune of

Fig. 2.2. Pearl-embroidered *cuffia*. Florentine School, *Portrait of a Lady in Red* (fifteenth century). National Gallery, London.

Florence. In 1316, they united briefly with the buckle and clasp makers, but they later became aligned with the mercers in the Arte dei medici, speziali e merciai.[58] In the fifteenth century, cuffie became more substantial, made of silk brocade or wool, even fully embroidered with pearls, and covered the hair completely, as shown by the fifteenth-century Florentine profile image of a young woman dressed in red, wearing a pearl-embroidered cuffia, in Figure 2.2.

MALE CLOTHIERS AND THEIR WORKERS
IN THE MAJOR GUILDS

On the other end of the clothier spectrum were a range of specialty clothiers who had alliances with the major guilds and had maintained an elevated reputation by their association with luxury from the beginning of the Commune's history. These craftspeople were subject to the communal sumptuary legislation, which became increasingly strident in the fifteenth century, especially as regards the clothing of women.

The *Vaiai* and *Pellicciai* | Furriers are mentioned in communal documents as early as 1138.[59] The fur trade itself required an initial large capital investment for the importation of exotic furs and therefore attracted well-connected businessmen who, from medieval times, had served a noble clientele.[60] In 1317, an association of two fur specialties (the *vaiai* and the *pellicciai*), created the guild that became the Arte dei vaiai e pellicciai, one of the first merchant associations of Florence and one of the original seven major guilds. Vaiai enjoyed a certain social status as suppliers of fur to the papal court at Avignon in the early fourteenth century, but in Florence it was mostly used for linings. The vaiai had exclusive rights to work with *vai*, the fur of the large gray European squirrel. They also traded in rabbit and ermine, both widely used for linings. Pellicciai worked with less expensive pelts, dealing primarily in fox and wildcat in the fourteenth century and later adding marten to their inventory.[61] Robert Delort has estimated that by the end of the fourteenth century, more than a million pelts came to the West from Russia and Poland each year to supply the luxury clothing industry.[62]

By the fifteenth century, the members of the furriers' guild ranged from rich import dealers to hands-on craftsmen who made a living dressing the pelts themselves. In 1427, furriers resided more or less equally in all four quarters of the city: 32 percent in Santo Spirito, 26.5 percent in Santa Maria Novella, 25 percent in San Giovanni, and 14 percent in Santa Croce. Some ninety male heads of household identified themselves as vaiai, which made furriers one of the five most numerous clothes-related occupations in the city, after shoemakers, used-clothes dealers, retail merchants, tailors, and gold-smiths.[63] Three examples from Santa Maria Novella serve to show that furriers seem to have done well despite sumptuary restrictions. In 1457, two brothers, Agostino and Filipo di Domenicho d'Agostino, in business in Santa Maria Novella, assessed their shop inventory (probably in fur pelts), at 262 florins, or about 20 percent of their total worth.[64] Further down the economic scale were two other practitioners of the trade, Antonio di Daddo and Antonio di Gusto di Giovanni. Antonio di Gusto had a shop in the Via del Garbo, which he rented for 13 florins a year from Mona Ginevra, widow of Lorenzo "Il Vecchio," brother of Cosimo de' Medici. This fifty-year-old furrier had a wife of thirty-four and two sons, aged six and ten. He owned Monte shares, which he had inherited from his mother, and had a net worth of 68 florins.[65]

The other Antonio died in 1480, leaving a wife named Bartolomea and two sons, aged four and six. His only assets were his *debitori*, who owed him about 50 florins. An inventory done by the officials of the Pupilli listed this more modest vaiaio's worldly goods, beginning with a copper basin, small pan, a cauldron and a pair of tongs (probably all equipment used in dressing the furs), then moving to his household goods (a bed, pots and pans, a few sheets, towels, and tablecloths), and the family clothing. Antonio himself only owned four fur linings, two of fox, and one lined gown (*gonellino*). His own cape (*luccho*) had no fur; instead, this furrier had made do with a lining of black taffeta.[66]

The actual creation of fur garments was not done by the furriers who dressed the pelts, however, but by tailors, doublet makers, and seamsters and seamstresses, who fashioned fur linings. Records are full of references to fur pelts being purchased and consigned to tailors to line cloaks and mantles, make decorative borders, and finish headwear, especially cappucci. For exam-ple, in 1447, Marco Parenti bought twenty-four and a half braccia of crimson velvet, thirty-three braccia of two sorts of lining fabric, and thirty-two buttons from various tradesmen. In addition, he paid a little over 12 florins for 188 fur pelts (*lattizi*) from a "Franco vaiaio." All this he turned over to his tailor, one Andrea di Giovanni, who had the job of fashioning a sleeveless overgown (*giornea*) from these materials; the fur was used as a lining and was visible only at the hem of the garment.[67]

The *Orafi* and *Gioellieri* | Goldsmiths and jewelers also enjoyed a certain cachet by being associated with the luxury trade, and their output was also strictly regulated by sumptuary legislation. They constituted a tier of minor members of the Por Santa Maria and provided a wide range of chains, rings, pendants, brooches, gemstones, and settings. The mainstay of their business was the production of wedding rings, however, the quality of which was assured by guild statute, which prohibited the use of imitation gems.[68] In 1427, almost half of the city's 100 goldsmiths resided in the quarter of Santo Spirito, especially in the gonfaloni of Scala and Drago Verde, and later, under the grand dukes, there was a concentration of botteghe on the Ponte Vecchio, where the fumes from the sulfur employed in the gilding process could waft down the river.[69] The remainder of the goldsmiths were almost equally divided between San Giovanni (25 percent) and Santa Maria Novella (20 percent), with only seven living in the quarter of Santa Croce.[70] Most of the craftspeople did not live any great distance from where they worked, and in fact living and working quarters often were one and the same. Florence Edler de Roover notes that the warpers who worked as sottoposti for setaiuolo Andrea Banchi lived within a two-to-three-minute walk of his bottega, for they often received warp thread in the morning and returned it by evening of the same day. His weavers, however, were spread out across the Arno in Santo Spirito, where they wove on home looms, sometimes for months on end before reconnecting with him.[71]

In spite of the status of their products, goldsmiths worked in the ambivalent atmosphere of tremendous communal sumptuary restriction on home consumption, and at the same time, intense local pride in their competition for the export trade. Davidsohn wrote that all the jewelry pieces they made were outlawed in the city—the miniature realistic birds, griffins, ships, and castles of enameled gold, the flowers of precious metals. But they did find a limited home market in any case, as the artwork of the Quattrocento can attest.[72]

The *Farsettai* | One specialty that had enjoyed a certain status since the thirteenth century was the making of doublets. Men wore them over their undershirts, as tailored vestcoats fitted to define the contour of the upper body, and under their longer tunics. Figure 2.3 allows us to see the general outlines of a *farsetto*, usually hidden under robes, in a mid fifteenth-century study for a figure of David by Ghirlandaio. A farsetto was a relatively expensive, closely cut garment, which required personal tailoring, making this craft somewhat analogous to a combination of vest and suit coat making today. It could be made of wool, silk brocade, or velvet, and was quilted by female workers with cotton batting called *bambagia*.[73] In 1449, Bartolomeo Pucci had a doublet of green velvet worth five florins listed in his goods; his brother Francesco owned two doublets, the first of black velvet, valued at four florins, the other of velvet dyed with kermes, valued at six florins.[74]

The tailoring specialists who made this quilted garment (worn by and large by males), appeared, as we saw in chapter 1, in the early matriculation lists of the Por Santa Maria. Beginning in 1296, two farsettai had joined this guild, and between 1310 and 1325, an additional forty-six matriculated. Between 1325 and 1430, the membership of the doublet makers dramatically expanded, with 259 additional farsettai joining, including two who worked only in English *garbo* wool, another pair working as both doublet and quilt makers, and one doublet maker who had emigrated to Florence from France.[75] While tailors had been relegated to associations with minor guilds by the late 1200s, the doublet makers stayed within this elite guild well into the fifteenth century.[76] In the third quarter of the fourteenth century, this craft temporarily achieved its own guild after the revolt of the Ciompi in 1378, before it was swept away in the reestablishment of oligarchic control in 1382.[77]

By 1427, only fifty-eight heads of household listed their craft as doublet makers, and out of these, four were women, two in Santo Spirito, and two in Santa Maria Novella.[78] These female doublet makers would not, however, have been independent guild members. No female names appear on the matriculation lists. More likely, they would have taken over their husband's craft upon his death, but their continuance of the often family-sustaining business would have been severely hampered by their not being allowed to take on apprentices or employ male workers.[79] Of the total number of farsettai in 1427, almost half resided in the quarter of Santo Spirito, almost one-third in San Giovanni, and only five in Santa Croce.[80]

Fig. 2.3. Male wearing a *farsetto*. Ghirlandaio, *A Study for David* (mid fifteenth century). Location unknown.

Thirty years later in 1457, of eight doublet makers who submitted tax declarations (*portate*) in that year, over half owned a house, had additional land either in town or out in the countryside, and had a net worth of 100 florins or more. In the gonfalone of Lion d'Oro in San Giovanni, one Simone di Antonio di Nicholo was worth 499 florins and in addition to his residence on the Via Guelfa owned a second house in town and eight pieces of land.[81] By midcentury, three-quarters of these craftsmen filed taxes in the quarter of San Giovanni, center of the clothier shops for the city.[82]

The *Ricamatori* | A fourth specialty craft closely aligned with the luxury trade was that of embroiderer (*ricamatore*). This designation typically denoted a male embroidery dealer, not to be confused with a young cloistered woman or mature widow at home plying needle and silk floss for hours on end. Embroidery was big business in Florence in the Quattrocento. It was not only used for wedding finery, festival dress, and children's clothes, but also for ecclesiastical vestments, liturgical hangings, and communal banners, and embroidery firms commanded high prices for specialized projects and kept shop workers and female embroiderers (*ricamatrice*) busy working from their homes. Vasari tells us that Botticelli developed the *commesso* technique of embroidery, used in many religious hangings, by which figures or designs were embroidered onto a piece of fabric and then appliquéd to a larger hanging. The baldachin housed in Orsanmichele, adorned with many entirely different renderings of the Madonna, used this fifteenth-century stitching innovation.[83]

In 1427, the quarter of Santa Maria Novella seems to have been a hub of the embroidery business. Roughly 30 percent of those clothiers in the embroidery or mending crafts resided here, along with the only cotton-wool maker to note her occupation in the city tax records. This quarter also contained 50 percent of the city's total population of uncloistered female religious, who often did needlework from their homes.[84] One successful embroidery firm in the quarter of San Giovanni, home to another third of the embroiderers/menders in the city in 1427, was owned by Lorenzo di Fede, whose shop was in the Piazza of the Parte Guelfa, which he rented from the Parte for 9 florins a year. Lorenzo assessed the contents of his shop as worth only 50 florins, with approximately another 100 florins owed him by over sixty customers, the largest debitori being churchmen, such as one "Messr Riciardo abate di Valle Onbrosa," who owed him 40 florins, and "Messr Batista priore di Santo Ianni da Orvieto" who owed only a fraction of that amount. For Lorenzo's own personal debts, in addition to the three silk merchants to whom he undoubtedly owed money for silk (the companies of the Ferantini, Peruzzi, and Charducci), he also listed the embroiderers who worked for him. He records three men, Michele di Biagio and Andrea di Giovanni, "chon meccho in botegha," and a third male embroiderer, Chosimo di Michele. He also employed two women, Mona Ginevra di Giovanni and Mona Chaterina, herself the widow of an embroiderer, "Antonio richamatore." To the women alone, Lorenzo owed almost 20 florins.[85]

One of these embroiderers, Mona Chaterina, owned her own house in Borgo San Frediano, where she lived with her also-widowed daughter Mona Lisa, tucked in between the convent of Montengmano and the monastery of Santa Maria del Carmine. She owned a second house in the same neighborhood, which she rented out to one Baldassare, the son of a female cloth worker, for six lire a year. This rent was counted as part of her net worth by the officials of the Catasto, along with her debitori list, topped by her renter, who not only owed her two years' back rent but also a loan of five florins.

Chaterina's other debitori included three individuals associated with the clothing business for whom she may have done sewing—Mona Tulia, a tinsel maker (*orpellaia*), Piero d'Antonio, a painter, and Piero d'Iachopo, a weaver, who together owed her approximately 34 florins. Lastly, four different embroidery firms were in her debt, including our Lorenzo del Fede. Altogether, these firms, all male-owned, owed Mona Chaterina about 25½ florins in back wages. Counted with her other debitori and rental property, her assessable income was 112 florins.[86]

Twenty-one years later, in 1448, embroidery concerns were doing well. Giovanni Gilberti, a well-known and respected Florentine embroiderer (*ben conosciuto e stimato ricamatore fiorentino*), discussed in Chapter 7, asked Francesco Castellani for 50 florins to embroider the sleeves of a *cioppa lucchesima* for his wedding to Lena Alamanni.[87] The year before, Marco Parenti had spent over 100 florins on gold and pearl embroideries for two gowns, a *cappuccio*, and fringes on collars and wristbands for his wife, and at least four embroidered dresses for his daughters.[88] Compared to the cost of the materials, however, the embroiderer's fee itself was modest. While an embroidery firm such as Niccholo d'Antonio e Chompagni richamatori was getting more than 37 florins for the gilded silver and pearl embroideries done for a woman's outfit, the actual wages of the embroiderer who worked for the firm, such as "Bonifazio richamatore," who filled some of Parenti's orders, was but a fraction of this, from 2 lire to about 3 florins per piece.[89]

OTHER CLOTHIERS IN THE GUILD SYSTEM

The *Cappellai* and *Berrettai*. | Hatmakers and cap makers had formed a corporation in 1316 in Florence, but two major guilds, the Por Santa Maria and the Arte della lana, moved to incorporate them. The Por Santa Maria imported and marketed hats and caps from Germany and France, and the Arte della lana competed to win control over local production of hat and cap makers, to regulate their materials and their botteghe.[90] The cappellai were subsumed in a special *membrum* of the Arte della lana in the later fourteenth century, and the berrettai came under the dicta of the Por Santa Maria.[91] In the Catasto of 1427, only four individuals in the city listed their craft as cappellai. This may indicate the relegation of this craft to informal status, making it a secondary occupation carried on under a head of household who bore the burden of the tax declaration for the family and was involved in a more lucrative trade.[92]

The *Calzolai*, *Pianellai*, and *Zoccolai*. | The last category of clothier in the Florentine marketplace, the shoemakers, were the most numerous. The Arte dei calzolai included shoemakers, slipper makers, and clog makers, and their numbers had initially made it one of the twelve major guilds, but it was relegated to minor guild status when the numbers of major guilds was cut down to seven by the changes enacted through the Ordinances of Justice in the late thirteenth century. The numbers of those who gave calzolaio as their occupation in 1427 was 264, still outnumbering the next most numerous occupation, the rigattiere, by some 104 people.[93]

Forty percent of shoemakers resided in San Giovanni, and 30 percent in Santo Spirito, with the remainder divided equally between the other two quarters. Interestingly enough, some 7 percent of the shoemakers and a full

40 percent of the slipper makers who declared themselves as heads of households on their tax forms were women.[94] No one seems to have paid their
shoemakers for the footwear they made, however, and their families must
have subsisted solely on credit, for the debitori lists of shoemakers in the
volumes of the Catasto regularly run a dozen or more pages, with about sixty
names per page.

The Florentine marketplace for clothing and accessories was, then, composed of a wide range of craftspeople and merchants, representing every
stratum of the urban world of work. Some occupations fell under the control
of the major guilds and were associated with luxury, others with the more
utilitarian production of the minor guilds, and still others were outside of the
guild system altogether. The next chapter tracks down the elusive tailors,
whose place continually shifted within this system, for a closer look at their
place in the socioeconomic milieu of the fifteenth century.

THREE

TAILORS IN

FIFTEENTH-CENTURY

SOCIETY

TWO TAILORING BROTHERS

In the mid fifteenth century, tailors seem to have belonged to a new "middling" group of artisans, reflecting what some historians have argued was an improvement in the standard of living and even a prosperity of sorts for certain skilled occupations in Florence.[1] This period of relative prosperity, paradoxically, coincided with a widening of the socioeconomic gap between rich and poor throughout the Quattrocento, with the upper ranks of Florentine society becoming increasingly display-conscious and aristocratic. Certain artisans who designed, created, and supplied the luxe to these ranks found the opportunity in these new consumption practices to better their own lots financially, however, and make a respectable living. In 1457, in the quarter of Santo Maria Novella on Via dei Fossi, lived two such brothers, Agnolo and Giovanni d'Antonio d'Agnolo (originally from San Gimigniano), and their family, which included wives, children, and widowed mother. They worked together as tailors and made clothes for Marco Parenti and his family for over thirty years in their bottega in the Arte degli speziali, next to Santa Maria Nuova, which they rented for 20 florins a year from Luigi and Giovanni Quaratesi.[2] On Agnolo and Giovanni's list of debts appears the name of the silk merchant Salvestro di Roberto Pitti, from whom they apparently bought silk, and to whom they owed some 97 florins. At the other end of the scale, the brothers owed some 80 florins in back wages to their employees who appear as well (male workers in their shop or female workers doing piecework at home). Their tax declaration also lists their debitori, people who owed them for services rendered, who for more than one tailor stretched into the hundreds and for some included people from the highest strata of Florentine society. Agnolo and Giovanni's debitori list in 1457 numbered 232 people, among them (beside Marco Parenti and his father) scores of the city's most illustrious families, including the Pitti, the Rucellai, and Mona Alessandra Macinghi negli Strozzi, Parenti's mother-in-law herself.[3] It also listed members of all the families of the Medici faction, except for two, the Soderini and the Pazzi. Apparently, sartorial cohesion was desirable in political cohorts, and beware the holdouts.[4]

Agnolo and Giovanni themselves were not poor. In debitori and property, including a farm of approximately 120 acres (staiore) in Settimo, they had a net worth of 787 florins.[5] But with two wives (Brigida and Piera), fourteen children ranging in age from sixteen years down to one month, and their sixty-two-year-old mother, Mona Bernarda, living with them, their allowed deductions more than counterbalanced their income (200 florins per mouth), leaving the brothers to pay only 8 soldi in tax.[6]

TAILORS AS A GROUP IN 1457

Tailors' Estates | In 1457, the assets that made up the bulk of tailors' estates began with the family house, which 82 percent of tailors surveyed owned. Almost 30 percent of these tailors rented these houses out (for 2 to 10 florins a year), however, and either rented other accommodation in the city for themselves or lived on their property in the country. About 40 percent lived in neighborhoods on the outskirts of town in the quarter of Santo Spirito. The Oltrarno gonfalone that had the highest concentration of tailors at midcentury was the working-class neighborhood of Drago Verde, with eight; six more lived in other gonfaloni of Santo Spirito.[7] Along with the gonfalone of Chiavi, in the outer regions of San Giovanni, these two districts of Florence also had most of the tailors outside the guild system in 1404.[8] Perhaps surprisingly, however, five of these Oltrarno tailors had an assessable worth between 221 and 1,068 florins. At the same time, only about 15 percent of the tailors of Florence lived in Santa Maria Novella, and almost none in Santa Croce, except for one Andrea di Lotto, who was retired (see Table 3.1). Tailors' botteghe were, however, typically in the center of the clothiers' district of San Giovanni, in the Mercato Vecchio, the Via Porta Rossa, and the Piazza of the Parte Guelfa. Alessandro Stella has noted that with the growing polarization between rich and poor in the city, came a concomitant change in patterns of residence, with the wealthy in the center and the poor and immigrant communities at the periphery.[9] Small service workers such as barbers and servants lived in the primarily oligarchic neighborhoods in the center, however, because they needed easy access to their employers.[10] What we see for tailors is a split between workplace and place of residence. They needed to be close to their oligarchic clientele for fittings and service but lived in neighborhoods on the outskirts of town.

The value of the primary residence of those who owned and lived in their own *casa* or *casetta* was not included in their taxable income, and adding this to their gross assets pushes tailors as a group further up the economic scale.[11] Of the thirteen richest tailors, ten owned property in addition to their primary residence, and nine had farms, some of which were worked (with a house for the worker on the land), planted with vines, olive trees, or fruit trees, while others are simply described as "wooded." Agnolo and Giovanni's farm, as we saw, was as large as 120 acres. Even tailors with very modest estates sometimes had additional land outside of town; out of a group of the five tailors included in Table 3.1 who had a net taxable worth of only between 36 and 100 florins, all owned land, and four had vineyards.[12] Almost 15 percent of tailors had shares in the communal Monte, and one had shares in the dowry fund, the Monte delle doti, which in this case set aside money for a granddaughter's dowry. One of the other richest in this group was a tailor's widow, sixty-year-old Mona Lucia, *vedova* of Leonardo di Bartolomeo, who owned a house in the gonfalone of Lion Bianco in Santa Maria Novella. Lucia listed only a twenty-year-old nephew and an older sister as deductions on her tax declaration, but her husband had left her with assets worth 1,122 florins, consisting of a house in town, two farms in Prato, eight additional pieces of land, and a vineyard, which she gave to San Domenico in Prato.[13]

Personal Effects | As far as personal possessions went, tailors' estates were modest. A tailor's accumulated family effects consisted mainly of household utensils, clothing for the various members of the family, a few family trea-

TABLE 3.1
Tailors' Demographics (Florence, 1457)

NAME	ASSESSABLE INCOME (IN FLORINS)	(GIVEN) RESIDENCE (QUARTER, STREET, PARISH, GONFALONE)	(GIVEN) BOTTEGA
Antonio di Domenicho di Pagholo	1,861	S. Spir, Via della Chiesa, Drago Verde	(none given)
Mona Lucia, widow of Leonardo di Bartolomeo	1,122	(Prato) pop. S. Piero Forelli	(none given)
Antonio di Jacopo di Miche, called "Barberino"	1,068	S. Spir, pop. S. Fred, Drago Verde	S. M. sopra Porta
Giovanni d'Antonio di Giovanni	853	S. Giov, Piazza d. Parte Guelfa	P. d. Parte Guelfa
Agniolo e Giovanni d'Antonio d'Agniolo di Toro di Sangimigniano	787	S. M. Novella, Via de Fossi, L. Rosso	Arte d. Speziale
Bartolomeo d'Antonio	397	S. Spir, Via Mozzi, Drago Verde	P. d. Parte Guelfa
Bernaba di Francesco di Mechuci	338	S. M. Novella, Via del Sole, L. Bianco	(none given)
Cristofano di Pagholo	325	S. Spir, pop. S. Pier Gattolino, Ferza	Mercato Vecchio
Domenico di Giovanni	288	S. Giov, pop. S. Pier Maggiore, Chiavi	(none given)
Gunto di Piero di Chino, called "El Zuca"	264	S. Giov, Via del Ciliegio, Chiavi	(none given)
Simone di Lorenzo di Simone	249	S. M. Novella, pop. S. Andrea, L. Rosso	Mercato Vecchio
Mona Piera, widow of Ventura di Ceffo	240	S. Giovanni, Via Larga, Lion d' Oro	(none given)
Antonio di Domenico	221	S. Spirito, Ferza	Santo Spirito
Domenico di Giovanni	192	(none given)	(none given)
Domenicho d'Andrea di Rinaldo (retired)	168	S. Giovanni, Vigna Vecchia, Bue	(none given)
Mona Andrea, widow of Cione di Cavalcante	143	S. Spirito, pop. S. Felicita, Scala	(none given)
Jacopo di Filippo	132	S. Giov, Via San Gallo, Lion d' Oro	(none given)

Name		Residence	Shop
Bartolo di Michele	107	S. M. Novella, pop. S. Pancraz., L. Bianco	(none given)
Antonio d'Angnolo di Martino	100	S. Spirito, Via Maffia, Drago Verde	Porta Rossa
Filippo di Pagholo	100	S. Spirito, Nicchio	(none given)
Giuliano di Donato	64	S. Spirito, Via Gualfredotto	Porta Rossa
Pagholo di Bartolomeo	64	S. Spir, Borgo S. Jacopo, Drago Verde	(none given)
Tomaso di Migliore	62	S. Giovanni, Piazza de Peruzzi	(none given)
Niccolo di Lucha	54	S. Spirito, Drago Verde	(none given)
Giusto di Benedetto	50	S. M. Novella, pop. S. Martino, Unicorno	(none given)
Andrea di Lotto (retired)	36	S. Croce, pop. S. Martino, Ruote	(none given)
Mona Checha, daughter of the late Mona Betta, widow of Francescho Fallchucci	0	S. Giov, Via San Gallo, Lion d' Oro	(none given)
Miniato e Bartolomeo di Baldo di Miniato	0	S. Spir, pop. S. Pier Gattolino, Ferza	Arte d. Speziali
Lione di Simone di Francia	0	S. Spirito, Drago Verde	(none given)
Giovanni di Antonio	0	S. Spirito, V. Camaldoli, Drago Verde	(none given)
Domenicho di Rinaldo di Neri	0	S. Giovanni, Lion d'Oro	(none given)
Bartolomeo d'Antonio (retired)	0	S. Giov, pop. S. Pier. Maggiore, Chiavi	(none given)

Total (known) Residences		Total (known) Shops	
Santo Spirito	14	Santo Spirito	1
San Giovanni	10	San Giovanni	8
S. Maria Novella	5	S. Maria Novella	2
Santa Croce	1	Santa Croce	1
Prato	1	Prato	0

SOURCE: ASF, Catasto [1457]

sures, and the essentials of the tailor's shop. An inventory of the estate of one
Michele di Giovanni di Betto, a tailor from Pisa who was working in Florence
in 1479, shows the extent of his goods. After his demise, the officials of the
Pupilli, being legally concerned with the well-being of the children (Vin-
cente, aged four years, and Michele, aged six months), listed all of his possessions.[14] They began in the bedroom with the beds, mattresses, linens, pillows,
and chests, then moved on to clothing (a modest wardrobe of five or six
gowns, some hats, and children's clothes); precious items (a pair of crystal
saltcellars, an ivory comb, a silk-embroidered handkerchief, a flowered veil);
jewelry (two gold rings, a string of coral, five silk belts decorated with silver);
furniture (coffers, a table, cupboards, a cradle, and a tailor's table, or *descho da
sarto*), kitchen utensils (spoons, pots, copper washbasins, fireplace tools,
lamps, six candlesticks); and devotional items (an altar, a plaster-of-Paris
statue of the Virgin Mary).

A few items in his family goods may indicate a rise in the status of tailors as
a group in the mid-to-late Quattrocento. These included a pair of chests
painted with the "arms of the house," the Virgin Mary statue, which also had
the "arms of the house" in relief, and a wooden table measuring four braccia,
again with the family arms.[15] What these "arms of the house" of the tailor
might have consisted of is not known, but that there was evidently a developed sense of familial identity in a working tailor's family is noteworthy in
and of itself. Family coats of arms were normally associated with old lineages
of distinction or with newly made wealth, certainly not with artisans, who
were for all practical purposes marginalized in the lesser guilds. However, a
large pair of stylized scissors (*forbici*) in full color, evidently a tailor's personal
blazon, also adorns the first page of an unpublished poem on Savonarola from
1498 by one "Giovanni sarto fiorentino."[16]

UPWARD MOBILITY

Stella's figures for 1352 and 1404 show an upwardly mobile trend for tailors as
a group.[17] By 1427, the more than 100 tailors who submitted tax declarations
to the city officials had an average net worth of 154.6 florins, which ranked
the occupation of tailor only nineteenth in the city, behind metal mongers,
masons, and woodworkers, among others.[18] However, by 1447, we see in-

dications of a rise in prosperity. In that year, Marco Parenti paid the sum of 19 lire 8 soldi to the tailor Andrea di Giovanni da Bibbiena for two garments for his bride's trousseau. These were very special wedding outfits, but the fee was for the tailoring alone and did not include any materials, all the fabric and notions having been supplied by Marco himself.[19] This is even more remarkable given that the fifteenth century was a period of relative price stability.[20] As high as that may have been for labor at the time, contrast the amount paid to the tailor with the total cost of the garment, however, which came to over 102 florins, including cloth and ornaments.[21] This suggests that while the rich were spending ever more conspicuously, the earning potential of artisans was also relatively higher.

Ten years later, by 1457, of those who did possess taxable assets, the average Florentine tailor's net wealth was approximately 357 florins.[22] From a group of thirty-four tailors (including three tailors' widows and one surviving daughter) who carried their tax declarations to the office of the Catasto in 1457, ten had a net worth of over 250 florins.[23] As a group, their taxable wealth ranged from a high of 1,861 florins down to those who listed themselves as totally without assets. The painter Andrea del Sarto (1486–1530) exemplifies the tailors' rising prosperity. His great-grandfather had been an agricultural worker (*lavoratore di terra*) near Fiesole, and his grandfather a weaver in the city; his father became a tailor (hence his son's surname), and by the late Quattrocento, Andrea himself was a much-sought-after artist.[24]

ONE OF THE RICHEST TAILORS IN 1457

We can see how one sarto's social position evolved in the course of thirty years, between 1427 and 1457, based on the fruits of his chosen occupation. Antonio di Domenico, our richest tailor in 1457, had lived on Via della Chiesa in Santo Spirito for at least thirty years. He had taxable worth in farmed property, land, and Monte shares, as well as money in the Monte delle doti for his granddaughter. This man had not only made his own living in tailoring but set up both sons in business. In 1427, at the age of thirty-seven, Antonio had had a taxable worth of 814 florins. Some thirty years later, at the age of sixty-eight, he was worth 1,861 florins, having more than doubled his assets. He still lived in the same house, but had turned his half-ownership of a second house in the same quarter on Via Sant'Agostino into a full ownership and added a farm of some twenty-six acres, worth over 310 florins, and a vineyard of some fifteen acres, valued at over 120 florins, to his real property.

Antonio had a shop in the center of the old city, which was located in Via Porta Rossa in the quarter of San Giovanni, and the list of customers who owed him money in 1427 included many of the powerful elite of the city, such as members of the Panciatichi, Albizzi, Tornabuoni, Popoleschi, Strozzi, Pazzi, Guidetti, Corsi, Cavalcanti, del Bene, Salviati, and Rucellai families, and even Giovanni di Bicci de' Medici. By 1457, Antonio had been retired for six years (he lists himself as "fu sarto") and no longer had a bottega. He had spent 500 florins to buy a silk shop under the aegis of the major guild of the Calimala for his older son Bartolomeo, aged twenty-eight, and had spent about 33 florins for furs to set up his younger son Francesco as a furrier (a venture that had failed, Francesco going bankrupt). In 1427, Antonio's wife Bonda, aged fifty-four, was still alive, as was his older brother Pagholo, aged seventy-three, who lived with them. Antonio's Monte shares had grown from 372 florins in 1427 to 456 florins in 1457, and he also had 200 florins invested in the Monte delle doti for his granddaughter, the daughter of his son Bartolomeo.[25] We see here indications of a successful career, with the rewards of stability, increased property, and monetary investments.

THE STRUCTURE OF WORK

Other tailors, however, were in less prosperous circumstances. In 1457, in spite of an upward trend for many, some 18 percent of Florentine tailors surveyed listed themselves as *miserabili*, completely lacking any resources, save the daily toil of their hands, the dwelling in which they lived, and the children they had borne—true fifteenth-century proletarians.[26] Some 40 percent of this sample found work in the shops of more successful, perhaps more skillful or experienced practitioners of the trade. Tailor Antonio d'Agnolo, likely the father of the brothers Agnolo and Giovanni, took on such a worker on August 2, 1452. He wrote in his logbook, "Richordo chomo ogie questo di 2 de agosto Bernardo di Piero viene a stare chomecho a botegha per gharzone e debe sevire la botega di die e di notte . . . e debe istare ano uno e debe avere per lo salario suuo lire otanta dachordo cho Piero di Michele suo patre."[27]

That is, the youth Bernardo was brought by his father Piero to the tailor Antonio who accepted him as a worker in his shop for one year. He did not outline specific duties here in writing but stipulated that the young Bernardo would be on call day and night and be paid 80 lire per year (approximately 16 florins).

This youth apparently served him well, for in the years subsequent to his hiring, Antonio d'Agnolo's volume of business increased dramatically. In 1450, three years before the young man came to work for him, Antonio had recorded making fifty-five garments for sixteen clients; the next year, seventy-eight garments for twenty-four clients; and the next, sixty-seven garments for sixteen clients. In 1453, however, the year after Bernardo came to work for him, his production level jumped. Together, they made 132 garments for some thirty-eight clients, with the years following continuing to reflect this approximately doubled output.[28]

The Bottega | Only the basics of the trade were to be found in a tailor's shop.[29] Tailoring was evidently an art that relied primarily on skill with scissors and needle, not an inventory of goods.[30] The inventory of a tailor's shop lists only "a large chest, another chest and a clasp knife, a cutting table for large pieces of cloth, two wooden mannequins and some tailor's coarse linen cloth" for fittings, and "other little things," which were not recorded.[31] Neither a scissors nor cloth (except for the tailor's canvas) is noted. Perhaps they were too valuable to be left in the shop.[32]

Prices Charged | From Antonio's logbook for the years 1445–55, we can see clearly the range of prices he charged. Over this ten-year period, he worked for at least 168 different customers, making more than 800 garments.[33] In 1446, for a dark reddish brown overgown with long sleeves (*cioppa monachina*) and a flounced gown with a train, Antonio charged only 8 lire; at 4 lire each, this was well within the 1415 restrictions.[34] However, a wedding dress made in 1448 for a young woman marrying a cloth weaver named Giovanni—plus two gowns for the bride's sister—cost the father more than 8 florins *grossi*. This ensemble included a sleeveless gown of azure blue, a pair of green velvet sleeves, thread, and a length of white silk for the bride, plus a white cloak of linen or cotton and a second azure gown for her sister (who was perhaps a member of the bridal party).[35] The father, one Bartolomeo Natti, must have been stretching his clothing budget to its limit, for he could only have been a minor guildsman at best if his daughter was marrying a cloth weaver.[36] Further, with the florin *largo di grossi* worth 20 percent more than the florin *di suggello*, equaling around 7 lire in 1450, this father paid over 67 lire for four garments and some silk. To give an idea of what this amounted to, in 1447, 67 lire had bought fifty-two brace of capons, 530 loaves of white bread, 140 eggs, and half a barrel of red wine for a wedding feast.[37]

Clientele | Antonio d'Agnolo had handled a clientele with an extremely different profile from that of his sons Agnolo and Giovanni a generation later. Whereas his sons' debtors would include the richest oligarchs of Florence, the father's consisted primarily of people identified in his records by occupation. Perhaps his own business experience gave his sons entrée to a more sophisticated clientele. Of his *debitori*, 18 percent were women and 8 percent were foreign. The average customer bought 3.5 garments, some 20 percent were kinsmen of other clients (3 percent were actually husband and wife), and over 60 percent were repeat customers. Most of his business was with retailers, for whom he apparently made ready-to-wear items, like the ready-made sleeves depicted in the otherwise spare fifteenth-century bottega in Figure 3.1. Although they constituted only 3.5 percent of his total customer base, these shops each bought 40.8 garments a year on average. Antonio employed two or three male workers in his bottega and otherwise hired women to do piecework at home. He grossed approximately 60 florins a year, out of which he had to pay rent on his shop, guild dues, and, eventually, his workers.[38]

RELATIONS WITH CLIENTS

Tailors and their clients necessarily did business on an intimate basis, given the nature of their work.[39] It seems, too, that there were socioeconomic connections among tailors and between tailors and their clients that went beyond the business level. Ronald Weissman has written that social relationships of this period were overlaid with traditional networks of patronage that riddled society and personalized most, if not all, relations.[40] He argues that artisans and shopkeepers attempted whenever possible to convert all neutral business relations into ties of "obligations, gratitude and reciprocity."[41]

Fig. 3.1. Tailors' shop. Castello di Issogne, *Negozio di tessuti*, detail of tailors (fifteenth century).

Patronage | Much work has been done in the past twenty-five years on the character of patronage networks of *parenti, amici e vicini* in Florentine urban neighborhoods.[42] The network of personal relationships that began with one's own relatives and extended family, then radiating out to include friends and the residents of one's neighborhood (*vicinanze*), defined the close-knit atmosphere within which a person worked and did business. Every aspect of a Florentine city-dweller's life was lived under the neighbors' gaze. Dale Kent and F. W. Kent have written that "the intimacy of the local world, the public nature of life in the crowded quarters of this comparatively small city, under the constantly observant eyes of friends and neighbors, made it necessary to go to extraordinary lengths to conceal . . . wealth," and that in neighborhood politics, "the impact of judgments and actions could never be ameliorated by distance or by attribution to an abstract authority; [rather] these confrontations were highly personal."[43] The smooth running of the economy of the city depended on cooperation between its sectors, and even if many tailors worked in one place and lived in another, this does not mean that they were excluded from either neighborhood network.[44]

Letters | There is evidence that tailors participated in patronage linkages initiated through business relations, which were then personalized. In a groundbreaking study, Molho identified networks of patronage in Quattrocento Florence as "a series of parallel hierarchies" of ties of "mutual interdependence" between the upper classes, but he did not see these networks as extending vertically, uniting upper with lower classes in a hierarchy to which artisans such as tailors and their clients belonged. Subsequent work done by Weissman, Nicholas Eckstein, and others, however, suggests closer links between various strata socioeconomically, especially on the neighborhood level.[45] Sharon Strocchia has noted, for example, the personal quality of the relationship between the very rich Filippo Strozzi and the construction workers whom he kept continually employed for years on end building his palace in the 1490s.[46] A few letters between tailors and their elite clientele survive from this period. In spite of an increasing "aristocratization" of the families of the rich (as one historian has termed it), there were evidently complex affective bonds between workers and those for whom they labored.[47] In February 1472, for example, one Filippo d'Andrea, a tailor from

Bologna currently residing in Viterbo, sent a personal letter to Lorenzo de' Medici in Florence. Filippo began his note with an expected formulaic greeting, "Gran stima e auguri me salute raccomandationi . . . ," etc. What is perhaps not expected is the wording of his next phrase, which begins "sotto brevità e domestichamente, io vi scrivero uno grande servizio ch' io vi domando," that is, "briefly and familiarly, I write to ask you a great favor."[48] Asking a favor of a member of the Medici family in the second half of the Quattrocento was in and of itself certainly nothing unusual. Conceivably, any member of this family on any given day received multiple similar requests for favors, words of recommendation, or just downright charity.[49] But what was unusual was the tailor's choice of words to this heir-apparent of the sociopolitical leadership of the city. That is, he writes unabashedly "domestichamente," in an intimate manner.

And furthermore, this tailor does not make a desperate, life-or-death appeal to Lorenzo, such as to help extricate some hapless *fattori* of his from Florence's Stinche prison (although there is a letter from another tailor to Lorenzo to that effect).[50] Rather, he asks Lorenzo calmly to assist him in obtaining a position, "qualche offitio," for a kinsman of his, which the young Medici could do simply by writing a couple of letters of recommendation to certain designated men. He suggests that Lorenzo could write "a Roma a Giovanni vostro" (to his maternal uncle, Giovanni Tornabuoni, manager of the Medici Bank there) and "e simile a Monsignor Orsini" (to one of Lorenzo's own Roman in-laws who was well-connected in the Curia). Both of Lorenzo's kinsmen would then presumably use their local connections to line this man up with a job. Filippo even suggests the type of office his kinsman could work in, "l'offito del conservatore dela ghabella o simili l'offitii."

Both the request and the language in which it is couched are remarkable. Neither betrays the slavish groveling that might be expected in a letter from a low-ranking guildsman (at best) to a member of the Florentine elite. Furthermore, that the letter exists in this form at all is perhaps noteworthy in terms of class relations. This tailor does not hesitate to suggest to whom Lorenzo should write his letters of recommendation, which demonstrates an assured and intimate knowledge of Lorenzo's relationship with Medici affine groups on both the Tornabuoni and Orsini sides of the family, and his suggestion as to how his kinsman might be employed bespeaks at least a cursory grasp of the workings of local government. He knows what type of job—a highly lucrative one, as it happened—would suit his relative.

Even the signature on this letter has a certain degree of self-possession, although standard and formulaic. Filippo signs himself "per loro servitore Filippo d'Andrea sarto da Bologna abitante in Viterbo," etc.—a deferential close, but one that also expresses the writer's sense of his own identity.[51] In two short lines, we learn, not only his name, his occupation (sarto), where he is from (Bologna), and where he is currently living and presumably exercising his trade (Viterbo), but also that he considers himself to be in some sort of relationship to "Il Magnifico," that is, "loro servitore"—a position that in itself carried a not insignificant degree of honor—any connection to one in power carrying with it an implied acknowledgment of that relationship on the part of the one being honored.[52]

This letter presumes on a business association in order to extend the relationship from the economic realm into the social.[53] But such a connection between economic and social was commonplace at this time. It is only our own contemporary experience of a separate economic realm that leads us to cleave economic and social in two and then be surprised when they fold back together.[54] In this case, the tailor and Lorenzo were obviously on intimate terms, with Lorenzo at or near the top of a patronage network of which Filippo considered himself to be a part. We have no record of whether or not Filippo's request for a job for his relative was ever met, but that is unimportant here. What is important is that this tailor perceived himself to have Medici connections and acted upon them. This letter would satisfy even a very strict criterion for what constituted a patron–client relationship, which Molho says did not necessarily hinge on what goods a patron had for his client, but rather "on his ability to bring his clients in contact with other individuals capable of honoring their requests."[55] Lorenzo here was being asked to act this part, that is, the part of broker, not of employer.

Another letter, this time addressed to Lorenzo's mother Lucrezia Tornabuoni some five years later after she was widowed, displays the wide range of requests that came through artisan/oligarch patronage networks. In a typically multivalent plaint, written in the summer of 1477 to Lucrezia while she was at the spa of Bagno a Morba, a tailor's widow, one "Katerina donna di Nicholaio di Piero sarto," begged Lucrezia for help of a most basic nature, while at the same time attempting to authorize herself as a distant affine.[56] She opens with the words "Karissima quanto madre . . . " ("Dearest as a mother . . . "), creating an intimate tone even more quickly than in Filippo d'Andrea's letter to Lorenzo. Asking for cloth so that she can make herself a shift ("una sottana"), this tailor's widow pleads her case by including the information that her late husband has left her with four children, two of whom are ill. Her appeal is based on extreme necessity ("grande bisogno"), and her approach to Lucrezia is personal.

Katerina identifies herself as the daughter of Messr Giovanni's sister-in-law Mona Nadda and, in addition, as the sister of a woman with whom Lucrezia had routinely been friendly when she was in Volterra "for the first time."[57] This tailor's widow is then not only an in-law of Lucrezia's brother Giovanni Tornabuoni but also the sister of a good friend of Lucrezia's in Volterra. On the one hand, she is a needy artisan's widow, with not even enough cloth to make herself a plain shift, but on the other, she is tenuously related to the Medici family itself. She has smoothly qualified herself as in some way part of Lucrezia's intimate circle, thereby hoping to establish Lucrezia's moral obligation to assist her.[58] Dale Kent has recognized this technique of *amici* seeking to incorporate themselves into a kind of extended kin group and appeal to familial solidarity to advance the applicant's case.[59] This letter could hardly exist in a cash-nexus economic system such as we have today, and if it did, it would be considered at best inappropriate and at worst demeaning. In a modern economic system, Katerina's sarto husband would never have been more than a "hand" to any rich family for whom he fashioned clothing. Here, instead, we have evidence of close personal relationships between tailors and their elite clients.

Catasto debitori lists | The largest asset that many a tailor possessed, and the element of his estate that may have been in fact the most valuable in more ways than one, was his debitori list; that is, the accounting of all the people who owed him for services already rendered. Weissman has commented on the extensive lists of debtors preserved in the documents of the time.[60] For some tailors, this list ran into the hundreds of customers and provides an interesting profile of their clientele.[61] John Davis describes the traditional Mediterranean practice of extending credit as a way not only of ensuring goodwill but of crafting a career as an artisan patronized by and respected in the community.[62] Tradespeople became "big men" by giving credit, everyone expected to have credit, and the marketplace at times seems to have run solely on credit. (No one ever seems to have paid their shoemakers, whose debitori lists in the Catasto can run to twenty pages.)

Tailors, too, participated fully in this practice. Many outfitted extended kin groups (such as the Bardi, Pitti, Capponi, Tornabuoni), and members of oligarchic families were sometimes in their debt for twenty or thirty years. Tailors regularly wrote notes on their tax declarations begging officials to consider these debts old and not to count them at full value. Whether or not the officials chose to heed these plaints seems to have been a matter of personal discretion.[63] Women were afforded credit, too, and regularly appear on the lists under their own names. These female customers never constituted more than 1 or 2 percent of a tailor's customers and included some widows, the majority of whom still perhaps tended to patronize independent female seamstresses rather than male tailors.

Tailors generally extended little credit to foreigners, for few appear on the lists; usually less than 2 to 3 percent of the total. By way of contrast, however, the tailor brothers Agnolo and Giovanni served an unusual number of foreign customers, in addition to many members of the Florentine elite. A full 10 percent of their clientele came from outside the city, ranging from Castelfiorentino, Cortona, and Lucca to Sangimignano, Settimo, Vico, and Como, a fact that speaks of their reputation as Florentine sarti par excellence.[64]

Members of the same family tended to patronize the same tailor. Agnolo and Giovanni themselves sewed for four members of the Adimari family, four Bonsi, four Rucellai, five Busini, five Vettori, and eight different members of the Pitti family, among their 232 customers. They also had the distinction of outfitting all of the members of those men Benedetto Dei identifies as "the Medici faction" in 1458 (except for the Soderini and the Pazzi, as noted earlier).[65] Another tailor, Gunto di Piero di Chino, known as "El Zuca," not only cut and stitched for five members of the Bartoli family, including two sets of brothers, but also for three generations of the Bonnamini family: Niccolò, Zanobi di Niccolò, and Messr Jacopo di Zanobi di Niccolò.[66]

One tailor, in particular, seems to have specialized in serving family groups. This was Bernaba di Francescho di Mechuci of Santa Maria Novella, gonfalone Lion Bianco. Bernaba lived centrally with his wife and three children in the Via del Sole and outfitted multiple members of the Altoviti, Buondel-monti, Corsi, della Luna, Ginori, Medici, Rucellai, Strozzi, and Tornabuoni families. In addition, he served thirty-four other families of the oligarchic inner circle.[67] Smaller tailoring businesses, such as that of Bartolomeo di Antonio of San Giovanni, gonfalone Chiavi, only sewed for a limited num-ber, in his case a total of six families: the Albizzi, Bardi, Capponi, Donati, Popoleschi, and Tanaglia. Seven of his customers were from the Albizzi family alone.[68] There is no clear evidence that one house used any one tailor exclusively, but it is clear that family groups tended to rely on a trusted tailor's expertise. Individual households of an extended family used succes-sive tailors over time, one replacing the next when the first was no longer active.[69]

The Medici employed many tailors and perhaps had those who worked exclusively to serve their exceptional needs for public clothing. Six tailors (and one embroiderer) from Milan are named for payment from the Medici bank account in two pieces of their correspondence.[70] These tailors were not all Milanese, however; four are listed respectively as "da Casale," "da Arona," "da Galia," and "da Trivio." The court city of Milan would, however, have provided a tailor with an even better living. By 1515, Duke Lorenzo de' Medici would keep five tailors busy himself, including a "Bernardino Napo-letano," from Naples.[71]

We also know from another letter that, not surprisingly, the tailors who worked for the rich did come to the family palazzo for private fittings. A letter of November 5, 1457, from the frequent Medici correspondent Gio-vanni di Luca Rossi to Ginevra degli Alessandri, wife of Giovanni de' Medici, informs her that a young woman, perhaps about to marry into the family, has been seen and fitted, in the presence of her mother. "The young woman came to Florence with her mother [she had come to Careggi, one of the Medici villas], and the tailor has come and seen the gown on the back of the girl and marked the design and taken the measurements . . . they say they are very happy," he writes.[72] While women of most families would have had their clothing cut by female seamstresses, and perhaps even sewn up by the women of their own families, fashioning important gowns for the elite patrilineages of Florentine society required a tailor's sure cut and professional mien. Here, the gown was deemed crucial enough to be designed and measured on the young woman herself, with no wooden mannequin standing in.

As clothes became more fitted and display clothing with a high degree of ornamentation came to be in demand, those tailors who could wield their scissors well were amply rewarded, for personal, familial, and communal honor were all at stake. Chapter 4 takes up the connection between clothing and honor to examine the ways in which the elites made use of the fruits of Florentine luxury-trade production to make this honor publicly visible at crucial times in their own family strategies within the public life of the Commune.

II

FAMILY HONOR

T A I L O R I N G

F A M I L Y   H O N O R

CLOTHING THE CITY

Much has been written on the notion of honor in Mediterranean
cultures. As Piero di Giovanni Capponi put it in the fifteenth
century, "La vita senz'onore è un viver morto" ("Life without
honor is a living death").[1] Julius Kirshner has said that in Florence, honor for
men was achieved through one's family reputation, in which wealth, impec-
cable ancestry, and having held high communal office combined to give one
"a form of moral authority" by which "to challenge the rest of the world."
The respect given to one of honorable repute was then internalized by that
individual and claimed as a right.[2] But in order to retain honor once gotten,
ah, that was the rub, for honor needed to be demonstrated continually, on
every public occasion. Kristen Neuschel has written that a member of a
community of honor is preoccupied with the notice of his "equals," and that
since his life is focused on a series of public events, honor has to be acted out
daily in order to be efficacious. One is constantly on the public stage, forever
courting the public opinion of one's peers so that they will continue to see
one as worthy.[3]

In his *Memorie,* Marco Parenti characterized the years of Cosimo's domina-
tion of Florence, from 1434 to 1464, as good and prosperous times. He chose

to illustrate this prosperity by describing how they had dressed in those days. From his memory, he drew a general composite picture of the special occasions upon which Florentines would wear their finest garments; garments that did honor to themselves, their families, and most of all, to their city. "Many festivities [were] celebrated. . . . with . . . women magnificent in dresses of silk, embroidery, pearls, and jewels," Parenti writes. "At these festivities the women were numerous and the youths were dressed in varied and very rich liveries. Men of all ages dressed themselves ordinarily in the finest clothes in beautiful cloth of rose color, or violet, or black, and every color of silk and rich linings."[4]

For Parenti, the most enduring visual image of the prosperity of the Commune was the clothing of its citizens. A Renaissance man of virtù was under the gaze of the community, for being *seen* was central to the experience of commanding the judgment of all—that is accruing honor and avoiding shame.[5] The Florentine humanist Leon Battista Alberti could write in all candor: "I will not say [that poverty] wholly hinders a man, but it keeps his virtue . . . hidden away in obscure squalor. . . . It is thus necessary that virtue should be supplemented by the goods of fortune. Virtue ought to be dressed in those seemly ornaments that it is hard to acquire without affluence and without an abundance of the things that some men call transient and illusory and others call practical and useful."[6] Riches made virtù visible, and honor was the result.

Of course, honor for women was something else entirely. Paolo Sassetti believed that an honorable woman "fecce onore a casa nostra, sempre" ("always brings honor to our house").[7] Patricia Simons has written that because Florentine women of the upper classes lived within a community of honor defined through the male lines, they became valuable "commodities," whose appearance was constantly subjected to the critical assessment of their peers.[8] Elaborate display clothing for women became essential in public in order to recharge their ongoing task of visualizing not their own virtù but the virtù of their male kin (be it father or husband), which was continually in danger of being used up; where one sartorial faux pas in public could theoretically undo months of accumulated honor.[9] Furthermore, as Klapisch-Zuber has explained, the clothing of elite women had to be acquired through the largesse of the men, or at least to appear to be acquired that way. The only goods that a woman acquired "honorably" in her own right were her paternal dowry and trousseau, given to her by her father or male kinsmen.[10] Anything associated with female transmission or female work degraded the "honor" of the goods. Eventually, even the clothing that an honorable woman wore out in public was all fashioned by men, the work of male tailors charged with creating the public outfits; seamstresses making the personal linens hidden beneath the stiff brocades.

FAMILY LOGBOOKS

In order to discern the intense interest and care lavished upon their garments by the rich families of Florence, we have only to turn to their family logbooks (*ricordanze*), in the pages of which their clothes are lovingly detailed. As a matter of practice in the Quattrocento, the clothes that were part of significant events in the family's life were recorded in these accounts and are abundantly listed for the fifteenth century. Aside from being narratives of family life, usually beginning with marriage, these books were also formal records of family possessions, each significant item being duly set down with an eye to posterity.[11] Families saw their clothes as one of the most meaningful aspects of their continuing identity, a self-consciously created collective persona that they conscientiously and at great expense developed over time. Using the logbooks, the details of the coming into being of an important piece of public clothing can be followed, which can tell us much about the clothing process and its purpose. All this took place with much focused family attention. Florentines spent a remarkable amount of time and money on their clothes, especially on outfits they wore outside the home on important occasions, in the public streets and piazze of their city.

ATTITUDES TO DRESS

Alberti makes the concern and even anxiety about clothes explicit in his *I libri della famiglia* (1433), which lays down guidelines for the proper governance of a household and family in Renaissance Florence. Alberti advised the head of the household to be very involved in the clothing of his (or her) family, counseling attention to what each member wore, family and servants alike. In

book 3, the character Giannozzo instructs his grown nephews on the importance of clothes, saying that among his *first* considerations ("fra' miei primi
pensieri") as head of the family would be to keep everyone in his household
well dressed, according to his station ("quanto a ciascuno si richiedesse
onestamente"). He also emphasizes the importance of spending time and
money on one's clothes. If he, as the head of the household, failed to do this,
he reasons, then everyone would hate him and talk behind his back, and he
would be considered a miser. "It would be no true thrift, therefore, to dress
them less than well."[12]

Uncle Giannozzo also explains why it is important to clothe members of
one's own patrilineage especially beautifully, stressing how a "bella vesta"
ennobles one's appearance for public occasions. "We want to have beautiful
clothes. Since they do us honor, we too should have some consideration for
them."[13] He implies here a certain reciprocity between a garment and its
wearer; that somehow one's clothes could work for or accomplish something
for their owner (as a good servant would do). Clothes, then, would work for a
man to the extent that their owner had taken the proper amount of time and
pains clothing himself. Giannozzo advises that before venturing out, a man
should try on his best public garments at home to see what effect they have on
his appearance. Above all, Alberti recommends that one cultivate an acute
awareness of the image one wishes to project with one's clothes. By way of
contrast, in his *De re uxoria* of a dozen years earlier (1416), the humanist
Francesco Barbaro wrote to advise Ginevra Cavalcanti, the young bride of
Lorenzo "Il Vecchio" (brother of Cosimo de' Medici), on the behavior
proper to a dignified wife. She should develop a certain personal objectivity
about *herself,* but not about her clothes. Instead, she should concentrate on
her physical demeanor *in* her clothes, developing a self-reflexive ability to *see
herself being seen,* and so be able to adjust her public comportment appropriately, to convey an honorable impression in the public eye.[14] A woman's
personal identity needed to be submerged within a sociocultural strategy laid
out for her and then internalized.

OCCASIONS DEMANDING NEW CLOTHES

Feast Days | In Florence, all public events warranted special attention to
clothing. The occasions for which clothes were specially made fell into three

distinct categories: holidays, officeholding, and rites of passage. First and most numerous were the feast days of the ecclesiastical calendar, which were celebrated with various events: parades, shows, horse races, and dinner parties, among others.[15] In Florence, the major sartorial display was possible during the spring festive season, which started on May Day and culminated with the Feast of San Giovanni on June 24, when the Commune celebrated its ancient victory over the Aretine Ghibellines in 1298 at Campaldino.[16] Alberti wrote specifically that on these communal occasions, the leading Florentine families that formed the most visually splendid and therefore most honorable part of the larger crowd needed rich new garb.

The chronicler Goro di Stagio Dati, among others, details the preparations for the festival, writing that "two months in advance the making of the palio is begun, and the clothing of the servants, banner-carriers, and the trumpeters."[17] He conveys the excitement of the holiday by describing how both the city and its citizens were dressed. Of the beginning of the festival on June 23, the Vigil of San Giovanni, Dati writes:

> In the morning all the Guilds have displays outside their shops of all their rich things, ornaments, and jewelry. They display enough gold and silk cloth to adorn ten kingdoms. . . . Then, after midday, and when the heat has passed, all the citizens collect by gonfalone . . . richly dressed. . . . The streets through which they pass are all bedecked, from the walls to the seats . . . which are covered with silk . . . and all are filled with young women and girls dressed in silken clothing and adorned with jewels, precious stones, and pearls. And this offering is enough to block out the sun.[18]

With at least twenty such feast days celebrated by the Commune each year, the tailors and specialty craftspeople undoubtedly owed a portion of their total business to the preparation of rich Florentine families for this display. Families had to buy cloth and materials and commission clothing from their tailors well in advance of a specific event, for much time was required to complete an elaborate outfit.

Entries in family logbooks noting purchases of cloth and jewelry along with commissions to the tailors were regularly made all year round, making it difficult to single out which garments were made specially for specific festivities. One fifteenth-century example from the *ricordanza* of the Infanghati family in 1417 details the purchases of jewelry, buttons, and clothing ornaments bought on a continual basis between May 31 and November 26 of that year. These expenses totaled over 73 florins. In the same year, between March 27 and September 16, the Infanghati made regular cloth purchases for all the members of the family. These ranged from luxury fabrics such as fine scarlet woolens (*rosato di grana*) to cloth for linings and stockings (*perpigniano scharlattino*). They also bought the dark *monachino* fabric used for widows and mourners. For this yardage and other pieces, a total of 104⅓ braccia of cloth, they spent well over 140 florins, the equivalent of roughly a year's salary for the second chancellor of the Florentine republic (see Table 5.1).[19]

Once a family purchased the cloth, the tailor often came to the house (for women) to take measurements, pick up the fabric, and begin the cut of the garment. Parenti's logbook records the commissioning of clothing from his family tailors stretching over some thirty-two years, between 1448 and 1481. At least half of the time, tailoring of clothes began in January or early February of a given year and ended in November or even December. In other words, there does not seem to have been in Florence a flurry of clothes making at any one time of the year; instead, there was an ongoing close attention paid to dress.[20]

Communal Office | More important personally for the Florentine families were the occasions when a member of the family was chosen to serve in communal office and in so doing was visually highlighted as a representative of his line. At these times, a man's dress was critical. Alberti writes of proper dressing for civic responsibilities in the commune of Florence, stressing that "good clothing for civic life must be clean, suitable, and well made—that's the main thing. Joyous colors are proper to wear, whatever bright colors suit the wearer best, and good cloth is imperative."[21] In fact, he draws attention to the overgown his fictional character is wearing, saying, "Look at this. . . . I have spent a good many years in it. . . . now, as you see, it is still not too bad for everyday use. If I had not then chosen the best cloth in Florence, I might have had two for the price, but I would not have been as well dressed in them as I was in this one."[22] Alberti's advice probably echoed the sentiments of many citizens of the Commune, which had been manufacturing textiles for hundreds of years. In such a cloth-sophisticated milieu, every subtle distinction between grades of fabric was undoubtedly known and evaluated in quotidian encounters on the streets of the city and in the rooms of the Signoria. Figure 4.1 shows a man in the refined public dress of fifteenth-century Florence in a painting by Andrea Mantegna (1470–75).

Being chosen as either a government prior or part of a Florentine embassy called for significant attention to, and expenditure on, new clothes.[23] Bartolomeo Masi recorded the preparations in 1493 for outfitting the embassy, consisting of six young Florentines led by Piero di Lorenzo de' Medici, dispatched to congratulate Rodrigo Borgia on being elected Pope Alexander VI. He writes that they went to Rome very sumptuously dressed, with carriages and over 175 attendant squires and grooms, also beautifully outfitted. While there, the Florentine ambassadors made it a point to change clothes continually, he notes, so that no one in Rome ever saw a member of the Florentine embassy in the same outfit from one day to the next, and this did them great honor.[24] Marco Parenti also had to foot the bills for these types of outfits. In 1477, when the Commune chose the still *giovane* Piero di Marco Parenti to represent Florence at the wedding of King Ferdinand of Naples as part of the Florentine embassy (along with Messr Bongianni Gianfigliazi and Pierfilippo di Messr Giannozo Pandolfini), his father Marco spent lavishly to outfit him in the best crimson cloth.[25] Piero was representing the republic of Florence, and even though his cloak (*mantellino*) had a luxurious fur lining, it was a plain, rich red, with no pattern or embroidery. It would not serve the purposes of the Commune if its male representatives, even its young men, were too conspicuously dressed, or in any way visually resembled the courtiers of the princely cities of Milan or Mantua, or worse yet, the commune of Siena, known in Florence for its fops. As Alberti's Giannozzo commented, "the slashed garments and embroidery that one sees on some people have never seemed attractive to me except for clowns and trumpeters."[26]

On August 7, Marco purchased a lining ("una fodera di lattizi") for Piero's mantellino from one of the most successful retailers in town, Tomaso di Pagolo e Compagni rigattieri, whose owner was listed by Benedetto Dei as one of the richest men in Florence in 1472.[27] The lining was made of about 300 half pelts, by one "Donato vaiaio." Six days later, Marco went back to the retailer for one more filet, undoubtedly to complete the job.[28] The fluidity of

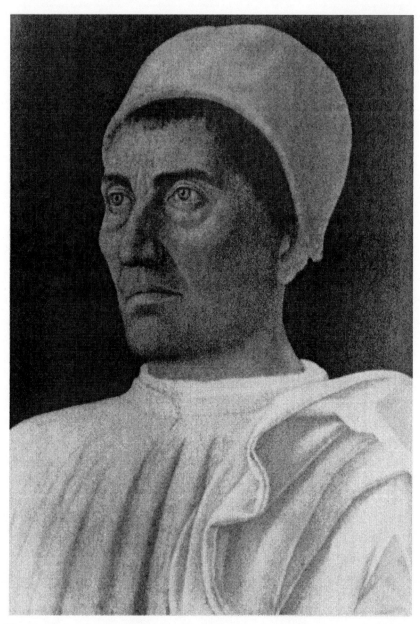

Fig. 4.1. Dress of the political elite. Mantegna, *Portrait of a Man* (1470–75). Uffizi, Florence.

the social structure of the Commune demanded a certain amount of personal control, a studious refinement in appearance by those chosen to hold power. Machiavelli wrote that Cosimo himself affected "great simplicity" in dress but also observed with realistic shrewdness that "two lengths of rose-colored cloth make a man of means" ("two lengths" being the amount needed to make the cioppa of a government prior).[29] Luxurious fur was best kept hidden, as was the labor-intensive nature of the process one went through in order to appear refined.

Public Life | Vespasiano describes many public figures in Renaissance Florence.[30] One of them, Lionardo Bruni, was the quintessential *uomo nuovo*. As a humanist scholar, he had ascended to the highest ranks of civic honor, being named chancellor of the Florentine republic in 1427 (making him one of Europe's earliest humanist statesmen).[31] Perhaps thinking of presenting Bruni as a paradigm of urbane gravity (maybe even a bit too grave), Vespasiano writes: "There was, about Messer Lionardo, a most solemn aspect. He was not tall, but of medium height. He used to wear a full-length scarlet woolen gown with sleeves that were lined at the openings, and over his gown, he wore a full-length rose-colored cloak, open at the sides. On his head, he wore a rose-colored hat, at times with the fabric hanging down on one side. He used to walk through the street with the greatest seriousness."[32] Visually, Bruni certainly embodied the dignified aspect that an upper-class Florentine man was supposed to display publicly on the streets of the city. Clothed in fine rich red cloth, with sophisticated yet unpretentious headwear, confidently worn—in all, a vision of the studied restraint of the cognoscenti.

Women in Public and Private | The term "studied restraint" would not, however, describe the public clothes the upper-class women of Florence wore for public occasions such as weddings, baptisms, and funerals, when to display their husbands' wealth, they dressed as "sacred dolls," as Trexler has memorably put it.[33] Not holding public office, women normally carried out their duties within the private realm of the family. Alberti also had definite ideas about women's dress. Female garments could not be seen as reflective of a woman's essential character, but rather of the role she was to play. In other words, it was important for a woman to understand that she had one utilitarian, sometimes quite physical role at home, and another, quite decorative role when she was being honorably displayed in public, *a fuori*. Cristelle Baskins writes of the "mannequin-like identity" of the Renaissance woman, who, in changing costume, took on a new outward persona invented and promoted by her male kin. Underneath, of course, she was essentially unchanged, simply playing a specific public role.[34] She was to be a chameleon.

Alberti does not specifically encourage expenditures on women's clothing but rather on training her in her duties as a wife. Instructing his nephews in wifely management, Giannozzo draws on his own personal experience as a husband with a young bride. The uncle explains that he taught his own wife not to emphasize her dress per se, but rather to concentrate on the job she had to do and to dress appropriately while doing it. Outside the house in the streets of Florence, she was to bring honor to the family name by walking with measured step and wearing gold brocade. At home, she was to be found busy with a distaff, hair tied up in a kerchief ("il capo fasciato"), attending to the household chores (*cose casalinghe*).[35] It was certainly a difficult balancing act between two fundamentally different personae. Figure 4.2, an unusual image of a plainly dressed young woman attributed to Botticelli (ca. 1478), depicts this type of outfit, very rarely recorded in Renaissance art.

This often physically demanding and never-ending "woman's work" was pointedly detailed by San Bernardino of Siena, who preached a fiery series of lenten sermons in Florence in the early decades of the Quattrocento, and whose female audiences often numbered in the thousands: "The good housewife is one who looks to everything in the house," he says. "She takes care of the granary and keeps it clean, so that no filth can enter. She sees to the oil jars, bearing in mind, this is to be thrown away, and that kept, . . . She sees to the salted meat, . . . she cleans the meat, . . . she causes the flax to be spun, and then the linen to be woven. . . . She looks to the wine barrels, if any are broken or leaking."[36] Obviously, she was not wearing the gold brocade!

So disparate were these two female roles, one private, one public, and such a world apart from the male realm, that Alberti conceived of a clever way to best explain to the young wife (and nephews), just how separate her two essential selves must stay. To illustrate his point, Giannozzo mentally dresses up his wife in the clothes proper to both of her roles, and also, for good measure, with the accouterments of a man. He then fantasizes her parading

Fig. 4.2. Woman *a casa*. *Portrait of a Woman,* attributed to Botticelli (1478). Galleria Palantina, Pitti Palace, Florence.

behind her own servants through the streets of Florence, dramatizing how incongruous all three personae (public female, private female, and male) would be, simultaneously displayed: "Well, my dear wife, . . . suppose it were a solemn holiday and you went out in public . . . and you wore a brocade gown, and your head tied up. . . . and bore a sword at your belt, and carried a distaff in your hand. How do you think people would look at you?" He has his wife reply, "Surely . . . I'd be thought mad, poor me, if I dressed like that."[37] Alberti's point about the need to keep public, private, and gender roles discrete and separate, was shrewdly made. Even the young, malleable wife knows she would look absurd wearing the clothes appropriate for each role simultaneously. The subtext here, of course, is that she must remember the role to which she has been assigned and play it.

Rites of Passage | Family rites of passage, which were treated in Florence as personalized public statements of honorable continuity, were arguably the most important and potentially most expensive set of events for which new clothes had to be made. At weddings (discussed more fully in Chapter 6), the most decorative event of Florentine life and a woman's most important public appearance, no personal extravagance was considered too showy. Communal sumptuary laws regulating dress were not directed toward the bride herself during the wedding, as she was not yet subject to the sartorial restrictions of an adult woman, leaving her free to shine as the proper center of attention. Regulations focused instead on controlling the proceedings surrounding her. Laws limited the kind and quantity of food served, the value of the gifts that could be distributed, and the number of guests and jugglers. The clothes of the guests were also subject to the normal sumptuary restrictions.[38]

Funerals, too, were important occasions for ritual dress. We know from both family logbooks and sumptuary legislation that in the fourteenth and fifteenth centuries, the dress of the corpse was always a concern. Gender was an important consideration. As Ronald Rainey has shown, in the Trecento, a male corpse, dressed in plain white wool lined in linen and wearing a lined cloth cap, was to be borne in limited mourning display to the church, where the services were also restricted by law. Only the funerals of knights and judges (which were considered public occasions) were allowed more ritual display. Women were also honored upon their deaths, but with less opportunity for show. Like men, they were to be clothed very simply in plain white wool, and restrictions for women were more carefully spelled out. They were allowed no head covering worth over 40 soldi, no garlands of flowers or herbs, and no plaits or ringlets of false hair. In addition, it was forbidden to adorn a female corpse with silk, silver, gold, or rings of any kind. The fine for exceeding these limits was set at 100 lire, four times what it was for men, and was to be paid by the deceased's husband, father, or brothers. Only female relatives were allowed to go back to the church the day after the funeral to pray for a dead kinsperson.[39]

The dress of mourners was also prescribed in the fourteenth century, and was typically made of drab *panno monachino*, which was bought and distributed by next of kin to both relatives and household servants. But some personal judgment in mourning dress was apparently tolerated. Margarita Datini and her sister discussed their outfits for the funeral of an old friend who was not a family member in a letter of 1393, attempting to decide whether or not the extravagant *mantello grande* (a cloak that hung to the ground and had a hood that covered the bereaved person's face) was necessary. They concluded that wearing an "unlined cloak" with their faces "decently veiled under the hood" would suffice, because they were not close relatives or personal servants of the deceased.[40] If the deceased had provided for mourning clothes for the females to be paid for by his or her estate, that request could be honored. In 1464, upon the death of Cosimo de' Medici, the four widows and five servants listed in his family records as members of the household all received cloth for mourning clothes from the immediate family.[41]

At the beginning of the fifteenth century, laws concerning funeral display did not immediately change. The communal regulations governing funerals that had been passed in the Trecento were simply incorporated into the communal statutes of 1415. It was not until 1473 that these laws were revised, reflecting the increasingly display-tolerant mores of Medicean Florence. These revisions gave greater latitude to the dress of the corpse and the funeral procedure itself. For example, the funerals of public officials and doctors of law and medicine were allowed banners bearing the deceased's family coat of arms and the emblem of his profession or public office. The corpse could also be dressed in any way deemed appropriate by the deceased's family and could be borne in procession in an open casket. Often, the dead were dressed in the habit of either a confraternity or a religious order.[42]

But the revisions of 1473 also put into place more restrictions on the dress of mourners (*vestiti a lutto*). There seems to have been a marked preference among the elite in the Quattrocento for spending on mourning clothes rather than candles, and as Sharon Strocchia has pointed out, by 1423, mourning cloaks (normally 10 bracchia for a man and 12 bracchia for a woman), had become "huge," with one listed for a woman at 14 bracchia and another (also for a woman) at 26 bracchia.[43] Between 1415 and 1464, trains were allowed to grow, and by 1450, mourning outfits had become so expensive that instead of buying the clothes (which would only be used once), they could be rented for the occasion. Finally, in 1473, a three-tier hierarchy of mourning clothes (from the "deep mourning" represented by the *panno nero imbastiti* to normal black clothes, to "dark" clothes, which could include brown) was put into place. While the new legislation recognized "the new spending habits of the elite," these habits were now manipulated to control display in specific ways and seem to have promoted patrilineal interests. For example, after 1473, only one adult woman from the family of a deceased woman was allowed "deep mourning," and legislation gave preference to the wife of her eldest brother over her own sister.[44] If no specific provisions had been made for mourning garb, then the limit for a woman was set at twelve braccia of dark woolen cloth, out of which she was allowed a cloak, overgown, head covering, and two veils.[45]

Isabelle Chabot notes that widows' garb especially became the focus of severe scrutiny, sumptuary law taking a moral turn.[46] By the 1470s, the Commune watched over not only the length of the train on a widow's over-gown but also the dip of her neckline. A widow was commanded to remain buttoned up, not to expose her breasts, and to wear no stylish fur trim on her gowns. The minutely delineated Quattrocento sumptuary laws on widows' clothes indicate communal concern with these now unattached women advertising and even flaunting their availability through their clothes.[47] Even in mourning and death, clothes were either designed to send or inadvertently sent a powerful message to the living. It was this power that the communal sumptuary laws sought to control and channel.

AMOUNTS OF CLOTH

Generally speaking, the more cloth one wears (thus enhancing one's volume), the more serious and indicative of high social status one's outfit is. (See

Appendix 3 for the cloth required to make selected garments in Renaissance Italy.) In Florence, the old Tuscan motto "He who has little cloth wears short clothes" seems to have held true.[48] Servants and slaves had smaller and shorter costumes. From as early as 1322 on, sumptuary legislation had forbidden female nurses and servants to wear gowns that touched the ground or hoods that concealed their faces and necks.[49] Servants needed to be clearly visible at all times. Fifteenth-century servants' skimpier dress is portrayed in the background of a religious scene in the detail from *The Inebriation of Noah* by Gozzoli (1450) shown in Figure 4.3 (Camposanto, Pisa). Cloth was reserved for the "honorably" rich, who fashioned their garments generously (while still maintaining a judicious proportion between themselves and their ensembles). Outside of Florence, however, overweening pride occasionally did win out, often in a court setting. For example, at the marriage of Bianca Maria Sforza to Emperor Maximilian in 1493, the bride, in her voluminous wedding gown, with long sleeves, has been described as "that poor princess, who was dispatched like a sumptuous doll dressed to play the part of an empress." Indeed, in the early sixteenth century, one thirteen-year-old nubile noblewoman was so weighted down by her bridal attire that she could not walk, and a constable had to be called in to carry her into the wedding ceremony in his arms.[50]

Inasmuch as being seen, being under the gaze of the community, especially one's relatives, friends, and neighbors, was central to being thought of as honorable, Florentine tailors cut overgarments for the upper classes big enough to amplify the opportunity for magnificent display without having to resort to any undignified fussiness.[51] The sense of visual bulk thus created suggested an honorable physical and social dominance for the men and a correspondingly appropriate gravity and general fecundity (without revealing any specifics) for the women.[52] J. C. Flugel observes that long, heavy clothes, and especially "garments that fall in ample folds about the feet, necessarily hinder movement and make rapid walking impossible. They compel the wearer to adopt a solemn, measured gait and impart dignity by suggesting that he [or she] has no need to hurry."[53] This was just the effect a well-clothed member of the Florentine oligarchy would have desired.

Despite the fact that the upper-torso garments worn in the informal domestic sphere of the family were form-fitting (the doublet for a man and the

Fig. 4.3. Servant dress. Detail from Gozzoli (fresco),
The Inebriation of Noah (ca. 1450). Camposanto, Pisa.

bodice [*busto*] of an ankle-length dress for a woman), overgowns and mantles worn outside by men and women's skirts and public cloaks were full. The Trecentesca clothing term *cottardita* still appeared as a category in the communal statutes of 1415 and denoted an amply cut long gown that was magnificent or showy, plainly, *una cotta ardita*. "He wears a cottardita because he is gallant," an old saying opined, with the multiple meanings of brave, noble, high-spirited, and daring.[54]

For women's clothes, more fabric than even for men's seems to have been used by the wealthy in Florence. In 1447, Parenti records an enormous amount of cloth, some thirty-five braccia, for one women's gown, "una roba da donna," which could have included a small train that would emphasize her movement on the street, and also keep that movement honorably slow.[55] The average amount of yardage needed to make the sleeveless overgown (*giornea*) for a woman's formal daytime wear was around twenty braccia—still a lot of cloth. Even the simple long dress worn by a woman, the *gamurra*, required eight braccia alone, enough fabric to make a ball gown today.

Renaissance art often shows women holding a good handful of the ample yardage of their skirts in front of their abdomens. This mannerism, which both facilitated walking and hinted at fecundity, may have originated in a self-conscious attempt to conceal pregnancy that women continued to affect even when not pregnant or past childbearing. The Ghirlandaio fresco of the Birth of John the Baptist from the Tornabuoni Chapel at Santa Maria Novella contains the image of a middle-aged woman, possibly Lucrezia Tornabuoni, mother of Lorenzo Il Magnifico, posed in this way. Working-class women, usually with their hands full of things *other* than fabric, achieved the same casually fecund look by pulling their overskirts up over a belt to create a pouf of fabric (and in so doing, revealed a wide band of underskirt beneath, usually of a contrasting color).

Garments of prosperous men also echoed this generous cut. A Medici account book from December 1515 notes twenty braccia of velvet cloth for one gown ("uno saio di velluto da huomo"). Twenty-six braccia of cloth of spun silver ("tela d'argento tirato") for another gown of even grander proportions was consigned to a tailor, Maestro Francesco, for a formal entrance costume ("una vesta per l'entrata") for Duke Lorenzo.[56] Clothes were not only physically large but formed the bulk of Florentines' personal effects, as we shall see below. It is no surprise, then, as Klapisch–Zuber has pointed out, that women cherished their garments, even though knowing full well that they would probably eventually be sold. In practical Florence, because clothing was so excruciatingly essential for rituals demanding public display of familial honor, expensive garments seem to have been valued by the head of the family only in the context of a specific social and political agenda (marriage alliance, political office, funeral display). When that occasion was accomplished, Florentines cashed in their clothes with surprising ease and focused on a new challenge.[57] The next chapter looks at these family wardrobes from a financial point of view. How much did this all cost?

FIVE

FAMILY FORTUNES

IN CLOTHES

The Parenti, Pucci, and Tosa

SPENDING THE FLORINS

The Florentine elite spent a lot of time and effort on tailoring, cloth, and decorations. But how much money did they actually spend? Their own marketplace for clothing and accessories, both imported and domestically produced, was among Europe's largest, with almost 900 heads of households declaring a craft or trade relating to clothes, shoes, hats, belts, or jewelry in 1427.[1] Communal officials passed sumptuary legislation repeatedly, revising the statutes some thirty-four times in the fifteenth century alone, a testament to the fact that Florentines created occasions to wear the extravagant products of their own cloth and accessories markets.[2] This chapter looks at just how much and how often rich Florentines spent their money on clothes for display, what factors were important in driving up the costs, and how much of a family's wealth was spent on this most personally flamboyant aspect of Renaissance consumerism. Did women dominate the family clothes budget, demanding that family fortunes be spent on jewelry and gold brocade? Diane Owen Hughes has pointed out that Franciscan Observant friars such as Giacomo della Marca (1416–76) preached that wives were so demanding of their husbands for jewelry and luxury accessories that clothes were pawned to Jewish pawnbrokers (*prestatori*), creating rich Jews and impoverishing Christian husbands.[3] Is it possible that the men of Florence were just as guilty when it came to indulging themselves in sartorial display, notwithstanding the modestly dressed males in the portraits of the period?

The high cost of luxury clothing in fifteenth-century Florence can be attributed to many factors, including the processes involved in cloth and clothing production, which were limited by human-powered looms, hand stitching, and time-consuming ornamentation. From the expense of the yardage and the cost of dyestuffs to the wages of the tailors and weavers and the precious materials used by the embroiderers, numerous elements contributed to the extraordinary amount of capital needed to produce these garments for the men and women of the upper class. Good cloth, both silk and wool, was expensive. Florentine fabric could run from almost 3 florins per braccio for fine wool up to 20 florins per braccio for velvet brocades with gold or silver threads.[4] To put this cost in perspective, in Renaissance Florence between the years 1440 and 1480, a family of four could live at a basic level on 56 to 70 florins annually.[5] (See Table 5.1 for annual wages for a variety of occupations.)

Silk Production | Silk cloth was the most costly fabric. The production of locally produced silks had steadily grown from the end of the fourteenth century, when skilled exiled Lucchese weavers found employment in Florence.[6] Expansion into the luxury market was aided by the reunification of the Church after the Great Schism, 1378–1417, when as bankers to the papacy, Florentine merchants dominated literally every aspect of the Church economy, including the supply of fur and elaborate ecclesiastical cloth to the papal court, which knew no sumptuary restrictions. By 1429, the city was giving tax relief to reelers and spinners of silk who relocated in Florence and encouraging the planting of mulberry trees in the countryside.[7] Although the wool industry would still dominate the cloth market of Florence until the end of the fifteenth century, by the first decade of the century, Florentine setaiuoli were also providing luxurious silks, velvets, and brocades, along with damasks, satin, and taffeta, to a ready market, not only at home, but at the courts

TABLE 5.1

Estimated Annual Earnings in Quattrocento Florence

OCCUPATION	ESTIMATED WAGE*
Successful lawyer	200–500 florins/year
Famous university professor	200–500 florins/year
Bank manager	100–200 florins/year
Weaver of brocaded velvet	170 florins/year
Church benefice holder	160 florins/year (varied widely)
Second chancellor of Florence	100–150 florins/year
Brunelleschi (foreman, Duomo, 1430s)	100 florins/year
Official of the Catasto (1427)	96 florins/year
Treasury official	80 florins/year
Weaver of damask	75 florins/year
Average university professor	74.5 florins/year
Communal accountant	72 florins/year
Tailor for middling class (1445–55)	60 florins/year
Strozzi palace construction foreman	60 florins/year
Average construction foreman	51 florins/year
Weaver of wool	43 florins/year
Weaver of plain taffeta	38 florins/year
Carpenter	36 florins/year
Unskilled laborers	27 florins/year
Retired pensioners (basic subsistence)	24 florins/year

*These figures can only be estimates, as a variety of artisans from the lower ranks were usually paid in silver lire, and the value of the gold florin fluctuated daily against the soldi (20 soldi/lira). Rates went from 1/77 in 1400 to 1/137 in 1499. See Goldthwaite, *Building of Renaissance Florence*, appendix 1, pp. 429–30, for fluctuations of the value of the florin between 1252 and 1533.

of northern Italy, France, and England, in Naples and Rome to the south, and in the harems of Turkey to the east.[8] Now, in addition to the heavy silk samites (*sciamiti*) and delicate sendals (*zendadi*) coveted in the Trecento, the Quattrocento silk industry in Italy developed new products with which to compete in the international marketplace.

The first new category of cloth consisted of fabrics woven locally in imitation of foreign cloth, such as damask (*damaschino*), a monochrome figured textile with a satin weave thought to be initially from Damascus, which in the fifteenth century also began to be woven on Florentine looms. Florentine weavers also produced shot silk (*cangiante*) with a taffeta weave, which achieved great popularity in the Renaissance due to its changeable color with warp and weft threads of two different hues. In the light, the lighter color was more evident, while the darker color predominated in shadow. Fashionable combinations of warp/weft threads for shot silk were red and green or red and yellow, and painters depicted this reflected duality in the cloaks of many Renaissance figures.[9] The cost of damasks ran from 3 ½ florins down to 1 florin per braccio, while taffeta cangiante could be had for 15 soldi per braccio. (Keeping even this lowest cost in perspective however, 2 soldi was estimated to be the price of a man's daily ration of food throughout the fifteenth century, so that two feet of taffeta was roughly equal to one man's food for a week.)[10]

Velvets | The second category of silk fabric that reached its ultimate refinement in Italian workshops was velvet, which was often figured or brocaded. Rich Florentines chose three types of velvet for their best clothing. There were first of all, the voided velvets (*velluti rasi, zetani vellutati,* and *velluti inferriati*). A voided velvet had a single-height cut pile that contrasted with a voided pattern, the satin ground showing through. These velvets ranged from 2 ¼ to 3 ½ florins per braccio, as did the second type, the figured velvets (*velluti operati*), combinations of cut and uncut velvet pile, with either a satin or brocade ground. The third and fourth types of velvets could reach the 4 to 5 ½ florins per braccio range. These were the multiple-pile velvets (*velluto altobasso* and *velluto rilevato*), with the higher pile absorbing more light and appearing darker, and velvets with cut and uncut piles of two or more heights, that is, *velluto cesellato*, with the uncut (*riccio*) piles higher than the cut (*tagliato*) piles, and *velluto ricamo*, with the uncut piles lower than the cut.[11]

Cloth of Gold | The third category of luxury silks were silk velvets to which gold or silver threads were added across the loom as a supplementary weft.[12] In Florence, families purchased these fabrics primarily for women's clothing for very specific uses, especially weddings and trousseaux. Two metallic fabrics should be mentioned here. First, there was *velluti allucciolati*, in which the metallic weft was raised higher than the silk pile to form little loops that reflected the light and produced a sparkling effect, clearly shown in the stylized pomegranate design of the young woman's elaborate sleeve figured prominently in the *Portrait of a Lady in Red* in Figure 2.2. Second, there was the more intense *velluto riccio sopra riccio*, which had metal loops grouped together to form a solid-looking gold or silver shape raised higher than the velvet ground.[13] With the addition of threads of precious metals, the latter fabrics could run up to 20 florins per braccio.[14] The fashion in fifteenth-century Florence was to make only the sleeves of a gown of this most expensive brocade, sleeves being routinely detachable after 1450.

Silk Weaving | A big element in the high cost of silken cloth was the time it took to weave using hand-powered looms. Figure 5.1 is a detailed fifteenth-century illustration of a Lucchese draw loom. The creation of figured silks and silk velvets on draw looms had become quite complex by the mid-to-late 1400s, and the amount of fabric that could be produced by one craftsperson in a given time was extremely limited. It took a skilled weaver approximately six months to weave fifty braccia of three-pile brocaded velvet cloth, or about enough for two *giornee* (a *giornea* was a full-length sleeveless overgown). Fifty braccia of damask took about two months to make; fifty of taffeta, four and a half weeks.[15] Fine cloth was a labor-intensive art product and commanded a good price in any commercial marketplace. Furthermore, Florentine silks were known for their small-scale stylized floral patterns, which we can see in the paintings of Botticelli (possibly showing early Chinese influence), and demanded the consummate skill of highly trained weavers.[16]

Raymond de Roover noted that relations between setaiuoli and their weavers were better than those between lanaiuoli and the weavers of wool. This was due in part to higher wages for silk weavers and more genial labor relations between the silk industry labor force and the owners, who had difficulty replacing disgruntled skilled weavers and therefore strove to keep them relatively content and productive.[17] The weaving of silk cloth was a significant part of its final cost, from 7.5 percent for plain taffeta up to 26 percent for a satin velvet. On average, however, the weaving of a silk-based cloth accounted for one-fourth to one-twelfth of its cost. On the other hand, if the fabric, whether silk or wool, was dyed with kermes (the most expensive of dyestuffs), the percentage of the final price attributed to the cost of weaving dropped significantly; generally to about 6 percent.[18]

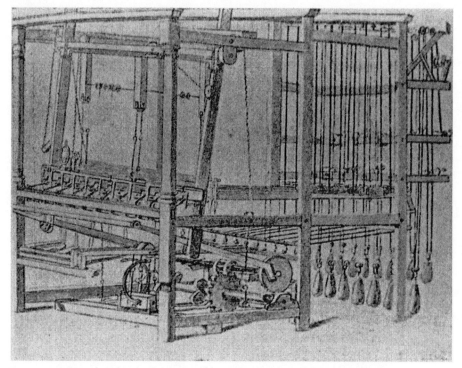

Fig. 5.1. Lucchese draw loom. C. Martini (fifteenth century). Archivio di stato, Lucca.

Woolens | Woolen cloth was the other luxury fabric choice. In Florence during the post-1434 era of Medicean dominance, Cosimo initially set the tone for male clothing, as we saw in Chapter 4, with a certain restrained republicanism demanding simplicity. But it was an elegant simplicity, with crimson mantles and pleated robes created from the finest wools and the most sophisticated professional tailoring.[19] As with the silks, many categories of woolen cloth had begun as Florentine imitations of foreign fabric, as Florence developed its own wool industry from the beginning of the thirteenth century. In the Trecento, the imitation had been *panni tintillano,* which, while not necessarily a luxury fabric per se, was probably superior to other Florentine productions of the time. By the Quattrocento, Florence was also weaving *saia* and *perpignano,* and in 1491, the Commune finally issued a ban on importing any luxury cloth not worked in Florence.[20]

Hidetoshi Hoshino has published the prices fetched for these fine wools, sold by the piece (or *pezza*, equaling twelve to fourteen braccia), which could range anywhere from 2½ florins a braccio for *panno lucchesino* (a scarlet cloth of English wool produced by the Convent of San Martino in Florence), down to dark perpignan cloth, *perpigniano chupo*, for a little over 5 lire per braccio. The garbo cloths could be had for as comparatively little as 13 soldi per braccio.[21] A major reason for the price differential between silks and woolens was that although the production of wool required at least twenty-seven different processes (compared with only nine steps for silk), the entire labor force, with the exception of the wool weavers and dyers, was relatively unskilled and badly paid; even the weavers and dyers were compensated poorly in comparison with silk workers, who were relatively well paid and highly trained.[22]

DYESTUFFS

The second factor that contributed significantly to the ultimate cost of a cloth was the dyestuff used to color it. Almost all silk floss was dyed in the thread, and *tintori* of silk specialized in this fabric alone. White silk was the only color not achieved with dye. Instead, the silk was bleached and the pearly white color achieved by exposing the washed and degummed silk to sulfurous acid fumes in a closed chamber.[23] Some woolen fabric was "dyed in the wool" early in the manufacturing process (after it had been cleaned, sorted, washed, and cleansed of impurities, the fourth step in the twenty-seven-step procedure). Most wool, however, was dyed after it had been first carded, spun, woven, fulled, and sheared, on the twenty-first step, before it was stretched, dried, mended, napped, folded, and packed for shipping.[24]

Reds | Red was by far the favored hue of the clothing of this Renaissance city and others, as Luca Molà has shown us for Venice.[25] Florentines developed a visual hierarchy of reds based upon the price of the dyestuff, and the subtleties of this hierarchy in cloth color would have been read easily by any native. In the fifteenth century, the highest quality and most intense dyestuff for crimson red was *chermisi*, or kermes dye. It was also the most expensive dyestuff and was never wasted on inferior cloth, being used in Florence for silk velvets, damasks, and the best-quality woolen fabrics.[26] At this time, kermes was imported in long-lasting powdered form from the East, where it was obtained from the desiccated bodies of a species of kermes shield louse, probably *Porphyrophora hameli*.[27] Jacqueline Herald writes that kermes also provided the deep scarlet that Pope Paul II adopted in 1464 as "cardinals' purple" after the fall of Constantinople to the Turks in 1453 cut off supplies of the traditional purple murex source in the eastern Mediterranean.[28] Due to the need to use great quantities of dye and also more than one dye bath, kermes was very expensive. To color one pound of silk with kermes (two dips) cost 40 soldi, more than three times as much as for a "Scottish" yellow or a "cornflower" blue color, and almost twice as much as a vermilion red.[29] To dye 100 pezze of wool with kermes cost an impressive 35 to 40 florins.[30] At these prices for chermisi dye, it is easy to see why every price list of fine cloth, from brocades and velvets to damasks and satins, was headed by a *di chermisi* fabric as the highest priced.

The second most prized red came from what was called *grana* (grain), also from the cochineal insect, but one of two Mediterranean species, *Coccus ilicis* or *Kermococcus vermilio*. Pliny had written that the best varieties of these insects were from Portugal, Spain, Tunisia, and parts of Asia Minor.[31] Found nearer to home and used since medieval times, grana was only about half as expensive as kermes. Grana produced a scarlet or carmine red, often referred to as *rosato* in family bookkeeping.[32] Other reds used as dyes were "*lacca* red" also derived from insects; *vermiglio* from *verzino* (a dyestuff extracted from the wood of various trees native to South America and the West and East Indies, collectively known as brazilwood); and lastly, the red from *oricello*, the red dye called "orchil" in English, obtained from lichens. It cost about 25 soldi per pound to dye silk with these lesser reds, about 6 to 7 florins to dye 100 pezze of wool.[33]

Other Valued Colors | Besides red, there were other colors that were considered appropriate to demonstrate a certain urbane male dignity in clothing. These were the dense *morello* black, purple (*perssi*), and the dark blue violet *pavonazzo*, or *pagonazzo*, all used in male public dress in Florence. In woolen cloth, the pavonazzo color was obtained with the grana dye, a costly 25 to 28 florins per 100 pieces, followed in cost by the morello and perssi at 17 to 20 florins for 100 pieces.[34] In silk, the most coveted hues were the rich blue *alessandrino* and the blue violet pavonazzo. The only color that could rival the cost of red chermisi was alessandrino, which also sold for 40 soldi per pound. The making of alessandrino required the three different dyestuffs of orchil (*oricello*), indigo (*indaco*), and madder (*robbia*) to attain its deep blue hue.[35] The blue violet pavonazzo color could be attained in silk by using either chermisi, grana, or verzino, all three of which were almost as dear as alessandrino blue or crimson, costing 35 soldi to dye one pound of silk cloth.[36] Any meaning traditionally assigned to a color had by the fifteenth century in Florence been subordinated to the realities of the costs of that particular dye color in the commercial marketplace. Goldthwaite makes the point that the logbooks kept by wealthy families detail how they spent their money throughout their lifetimes but not how the money was earned. Evidently, upper-class Renaissance Florentines were more identified with expenditure. By spending, they turned their wealth into objects that enhanced their personal honor. In the process, they hoped to transform themselves.[37]

EXPENSES FOR SPECIAL OCCASIONS

Given that the price of fine-quality cloth reflected not only the amount of time it took a skilled weaver to weave it but also often the costliness of an imported dyestuff handled by a second skilled group of craftsmen (the dyers), just how much of this cloth did the rich merchant oligarchy of Florence buy and how much did they spend to tailor it into their clothing? It is not difficult to discover how much Florentines paid for clothing made for special occasions such as weddings and feast days, on being named to government posts, and even for costume parties. Sumptuary legislation not withstanding, Florentines still spent lavishly on dress.

Communal Office | In 1450, Parente Parenti, Marco's father, was chosen to serve in the Signoria as a prior.[38] This was a communal honor widely distributed over some 2,000–3,000 males of the ruling class, but an honor that nonetheless called for the right costume.[39] Parente was already over seventy years of age at the time of his selection, and his official robes for the priorate were ordered by his son Marco, who recorded in his logbook, "and on the first of November, 1450, for making a scarlet cioppa with open sleeves lined with marten fur, for my father Parente when he was elected to the Signoria. . . ."[40] No amount of payment is listed here, but we can calculate it, as we do know how much each element of this garment would have cost. First, the communal statutes of 1415 had limited the amount a tailor could charge for fashioning a cioppa to 3 lire 13 soldi, but that by 1450 (when Marco ordered this cioppa), tailors were routinely charging 4 lire. This was the smallest element of the final price tag for a luxury garment such as this, however.

The materials, on the other hand, were very costly. The cloth was the most expensive element in the final cost. "Two lengths" were necessary to make a cioppa of substance (that is two pezze of cloth, or about twenty-four braccia). In addition, priors wore a red near the pinnacle of the fifteenth-century hierarchy of colors, that is a rosato, which required expensive grana to produce. With rosato di grana wool cloth at 8 florins per canna, the fabric for the cioppa would have cost approximately 64 florins. Secondly, fur trim (or at least fur lining) was considered necessary for a public official's gown. Marco would have needed the fur of about fifty martens (twenty-five per sleeve) at 40 soldi each, which totaled almost 3,000 soldi, or 35 florins, for the fur.[41] Adding these three elements together—tailoring, cloth, and fur—we arrive at a hefty final cost of 99 florins and 4 lire for one prior's cioppa.[42] Undoubtedly, selection for the priorate was one of the highlights of a public life in Renaissance Florence and considered an honor worthy of 100 of one's hard-earned florins in clothing.

Ambassadorial Duties | Being chosen to participate in an ambassadorial foray was perhaps even more prestigious a communal position. It certainly indicated that one's family had arrived in local importance and was deemed worthy of representing ones peers. Again, the Parenti family had the opportunity to serve in this capacity, and Marco, as usual, assiduously kept track of what he spent. "I record this day, August 7 [1477], the shopping done for my son Piero when he went as a youth with our embassy to Naples for the wedding of King Ferdinand," going on to list not only the expenses involved with making his son's clothing but also the purchase of the horse he was to ride, along with its furnishings.[43]

The mantellina that Piero was to wear was made of silk with a satin weave, dyed with kermes (*zetani raso chermisi*). For nine braccia of crimson satin, Marco paid 13 florins *larghi*. To make a fur lining, he purchased about 300 half pelts of gray squirrel (*vai*) for 9 florins larghi, from the rigattiere Tomaso di Pagolo e Compagni. The cost for the overcloak in cloth and fur came to 22 florins larghi. But Piero also needed three types of undergowns for his sojourn, a *gonnellino*, a *gabbanella*, and a *catalano*, plus a new doublet. For the three undergowns, two of which were to be made of dark blue-violet velvet (*velluto pagonazo*) and one of red wool (*panno luchesino*), Marco paid over 50 florins, for a total of forty braccia of cloth.[44] For lining, Marco purchased fifteen pounds of two types of linen cloth (*valescio* and *guarnello*), 15 lire for both. To provide visual relief from this relentless display from the red spectrum, Piero's doublet was to be of a contrasting green silk (three and a quarter braccia), which came to an additional 3½ florins. Together, Marco spent almost 54 florins for the three undergowns and farsetto in materials alone.

Completing Piero's outfitting, Marco also paid out 10 florins more for hose of unrecorded color and for sewing materials. The entire ambassadorial wardrobe came to over 92 florins. The cost of all five items of clothing plus hose was comparable to only one prior's cioppa, but cost is not the only factor to consider here when assessing its value. Piero's main item of clothing, his ambassadorial overcloak (*mantello*), was of chermisi red, whereas his grandfather's cioppa for the priorate, twenty-seven years before, had been of the less expensive rosato.[45] As prior, Parente Parenti would mostly have been seen at close range in the rooms of the Signoria and the narrow streets of Florence, where the quality of *cloth* of his cioppa (probably of the finest San Martino wool) would have been judged, rather than the *color*. Doubtless it was more important for Piero, as part of an embassy coming from afar, to appear in chermisi red. Certainly, Florentine ambassadors always put the Commune's best sartorial foot forward, even the *giovane* among them, such as Piero Parenti. Vespasiano wrote that when Piero de' Pazzi was chosen ambassador, no other representative had "ever left Florence in such stately guise," and that he "traveled in such state that every day he would change his sumptuous attire once or twice, and all his attendants would do the same. . . . all clad in handsome new garments, with silk cloaks, sleeves embroidered with pearls of great value."[46]

Maschere | Costume parties and masked events held in the late fourteenth and fifteenth centuries by influential families demonstrate that these private social diversions were also serious display opportunities in Renaissance Florence.[47] Descriptions of costumes for specifically named affairs are listed in Duke Lorenzo de' Medici's wardrobe account book for 1515 in a special section that separated such festive outfits from other clothes. Under the heading "Illustrissimo Signore Lorenzo de' Medici per conto di maschere," the cloth, fur, masks, hats, hose, embroidery, tailoring, and matching horse trimmings bought for the duke are listed.[48] (See Table 5.2.) Not only did Lorenzo buy special masks in Milan (thirteen masks for 4 ducats), but he spent generously on soled hose. On May 23, in addition to paying about 1½ ducats for turquoise cloth to make two pairs of hose to match his silk outfit of turquoise and red, he then paid some 27 ducats to have the hose decorated. This ornamental work was done by a "Nasi, *battilori*" (gold-beater) from whom Lorenzo bought five and a half braccia of fine spun-silver cloth, and whom he paid to stitch fringe and other decorations onto the hose. These masks, outfits, and fancy turquoise stockings were all fashioned especially for a costume event at the Palazzo Salviati in May.[49]

For this year, Lorenzo's account book specifies purchases of cloth, clothing, and accessories for three events; the maschere at the Salviati palace, a second costume party organized by Lorenzo himself and Filippo Strozzi, and a third for the winter celebration of Carnivale. Detailed entries with costs and names of purveyors run four pages in his account books, and the purchases totaled some 534 ducats (florins), 4 soldi, and 10 denari for one year's festivities alone. For example, Maestro Jachopo da Faenza, calzolaio, was paid 12 ducats on August 1, 1515, for shoes. We do not know how much he got per pair, but a piece of white velvet for one pair cost the duke 2 ducats alone. The amount paid for tailoring in this year was about 15½ florins, not a small amount, but less than 1 percent of the duke's total expenditures on cloth and clothing for the year. He did, however, remember one tailor, Maestro Francesco, at Christmas time, giving him a gift of 10 ducats.[50]

Nuptials | But more important than public office or parties was the joining of two families in marriage. For this event, we have our most detailed information on amounts spent for the clothing (*vestizione*) of the brides. Florentine

TABLE 5.2

Duke Lorenzo de Medici's Wardrobe Expenditures in 1515

	FLORINS (DUCATS)	SOLDI	DENARI
Cloth	3,385	2	4
Embroidery	67	19	12
Fulling cloth	1	10	0
Fur	1,278	19	8
Hats	22	5	4
Miscellaneous	174	6	2
Shoes	43	3	7
Stockings	49	6	15
Tailoring	35	15	1
Total	5,054	89	5

SOURCE: *Archivio di stato Firenze* CXXXII, MAP, fols. 1R-6R; 30R-32V.

NOTE: Between October 31, 1515, and May 12, 1516, Lorenzo de Medici also spent an additional 530 florins, 13 soldi, and 5 denari on costumes (including cloth, ornaments, embroidery, hats, and shoes) for two *maschere* and Carnival. In addition, for a further total of 2,628 florins, 1 soldo, and 7 denari, he made gifts of cloth to (a) young men accompanying him to Milan (14 outfits for 750 fl.), (b) the *guardia* of Florence for *giubbe* (doublets) for the entrance of Pope Leo X in 1515 (202 fl.), (c) grooms, horsemen, trumpeters, and tambourine players as Christmas presents (41 fl.), (d) "fra Giovanni" for a "spagniuolo cappellano del papa e una tonacha e mantello e scapulare" (a papal outfit, requiring 32 braccia of "panno monachino, panno bianco, saia di lilla," which cost 19 fl.), and (e) his house tailor, Maestro Francesco, at Christmas (10 fl.).

women made the most visual statement of their lives in their wedding appearances, and their display-conscious families lavished money on multiple bridal outfits to enable their daughters to display the honor of their lineage on their backs. Two aspects of clothing expenditure emerge from the various festivities deemed necessary to present familial honor: the dowry (*dote*) including the trousseau (*donora*), and the husband's counter-trousseau of additional gifts of adornment to his bride.[51] A trousseau in this period would have cost roughly about 110 florins for gowns, jewelry, headpieces, and shoes.[52] When Andrea Minerbetti recorded the marriage of his eldest daughter in February 1511, however, he noted having paid some 2,000 florins in dowry over a year and a half, of which he labeled 280 florins, or 14 percent, "di uso di donora"; he then added another 520 florins to this enormous amount.[53] In an earlier case, the second informal gift of clothing supplied to the bride by the groom was added. In 1447-48, Marco Parenti spent over 560 florins on his counter-trousseau for his bride Caterina. He had two embellished gowns made of the finest fabrics and one fur-lined cloak with a fringed and embroidered cowl. Caterina also received two headdresses, a brocade belt worked with silver and gold, a pearl necklace, and brooch. Marco's gifts of clothing were fashioned of fabric dyed with kermes and worth at least a good-sized working farm in the Mugello.[54] Counter-trousseaux are examined more closely in Chapter 6.

PATTERNS OF SPENDING

If special events such as these called for such expensive outfitting, what was the clothing budget, not for an ambassador or a bride, but for an entire family over time? One could posit that given such an emphasis on sartorial display, a continual concern with dressing well and even dressing to display familial virtù, would have been a fact of life in Quattrocento Florence. As we saw in Chapter 4, Florentine families do not seem to have had clothes made once or twice a year; rather, cloth was bought and tailors, doublet makers, hatters, and seamstresses were commissioned year round. So, how much did a family spend, and did this year-round making of clothes tip the family budget precariously toward what some historians have seen as the freezing of "excess capital" in luxurious display, thereby eroding the pool of communal funds available for commerce and trade? Could such consumption have contributed to and even hastened a crisis in the Florentine economy?[55]

The Parenti Family | Taking as a base the generous, even excessive, amount spent by Marco Parenti on his bride Caterina, one might expect a continuance of such an indulgence in luxury clothing on his part. Marco's diary provides an interesting overview of what he actually spent on garments for his family from the years 1447 to 1464. The first year of his marriage to Caterina Strozzi, including their wedding, the expenses for her clothes alone were extremely high, as we have seen. But in the second year, expenditures fell to about 88 florins, a mere 16 percent of the amount of money spent in the first year.[56] In the following twelve-month period (1449), he spent even less. Marco bought only one garment all year, a *saia* for Caterina dyed with grana, on which he spent about 37½ florins. We see clothing expenditures dramatically dropping from a high of around 560 florins to 37½ florins—a decrease of around 93 percent.[57] For the next two years, Marco's annual budget for clothes hovered around at 90 florins, aside from the extraordinary expense of an additional 100 florins for his father's cioppa for the Signoria. In 1452, however, his purchases dropped to a little over 18 florins for the year (for two *cioppette* for his young son Piero).

The same pattern appears in 1453 and 1454, when Marco spent an average of about 136 florins a year, followed by two years of spending literally nothing. Specifically, in 1455, he had a new bodice put into a *chotta* (cotta) for Caterina (for approximately 1½ florins), and in 1456, he did not record buying anything at all.[58] Just two years later, in 1458, Parenti's gross assets in real estate and Monte shares totaled about 2,700 florins, which certainly did not put him at the financial pinnacle of the Commune but did place him among those expected to express their honor in their clothing.[59] His expenditures on clothing, however, while high, were not ruinous.

In his repeated efforts at honorable sartorial display for his whole family, Marco's clothing costs continued to vacillate back and forth in a similar pattern over a nineteen-year period: upward spikes due to the additions to his growing family, downward plunges perhaps in compensation. By 1465, Marco had spent a little over 2,000 florins for his family wardrobes, or approximately 106 florins per year.[60] His three daughters' expenses did not begin to press upon him with the demands of dowries and trousseaux until 1470, the year Ghostanza, his eldest, married Filippo di Lorenzo Buondelmonti, with a dowry of 1,166⅔ florins *larghi* and a formal donora that cost 110. This would have been added to his clothes budget for the year, no doubt causing him to compensate the following year by again cutting back.[61]

Marco evidently juggled his purchases to stay within some sort of budget, and the pattern of his spending on display shows that its importance was limited to certain key events. Just three years into his marriage, for example, he was already having clothes repaired and remade to save money. One of the flowered blue and white gowns from Caterina's trousseau was refitted with a new bodice.[62] Over half Marco's commissions to his tailor, Agnolo d'Antonio, in the seventh year after his marriage were for remaking garments. The only gown for Caterina was made of used cloth The two completely new (and pricey) garments made that year were two cloaks (*ucchi*) for Marco himself, one of wool dyed with grana, lined with the soft underbelly fur of gray squirrel, the other of black velvet, lined with marten fur. For these two cloaks alone, Marco would have paid close to 177 florins. His expenditures for Caterina, on the other hand, totaled about 10½ florins, a far cry from her bridal expenses.[63] The showy clothes that had been part of his bridal gift would be thriftily taken apart forty-three years later and the precious ornaments sold to the rigattiere.[64]

FORTUNES IN WARDROBES

In addition to obtaining a diachronic view of the patterns of purchasing clothes over time from the ricordanze, family inventories can give us a synchronic view to tell us another story about clothes, that is, what each family member owned in the way of clothing at any given time and how much the officials of the Commune deemed this clothing to be worth.

The Pucci Family | An inventory of the household effects and personal real estate holdings of the Pucci family was taken in 1449 upon the death of the paterfamilias, Puccio Pucci.[65] The members of the Pucci family were loyal friends and partisans of the Medici, and Lauro Martines notes that as members of the powerful "inner circle," they increased what began as quite a modest patrimony in the first quarter of the fifteenth century into a large fortune by astutely buying and selling Monte shares based on information to which an insider would have had access.[66] Upon Puccio's death, he left not only his widow (née Bartolomea Spinelli) and two young children but also four adult sons (three married with children) and four married daughters.[67] The four married daughters lived elsewhere with their husbands, but Bartolomea and Puccio's married sons and their families lived in the Pucci family homes in Florence on the Via dei Servi and outside the city in Uliveto, along with the couple's own minor children. The possessions of Puccio Pucci's heirs (rede), a total of eleven family members, were inventoried in 1449. From these inventories, it is clear that clothing formed a large part of the whole family's household possessions, personal items typically being limited for women to sewing supplies (a pair of knives, needle cases, thread, yardage), toiletries (an ivory comb, a string of coral or amber, ribbons), and devotional items (a breviary, a holy doll). Men seem to have had even fewer personal items—a few books, gemstones, devotional items, and in some cases, military gear, such as armor, swords, helmets, and horse trappings.[68]

The total inventoried family property, including real estate, was appraised and listed as worth approximately 5,771 florins.[69] Of this amount, only 1,809 florins, or some 31 percent, was in real estate. Household effects and wardrobes made up other 69 percent of the total, that is, around 3,962 florins, and of this amount, 2,196 florins was accounted for by clothing and jewelry. These figures show that the wardrobes of the eleven members of the Pucci family were worth 17 percent more than the Pucci real estate, and, in fact, represented almost 40 percent of the total inventoried family property. Of course, this 2,196 florins in clothes and jewelry was somewhat unevenly spread among the eleven surviving members of the family, with the clothing wardrobes of the married sons' wives hovering around 324 florins each (including jewelry), while the value of the men's wardrobes averaged less, at about 170 florins each.[70]

The Tosa da Fortuna Family | While the inventory of the Pucci does provide us an insight into a family perhaps of a little more means than that of Marco Parenti, the total amount of capital invested in clothing and adornments, while large, is not breathtaking. For a family of comparable means, we may turn to another Florentine family, the Tosa, listed by Dei as one of the most glorious and powerful of 365 top lineages in the city by 1472.[71] An inventory completed in 1429 by the Pupilli upon the death of the head of the household, one Albizo del Toso da Fortuna, opened the private rooms, chests, and closets of their family homes in Florence and Fortuna to inquiring eyes, with the two officials listing appraisals, which was not usually done. They noted a value for each item of substance, then organized like items of lesser value into lots, which were given a lump sum value.[72] Not only were the clothing and personal effects of Albizo's widow Marietta and children listed, but also those of two other kinsmen (probably brothers), living under the same roof along with their wives and children, and, lastly, a small collection of clothes found in one of the upper rooms of the house, possibly belonging to a female servant or slave.[73]

The two most expensive garments owned by the Tosa family members in 1429 were gowns of green velvet embellished with silver ("tutto fornito d'ariento"), found in the rooms of Toso and his kinsman Lotto respectively, which were assessed at 65 and 70 florins each. Obviously, the decoration with precious metals would have driven the prices of these garments up. In addition, each had a gown of kermes-dyed wool ("alusanze"), which the officials appraised at 60 florins apiece; and furthermore, Lotto and another kinsman, named after the deceased Albizo, both had overgowns dyed with grana ("cioppe rosate") and lined with fur, which were valued at 40 and 45 florins, still heady sums of money. The only other individual pieces of clothing for which we have assessments in this price range are two overgowns of black velvet lined with taffeta, which were valued at 40 florins apiece. A large price gap then opened under this for the many other garments counted.[74]

Two of the *least* expensive pieces of clothing individually appraised belonged to women in the family, specifically, a gray lined overgown ("una cioppa bigia foderata da donna"), valued at about 1 florin, and a plain brown gown ("uno sacchetto monaco da donna"), valued again at about 1 florin. The remainder of the garments that were identified as women's garb (that is "da donna" or "da parto," indicating a maternity dress), ranged from 14 florins for a scarlet gown with open sleeves ("uno saccho rosato chon maniche aperte") to 6 florins for a gray gown with silver trim ("uno saccho bigio . . . chon ariento").[75]

The only other extremely expensive items in the Tosa family wardrobe inventories were the rings. Toso himself had a small silvered jewel case ("uno forzerino inarientato"), which contained six rings: two with spinels, two with sapphires, one with a large pearl, and the last with an emerald, all of which, together with the case, were estimated at 95 florins. Albizo had a total of ten rings but no jewel box: two rings with diamonds, two with large emeralds, two with large spinels, three with sapphires, and one with a large pearl. All these, however, only added up to 70 florins.[76] The other family members had only ornamented belts, which were arranged by the officials in groups of five or six and appraised at around 20 florins for each group.

Including clothing and jewelry; yardage, linens, and bedding; furniture and brassware; kitchen and stable trappings, and stores of wine and grain, the family's possessions were worth a total of about 3,462 florins. Of this, clothing and jewelry represented approximately 58 percent, or about 1,994 florins. We do not know the family real property included in this inventory of household effects (*masserizie*), but if the ratio is assumed to be the same as in the case of the Pucci family, the family fortune would be enlarged by about a third, with clothes and jewelry remaining the most important items.

The inventory of the family of Albizo del Toso da Fortuna shows an extensive wardrobe, in which the value of the jewelry and clothing of at least four adults with their untallied wives and children totaled about 2,000 florins. A few garments were even worth up to 80 florins apiece, a sum equal to a year's wages for many professions, such as a treasury official, weaver of damask, university instructor, accountant, or tailor.[77] However, by 1500, some seventy years later, expenditures on clothing for the very wealthy had increased beyond this level of indulgence, indeed, beyond all caution. Duke Lorenzo de Medici spent an exceptional amount of money on his personal attire in 1515. While we do not have the exact amounts for more than a few specific garments, the duke spent some 3,385 ducats (florins) on cloth that year, and some 1,278 ducats on fur. Embroidery cost him 67 ducats, and shoes and stockings totaled 92 ducats.[78] In Milan, he purchased at least 302 ducats worth of marten fur linings, cloth of turquoise velvet, silver thread, and Milanese-made hose. The hose were embroidered and lined, and cost 1½ ducats a pair.[79] On one piece of black damask headgear alone (a *cappuccio*), Lorenzo splurged, even for him, spending a full 17 ducats for the long, wrapped hat.[80] But while individual accessories in ducal Florence were expensive, nothing could compare to the outlay of the princely courts.

A BRIEF COURT COMPARISON: LUCREZIA BORGIA D'ESTE

Rich Florentines may have spent generously to display themselves and their lineage, but they do not show the same level of self-indulgence that was possible in the court cities of the time. One court comparison will have to suffice here. An inventory of the wardrobe of Lucrezia Borgia, taken upon her espousal to Alfonso I of Ferrara in 1502, shows the lengths to which the very rich went to present an honorable façade at court. Lucrezia and her father Rodrigo, as Pope Alexander VI, had intimate dealings with the Farnese, and by marriage, with the descendants of the Pucci family, whose household inventory is detailed above.[81] Lucrezia's inventory, however, reveals astonishing totals spent for one person's clothes, shoes, accessories, jewelry, and yardage.

Among other items of clothing, Lucrezia herself owned some eighty-four gowns, twenty cloaks or robes, twenty-two headdresses, thirteen belts, thirty-three pairs of slippers, and fifty pairs of shoes. Her jewel cases contained some 1,900 pearls and almost 300 gemstones, including diamonds, rubies, and spinels. She also had on hand almost 5,000 braccia of satin, silk, velvet, brocade, and cloth of gold, in addition to sixteen and a half pounds of other silk and taffeta, with certain pieces specifically designated as belonging either to her or to one of her two young sons still living with Borgia family relatives in Rome.[82] Our limited sources for her include one inventory that tantalizingly gives no monetary totals, but we do know that she came to this marriage with a dowry of at least 300,000 ducats (not including an additional 100,000 ducats in jewels, linens, and horse and mule trappings). One "trimmed" dress in her trousseau was valued at some 15,000 ducats alone, and it also contained some "two hundred costly shifts, some of which [were] worth a hundred ducats apiece." Even the detachable sleeves of some of her gowns cost 30 ducats each.[83] The Ferrarese ambassador, Gianluca Pozzi, wrote to Duke Ercole, Lucrezia's future father-in-law, that it was going to take "a number of vehicles which the Pope had ordered built in Rome and a hundred and fifty mules" to bear Lucrezia's trousseau for the thirteen-day trip from Rome to Ferrara.[84] Not counting her jewelry, this trousseau was worth at least 50,000 ducats in clothing and accessories.[85]

In Florence, however, display was event-based, and with the aristocratization of society still in process, attempts were made to balance a high-outlay year by cutting back in the subsequent one. Chapter 6 looks at the extremes to which Florentine husbands and families did go in a typically "high-outlay year," such as when bedecking a bride. Examples from the Castellani, del Bene, and Strozzi families will serve to highlight the specific message conveyed by the appropriate clothing.

SIX

THE MAKING OF
WEDDING GOWNS

T ension and interest ran hand in hand when an important marriage
alliance was in the offing and conflicting interests collided headlong
into each other, pitting the need to conserve family patrimony
against the pressure to spend lavishly in the increasingly market-oriented
economy of Renaissance Florence. The sartorial splendor deemed essential
for an honorable public appearance inevitably involved the families of the
ruling classes in a contest for visual primacy in which there seemed to be no
logical limit to the time, attention, or money that might be expended.

COMPONENTS OF THE MARRIAGE PROCESS

The first public event in the marriage process that called for a special outfit in
fifteenth-century Florence was the espousal (*sposalizio*), traditionally held at
the bride's family home, where her natal family hosted a dinner for their
relatives and the relatives of the groom.[1] As Klapisch-Zuber notes, the bride
and groom exchanged vows of consent (*verba de praesenti*) and the bride received wedding rings from her husband and his family in an informal ceremony known as the "be-ringing" (*anellamento*).[2] The second event was the
actual wedding (*nozze*) itself, the celebration of which could be delayed until a
family had amassed the daughter's dowry. Before the fifteenth century, the

dowry had been transferred to the groom upon completion of the sposalizio, but as dowries soared in the Quattrocento, the actual wedding might be delayed for a year or even longer after the engagement while the bride's family amassed the dowry amount for the groom. It was not unusual for the groom to need these dowry funds to "dress" his bride for the event itself, as the adornment of the woman became increasingly important. With the dowry transfer from bride's family to groom, however, the nozze could proceed.

The nozze normally began with the *ductio*, the public event in which the bride was led through the city on horseback from her family's house to the house of her new husband, accompanied by her family entourage. This was the most crucial display moment of the entire wedding procedure, because it provided the best opportunity for the public to see the bride, who sartorially embodied the honor of the entire social transaction.[3] Dazzlingly dressed and seated on the traditional white horse, she was slowly paraded through the streets of Florence. As an unmarried young woman, she did not yet have to wear a cloak (*mantello*) over her cioppa (which would normally hide the gown of an adult women in public), and her wedding finery would have been available for all to gaze upon.[4] At their destination, she and her family would then be met by the bridegroom, his family, and their friends, where the next stage of the nozze, the ensuing dinner and festivities, would begin. In the fourteenth and fifteenth centuries, not only the procession, but the wedding festivities themselves were the targets of repeated sumptuary legislation, which regulated all aspects of ceremonial display, from the number of guests and number of courses eaten to the type of foods that could be served, the extent of the entertainment allowed, and the extravagance of the gifts exchanged.[5] These festivities, however, which not only included the bride and groom and their immediate families but also the extended kin group of the families involved, created an increasing demand on everyone to be beautifully clothed, thereby contributing honor to the event. The pressure for everyone involved in this heightened social transaction became so great that invitees complained that they had "nothing to wear" and sometimes even decided to forego the celebration altogether.[6] When, under Lorenzo "Il Magnifico," these final festivities tended to become more private and were sometimes eliminated altogether, perhaps it was not simply an example of tightening Medicean control but also the beginnings of social unease about escalating economic display.[7]

A GOWN FOR A SECOND MARRIAGE: THE CASTELLANI

In the 1448 case of Lena Alamanni, the story of whose wedding gown opens this book, the price her husband-to-be Francesco Castellani paid for the basic dress, before the elaborate decoration was applied, is not known.[8] But another family logbook of a year earlier lists a similar gown, "una giornea di zetani vellutato di chermisi" ordered for the sixteen-year-old Caterina Strozzi (a kinswoman of Castellani's deceased first wife, Ginevra). Caterina's wedding vows to Marco Parenti had been made in 1447, as we saw in the previous chapter, and with his counter-trousseau, had cost him over 560 florins. For the public wedding ceremony and procession, among other garments, one giornea from this gift had been commissioned from the same tailor that Castellani used (Andrea di Giovanni da Bibbiena) and cost over 100 florins, including fabric, lining, buttons, and fur.[9] Figure 6.1 shows an elaborate wedding cioppa in a detail from a cassone painting by Giovanni di Ser Giovanni called *lo Scheggia* (ca. 1450).

We do not have full records of the costs incurred for the clothes for Francesco and Lena's wedding, nor do we know the origin of the funds. We do know some things, however. First of all, added to the presumed dowry and trousseau that Lena would have brought as a bride, Francesco had additional wedding clothes made, undoubtedly for the ductio. Many historians have looked at the vexed issue of the husband's lavish counter-trousseau as a form of customary "gift," and at what the societal and interfamilial dynamics were behind this so-called *donatio*. But first I would like to examine the process of clothing the bride itself. We can deduce that Lena's cioppa would have cost more than Marco Parenti had paid for Caterina's giorna, because while a giornea was sleeveless, a cioppa was sleeved and would thus would have taken more costly fabric, more time, and skill to fashion. But labor was still cheap, while materials were dear, and the tailor's fee was a minor expenditure.[10] For Parenti's dress it had been 9 lire 13 soldi.[11]

Ornamentation | But this was just the beginning of the creation of Lena's gown. In December 1448, when the tailor had made the basic garment, elaborate surface ornamentation was added, consisting of an original embroidery design. In Florence, a cioppa such as this was worn over a gamurra. It was a woman's formal outer garment, one of her most public pieces, and it

Fig. 6.1. Wedding *cioppa*. Detail from cassone painting, Giovanni di
Ser Giovanni detto "lo Scheggia" (ca. 1450). Galleria dell'Accademia,
Florence.

therefore, needed to be as visually eloquent as possible, as adornment went
hand in hand with honor.[12] The Castellani were one of the top 200 or so
Florentine merchant elite families, so Francesco turned the cioppa over to the
well-known and esteemed ("ben conosciuto e stimato") embroidery firm of
Maestro Giovanni Gilberti for decoration. The embroidery firm and Francesco immediately argued about the price however; it wanted 50 florins but
Francesco only wanted to pay 38 to 40 at the most ("al più"). Francesco called
in a kinsman of Lena's to settle the price, one Luigi di Boccaccino Alamanni,
who acted as arbitrator.

Materials | But this initial disagreement did not deter the project, and on
December 10, Francesco went about assembling the materials necessary for
the embroidery. He began with the pearls (weighing thirty-four ounces,

twenty-two and one-half denari), the embroidery firm promising in turn to keep close track of all the gemstones, silken gold thread, and small silvered ornaments ("le scaglie e i tremolanti," being made by a goldsmith, one Piero di Chimenti), in the shop.[13] Then, in the presence of the tailor and an accountant, a certain Giovanni del Miglore, the bridegroom and the firm agreed that they would see how the work on the gown progressed before deciding on the final price. Work on the ornamentation finally began early in 1448.

Design | And work it would be, for Francesco Castellani had requested an elaborate and fanciful embroidery design of his own creation for his new bride Lena, a design so ornate that it would take many months to complete. For this second marriage, Francesco wanted silver and pearl embroidery on the large, stiffened, upturned collar of the cioppa, as well as on the belt (*cintola*) and the sleeves (*maniche*). In his family ricordanza, Francesco wrote out his design in meticulous detail. On the bodice of the dress, near the shoulders, he envisioned the heavens, with the sun and its large rays of gold. Under these rays, about halfway down the sleeves, there was to be a large eagle of gold and pearls, flying toward the rays of the sun, as if to renew itself. Spilling over the entire bodice and sleeves, he wanted feather designs made of gold and pearls, and smaller rays with sparks of gold and pearls all around, embroidered in the same style as the large rays.[14] (The detail from Ghirlandaio's *The Birth of the Virgin* [ca. 1486–90] in the Tornabuoni Chapel shown in Fig. 6.2 illustrates remarkably similar embroidered ornamentation on a Tornabuoni woman's gown.) To complete this design, Francesco personally assembled all the materials and either delivered them or saw to it that they were delivered to the shop of the Maestro Giovanni. Francesco also oversaw the making of the special "scaglie e tremolanti" by the goldsmith, which would add to the glory of his vision.

Ancillary Garments | However, this project was not the only job given to the embroidery firm of Giovanni Gilberti. Two more pieces of embroidery, which would decorate other items in Lena's ceremonial wardrobe, were added. The first, an order for a pair of sleeves ("uno paio di maniche") to be pearl-embroidered for a shorter blue violet cioppa ("una cioppetta pago-

Fig. 6.2. Surface ornamentation on *cioppa*. Fabric detail from Ghirlandaio, *The Birth of the Virgin* (ca. 1486–90). Tornabuoni Chapel.

naza"), was handed to Maestro Giovanni three months later, in March 1448. The firm was to use pearls, gold and silver thread, and silver "tremolanti" in its work, a percentage of which were to be supplied by Castellani, the rest by Gilberti's firm itself.[15] A second job, added in April 1449, was to sew two strips of rich blue cloth of *allexandrino* in silver thread, to be used as contrasting ornament for the pearl-embroidered blue violet sleeves of the cioppetta. These were certainly not commissions of the complexity of the first but would nonetheless have involved many hours of work on the part of the craftspeople working for this concern.[16]

Maestro Giovanni Bows Out | In July 1452, when Castellani recorded finally settling his account, neither he nor the master embroiderer had ever met. In fact, Maestro Giovanni had died before the commissioned embroidery was completed, leaving the unfinished work somewhere in his shop, along with all of Francesco's pearls, silver and gold thread, and silver spangles. Francesco now had to recover the gowns and the precious materials he had entrusted to the firm. He sent his family agent, Nofri di Nicolo degl'Agli, to settle accounts with the man who was acting on behalf of the heirs of Maestro Giovanni, one Lodovico di Paolo, prior of Santa Maria sopra la Porta. In the presence of another family friend, Maso Alessandri (as well as two other embroiderers who were brought in to evaluate the work that had been completed), the two men appraised its value at 85 florins. This was more money than a treasury official in Florence would make in a year. After paying some 18½ florins to settle an account of Giovanni's in Perugia, Castellani was deemed to have paid in full and was able to take his partially embroidered garments back home.[17] To enable Castellani to recover at least the cost of the expensive pearls (and undoubtedly because the occasion for which Lena needed to be thus adorned had passed), a prior, one Lodovico di Paolo, then took apart the "cioppa d'alto e basso chermisi" by hand and stripped it of all decorations. The dress was either sold to a used-clothes dealer or the fabric refashioned into another garment. Four years later, in May 1456, Francesco called in a jeweler, Bartolomeo del Lavachio, to weigh the pearls, and with the help of a cloth dyer, Matteo di Puccio, and the poet Luigi Pulci (a close friend of the Castellani family), agreement was reached as to their market value. The pearls that were to have been suns and rays and eagles flying were now divested of any transformational value and became once more simply an economic asset. Being weighed, they totaled 30 onciel 15 denari (4 on. 7½ d. being left unaccounted for) and were entered into the Castellani account book among other family financial transactions. For enough cloth to make the cioppa, Francesco would have invested close to 71½ florins. A cioppa took about thirteen braccia of fabric to fashion, and "alto e basso chermisi" cloth cost close to 5½ florins per braccia at midcentury. We also know that the embroidery set Francesco back 40 florins "al più," but the embroidery materials cost a small fortune, including not only gold and silver thread but also some 35 ounces of pearls "da richamare," which, at about 6½ florins per ounce, would have amounted to approximately 227½ florins. Adding the hiring of a tailor to put it all together (a minuscule amount of about 10 lire), this one gown would have cost Francesco about 300 florins, not including lining or thread.[18]

Francesco's project thus ended in a fiasco. The pearls remained untransformed by his imagination, and the cioppa never saw the light of day in any piazza in Florence; an unsuccessful mission to bring glory to his bride, and by doing so, to himself and to his house.

A WEDDING DRESS: THE DEL BENE

A similar lengthy dialogue concerning a young woman's wedding dress can be seen in a series of letters between members of another old Florentine family, the del Bene, in February 1381. Letters between two cousins, Giovanni d'Amerigo and Francesco di Jacopo del Bene, show that it was not always the head of the household, or even the men of the family, who made the ultimate decisions regarding a woman's clothing.[19] In this case, the women were apparently vocal in the family discussions. Marriage negotiations had been concluded for Giovanni Del Bene's daughter Caterina to wed Andrea di Castello da Quarata. Now her family faced the all-important decision of how to dress her for the wedding. Caterina herself wanted an elaborate satin gown, which seemed to her father Giovanni too lavish. Complicating matters, her cousin Antonia, also of marriageable age, was jealous of Caterina's wedding and proposed extravagant dress, because negotiations for her own betrothal had recently fallen through. In a letter to Antonia's father Francesco, Giovanni worried, "I also think that Antonia may be upset when she sees Caterina's beautiful gown."[20] Obviously, the feelings of the female members of the family, even daughters, were of concern, and a matter of formal, written discussion here between two fathers.

In contrast to the Castellani gown and accessories discussed above, this Del Bene dress was to form a part of the girl's dowry and involved not her husband-to-be but members of her own natal family, male and female alike. At least eight relatives were concerned with the decision about the gown, as well as with how much her dowry as a whole should be and when and where the marriage should take place. After many letters and much negotiation, Giovanni wrote to his cousin Francesco that "the women have decided that Caterina's dress will be made of blue silk [i.e., not the satin that Caterina preferred], and that the gown will constitute part of the dowry."[21] Apparently, the jealousy over the dress had been quelled and divisive feelings between Caterina and Antonia had been ameliorated by other family females, who had chosen a compromise dress for the bride—still fancy enough to satisfy her and the demands of the occasion for which it had been made, but not the satin she wanted. Evidently, even if the clothes were designed for a public occasion as crucial to a family as a wedding, the views of the women of the family could be considered in the final decision.

A WEDDING ENSEMBLE: THE STROZZI

In fact, in at least one case, the materfamilias, in the absence of a husband, was centrally involved in judgments concerning clothes. Alessandra Macinghi negli Strozzi, whose daughter Caterina we have already seen having her wedding dress made, had been exiled from Florence in 1434 along with her husband, Matteo di Simone di Filippo Strozzi (1397–1435), after the return of Cosimo de' Medici. They had gone to Pesaro, where Matteo and three of their children had died the following year, leaving Alessandra a young pregnant widow. She returned to Florence, where her last child, Matteo, was born, to raise her surviving two daughters and three sons.[22] When the boys came of age, they joined their Strozzi kinsmen in exile in Naples, but Alessandra stayed behind with the girls, where she shouldered the responsibility of actively managing her sons' patrimony.[23] The socially savvy mother here was

Fig. 6.3. *Ghirlanda* of peacock feathers. School of Pollaiuolo (mid fifteenth century). Uffizi, Florence.

not only deeply involved in appropriately adorning her daughter Caterina for
the biggest public event of her life but also later successfully provided a second
daughter, Lesandra, with a suitable spouse and dowry, thereby promoting
Strozzi family honor while conserving her Macinghi dowry and the Strozzi
patrimony as best she could.

In 1447, after she had completed arrangements for her daughter Caterina
to wed the up-and-coming Marco Parenti, Alessandra wrote to her son
Filippo in exile in Naples to describe his younger sister's wedding ensemble,
especially the gown of "zetani vellutati di chermisi" being assembled by the
groom. The mother's personal triumph in the dress being prepared for her
daughter is undeniable. Caterina would wear the most beautiful clothes in

Florence (" 'l più bel drappo che sia in Firenze") "when she goes out," Alessandra enthused to her son, and would "have on her back" the equivalent of more than 400 florins in the shape of a gown of crimson silk velvet, decorated with two long braided pearl trims (*trecce*), and a headdress of peacock feathers and pearls. (Fig. 6.3, a fifteenth-century School of Pollaiuolo drawing in the Uffizi Gallery, depicts a comparable *ghirlanda* of peacock feathers.)[24] That Alessandra thought about her eldest daughter's clothing in such specifically monetary terms, using florins as a metaphor for her wedding outfit, can be read as a sign of the overcommercialization of upper-class Florentine bridal *vestizione* in the mid fifteenth century.

MAKING THE CLOTHES

Clothing oneself and one's family in fifteenth-century Florence was complex and time-consuming, especially for the families of the upper class. Marco Parenti recorded the entire process in his logbook. One can thus trace the fabrication of a piece of clothing over time, as well as the number of steps involved.

Recordkeeping | Parenti listed each of the garments under its name, such as "Una roba" or "Una giornea," noting the cloth, from whom it had been purchased, and the price. Next followed the fabrics or furs used for the lining, along with any fur trim, fabric for facing, ribbons, laces, jewelry, metalwork, or feathers to decorate the ensemble. Important sleeves, often the most fashionable part of an outfit, usually warranted an entry of their own. In addition, makers of doublets, shoes, slippers, headdresses, berets, cowls, purses, belts, velveteers, jewelers, and pearl dealers were listed by name, as well as the retail shops from which Parenti purchased materials and sewing notions.

Shopping | When Parenti began the process of putting together Caterina's wedding clothes, it was the summer of 1447. He made an entry on August 8 that began "una giornea di zetani vellutato di chermisi della donna" (a sleeveless overgown of crimson silk velvet, open at the sides, for a woman), under which he painstakingly recorded the entire procedure for getting it together. The first step was to obtain the basic fabric for the gown, which he supplied from his own silk firm, "Marcho Parenti et Chompagni."[25] On the same day, he also got the lining material of red cloth, *valescio rosso,* from a retailer. One week later, on August 16, he bought another type of lining fabric, a *guarnello,* from the same retailer; thirty-two eyelets (through which the garment's lacings would be threaded) from a goldsmith; and more fabric for the gown, which he had to buy from another cloth merchant, one Zanobi di San Martino.

The Tailoring | Ten days later on August 26, Parenti took the materials to the tailor, Andrea di Giovanni da Bibbiena, to whom he gave an initial payment to begin fashioning ("per fornitura") the wedding ensemble.[26] Very early in this entire process, although not recorded in this logbook, the tailor would have been summoned to where the family lived to begin putting together the gown. In the presence of her mother and/or female kin, a fitted pattern of sorts would be created on the girl herself from the kind of coarse cotton or linen tailor's cloth we saw listed in a shop inventory in Chapter 2.[27] This pattern would have been made for the all-important cut, and the procedure was undoubtedly as efficient and closely monitored as possible. Sumptuary laws prevented any radical departure from traditional lines, and any subtle gown innovations could be tried out later on wooden mannequins (*huomini di legno*) in the tailor's shop. The inevitable intimate contact involved between a nubile upper-class woman and an artisan of lower rank gave rise to salacious verse. "The deceit that they [the tailors] use with these counterfeit cuts, always cutting round the bodices so they fit well; one must put a hundred conditions on these peculiar beasts," an anonymous fifteenth-century poet wrote of such fittings.[28]

Rather than being paid in silver at the outset, Andrea di Giovanni was given one gold florin *largo.* The job also included a gown (*cotta*) of the same fabric, which had its own entry in the logbook, with its own specific litany of painstaking realization. Having left the materials at the tailor's shop and made an initial deposit, Parenti then promised a second payment of 7 lire for sewing the gown ("per chucitura da giornea"), and 7 lire 10 soldi for making another gown ("per fattura di una cotta") two days later, on August 28. These amounts were entered in silver money of account. The total cost of tailoring the two garments was to be 19 lire 6 soldi.[29] Marco then waited until September 11 to buy 188 little furs (*lattizi*) from Franco the furrier to hem and border the gown, which then needed to be finished by the tailor. That was the process for just the outer garment of the ensemble.

More Shopping | He went through a similar process for the cotta his bride would wear under the sleeveless overgown. It, too, needed lining fabric, cotton wool for quilting the bodice, 120 gilded singlets for the dress itself, and 100 small singlets for the sleeves alone. The cotta also had embroidery and thirty-six lattizi furs for decoration, as well as a fringe and ribbons of green and gold, which Parenti bought by the braccia. Together, the two gowns cost him over 174 florins.[30]

The other items included in the wedding ensemble each had *their* own entries as well. The headdress was embroidered with silver and pearls and decorated with eleven roses made of peacock feathers; metalwork was gilded and enameled with flowers of rose and azure and silver tinsel, which alone cost almost 8 florins. The total cost of the headdress came to just under 60 florins.[31] The basic belt was fashioned of crimson silk in a satin weave with gold thread dyed with kermes, and Parenti had spent 3 florins on it before he had it embellished with open embroidery work in silver gilt and added the buckle (*fibbia*) and metal tip (*puntuale*) of gilded silver, which had to be made by a goldsmith, costing another 10 florins, 5 soldi, and 2 denari. (Eleven years later, in 1458, he was able to sell the metalwork off the fabric belt for 25 lire, or around 7 florins—a little more than 50 percent of his original investment). For his bride's head, Parenti had a pair of pearl braids made ("un paio di treccie di perle") that would be wound over a padded roll (*mazocchio*), which would fit around Caterina's forehead. This would form the stable base for the more fragile and fanciful feathered ghirlanda. These pearl trims cost an additional 61 florins.[32]

Creating the Jewelry | Finally, on August 30, 1447, Parenti added the pièce de résistance, a golden brooch set with two sapphires and three pearls (one of which weighed five carats). Alone, this piece of jewelry, which Caterina would wear on the shoulder of her sleeveless overgown, cost Marco almost 40 florins.[33] No wonder his mother-in-law Alessandra expressed enthusiastic pride in Caterina's final outfit. The entire process was a major investiture of time, planning, effort, and expense on the part of both families. That those involved identified personally with the outcome of such a laborious process is not surprising. We do not know whether Caterina or Lena were consulted about their dresses, but we can see how intimately involved their kinsmen and women were, from the records left in family logbooks. This shows the power of the patrilineage in shaping and exploiting the most public marriage moment for maximum display and the critical importance of such display to make visible the honor of the occasion. Other less ceremonial pieces in the dowry trousseau may have had more input from the young women themselves and their natal families, but in any case, the decisions were still finally made by the family head.

. THE MANAGEMENT AND MEANING OF THE CLOTHES

The ownership and eventual disposition of the clothing of the family was another complex concern and had far-reaching implications for every member of the family, especially the wives. The gifts and countergifts constituted a highly ritualized exchange, the end result of which was the reestablishment of some sort of social equilibrium once the couple married and the transfer of the woman from one house to the other had been accomplished.[34] But by the mid 1400s, the nature of this social equilibrium in Florence had been transformed by an increasingly market-oriented economy.[35] What one was was not as important as what one *seemed* to be, or maybe these two were one and the same.

The Trousseaux and Counter-Trousseaux | In Quattrocento Florence, the trousseau a woman brought to her marriage was counted as part of her dowry.[36] But more than just the dowry changed hands, because marriage was supposedly an equal exchange, which would have been unbalanced if gifts only went one way. The husband and his line were already legally getting the woman, her domestic labor, and her children. With the dowry added to that (especially when dowries rose to 1,000 florins and above in the upper class), the husband's family stood to lose face, and its all-important honor, by not contributing something. Moreover, in the fifteenth century, even though the *donatio propter nuptias* (called the *morgincap* in Tuscany) was still legally required of the husband as a marriage gift (traditionally given to the bride as a reward for her virginity the morning after the marriage had been consummated), it was sharply limited to 50 lire. It could not begin to be an appropriate response to the enormous amount of dowry the woman had brought (in trousseau, cash, Monte shares, and even real property).[37]

The practice thus gradually developed of the groom bestowing a counter-trousseau on his bride in the shape of an additional wardrobe of clothes.[38] Marco Parenti spent more than the 500 florins in cash he had received in dowry from his betrothed Caterina's mother and brother on clothing for her, and it might be assumed that these garments, cut and made and decorated especially for her, and given to her to wear, then belonged to her.[39]

However, as Jane Fair Bestor has recently argued, the ceremonial garments that made up the counter-trousseau were not, in fact, gifts but loans. Although they were often purchased out of the bride's own dotal funds, they did not actually belong to her unless the husband made a specific point of legally transferring them into her name.[40] If he did not intend to give these ceremonial clothes to her as a gift legally, a husband was free to reclaim them after the occasion for which they had been made was past. The honor that accrued to the marriage from the adornment of the bride did not depend upon the actual ownership of the items or the gifting-of-the-bride process. Instead, what mattered most in mid fifteenth-century Florence was the *appearance* of the ceremony itself. If the husband was able to provide visual evidence of "honor" by properly adorning his espoused for this limited ceremonial time frame, then he had achieved honor for the union and, most of all, for himself personally. What was more important than actually giving his bride a lavish gift or gifts was the ability to provide the proper set of accoutrements necessary for an honorable social occasion, an honorable ceremony, an honorable transition. Everyone involved knew that his "gifts" could simply be loans for the day; might, in fact, be rented jewels and headdresses, already used in some other bride's wedding, but the critical issues were that there was enough *of* it and that it was finessed so as not to appear *obviously* rented or loaned. The bride had only a couple of years in which to wear these sumptuous garments in any case, at which time she would fall under the stricter sumptuary restrictions that regulated married women's dress.[41]

The important thing, then, for Florentine society was the honorable moment of transition. If the groom had the wherewithal to outfit the moment beautifully, then the future looked solid for the continuing honor of his union, which marked an extension of his own familial line. The only equilibrium that the passage of "gifts" from groom to bride needed to maintain was an *appearance* of an equilibrium, during the very short, heightened, public period of the wedding itself. This was where there was perceived danger to his lineage— that the groom might be too taken with his bride and gift her recklessly, thereby squandering familial patrimony by a monetary transfer to the bride in the form of *real* gifts.[42] But instead of the family being fatally smitten financially, the temporary wedding clothes of a counter-trousseau could, however, easily be retransformed from bridal display into simple family assets on a page in a family ledger as a husband saw fit. This is not to say that the entire amount of a woman's dowry did not still have to be returned to her (no matter what kind of finery the money was tied up in) upon her husband's death. But that was another matter. Agnatic relationships prevailed in this virilocal society, in essence leaving women out, with the visible exception of their dowry rights. Legally, a woman was entitled to receive her whole dowry back, including any amount that had been spent to adorn her for the transition to her husband's house. But as Isabelle Chabot has recently noted, legal maneuvers in the late fourteenth and early fifteenth century put increasing restrictions on female intestate succession in Florence, which was under communal statute. Daughters were disinherited in favor of sons and even nephews.[43] A deceased woman's dowry could also be taken from her children and given to her widowed husband.[44] Young orphans being robbed of their inheritance by unsympathetic kin cannot have been the *only* possible legal outcome in Florentine families, but it was certainly made easier in the Quattrocento. As Martines noted based on his studies of the fifteenth-century legal evidence, the most common legal proceeding involving a woman was that of a widow attempting to wrest her dowry from the hands of her deceased husband's relatives through her legal representative (*mundualdus*). Undoubtedly, many dowry amounts would still have been entangled in family business investments, real property, and often in the ritual clothing and adornments that had been made specifically for her but did not legally belong to her.[45]

If, in fact, certain items from the counter-trousseau were not sold after the wedding and were still in the wife's possession when her husband passed away, she may have believed she had claim to them, from having had use of them for so long, but legally, they were not hers.[46] In addition, Klapisch-Zuber has shown that upon a husband's predeceasing a wife, his family often viewed this clothing as part of their general family patrimony and were loathe to part with it, especially if the widow was young enough to be remarried into another (competing) lineage by her natal kin.[47] Of course, the husband's family's insistence that his widow leave the clothing would have been even stronger if the cloth or ornamentation bore the colors or motifs of his family.

Selling Clothes | As the usefulness of these garments passed (which sometimes happened very rapidly indeed), there were many options for their eventual disposal and reabsorption into the family assets. A husband could sell them, rent them out for a price to the families of other brides-to-be, or return them to the person from whom he had rented them. They could be stripped of their ornaments and sold piecemeal to pawnbrokers, whom preachers blamed for ruining family finances.[48] They could go to a used-clothes dealer or eventually even be auctioned.[49] Jewels could be taken from settings in brooches and necklaces and resold to a jewelry retailer, pearls cut carefully out of embroidery designs, gold melted down, fabric burnt to reclaim the silver. Clothes could, and did, dissolve into thin air.[50] Alberti's vision of clothes as tools or servants in his *Libri della famiglia* does seem to have been the guiding paradigm in Renaissance Florence.

In Caterina's case, Marco did not sell his wife's wedding clothes to a rigattiere until 1490, some forty-three years after they were made, and nine years after her death.[51] In other instances, however, garments were more quickly pawned. In 1452, Francesco Castellani sold two very ornate garments that had been made for his wife Lena, along with their fringe of gold and silk, gilded silver buttons, and ribbons with silver trim, to a pawnbroker, one Manuello da Volterra, for 51 florins *larghi*. Clearly, what had been her wedding clothing had been transformed into family capital. Castellani wrote at the foot of the entry that these gowns had been sold to help pay family taxes.[52]

Not only display clothing was sold, but other garments as well. Clothing inventories of deceased family members often show the subsequent sale of some or all of the items to satisfy the demands of heirs of the estate or of creditors. In 1451, after the death of Marco Parenti's parents, he sold major items of whatever was still saleable of their clothing to a used-clothes dealer, along with a couple of pieces of his own clothing, meticulously as always noting the owner of the clothes in the margins of the account book. Parenti raised some 242 lire, or about 60½ florins, by selling these clothes. He sold six cioppe, a mantello, an *uccho*, three pairs of red stockings, and an old fur lining of his father's; two blue gowns with black sleeves of his mother's; and two lined gowns of his own, all in the name of the heirs of his father's estate, in the presence of the officials of the Pupilli.[53] There is little written evidence in the generally male discourse in the family logbooks of any sentimentality associated with clothes, or if there was, merchant mentality overrode sentiment. The only hint of sentiment over a wife's clothing I have found is the fact that Marco Parenti waited many years after Caterina's death to sell her wedding outfit.

Other young females did not have to bear the tribulations of the marriage game in fifteenth-century Italy, being destined for another fate, the life of the convent. But even a convent-bound young woman needed to bring a dowry and trousseau to her celestial spouse. The next chapter investigates the dramatic sartorial contrast between being married or going to a convent for two Florentine half-sisters, Ghostanza and Maria Minerbetti.

SEVEN

TROUSSEAUX FOR MARRIAGE AND CONVENT

The Minerbetti Sisters

MARITATE O MONACHATE

The increasingly elitist nature of the upper ranks of Florentine society had a profound impact not only on the lives of elite males and guild-associated artisans who made a good living supplying the display and pomp but also on the women of the families, whose societal role was redefined by it. The disparity between public and private grew, and with it came a subsequent devaluation of what was relegated to the private, whether it be things or people. For a Renaissance wedding, as we have seen in the previous chapter, sartorial extravagance by those clothing the upper-class bride was expected and essential for the honor of the lineage. On the most important day in her life, a young woman around the age of seventeen would be accompanied by her male kin through the streets of Florence. She would make her way from her father's house to the house of her new husband with great festivity, thereby publicly marking a new socioeconomic and political alliance between her family and that of her groom. The bride would be wearing a richly colored, embroidered, multilayered ensemble, tailored of silk brocade or silk velvet, and might be adorned with jewels and a headdress of feathers and pearls. All eyes would be on this surface decoration, the dress splendidly stiff and full. The treasures of her dowry trousseau (*donora*) would have been safely patted and locked into elaborately decorated chest or chests (*cassone*), which, in her grandmother's day would have accompanied her physically as a symbol of her transfer from one house to another, but by the fifteenth century, were less publicly conferred without any ostentation. Nothing was to distract from the bride and her appearance. On that day, the young bride shone in visual splendor, with her trousseau containing extra gowns of silk satin with cut-velvet sleeves, separate fur linings, and an entire inventory of other clothing, linens, accessories, and personal items. This was all contrived to conjure up familial virtù and confer honor made visible by riches of substance that would impress the most jaded *raffinati*.[1]

If, however, the fate of a young girl (often a sister to the first) was not to live as a married woman but rather as a "bride of Christ," she was quietly led by her male relatives, often at an earlier age, with *no* show, through these same streets.[2] This occasion was not celebrated in Renaissance painting, and her destiny would be dramatically different. She would live her life in one of the city's many convents, which were clustered along streets in the less expensive areas of town, around the city gates.[3] She, too, would routinely wear an overgown for her journey through the streets, like her marrying sister, but instead of embroidered silk brocades and velvets, hers would likely be of plain gray wool. No pearls or feathers adorned her head. Instead, her hair was covered by a linen scarf. Her modest "trousseau," which convents required, along with a monastic dowry (*dota monastica*), nonetheless accompanied her, neatly folded in a wicker basket. She was, without fanfare, privately made a nun (*fatta monaca*) by her family, and retired from public view and any public role, at least for the near future, except, as Trexler notes, to piously pray for the future of the Commune.[4]

The fates of the daughters of the prominent Minerbetti family between 1506 and 1518 dramatically illustrate upper-class women's alternatives in the fifteenth and early sixteenth centuries in Florence: *maritate o monachate*, marry or become a nun.[5] Moreover, their trousseaux could not have been more different. Ghostanza Minerbetti, the eldest, had her espousal, while five of her younger sisters and half sisters were warehoused by their family as nuns. Increasingly throughout the Renaissance, dowry amounts soared, exceeding all fiscal boundaries of prudence. By the beginning of the sixteenth century, an upper-class female's dowry, essential for marriage, could easily be over

1,000 florins, or even as high as 2,000 florins. It being vitally important for the families of the upper classes to forge political alliances through marriage, some families found themselves in the position of being able to afford to marry only one daughter "honorably," while consigning other daughters "honorably" to a convent.[6] In fact, Andrea Minerbetti was able to successfully marry only about one-third of his many female progeny.

In order to discern the intense interest and care lavished upon trousseaux, we have only to turn again to the family ricordanze. Marriage was normally the first event recorded in a logbook, and the clothing commissioned for it typically formed a major, and undoubtedly meaningful, part of the entry. Every item of clothing, piece of jewelry, or other personal possession that was being transferred from one house to another was described in detail, and listed in the trousseaux. In the records of the Minerbetti family, Andrea di Tommaso began by entering an account of his marriage to his first wife, Maria di Piero Bini, in 1492.[7] A year after her death in 1499, he recorded his marriage to Ermellina Corbinelli, and after her death in 1509, to Antonia Sassetti in 1511. For each of his many daughters, Andrea entered their trousseaux and dowries, whether for marriage or convent. Here, clothes are constants, in between the records of the births and deaths of many children, the death of a parent, the buying of a house, an argument with a brother, or the consigning of a young daughter to a husband or a convent.

TROUSSEAUX COMPOSITION

The Trousseau | In Renaissance Florence, a bride's traditional source of clothing was her trousseau, which she and her family put together in the months before her the wedding. It was usually paid for by her father, or, in the absence of a father, by the acting head of household (as we have seen in the case of Alessandra Strozzi, acting in consultation with her exiled sons).[8] Among the rich, in the Quattrocento, a trousseau had two parts: a formal donora, whose value was legally assessed (*stimate*) by an outside broker as part of the dowry, and an informal donora, left unappraised (*non-stimate*) and made up of items of a more personal and less substantial nature.[9] As Klapisch-Zuber has noted, by the fifteenth century in Florence, the formal donora had been transformed from its traditional purpose, which had been to provide

a woman's personal clothing items and the family linens necessary for equip-
ping a new household. Instead, it became an inventory of display items
focused more on decorating the body of the bride herself.[10] It would typically consist of ornate gowns (from three to six for display purposes), such as
cioppe and giornee, ornamented with pearl embroidery or fur trim, and
often dyed with the crimson kermes, a belt of brocade with worked silver
ornamentation; a couple of hats or hoods (*berrette, cappucci*), a number of
embroidered underblouses, and some handkerchiefs (*fazoletti*). Also included
here would be small devotional books (expensively decorated) and any
jewelry.

Unappraised Items | The informal unappraised part of the bridal trousseau,
which often grew in relationship to the appraised portion in the fourteenth
and fifteenth centuries, was much more humble, but it might nonetheless be
extensive. It would typically include gowns of cotton (*di boccattino bianco*),
linen, or of plain thin wool (*di rascia*), as well as everyday personal linens such
as aprons, veils, headscarves, head garlands, stockings, socks, and towels.
Purses, shoes, slippers, yardage, cording, and ribbons were here, and also a
young woman's smallest and most personal items, such as hairbrushes and
combs, linen neck scarves, collars, and the like. In addition, here can be found
any small toilette items of silver or brass, such as a mirror, water basins and
ewers, an array of utilitarian items such as baskets and wooden chests and
boxes, and, finally, sewing paraphernalia: scissors, thimbles, pincushions, embroidery silk, distaff, and spindle.[11] Motivations for the increase in the unappraised part of the trousseau are unclear, but as Klapisch-Zuber has argued, it
may have represented familial attempts to ensure that these intimate items
their daughters brought with them into the marriage could later be retrieved
without question. By keeping a greater portion of a young woman's goods
out of the dowry, and away from the *rigattiere* who made the estimate, her
family avoided possible entangled seizure of these personal effects by her
husband or his family, and even their loss, which would break the link to
her natal family represented by her donora.[12] On the other hand, increasing
the unestimated portion of the trousseau could also be part of a strategy of tax
avoidance, lowering the value of the dowry and thereby reducing the contract
tax (*gabella dei contratti*) mandated by the Commune.[13]

THE MAKING OF A TROUSSEAU

In any case, in Florence, many specialists participated in the making of a young woman's trousseau. Traditionally, instead of guild-associated artisans working under the direction of the groom, such as we saw in Chapter 6, the women of the family oversaw the wedding trousseau. This, like the first type of project, would take several months of planning, negotiating, shopping, collecting, and needlework. The division of labor in these two clothing realms could not have been more gender-specific. However, we need to be careful to distinguish between the two parts of the trousseau in the fifteenth century. For although women had been in charge of the trousseau in the past, it is clear that by the Quattrocento, the appraised portion was controlled by the needs and desires of the males of the family and was actually made primarily by men. With the growing aristocratization of the upper class, the bulk of the utilitarian items and personal linens, which would have been made by women, were relegated to the unappraised portion of the trousseau.[14] Assisted by craftsmen, merchants, and dealers, the men of the family busied themselves with the highly adorned externals of marriage display provided by the dowry money and the appraised trousseau, while its female members oversaw the craftswomen who made the more intimate, personal items of the unappraised trousseau, which would rarely have been seen outside the private realm, being nearly invisible under the bride's clothes. The stiff, expensive quilted brocades and pearl-embroidered velvets, saturated colors, and jewelry and precious metals that the men dealt with contrasted sharply with the soft, often unbleached cotton and linen garments and household items made by the women.

The clothing in the unappraised part of the trousseau was all made by hand, with humble materials, for the most part, and took hours of monotonous needlework to hem. Some of these items could be produced within the household itself by family members and servants, while others would have to be commissioned from *camiciai*, seamstresses in Florentine convents or from the ranks of the female tertiaries of the city.[15] Almost every family in Renaissance Florence had at least one kinswoman who was a nun, and upper-class families typically had multiple kinswomen in convents. Female relatives often lived in the same convent, the older ones looking out for the younger. By

1500, there were some fifty or so convents in the city, with an average of about ninety-eight women per house.[16] Gene Brucker has estimated that by 1515, there were over 2,500 professed nuns living in the convents in and around the city, which would only have accounted for a portion of the total number of female convent inhabitants.[17] In 1470, thirty such convents were clustered together along several streets in the city. Each of the city's four quarters contained religious houses for women. In Santa Croce, convents were located on Borgo Pinti, beginning at the Piazza San Piero Maggiore, and also in the Via Ghibellina; in the quarter of San Giovanni, they began at the church of San Lorenzo and ran along Via San Gallo. There were also houses in Santa Maria Novella around Ognissanti, and on the Oltrarno in the quarter of Santo Spirito, near the Porta San Piero Gattolino (now the Porta Romana).[18]

THE MONTE DELLE DOTI

The trousseau a woman brought to her marriage, which counted as part of her dowry, ranged from 5 to 16 percent of its value, with the average being about 11 percent.[19] In 1427, a dowry would substantially raise her new husband's total worth, on average by nearly 23 percent.[20] Work done by Anthony Molho and Julius Kirshner has found that the stability of this percentage, even as dowry amounts soared throughout the course of the Renaissance, was aided in part by the establishment in 1424–25 of the Monte delle doti, a communal fund created to guarantee adequate dowries to families that had made a deposit in it when a daughter was still an infant or child.[21] As it was first structured, the fund would accrue interest for eight to fifteen years, at which time the Commune would pay the earned amount upon the marriage of the insured girl.[22] To allow time for the deposit or deposits (if more than one was made) to mature, the first payments into the Monte delle doti were made when girls were on average about five years of age.[23]

Daughters of upper-class families needed to marry well and marry young, so the decision of whether or not to enroll them was a crucial step in family planning. In 1437, the Monte was adjusted to accommodate enrolled girls who were to take vows. Instead of the family losing their deposit from one to three years after the girl entered the convent (as also would happen if a girl were to die), the capital invested in the dowry fund would be returned to the parents. Out of this amount, they could pay the monastic dowry required by the convent for each girl accepted.[24] From the late 1440s on, another option was made available to the families of enrolled girls who decided to enter a convent of their own volition, or, as more often documented, were deemed unlikely to make a marriage (due to physical or mental infirmity) by their family. The family could petition the officials to be able to replace the initial enrollee with a sister, to whom the Monte deposit could then be transferred, she marrying and the first girl being cloistered.[25] Many girls of the upper class were never enrolled, however, because multiple or infirm daughters were often consigned to a convent at a very early age, their fate having been decided.[26] Although they were certainly exceptions, at least among girls enrolled in the Monte, Molho cites a number of girls cloistered before the age of ten (4.5 percent), and there were extreme cases of girls being sent to convents as early as the age of three.[27]

A MARRIAGE TROUSSEAU

The trousseaux of those who married were normally quite extensive, including not only clothing but sewing and writing supplies and items such as chests, baskets, basins, and ewers. Andrea Minerbetti's ricordanza itemized each of his three wives' trousseaux, which run many pages in length, distinguishing between items assigned a monetary value (noted in the margin) and those left unestimated. Upon the betrothal of his eldest daughter Ghostanza in 1511 (at the age of eighteen) to Carlo di Tommaso Sassetti, Andrea provided her with a dowry of 1,200 florins (divided between 960 in Monte credits and 240 in cash), and a trousseau of 275 florins *di suggello*. In his records, Minerbetti detailed every piece of clothing in her trousseau, as was usual, noting the type of garment, fabric, color, and specific styles of gowns and sleeves.[28] Andrea had previously sent this daughter to a convent on two occasions before her espousal, the first time being the day after her sixth birthday, when her mother died on December 19, 1499. The second time was eight years later, at the age of sixteen, after his second marriage also ended in a death, this time that of her stepmother.[29] Klapisch-Zuber notes that the custom had developed in Florence by the fourteenth century of using the convent system in this way as temporary lodging for girls, especially when a father had been widowed and found it expedient.[30] Emerging from her convent in February 1511, Ghostanza was finally readied for marriage and provided with the elaborate ritual clothing that would equip her for public display. In addition to her "official" detailed trousseau, worth around 280 florins, her father gave her another 520 florins, which was listed directly under the amount paid for her dowry and the trousseau. The Minerbetti were part of the Florentine elite, and this marriage would have strengthened their alliance with the illustrious Sassetti family, so the additional amount was in all probability added for more clothing for the requisite ritual festivities.[31]

The first impression of the written description of her official (stimate) wedding trousseau is one of luxurious silk pastel gowns, fur linings, jewelry, and extra detachable sleeves to mix and match. Besides the requisite ornate silk overgown, hers of a carnation pink (gherofanato), lined and bordered with fur, Ghostanza had in her trousseau three other gowns (cotte), two of fabric called ciambellotto; one of these was light yellow (limonato) in color and the other white. The third cotta was of damask in a color designated as sbiadato, possibly a pale, watered blue.[32] She also had three pairs of detachable sleeves, one of heavy silk chermisi, another of crimson velvet, and a third simply designated as lavorato, or embroidered. These garments were only seven of her many clothing items, which ran two full pages in her father's logbook, including other gowns (lilac blue silk with flounced sleeves, green wool with lined sleeves of tan silk damask); as well as headdresses, belts, head scarves, aprons, linens, slippers, undergarments, and an appropriate Santa Margherita doll, "dressed in brocade with pearls," which had undoubtedly been passed down to her by her mother, a doll of the same description being listed in the mother's trousseau some sixteen years earlier in 1493.[33]

The second, unassessed part of Ghostanza's trousseau was even more extensive, and contained dozens of other items, whose worth was left unestimated, although they were of no mean value. More clothes, linens, and accessories were listed, including detachable sleeves, gold-embroidered stockings, and two pairs of wooden platform shoes (zoccoli) for wearing in the street. Included also were ribbons, purses, and gloves, as well as sewing and embroidery supplies (scissors, pins, silk pin cushions, and embroidery thread "of many colors"), silk appliqués of doves and flowers, and an angel embroidered in gold. Also here were many items fashioned of ivory, including a comb and gilded brush, the requisite distaff and spindle, and also a portfolio and ink-stand. Among other things, she was also given many baskets, two big marble basins, gilded chests of cypress wood, a tabernacle with painted saints, and two pairs of stockings with the family device worked on them. But female artisans' work did appear here as well in earnest, among the masses of linens amassed by her family, the multiples of which are quite impressive: eight aprons of new linen cloth, nine large veils, ten handkerchiefs, ten neckbands, eleven pairs of stockings, eleven hairnets, fourteen linen caps, and much, much more. She also had over twenty items made of silk: underblouses, purses, caps, neckbands and ribbons.[34]

A TROUSSEAU FOR THE CONVENT

For her younger sisters Ypolita, Francesca, Maria, Bartolomea, and Lucretia, life, and the way in which they would be outfitted for it, was a different story. Ghostanza's father Andrea recorded all the garments and linens that made up the smaller trousseaux he provided to these five daughters, just as he had for his eldest. Between 1506 and 1518, at between five and sixteen years of age, the girls were sent to various convents in and around Florence to be made nuns.[35] Ypolita was not yet five years old when she was consigned to the convent of Santa Marta a Montughi, outside the city walls. She had con-tracted German measles before the age of two, which had left her blind in her left eye. As her chances of being able to marry successfully were thus slim, her fate was decided very early.[36] These girls were "given to God," some before puberty, and would spend their days within the convent's confines, either eventually embracing a spiritual life and praying for the destiny of the Com-mune by becoming a nun or sister (*suora*) or simply residing there as a roomer (*in serbanza*), temporarily or permanently depending on the dictates of their families, often spending their days of stitching and sewing as best they could.[37]

This transfer of a young woman from her father to a new guardian (in these cases, not a husband, but a convent), was marked with the same ritual ex-changes as a marriage. Each convent, upon accepting a Minerbetti girl, re-ceived a *dota monastica* of 100 florins, listed as an alms donation (*per limosina*) to the convent, along with the girl's conventual trousseau. These conventual dowries were worth only about one-tenth of a wedding dowry and thus were affordable to a family stretched financially by having to dower many daughters. But it was in the trousseau, *not* in the dowry, that Andrea Minerbetti really saved his florins.

The dowries and trousseaux of the five daughters who entered convents were intended to provide the bare necessities for the girls' support, perhaps for their lifetimes. There would be no room in these girls' lives for finery designed for public display, and their trousseaux could scarcely have been more different from their sister Ghostanza's, averaging only around 20 florins each in clothes, fabric, and foodstuffs. They were essentially retiring into the domestic, private realm at a tender age and would take up only that aspect of a Florentine woman's life that had no place for luxuries.

It is only when we compare a bridal trousseau with one destined for a convent that we can see how display-conscious trousseaux had become for the upper classes in the fifteenth century. In a conventual trousseau, ornate items are absent. There is no color. All the clothing is gray, all the fabric black, white, or brown, and the cloth is of modest quality. The composition of these two types of trousseaux reinforces the notion that the trend toward appearance and outward display in the upper classes widened a gap between public and private dressing, especially for women. Conventual trousseaux allow us to see private dressing most clearly and visually recall Botticelli's profile portrait of a plainly dressed young woman in the Pitti Palace (Fig. 4.2). These *donore* consisted of a couple of basic house gowns (*gamurre*), plus undergarments, head scarves, aprons, handkerchiefs, slippers, and shoes. Girls bound for the convent also typically had yardage provided from which they would fashion future garments themselves. Usually, this cloth was of modest quality and of neutral color. For example, "black woolen cloth for clothes" ("saia nera per abiti") was listed in the Minerbetti family logbooks for each girl, along with "white woolen yardage" ("saia biancha").[38]

We can closely contrast such a conventual trousseau with one for a wedding by looking at the goods listed for one of Ghostanza's younger half-sisters, Maria. Born in 1501 to Andrea's second wife, Ermellina, she was eight years Ghostanza's junior, and had been named after Ghostanza's deceased mother, Maria. In 1506, not yet six years old, she was sent off to Santa Felicita, one of the seven convents run by the Benedictines in the city of Florence, located in the Piazza Santa Felicita.[39] On November 7 of that year, Maria cost her father only about 5½ florins for her trousseau, which contained, in addition to two dresses and a woolen cloak, everything she would need for her new life. She was safe, and safely out of public sight, along with two pairs of socks, two sets of washable personal linens, and eight each of underblouses, head scarves, and caps.[40] Maria's family provided her with six bath towels, four other towels, four aprons, four handkerchiefs, and an ivory spoon for her personal use at Santa Felicita. For chilly weather, she had two linings, two more pairs of shoes, a pair of gloves, and some slippers.

In the convent, the nuns would braid her hair, tie it off with thread, and clothe her in a gray woolen smock of *berettino* in winter and "coarse linen cloth of the same color" ("tela grossa di Lino tinta del medesimo colore") in summer.[41] She was to be anonymous and plain.[42] Her superiors and elders wore the heavier wool year-round, of another color of gray called *ceneritio*, the color of cinders, which represented their supposedly more intense state of humility and mortification.[43]

A girl living in a convent in Florence needed some type of annual support from her father or his heirs, either in cash or kind.[44] In Maria's case, sheets, tablecloths, towels, and dozens of yards of fabric to be used for unspecified utilitarian purposes began to arrive eight months after she did, and over the next eight years, supplementing the meager resources with which she had entered the convent, her father brought additional items: eighty-four yards of sheeting, forty yards of wool, thirty-six yards of white cloth, and thirty-three yards of linen. But no more garments. Maria was simply provided with drab brown yardage for her clothes ("monachino per abiti") and washable fabric for her undergarments ("pannolino per camice"). No tailor was needed here.

After she had been there for a year, her family gave Santa Felicita two paintings: one of a crucifixion, the other of St. Roch, a healer who was invoked as a charm against plague in the fifteenth century.[45] Molho has noted the popular belief in miraculous cures effected by these sacred images and relics among the many girls in convents who were infirm.[46] Two years later, more fabric was purchased and brought to the convent by her family for the making of Maria's habit, the black overgown worn by the Benedictines ("cioppa nera per la tonacha"). In Florence, most young women had to reach the age of twelve to fifteen years (if they were going to consecrate their lives to God and take the vows of chastity, poverty, and obedience) before they were allowed to wear the nun's habit (*tonaca*), made with yardage supplied by their own families.[47] Maria would have been around eight. Around Easter in 1510 and 1511, more personal linens and aprons, as well as food and candle wax arrived, and in 1514, there is one last entry: more thin, coarse linen. After that, the family ricordanza falls silent on the fate of this young woman.[48]

SELLING CLOTHES FROM WEDDINGS AND TROUSSEAUX

Like wedding dresses, the clothing and personal effects contained in a trousseau were not immune to financial liquidation. As Klapisch-Zuber notes, whereas in the fourteenth century, a widower had customarily returned a deceased wife's possessions to her natal family, by the fifteenth century, trousseaux items tended to be disbursed as part of the domestic goods of a household.[49] For example, in Minerbetti's records from January 1496, some four years after his first wedding, he records selling clothing to a used-clothing dealer for 230 florins, with which he promptly paid off a creditor, one Agnolo Pandolfini.[50] However, the clothes he sold were not his alone. Some were his and some had belonged to his father Tomaso, but others had been worn by his first wife, Maria, the mother of Ghostanza. Maria's clothes, which included items from both her own trousseau and the counter-trousseau Andrea had given her, fetched a hefty 60 florins. Among the items sold were eight of her gowns, including a white damask cioppa that had been listed first in her trousseau and had probably formed the centerpiece of her wedding clothes.[51] The only object that I found that could have been sentimentalized was the holy doll of Santa Margherita, which went from the deceased mother Maria to her to oldest daughter, Ghostanza, via her trousseau.[52]

By comparing the donore of two half-sisters from the same rich family, the extreme range of sartorial realities of the *classe dirigente* can be seen, and the toll paid by the women themselves, caught up in an increasingly display-conscious culture, better appreciated. Chapter 8 moves from the uses Renaissance Florentine society made of specific costumes for young women of the upper class to a discussion of the clothes themselves in all their intimate complexity and layers of meaning.

III

FASHION AND
THE COMMUNE

EIGHT

THE CLOTHES THEMSELVES

I rrespective of the wearer's social class, gender, or age, Renaissance Florentine outfits were composed of many garments and accessories layered together to form a coherent ensemble that could be altered for comfort, when the weather was warm or turned chilly, by subtracting or adding a layer. In addition to the cut and arrangement of the garments, overall shape and color were also essential aspects of a coherent visual message in this increasingly appearance-conscious urban society. Any attempt to reclaim and understand the many dimensions of historical clothing is, however, prickly with inherent problems. Roland Barthes's semiotic terminology of "technologic," "verbal," and "iconic" elements with regard to clothes can be applied here.[1] Clothing existed in three distinct realms, which all referred to one another, that is: the clothes themselves, writing about the clothes, and the manufactured images of the clothes. The last two realms, however, were by definition quite distant from what would have been the everyday visual reality of dress as seen in the streets of Quattrocento Florence.

The Actual Garments | First of all, we know that the clothes themselves (Barthes's "technologic" element) represented an important part of the material culture of the Renaissance. These clothes are, however, unavailable for analysis. Save for some embroidered ceremonial clerical vestments and eccle-

siastiçal orphreys, all we have left from fifteenth-century Florence are fragments of fabric. An elegant but sparse selection of very hardy brocade and
damask fragments and a few centimeters of carefully wrapped velvets are
scattered about in museum textile collections. Other than a shoe or two and
the more time-resistant jewelry, the clothing of fifteenth-century Florence is
gone.[2] And so, very few "technologic" artifacts are available for material
analysis.

Notwithstanding this void, historians of costume have traditionally written
about the vanished clothing of the past with an omniscient eye, describing it
in minute authoritative detail, as if they had actually *seen* the garments, and
yet omniscience is precisely what we do not have. In general, we must rely
upon the two ancillary realms where this clothing has been represented; the
written records and works of art that have survived. It is from these sources
that the richness of the garments must be gleaned, while these sources themselves present formidable obstacles to understanding the now-vanished second skins of cloth, fur, leather, precious metals, and lace.

Written Clothes | Tailors, patricians, clerics, and legislators alike invented
the vocabulary used to refer to the garments they created, wore, wrote about,
and passed judgment upon (Barthes's "verbal" element). Often, the quickly
changing clothing styles of the fifteenth century outpaced the written descriptions of them, and those who were forced to put pen to paper in the
service of clothes found themselves without adequate words with which to
work. The language of public sumptuary legislation lagged woefully behind the quotidian ricordanze of private individuals in its description of the
clothes, which still must have been a pale second to the actual garments. For
example, whereas Rubric LXXI of the Statuta of 1415 mentions only twelve
types of garments that tailors made, the family ricordanze of the fifteenth
century name over twice that many.

Barthes has discussed the problem of reducing a piece of clothing to its oral
version, noting that the conversion from material culture into language elimi-
nates the freedom afforded a piece of clothing visually. Language acts to
immobilize the perception of the garment at a certain level of intelligibility,
that is, it picks out those aspects of the garment that are deemed important to
notice (cloth, color, neckline, whether it has gussets or not) and then imposes

those choices on the reader.[3] Any student of the communal sumptuary legislation will recognize this conundrum immediately, as the choices made of
what to describe rarely give the reader the whole picture of the garment.
What can be discerned, however, may be indications of those elements of
fashion that were the cause of sumptuary concern, perhaps innovations in
style. Chapter 9 looks at these innovations.[4]

Clothing in Artwork | Moving from the written to the visual sources (the
"iconic" element) presents challenges. In the visual representation of clothing
in the art of this period, there are daunting uncertainties in matching the type
of garment pictured with the written descriptions. Because the fashion of the
clothes themselves was rarely the primary concern of the artist, not only is the
shape of a specific garment difficult to identify using the range of contemporary terminology, but, if there is color, it is too. Certainly, the subtle differences in fabric hue and texture described in written sources, are often impossible to discern in the brush strokes or charcoal lines of the surviving artwork.
However, through studying the artwork, it is possible to synthesize a general
picture of the dress of the urban population.[5]

OVERALL VISUAL IMPRESSION

Males | Based on pictorial and written sources, the clothes men wore in
public in Renaissance Florence appear to have depended on status and occupation. Artisans and shopkeepers dressed themselves in belted tunics and
haphazardly fitting hose of undistinguished color, and the *popolo minuto* often
wore soft caps called *foggette*, which those of upper rank (the *popolo grasso*)
disdainfully eschewed. To call a man of lesser status a *foggettina* ("poor little
hatted one") was a patrician insult.[6] Figure 8.1 depicts the Florentine popolo
minuto in a detail from Masaccio's *St. Peter Healing with His Shadow* in the
Brancacci Chapel (1430).

Those who held public office, roughly 5 percent of the urban population,
evidently clothed themselves, at least for their portraits, in amply cut, unbelted calf-length mantles and gowns (*cioppe* or *lucchi*) of a plain, rich crimson
woolen cloth, usually adding a rolled-up hood (*cappuccio*) of a corresponding
color.[7] The cappuccio was a complicated article of clothing fashioned by

Fig. 8.1. Males of the *popolo minuto*. Detail from Masaccio, *St. Peter Healing with His Shadow* (1430). Brancacci Chapel, Santa Maria del Carmine.

tailors, usually of the same fabric as the cioppa or mantello, and was worn in a variety of ways, depending on the style and flash of the wearer.[8] The crimson cloth would be dyed with kermes and well tailored; it was lined with silk in summer, and a fur lining was added in winter.

Vasari tells a story about the Florentine cappucci. He writes that Botticelli played a practical joke on a student, one Biagio, who had painted a copy of his life-size tondo of a Madonna and Eight Angels. Botticelli had already brokered its sale for six florins, and the student was bringing the buyer to Botticelli's workshop to see it. As a prank, Botticelli and another student "made several paper hats (like the ones the citizens wore) which they stuck with white wax over the heads of the eight angels that surrounded the Madonna."

When Biagio and the buyer came in, "Biagio looked up and saw his Madonna seated not in the midst of angels but in the middle of the councilors of Florence, all wearing their paper hats! He was just about to roar out in anger and make excuses when he noticed that the man he was with had said nothing at all [being let in on the joke beforehand] and was in fact starting to praise the picture . . . so Biagio kept quiet himself." The student subsequently accompanied the buyer to his house, where he received his six florins for the painting. When he got back to the shop, Botticelli and his other students had removed the hats, "and he found [to his amazement] that the angels he had painted were angels after all."[9] Apparently, in Renaissance Florence, cappucci had the power to transform angels into mere mortals.

The powerful leaders of the Commune wore soled hose, which was either black or matched their cloaks. The narrow-cut shoes with pointed toes fashionable in mid-to-late Quattrocento Florence were generally custom-made, either of calf leather with punched-out or tooled designs or of suede or lined fabric, with a heavier leather sole sewn on the bottom. Records of SS. Annunziata show repeated purchases of "scarpe di vitello" for the monks, bought for the amount of around ten soldi a pair in 1492.[10]

From the surviving artwork, it appears that Florentines wore little or no jewelry that would have been visible on the street.[11] On one Milanese ambassador's practice of sporting many golden chains around his neck, Bracciolini has his fellow humanist Niccolò Niccoli opine, "I say, those other lunatics let themselves be tied with one chain, while he instead is crazier, and not happy with only one."[12] Figure 8.2 shows conservatively dressed members of the

Florentine ruling class in a detail from the *Angel Appearing to Zacharias* by Ghirlandaio in the Tornabuoni Chapel.

This unadorned uniform of fine red woolen cloth (which changed only slightly during the fifteenth century) must have given the designated leaders of the city a certain generalized egalitarian appearance, an impression they were eager to convey. A letter from one of Cosimo's great-nephews to his father during the Medici exile in Venice in 1434 reveals the outward modesty of the everyday Florentine male dressing practices: "Here everyone dresses very finely, and I often go with Lorenzo ["Il Vecchio," his great uncle] to places where one must cut a distinguished figure, so that at the moment all my *usual* outer garments are of silk"[13] (emphasis added). Such outward ostentation in dress, while acceptable in the more cosmopolitan milieu of Venice, was not usual or desirable in Florence, which prided itself on its strictly conservative, republican image for men. Stella Mary Newton says that the use of the expensive kermes dyestuff was limited in Venice to silk cloth, however, whereas in Florence, perhaps contradictorily, kermes was also used to dye the finely cut woolen mantles worn routinely by upper-class men in public.

This uniform of sorts also directed all attention, not to the clothes of important men, which were of similar excellent cut and fabric, but rather, to their individual heads.[14] This can dramatically be seen in Figure 8.3, a detail from *The Calling of Saint Peter* by Ghirlandaio from the Sistine Chapel (1481). The ruling group accentuated their faces (and differentiated themselves), by wearing the wide range of headgear for which Florence was famous, from cappucci rolled in individually distinctive ways and berretti bearing personal jewelry—usually brooches—to a noteworthy variety of other caps and hats.[15]

Females | Women in Renaissance Florence cut another figure altogether. Over their cotton or linen underblouses, marketplace women, working women in the streets, and the wives of lesser guildsmen all apparently wore simply cut, calf-length linen or woolen gowns or shifts, which modestly covered the body from neck to wrist to calf. Usually, the outfits were belted with generous washable aprons (*grembiali*) to protect clothes from the contamination of the workday. Figure 8.4, a detail from *The Distribution of the Goods of the Church* by Masaccio, from the Brancacci Chapel (ca. 1425), shows females of the popolo minuto thus garbed. These shifts would have been

Fig. 8.2. Males of the ruling class. Detail from Ghirlandaio, *The Angel Appearing to Zacharias* (1486–90). Tornabuoni Chapel.

Fig. 8.3. Individuated male heads. Detail from Ghirlandaio, *The Calling of Saint Peter* (1481). Sistine Chapel, the Vatican, Rome.

either of a natural uncolored cloth or of inexpensive hues, ranging from *rancio di bianco* (a warm white color) to *cilestri di bianco* (a light blue) or even *scarlattini* (a light red). After they became threadbare or torn, working women continued to wear their precious clothes patched. In Figure 8.5, a detail from the *Inventario di un' eredità dei Buonomini* by the School of Ghirlandaio (late fifteenth century), working women are shown huddled in a doorway in patched gowns. Ironically, this image is from the Oratorio del Buonomini di San Martino, a prestigious Florentine wool-finishing firm.

In contrast, when venturing outside the domestic realm (going to or from church, or from one family abode to another), women of the richer merchant families presented themselves in voluminous multilayered draperies of richly woven and dyed cloth. Much of the luxe of an upper-class adult female's layered clothing would not have been visible on the street, however, for she would have wrapped a full-length cloak or mantle around her gowns outside the house (*a fuori*). The only place most Florentines might briefly have glimpsed a rich female in a formal outfit would have been from afar in the

Fig. 8.4. Females of the *popolo minuto*. Detail from Masaccio, *The Distribution of the Goods of the Church* (ca. 1425). Brancacci Chapel.

Fig. 8.5. Women in patched *gamurre*. Detail from School of Ghirlandaio, *Inventario di un' eredità dei Buonomini* (late fifteenth century). Oratorio del Buonomini di San Martino, Florence.

street, on her way to be married, seated in a family loggia or audience on a communal feast day, or, in the last decades of the century, in family chapel frescoes, only partially visible in the filtered light of a couple of the city's churches.[16] Otherwise, such women remained hidden from "common" eyes, eyes for whom they were not outfitted in the first place. Of course, within the privately "public" space of the palazzi of the rich, there would have been opportunity for an insider to gaze to his or her heart's content.[17]

On a woman's feet, cloth slippers were often worn "slipped" inside larger wooden clogs for walking in the public streets. Upper-class women also wore clogs with platform soles, called by their fashionable foreign name of *chopine*. These platform clogs could be fabric-covered and embroidered for festive outfits. On their heads, the females of the upper class, like their male counterparts, wore cappucci, but women rarely rolled them up about the head turban-style the way men did. Rather, they were worn as cowls, to shield the face and neck from view. Francesco Barbaro's *De re uxoria* insists that an honorable woman should remain covered and hidden ("coperta e nascosta") when in public view and should avoid meeting the eyes of any man on the street.[18] Certainly, the wearing of an ample cappuccio would have helped her do so. Fashion evidently demanded that cowl match gown. Margherita Datini complained to her husband that if she were to have a new cloak, she had to have a new cowl too, for she could not wear an old piece with a new one.[19]

The overall effect of a rich women in the street, covered from head to foot with expensive cloth, elevated on platform shoes, and always with her servants or kinswomen, appears to have been one of a rather large, sedately moving, imposing mass of fabric.[20] Kinswomen also possessed clothing cut from the same cloth, and when worn en masse on the street, this would have heightened the visual impact.[21] Of course, the figure cut by women of the upper class out in the streets was not what has been preserved in the portraits of the women of the oligarchy, which give us a skewed visual record of the normal appearance of most Renaissance females, poor or rich, an issue looked at in Chapter 10.

MEANINGS

Upper-Body Emphasis | Beside being of grand proportions, clothing for the rich had the luxury of being stylish. Most of the modish differentiation in these clothes was concentrated either on the head, the neckline, or the sleeves. This emphasized the upper region of the body over the lower, and, by association, the mental over the physical. In men's clothes, all cloth bulk and emphasis was on this upper-body region.[22] Headwear for both men and women in Florence was multiform and could be large, creating an impression of height and volume and providing an extension of bodily self, which projected a sense of power. Tall hats for men and bulbous headpieces (*balze*) for women (especially worn for ceremonial rites of passage) enabled both males and females to fill more public space, thereby extending their degree of personal control.

Necklines varied from very high (*alleuto* or *accollato*) for mature, married, or cloistered women to lower, rounded neckline styles for nubile girls, which a sumptuary revision of 1464 set at a sixteenth of a braccio from the "fork of the throat" in front, and an eighth of a braccio in back.[23] The shape of the neckline is not delineated in the written documents, however, bringing to mind Barthes's comments about the imposed choices language makes upon clothes in their written form. What *is* richly articulated in the literature, however, is the ornamentation sewn on around the neckline. At least twenty different terms referring to baubles and decorations for gowns are recorded in family accounts.[24] The Commune frequently updated its sumptuary laws to cope with these decorative innovations.

Finally, at least a dozen different types of sleeves, slashed and puffed, straight and gathered, narrow or full (but always full-length to emphasize arm movements in men and modest reserve in women) are mentioned in the Florentine documents of the time.[25] An average pair of men's sleeves required two and a half braccia of cloth, about a yard and a quarter for each arm. For women's sleeves from midcentury on, less fabric was used (only one and a half braccia for a pair of sleeves for a woman), which could indicate that this cloth was to make sleeves in the "new" style thought to be of Spanish court origin—that is, detachable sleeves, smaller and fitted, which tied onto the bodice of a gown with laces and were of contrasting rich fabric.[26] These new detachable sleeves then *themselves* came under sumptuary legislation, not because of their fullness, but because of their luxurious cloth, as we shall see in Chapter 9.

Lower-Body Similarity | Whereas the upper portion of Florentine Renaissance dress, especially the hats, necklines, and sleeves, was radically individualized, the lower parts of ensembles for both men and women of all classes were remarkably similar for each gender. Men all wore leg-hugging soled hose of stretchable perpignan cloth, more or less tailored, depending on what they could afford.[27] Women all wore gowns with full-length voluminous skirts of varying fabrics, perhaps, as Lawrence Langner has suggested, to inconspicuously accommodate regular pregnancies.[28] Alison Lurie writes of the contemporary phenomenon of jeans being worn with everything from plain white T-shirts to tube tops and Armani jackets that clothing that is all the same for a group from the waist down but different from the waist up suggests that "in their lower or physical natures these persons are alike, however dissimilar they may be socially, intellectually or aesthetically."[29]

The sartorial delineation of rank in Renaissance Florence would seem to bear out Lurie's hypothesis, because although the pursuit of fine cloth, expensive dyestuffs, and dignified, large headgear preoccupied the upper class, the cultural obsession with visualizing honor did not much extend to the nether regions of the ensemble for either gender. Moreover, this subconscious dichotomy between upper and lower body regions was accompanied by a gendered division among craftspeople. Men for the most part clothed the top half of the body, manufacturing hats, caps, cowls, hoods, jewelry, and certainly doublets, but making belts, hose, and slippers was traditionally the domain of women.[30]

ACTUAL WARDROBES

Layering | Arguably the most characteristic feature of Renaissance dress was its sumptuous layering. When fully outfitted, both men and women wore four layers of clothing, weather permitting. Tailors were able to convey complex visual expressions of luxury by deftly slashing or snipping away fabric at the neck, wrists, elbows, and sides of the garments thus layered, thereby opening windows through which to view the linings, patterns, and contrasting colors beneath; to our twentieth-century eyes, the juxtaposition is sometimes startling. As Quentin Bell has observed, the sumptuous nature of layered clothes, that is, their "conspicuously expensive character," is most enhanced through this cutting away, "so as to show how many things are being worn and what expensive things they are."[31] Part of the subtlety of the layered effect was, of course, the quick flash of a brilliant lining or the tease of an exotic fur as the wearer passed in the street. Rich women, as we saw in Chapter 4, added to this effect by bunching up the fabric of their skirts as they walked or stood, thereby revealing an underskirt of contrasting color or trim. Layered, lined, slashed, and bunched up though these ensembles may have been, the distortion of the human body was less pronounced in the clothing of Florence at this time than in the costumes of France, England, Germany, Spain, or even other Italian city-states. It was this practice of wearing layers of garments of thin fabric, one over another, that accounted for a more natural, if slightly enlarged silhouette in the costumes of Florence.

Men's Ensembles | The garments men wore are best considered using the terms they used in their own family records. Every man began with the *camicia*. This washable layer was full-sleeved, gathered at the neck and wrists, and long enough to be tucked into the tops of the hose, which (more or less) covered every man's legs and could button onto his shoes, if he were wearing them.[32] Over this went the constructed upper-body *farsetto*, which gave the male chest definition. Closely tailored and quilted for shape, this garment could be made of many kinds of fabric, from cotton or linen to velvet or brocade. In these two upper-body pieces, along with hose, a man's body was covered, but certainly not completely dressed.

The third essential garment was the tunic, which went by many names even within Florence itself. Tunics included the shorter *giubbia* or *villano* (increasingly and even sometimes scandalously shorter as the century wore on), the slightly longer *cioppa, cotta,* the traditional Florentine *lucco,* and the sleeveless *giornea* (originally a military garment).[33] These garments could also be of varying styles—narrow, gathered, pleated, or open in the front—and lined with either fur or silk for winter or summer wear.[34] And, finally, men *might* wear overgowns for warmth, luxe, or simply to cut a dashing figure on the street. Besides the old-fashioned *cottardite,* there were in addition amply cut *mantelli* and *robbe* or *sacchi.* Of all of these various shapes and styles, *mantello* seems to have been used as the generic term, with over twenty different types singled out in the communal statuta for regulation. Figure 8.6 shows two men wearing scarlet woolen mantelli in a detail from Masaccio's 1426 predella panel, part of the *Pisa Polyptych.*

Fig. 8.6. Male *mantelli*. Detail from Masaccio, *Adoration of the Magi*, predella panel of the *Pisa Polyptych* (1426). Gemäldegalerie, Berlin-Dahlem.

Women's Ensembles | Women's outfits, which had as many if not more requisite layers and differentiated garments, were even more specifically artic- ulated. Like men, the women began with the camicia, what we would call today (feminizing the garment name) an underblouse rather than an under- shirt. The gendering of a garment name, however, was something that Florentines as a rule did not do, although male and female cuts of a garment were apparently known in Renaissance Italy. For example, art historians have noted the marginal occupations of the women painted by Titian, as attested to in part by their wearing what possibly are "men's" *camicie*, with a decided degree of décolletage.[35] In Florence, only a few head ornaments had any gender exclusivity. *Balze, selle,* and *corne* were not worn by men, but even a ghirlanda could be a wreath sported by a male, and a berretta could be worn by a female.

Women's underblouses, whether of fine linen, inexpensive cotton, or a luxurious silk, were of natural unbleached color or pearly white, and visible at every opening of the garments layered over them—at the neckline, poking through the shoulder seams of the attached sleeves, at the wristline of the sleeves, and, after midcentury, often at the elbows. Slashed openings often even ran the entire length of the sleeve. Some bodices were fashioned of two pieces of cloth laced up the front with laces (*lacci*) threaded through eyelets (*maglie*), with the underblouse visible beneath the laces.[36]

Over a woman's camicia, she wore a simply cut, figure-revealing gown, either ankle- or floor-length; perhaps with even a small train (*strascico*) until the first decades of the fifteenth century. For everyday wear at home, this gown was of a modest fabric; a cotton, linen, or thin wool. These equiva- lents to our modern-day dresses went by a wide variety of names, from the fourteenth-century *gonna, gonnella,* or *sottana* to the later fifteenth-century *gamurra* or *cotta.*[37] For special occasions, these basic gowns could be of silk or fine wool, as we have seen, and in all but the most domestic of settings, they were worn partially covered with a third layer, the overdress. In the summer- time, this would perhaps be a sleeveless *giornea,* often of damask or silk bro- cade. We know how remarkable it was for anyone who was not a member of the immediate household circle to see a woman in her gamurra. Lucrezia Tornabuoni, who had gone to Rome in the spring of 1467 looking for an appropriate match for their son Lorenzo, wrote to her husband Piero in April that she had been able to see Clarice Orsini "in her gamurra," enabling her to better judge the young woman's figure and carriage.[38]

In the winter, the overdress would have long sleeves, this being the cioppa, and could be of silk brocade or cut-and figured-velvet. It was this third layer of garments on women that displayed the most opulence in terms of surface decoration, bordering, and extravagant sleeves of either generous proportions or rich, contrasting luxury fabric. This is the layer that was most often portrayed in the artwork of fifteenth-century Florence, because the young women usually shown did not yet wear the fourth and final layer, consisting of the mantello. This decorative third layer, made of damask or cut velvet, oversewn with additional pearl or metallic embroidery, was the layer that conferred honor upon the wearer (and by extension her family), since it served no utilitarian purpose. Lurie has noted that clothes that have obviously been decorated after the garment was made, whether by embroidery, the application of lace, or the sewing on of appliqués, are the most notable examples of status garments. Fabrics that contrive to combine "large areas of pale, easily soiled plain fabric with elaborate hand decoration" are especially prestigious, she observes.[39] With characteristic frankness, Alessandra Strozzi made all this quite clear in a letter to one of her sons about wedding-dress ornaments, saying, "Jewelry is the thing which must be well provided for . . . and if the fabric [of the gown] is not adorned with pearls, one must decorate it with other trifles [*frasche*] for which you lay out a lot, and this expense is just thrown away!"[40] With all the attention going to the "frasche" on the sumptuous fabrics themselves, little concern was directed to the wearer of the costume. The dazzle of the gold and silver threads reflected back onto the viewer his or her own societal reading. It was the clothes, or even the cloth itself, that people noticed; the social element of this layer were more important than the personal ones.

Out on the street in public view, unless it was unbearably hot, adult women of the upper classes, unlike the men, *did* require the fourth layer of clothing over these three layers, in the form of a cloak, which would be plainer than the opulent third layer and was designed to render the married upper-class woman *nascosta,* or hidden. This cloak went by the name of *mantello, lucco, sacco,* or *roba*—the same designations used for the male equivalent. Each of these four types of cloak was regulated by communal statute in the Quattrocento, and it is evident that mantelli were the most expensive to tailor.[41]

Although they may have been expensive and regularly worn, cloaks are not prominent in the pictorial records left by fifteenth-century artists, at least not on the women chosen by Renaissance Florentine society as paradigmatic of the honor of the republic. Married women did not serve as such paradigms. Renaissance artists and patrons focused instead on nubile young women who did not yet wear figure-concealing mantelli. In fact, more than one historian of costume has intimated that the putting on of the mantello acted as a sort of sartorial rite of passage for women, marking their moving from girlhood to womanhood upon marriage.[42] Most of the mantelli we do see are painted *all'antica* in scenes with religious subjects. The mantello is the preferred garment for the Virgin Mary, saints, and women in Renaissance portrayals of biblical events, but it is not usually shown worn by actual Florentine women. Figure 8.7, a detail from Ghirlandaio's *The Visitation* in the Tornabuoni Chapel (1485–90), shows religious figures wearing mantelli.

Children's Wardrobes | From the adult women, we turn to their children, who have not been singled out for discussion up until now. For the most part, from toddlerhood to puberty, young people simply wore smaller cuts of their parents' layered styles of clothes. The only real difference was the addition of an apron or smock (designated by many garment names, from *grembiale* to *cioppetta*), which protected garments from everyday spills and messes. Figure 8.8, a detail from Ghirlandaio's *The Resurrection of the Boy* in the Sassetti Chapel (1483–86), shows the public costume of an upper-class young girl. In family wardrobes, a child's garments are usually indicated by a diminutive ending on the garment name. Thus, an child-sized overgown becomes a *cioppetta, cioppettina, ucchetto,* or *lucchetto*; a hood or cowl, a *cappuccetto* or *cappuccino*; a cape, a *mantellino*; at-home togs, *gammurrina, gonnellino, guarnellino,* or *sacchetto*. Children also had tiny versions of linings (*foderetti*) and of the quilted vest (*farsettino*), and a young girl could have her own little headdress and belt like her mother's, called a *grillandetta* and a *cintoletta* respectively.[43]

Children, too, wore the camicia (with sometimes heavier *camicie da verno* for winter), but apparently no underpants until they were toilet-trained. Nursemaids, mothers, and older sisters cleaned up after them as best they could.[44] Their legs and feet *were* protected, however, by soled calze, while

Fig. 8.7. Female *mantelli*. Detail from Ghirlandaio, *The Visitation* (1485–90). Tornabuoni Chapel.

Fig. 8.8. Public costume of an upper-class young girl.
Detail from Ghirlandaio, *The Resurrection of the Boy*
(1483–86). Sassetti Chapel, Santa Trinita.

cuffie, berrette, or cappelline covered little heads.[45] Like their parents, they had nightgowns, some lined. In other words, almost every type of garment had its childish counterpart, with the exception of garments with specifically adult functions.[46]

Size of Wardrobes | Since a person's ensemble consisted of sumptuous layering, many different pieces made up a personal wardrobe. We know from inventories of family goods that the members of a household possessed multiple garments, with some interchangeable pieces listed separately (often sleeves, or one sleeve, linings, and belts), probably because they had been made separately. Adult wardrobes tended to be composed of some twenty to twenty-five pieces of clothing, not including linens. The wardrobes of growing children were understandably less extravagant, numbering between ten to twelve garments per child on average.[47] Antonio Pucci was unique in having noticeably fewer garments, but this military man did have a wide array of military gear and accoutrements, including six helmets, two of which were decorated with pearls, two with silver, and all with various figurative designs.[48] At the other end, sartorially speaking, was Lorenzo di Piero di Lorenzo de' Medici, the nominal head of the Florentine state, who had at least fifty garments of more than seventeen different types made for himself in a single year, and some seventeen separate linings, as well as placing fifteen orders for headgear, leg and footwear, and undergarments. He also had four garments embroidered and more than a dozen pieces of military-type gear crafted for him between July 18, 1515, and August 17, 1516.[49]

MATERIALS

Cloth | Renaissance Florentines combined velvets with silks, and lined brocades with satins, silks, and furs of many kinds. The most expensive silk brocades and cut and figured, multi-pile velvets were those colored with crimson and violet dyestuffs.[50] A wide array of woolens was also available to citizens, from fine English wool cloth (finished in Florence in the Convento di San Martino) to the relatively inexpensive stretchable perpignan jersey used for hose, with many grades in between.[51] Washable cotton, linen, and cotton/linen combinations, from plain *guarnello* to the worked *boccaccino*, were used not only for personal linens and underclothes but also for children's garments, at-home wear, and the clothing of servants and slaves. Alberti had advised in *Della famiglia* that everyone in the household be appropriately dressed; servants and slaves wearing clothing that bespoke their humble, but well-integrated, familial role.[52]

Furs | But there was much more to a garment than simply its fabric. In fact, in the complex ensembles of the upper class of fifteenth-century Florence, which offered ample opportunity for fabric patterning, furs, and jewelry, the basic fabric was only one element in a whole palette of fashion choices. Fur was considered essential for both warmth and luxury, and the ruling and professional classes wore a wide range of furs as both linings and trims. A government prior's cioppa needed a hint of fur trim for show and a fur lining for substance. These linings were constructed as independent garments, which could be used or left off as the weather or occasion required. By far the most commonly used furs were squirrel, rabbit, and dormouse (a large European rodent), but over twenty types of fur pelts were available in Florence by the mid 1500s, including fox, wildcat, ermine, sable, lynx, four species of wolf, three species of hare, and the European polecat.[53] The prized gray fur of the European variety of the large squirrel (originally native to Siberia, Russia, and Bulgaria) was called *vai*.[54] Renaissance Florentines made good use of this European fur source, employing at least four parts of the squirrel pelt to trim or line their clothing and headgear. The cuts were the *dossi*, or backs; the *pancie*, or soft white underbelly furs, which were smaller and therefore more expensive; the *teste*, or heads; and the *chodioni*, or rumps. Robert Delort has noted, however, the popularity of this fur, strong throughout the Middle Ages, waned after 1430, when marten and ermine were added to consumers' choices. After midcentury in Italy, the ratio of fur to cloth in an ensemble began to favor cloth, furs being relegated to linings and accent trims.[55] (See Table 8.1 for furs.)

Favored for heavier winter linings were the thick fur of the marten (*martore*), fox (*golpe*), and even polecat (*puzzole*). All were available locally. The more exotic and expensive imported ermine (*ermelline*), lynx (*lupi cerveri*), and sable (*zibelline*) furs were normally saved for trimmings.[56] The decorative use of foreign furs imported from the area of Russia dropped off after midcentury, when the capture of Constantinople in 1453 by the Turks closed supply lines

TABLE 8.1

Pelts Used for Lining, Borders, and Sleeves in Fifteeenth-Century Florence

---

Ermelline (ermine); strictly regulated by sumptuary legislation, imported through
  Constantinople until 1453 from the area of Russia

Gatto selvatico (wildcat); imported from Spain, used for trim

Golpe, or *volpe* (fox); available locally
  —*fianchi* (flanks)

Lattizi (literally "sucklings"); juvenile ermine?
  —*nel filetto da pie* (in filets by the foot)
  —*nel filetto di pancie da pie* (in filets of underbelly fur by the foot)

Lupi cervieri (lynx); exotic fur used for trim, imported from Russia

Martore (marten); available locally, thick brown fur used for winter linings
  —*bianchi* (winter white coat)
  —*nel filleti* (in filets)
  —*nostrali* (family-owned, privately skinned furs)
  —*uno chollarino* (a fur collar)

Pelle; generic, locally available fur used for linings, often *coniglio* (rabbit) or even *ghiro*
  (dormouse)
  —*bianche* (white)
  —*nere* (black)

Puzzole (pole cat) European relative of the North American skunk, available locally,
  used for linings

Vaio (large European squirrel); available locally, most commonly used fur, usually gray,
  also in red.
  —*chodioni di vai* (rumps)
  —*dossi di vai* (backs)
  —*dossi di vai rossi* (red fur backs)
  —*pancie di vai* (underbelly, usually white fur)
  —*teste di vai* (heads)

Zampe (paws); of many different creatures used
  —*bianche* (white, most prized)

Zibelline (sable); used for trim; strictly controlled by sumptuary laws, much like ermine
  and lynx, and also imported from the area of Russia

from the East.[57] But the Italians still got wildcat (*gatto selvatico*) imported from Spain, and pushed clothiers to find other ways to accent outfits in compensation. Eventually, tailors began to use figured silks in place of increasingly hard-to-get exotic furs.[58] Figure 8.9 shows a young Sienese man wearing a pet ferret as an ostentatious living fur in a detail from Domenico di Bartolo's *Pope Celestinus III Grants the Privilege of Independence to the Spedale* (1443).

CLOTHING COLORS

Color in clothes differentiated the great from the near great, as we saw in Chapter 5. The most intensely colored cloth used the most expensive dyes—and crimson, scarlet, red violets, blue violets, and purples, carried with them the association with luxury. Dyers also used less costly dyestuffs to produce a wide range of other hues. From brazilwood (*verzino*) they got vermilion; from woad (*guado*), orchil (*oricello*), and madder (*robbia*), reds, blues, and greens.[59] Indigo (*indaco*) produced a dark blue, and the fumes of sulfurous acid created pearly white silk. Florentines then bordered, faced, and lined these rich hues with strikingly contrasting colors; gold with turquoise, black and gold with white, green with crimson, tawny yellow with red violet, scarlet with ashen gray, achieving combinations of gowns and linings of bold juxtaposition. Bodices of gowns often contrasted wildly with attached sleeves; a purple bodice could be worn with red and green striped sleeves. (See Table 8.2 for clothing color combinations.)

Symbolism | By the fifteenth century, however, whatever rigid symbolism had been associated with color had been overlaid by marketplace considerations. For the most part, Florentine society eschewed the traditional literary and ecclesiastical associations such as those used earlier by Dante in his *Divina comedia,* where the theological virtues of faith, hope, and charity had been matched in the costumes of characters by the colors of white, green, and red.[60] Although in the late fourteenth and early fifteenth centuries, a handful of minor poets (among them Niccolò da Correggio, the Genoese Federico Fregoso, Venetian Mario Equicola, and Mantuan Pellegrino Moretto) wrote treatises themselves or collected rustic folk poems on the meanings of color, flowers, (and even fabrics), they intended these verses as simple "diverti-

Fig. 8.9. Young Sienese fop (with ferret). Detail from Domenico di Bartolo, *Pope Celestinus III Grants the Privilege of Independence to the Spedale* (1443). Spedale di S. Maria della Scala, Pellegrinaio, Siena.

TABLE 8.2

Fifteenth-Century Florentine Overgowns and Linings

GOWN	GOWN FABRIC	LINING FABRIC	AMOUNT IN BRACCIA*
vesta	brocatello bigio (gray brocade)	taffetta pagonazo (di chermisi) (blue violet taffetta)	3½ lbs**
saio	broccato (brocade color unknown)	taffetta paoanazo (di grana) (blue violet taffetta)	3 lbs
saio	brochato riccio (brocade w/gold)	raso pagonazo (blue violet silk)	16 braccia
saio	panno cotonato (biancho) (white cotton)	raso sbiadato (faded blue silk)	⅔ pezze***
saio	raso bianho (white silk)	teletta d'oro (tirato) (spun gold tissue)	17⅔ braccia
saio	raso tane, velluto tane (tan silk, tan velvet)	raso pagonazo (allucciolato) (violet blue silk with raised gold threads)	12¾ braccia
saio	teletta d'oro (spun gold tissue)	raso bianco (white silk)	16 braccia
saio	teletta d'oro (spun gold tissue)	domasco turchino (turquoise blue damask)	16 braccia
saio	teletta d'oro (spun gold tissue)	raso verde (green silk)	16 braccia
saio	teletta d'oro, velluto nero (spun gold tissue, black velvet)	panno biancho (white cloth)	14 braccia

*A braccio is approximately a yard in length.
**Taffeta was sold by the pound (12 ounces to the Florentine pound).
***A pezza is approximately 36 braccia in length.

menti."[61] Moretto satirizes any notion of stable associations with hue: "The color green reduced to nothingness / Shows that red has little certainty / and the will of black is crazy / White shows longing and its will spent / While yellow has hope on the ascent / Tan covers up foolish wisdom / As morel scorns death for affection."[62]

Even fabrics themselves came in for scrutiny in the folk poetry of the end of the fifteenth century. In a collection of anonymous works transcribed by Sanudo, we find what Vittorio Cian calls "poor poetry becoming almost an art in the service of industry": "Brocade conveys honor, velvet humility / satin, the highest grace / shot silk, fraud or instability / damask, a natural roughness / samite and sendals show simplicity/taffeta, talent and subtle levity / serge reveals meanness in all / wool and tabby, danger will befall."[63]

Uniforms | Only in uniforms—political, ecclesiastical, or social—was color frozen in a symbolic way, uniforms being the terminus ad quem of style.[64] While at the northern courts, young men in the service of a patron sported his colors, in Florence, a showing of family colors could be seen at maschere, Carnivale, weddings, and communal feast days. In addition, members of lay religious confraternities apparently moved as one in matching hooded robes of symbolic color (white sackcloth denoting humble flagellants, or *compagnie dei disciplinati*; black, burial groups such as the Compagnia de' Neri), with the hoods of both admitting only a "finger of light" out of which to see. Their belts were cords of hemp knotted several times; the disciplinati carrying ropes to whip themselves. Emblems worn on shoulder, sleeve, or cap identified the Florentine confraternities; gold crosses on circular black fields for the Compagnia di San Zanobi, yellow crosses on red backgrounds for the Compagnia di Santa Maria delle Laudi, caps with angel-and-dove insignia for the Compagnia della Santissima Annunziata.[65]

Clergy | Clergy, of course, wore the distinctive habits (*sacchi*) of their particular order, the Franciscans of Santa Croce garbed in mean fabric and going unshod in imitation of Saint Francis and his symbolic renunciation of the world.[66] Other orders spent more on clothes and, in fact, came under sumptuary criticism from their own Church administration. Archbishop Antoninus of Florence voiced concern about the trend toward luxurious clothing among friars in the text of his episcopal constitution in 1455. He reminded clergy that all elements of their vestments were to be humble; not be open in front, too short, or trailing on the ground. Their tonsure should also be modest, being the sign that set them apart from secular society. And, finally, jewelry, fur, silk, and fashionable doublets should have no place in their wardrobes. Any infraction of these restrictions resulted in a five-lire fine and the loss of the outlawed item.[67] From the domestic records of SS. Annunziata, it would seem that Antoninus's dicta not withstanding, some friars even slept in furs. By midcentury, the clergymen at Santissima Annunziata had leather shoes, woolen or woolen-jersey vestments (rascia or perpignan cloth) that were woad-dyed (which produced a *negro finissimo*), and nightshirts of fine linen, wool, and even fur (*guardacuori di bisiello, di panno di peluzo biancho, di pelle bianche*).[68]

The Ruling Oligarchy | In appearance-conscious Florence, members of the merchant oligarchy were anxious to eschew the limitations of uniform and the implied agreement to act in accordance with the rules of the group.[69] At the same time, they were also eager to embrace parameters set by the group as long as these allowed for a subtle individual expressiveness. The wearing of the crimson cioppe by politically active men was their way of showing themselves to be simultaneously both of and *not* of the group. Individual style, distinctive headwear, color of hose, mode of wearing the cloak, and mode of draping the cappuccio all individuated the "uniform" of the crimson cioppa.

To assign an overlying text to the color red, however, is to do an injustice to the complexities of Florentine society. Red, besides being the color of luxury, had at times also been associated with usury and with the shedding of blood. Red could mark prostitutes and in some places had identified Jews.[70] What one *might* notice to distinguish the deep crimson red of the priors' clothes of Florence from these other reds was a subtle modulation in hue. Whereas the red of blood, marking the usurer, prostitute, or Jewish "outsider," has often been associated with aggressive passions (like love, anger, and sex), Lurie argues that a saturated crimson color seems "to suggest a capacity for passion that, though deep and strong, is currently satisfied or dormant."[71]

Black | The color, or "non-color," of black, on the other hand, while today considered the height of elegance and dignity, did not yet read this way in fifteenth-century Florence. Very few overgarments (outside of certain eccle-siastical uniforms) were made of black cloth, and *morello di grana*, the most expensive dense black dye for either wool or silk, was only about half as expensive as chermisi and so lacked any special monetary cachet. Black was not considered a color, but rather an absence of color, and in Venice, so inappropriate for a communal official that special permission had to be ob-tained to wear it while in office.[72] It would not be until Leonora of Aragon married Ercole d'Este of Ferrara in 1473, followed by the wedding of Isabella of Aragon to Gian Galeazzo Sforza of Milan, that Italians connected the color black with wealth and refinement. When Lucrezia Borgia married into the house of Este in 1502, bringing with her some thirty black gowns (eleven of which were black velvet), the color would finally become the sine qua non of fashionable court elites.[73] The associations of black that *did* appear in early Renaissance Florence, however, and that still persist, are gloom, guilt, and death. Black garments made up the habits of nuns and the wardrobes of widows, along with the "widow's mark" of a horizontal black stripe on their unbleached linen veils. But just as often, we are likely to see a widow's cloak made of *monachina* (a dull hue of dark brown-red) or yardage distributed for funerary wear simply designated as "dark."[74]

Family Colors | Families seem to have favored certain colors, and family members on occasion dressed "all of a piece."[75] For example, in 1461, Marco Parenti, his wife Caterina, and their son Piero all had tawny, gold-colored cioppe of *mostanolione* made by the sarto Antonio d'Agnolo. Three years later, father and son dressed alike in sleeveless overgowns of scarlet. Still later, Ca-terina and her daughters Marietta and Lisa each ordered blue violet woolen gowns of *rascia pagonaza* with silk sleeves.[76] Also scattered throughout their family logbooks are at least twelve gowns and overgowns of blue and white, in addition to all of the trousseau garments Caterina initially brought to the family. The blues were either *azurre* or *allexandrino* and in more than one case also *fiorito* (flowered). Two of the most lavish of these blue and whites were in the trousseaux of Caterina's oldest daughters, Ghostanza and Marietta. Gos-tanza's gown is described as "a gown of white silk from the Levant, with sleeves of damask interwoven with blue and white," while Marietta's was "a summer gown of blue satin silk with white flowered silk sleeves."[77]

Needless to say, these color combinations were not serendipitous and may even have visually harked back to their roots on their Strozzi grandmother's (née Macinghi) side. The blue and white express neither the gold of the Strozzi impresa (three crescent moons) nor the gold and black of the Parenti imprese (wolf, rampart, or bear). A generation before, Alessandra Strozzi had assembled her daughter's trousseau of all blue-and-white garments, which Caterina then in turn continued to use for her own daughters' trousseaux. Perhaps the colors were part of a subtle feminine discourse between generations; a female legacy of color (as Klapisch-Zuber has suggested for another mother and daughter, who both came to their marriages with gowns of *limonato* yellow).[78] The Parenti young women, dressed in blue and white, however, would have carried a more overt color symbolism. Blue, traditionally signifying loyalty and the Virgin Mary, and white, purity.[79]

Polychromes | There was a wide range of colors available in Florence, including a noticeable attempt to describe polychromes or in-between colors. Florentines showed a penchant for changeable subtlety, and differentiated between many shades of basic hues, with their dark golden yellow (*mostanolione*), speckled (*spolverezata*), marble (*marmorini*), and smoky gray blue (*sbiadato*) colors.[80] They also developed the "shot" silk (*cangiante*), available in satin, brocade, and taffeta. But other colors were even more elusive, especially the color *pavonazzo,* on which there is still no consensus; it has been variously identified as peacock blue, peahen brown, red violet, blue violet, purple, and even "between blue and black."[81]

WRITTEN COLORS

In fact, the entire issue of color names presents difficulties. Hues of woolen cloth could have beautiful, associative names; *gherofanato di cilestrino* (carnation pink) and *rosa secca di turchino* (old Turkish rose) are both recorded in lists of dyestuffs. But wool manufacturers tended toward the conservative, preferring to reflect closely the specific dyestuff used. Wools are listed laconically as *chermisi, grana, rosato,* and the like. Exotic names for silk proliferated, however, as silk fabric eclipsed Italian woolens in the international luxury trade. Merchants attempted to lure customers to their wares with imaginative names such as "pink sapphire" (*rosa di zaffrone*), "gladiolus" (*giaggiolino*), and "peach blossom" (*persichino*).[82] These names, however, were not most often what was recorded in the contemporary family records of garment colors. There, we see more utilitarian designations for hue: *rosa*, *rosina*, *bianco*, and *tane* being common. Matching these two forms of discourse on color, written with very different purposes in mind, can be an educated guess at best. On the other end of this descriptive tradition, silk color names could also border on the rustic (names perhaps muttered by dyers), with the barnyard overtones of geese and chickens emerging in such names as "goose dung" (*schizzo d'oca*) and "foot of the capon" (*pie di cappone*). Such names recall the proximity of city and countryside and the realities of the lives of the *tinori* themselves (working sottoposti for the silk merchants), in the time when the Via Ricasoli was the Via del Cocomero.[83]

By the first decade of the seventeenth century, the Florentine silk industry had grown to specialize in serving the European elite, and with this direction, the names for silk blossomed luxuriously. Reds ranged from the beautiful—"angel wing" (*penna d'angelo*), "cherry" (*rosso ciliegia*), and "flicker" (*la fiammetta*)—to the grotesque—"wounded" (*incarnato*), "lung" (*il pulmone*), and even "tick" (*zecca*). Over twenty-nine names for red are known to have been used in the trade as early as 1629. Names for greens flourished with even more—some thirty-three different hues, from "parrot green" (*verde pappagallo*) and "festivity" (*festichino*) to "laurel" (*verde lauro*). Even "bad" greens had designations: "toad green" (*verde botta*) and "mossy green" (*verde della borraccina*). Blues, yellows, violets, blacks and whites all followed with their own elaboration.

Fashionable Names | But it was the neutral, dark, and gray colors to which silk merchants first gave evocative, and therefore undoubtedly fashionable, designations. In these names, allusions to interior mood and exterior place expanded color beyond Barthes's "technologic" aspect to a new psychological dimension, where fanciful connections could be made through the Barthean "verbal" aspect of clothing. For example, neutrals and darks are transformed from the negative fifteenth-century names of "dark" (*scuro*), "cinders" (*cenerito*), gray (*bigio*), and purplish black (*morello*) to the imaginative terms of the seventeenth century. "Smoke" (*fumo*), "felt" (*feltro*), and "throat of the dove" (*gorgia di piccione*) became refined names for grays; "shadow of the umbrella" (*scuro d'ombrello*), "dry leaf" (*foglia secca*), and "clove" (*garofano*), sophisticated browns. Neutral color names now collected the fashionable into an elite of international cognoscenti with silks called "Egyptian earth" (*terra d'Egitto*) and even "mud of Paris" (*fango di Parigi*).[84]

In the course of the Quattrocento, silks eclipsed woolens in the international marketplace, fashions became more fitted, and tunics shorter, and in spite of their inherent conservatism in dress, Florentines seem to have become increasingly caught up in display and ornamentation, especially for women of the elite. Chapter 9 turns to the Commune's reaction to these clothes, both morally and legally, in its sumptuary legislation and the development of special units who policed fashion. For the first time in European history, it was here in Quattrocento Florence that "fashion" was fully articulated and became the most widely available form of conspicuous consumption.

NINE

SUMPTUARY LEGISLATION

AND THE "FASHION POLICE"

SOCIETAL ORDER

T he strict external ordering of garments using sumptuary restrictions for policing who was allowed to wear what seems to have been most rigid where hierarchy did not rest on birthright; where it was literally believed that clothes made (or could make) the man.[1] The colors, shapes, and dimensions of the garments worn by the inhabitants of Renaissance Florence displayed a complex and multivalent vestimentary code, which expressed their values and beliefs. Simply put, clothing made social place a visual reality. Filarete (ca. 1400–ca. 1469) expressed his concerns regarding the appropriate clothes in his *Libro architettonico,* writing that in fifteenth-century society, the idea was widely accepted that a person's rank (or *qualità*) in society should be reflected not only in the structure of his abode but also in his mode of dress; larger and finer homes and clothing defined "larger and finer" men.[2] *Il libro del sarto,* a compilation of clothing styles and patterns printed in Venice in the 1580s, took this notion into the pictorial realm, attempting to illustrate some sort of natural sartorial hierarchy. Here, all "respectable" ranks of society were represented, from mounted knights to high-born women. Paulo Getrevi writes that in this first printed visualization of Italian high society, "every costume marks the single person of the scene in a definite gradation of the social scale, but speaks continually with the preceding and the following."[3]

In pursuit of the proper clothing, we have seen that the hundred or so tailors in Florence at any given time had lists of debitori that ran into the hundreds and constituted a roll call of the rich and powerful. Furthermore, by dressing the females of their families in a competitive dazzle of fabric design, boldly contrasting colors, surface embroidery, and family jewelry for important events, Florentine oligarchs were able to demonstrate to their families, friends, and neighbors a certain nonchalant largesse at one remove—on the bodies of their women. Inventories of personal possessions showed an inordinate portion of their total wealth was spent on clothes; 40 percent, as we have seen, was not unheard of. The communal government expended continual energy to rein in the extravagant fluidity of dress with its repeated passage of sumptuary legislation, but, flurries of statuta notwithstanding, fashion-consciousness did overwhelm the city, and clothing became, in the fifteenth and sixteenth centuries, ever more difficult to control.

FIRST SUMPTUARY LAWS

The first mention in Florentine records of a phenomenon called "fashion," of the need to constantly change and update one's (still-wearable) clothing, is probably to be found in Villani's early fourteenth-century *Cronica*. In lauding the wide-ranging sumptuary legislation passed in April 1330 (which he believed was much needed), Villani also warned that sumptuary laws seemed to spur fashion into being. "But in spite of all these strong ordinances, outrages remained; and though one could not have cut and figured cloth, they wanted striped cloth and foreign cloth, the most that they could have, sending as far as Flanders and Brabant for it, not worrying about the cost," he writes.[4] This was not the first sumptuary legislation the Commune had passed. Ronald Rainey puts that initial law (now lost) in 1281, and the first laws specifically regarding women's garments in the Consulte of 1290, which refers only to the registration of clothes.[5] In Florence, right from the beginning, concern to control clothing, and thereby properly mark social place, was played out through the women.[6] Fiscal concerns seem to have led to the early communal practice, which continued throughout the fifteenth century, of allowing men and women who wanted to dress elaborately to buy licenses from the city by paying a tax on their forbidden clothes, gemstones, precious metal ornaments, and pearls.[7] There was also an attempt on the part of the popular government to register any offending clothes that had been made before the laws had gone into effect and tag such garments with a communal lead seal (making them *vesti bullati* or *vesti timbrati*),which would force owners to have new, less showy attire made. This was tried first in Florence in 1290, according to Catherine Killerby, and required the advice and assistance of the craftspeople of the Florentine marketplace who had the expertise to make an accurate assessment of grades of fabric, qualities of dyestuff, weight of precious metals, and clarity of gemstones. They were drafted, however unwilling some may have been, into the service of communal officials.[8] Further sumptuary laws were enacted in 1299 and every few years thereafter.

Whereas the sumptuary laws of northern European courts were aristocratic in origin, Diane Hughes notes, the impulse to restrict splendor in clothing had a distinctly republican mien in Italy. Florentine sumptuary legislation started out as an anti-aristocratic move by newly empowered major guildsmen to restrict the sartorial power of the newly outlawed magnate families.[9] This impulse, of course, changed over time with the increasing display of the new "aristocrats," and in fact, as Marco Parenti remembered (p. 78), the popular Commune attempted to marshal its citizens' attire into its service whenever it suited the city's designs. Even early on, whereas the Commune acted aggressively to rein in individual display within the upper reaches of society, certain signs of luxe (jewels, pearls, gold, silver, exotic fur trim) could still be worn by some magnates (mounted knights) and selected professional orders (doctors of law, doctors of medicine, and their wives). On these occasions, clothing served to aggrandize not the individual but rather the community controlling the display. Here, dress assumed an entirely different function, as a splendid collective uniform. Trexler writes that while sumptuary laws were not suspended during the Feast of San Giovanni, for example, they also "were not enforced during celebrations; indeed it was a mark of honor to the personage being honored that the normal rules of dress were waived."[10] Individuals and even family groups were both temporarily submerged in this communal identity on these occasions.[11]

In 1322, the commune of Florence made its first large compilation all existing laws in the Statuti of 1322–25, which produced a sweeping list of restrictions on women's attire, setting limits on headgear and jewelry design, the numbers of gowns (four), types and amounts of fabric, quality of dye, and types of ornamentation allowed.[12] The woman's father or husband, who had bought the offending item, was to be fined 100 lire, but the tailor or seamstress who had made the gown was fined *double* that amount: 200 lire.[13] Officials could also search the shops of goldsmiths and tailors for restricted ornaments or garments.[14] It has also been pointed out, however, that any fine paid out for a woman by her father or a kinsman, no matter if she were married or unmarried, could later be taken out of her dowry funds either at the time of her marriage or at the restitution of her dowry upon the death of her husband. This put the burden of the sumptuary fine ultimately on the woman herself.[15]

Five years later, the Statuti of 1322–25, however wide-ranging their scope, were roundly trumped by the 1330 law so fervently endorsed by Villani. This piece of legislation was apparently the first attempt to put out a virtual firestorm of fashion activity and imposed the most extensive list of restrictions specifically on women's clothes.[16] In this early period, communal sumptuary legislation labored in vain to stem the influence of foreign styles, often tagged in contemporary sources as from "beyond" ("alla di là"), which had been unwittingly allowed to enter fourteenth-century Florence through the clothes worn by the wife of the first French podestà, hired in 1326, and also the second, in 1342.[17] We do know that regional styles could easily be distinguished in clothing from their descriptions in trousseaux inventories and letters of the time. Women write of "le camicie maschili a modo di Firenze," "fogia mantuana," "le vesti alla milanese," "le vesti alla romana," and even "le borse alla ferrarese e alla genovese."[18] Foreign influence could be detected especially in the design of a garment's sleeves, which would come under increasing scrutiny by sumptuary officials.[19]

THE UFFICIALI DELLE DONNE

In response to these foreign styles, on April 1, 1330, the Commune banned all ornaments for Florentine women, and proceeded to create the first tellingly named fashion police, the Ufficiali delle donne, which was charged with enforcing these bans. Six citizens were chosen to elect a foreign notary for the job, who was to have a salary and a staff from the communal government for his six-month term of office, during which he was to patrol the streets, bridges, and piazze of the city, on the lookout for women, children, and men whose garments were suspected of violating current laws.[20] Apparently, this duty was so undesirable that in 1333, the Commune decided to have the bishop of Siena appoint the foreign official, further distancing Florentine males from this job of policing their own.[21] From the autumn of 1343, we have the names of fifty-one women harassed and apprehended by the roving officials in only three days' work at the end of October. The records also contain elaborate descriptions of their clothes.[22] Six years later, a set of documents from 1349, undoubtedly representative of many more, details the vicissitudes of another Ufficiale delle donne, one Ser Donato di Piccolo di Giovanni of Monte Ramucino, who had set about his work after having had the required public proclamation of current sumptuary restrictions made in all the usual places.[23] Not only did he encounter evasive tactics on the part of some women, but active resistance from their male companions. If a woman ran into a church, she had sanctuary, and the official had to wait outside until she reappeared, no law enforcement official being allowed to enter the sacred space in pursuit of an offender.[24]

The sumptuary officials could be found doing their rounds in many areas of the city; locations noted in their logbooks included the churches of San Lorenzo, Santa Maria Maggiore, and the Cathedral, as well as the area near the Ponte Vecchio, the loggia of the Tornaquinci, and in various other streets and piazze of Florence.[25] Writing their descriptions in the required official Latin, however, the officials struggled to describe what they were visually encountering on the streets with the limited written language of the formal (and by then already inadequate) sumptuary legislation itself. This disjuncture of language would prove to be a key factor in the development of fashion innovation. In clothing, there would be new styles, new ornaments, new *everything*, to keep one step ahead of being the target for the clothing categories available to the sumptuary police.[26]

These officials focused their work on the excesses of female finery but could catch other offenders in their nets as well. Men, although rarely cited, could be written up for clothing excesses if their garb was deemed to be too feminine. For example, while we have no written records of citations for men wearing extremely short or figure-revealing tunics and codpieces, or hose partially unlaced (even though we have visual records), we *do* have arrests for the wearing of platform shoes or ruffles and pleats.[27] Even improperly ornamented children in Florence could be stopped and their parents fined.[28] The Ufficiale Ser Donato himself also kept a special section for craftspeople who were apprehended for selling goods and services for more money than was allowed by communal statute.[29] Tailors were, of course, particularly in the line of fire of sumptuary officials, as perceived co-conspirators in producing luxe; a tailor was apprehended in 1377 for having fashioned a prohibited item, another in 1397, one Biagio di Pace, for having produced a cloak with sleeves that exceeded the limit set for cloth yardage per sleeve.[30] This points to the problems of attempting to enforce prohibitions at odds with the very basis of the Florentine economy itself.

EXPANSION OF MAGISTRACIES

But the intrusive Ufficiali were not the only vehicle for the policing of excess in fifteenth-century Florence. Accusers could secretly place their written denunciations of suspected wrongdoing in one of the many denunciation boxes (*tamburi*) available in communal offices around the city, inside Orsanmichele and San Piero Scheraggio and in one of the columns of the Cathedral itself.[31] Andrea Zorzi writes that in fact around 50 percent of the cases prosecuted by various magistracies at the beginning of the 1430s originated in a secret denunciation.[32] Among guildsmen, artisans also operated as spies, giving their accusations to the magistrates of the Arti.[33] Not content with anonymous tips, however, throughout the later Trecento and into the Quattrocento, the Commune expanded its concern with dress by creating new official bodies of citizens to oversee sartorial practice. Not only was the dress of the body of the "honorable" woman their focus, but also as Hughes has shown, the control of less desirable marginalized groups within the community by the marking of their costume.[34] Sumptuary legislation turned from an earlier focus on fiscal matters and anti-aristocratic bias, shifting instead to a moral stance. As early as 1384, the Commune had made an effort to sartorially link prostitutes with the Old Testament passage from Isaiah that excoriates vain women with "wanton eyes, walking and mincing as they go, and making a tinkling sound with their feet," by requiring prostitutes to cover their eyes with veils (while wearing platform shoes and bells on their heads) to act the part of biblical whores.[35] Certainly, in Boccaccio's *Decameron* and the short stories of Sacchetti, Sercambi, and other *novellisti*, many plots turn on the deception of a woman of base worth and easy virtue masquerading in beautiful clothes as an honorable matron.[36]

The Ufficiali dell'onestà | In 1403, the Commune, in what has been seen as a response to a generalized fear of potentially disruptive sexual activity, created the Ufficiali dell'onestà, the first city police force specifically for the regulation of the prostitute population.[37] This magistracy, unlike that of the Ufficiali delle donne, was not composed of foreigners, but rather of eight Florentine citizens, two from each of the city's four quarters, who were chosen from the *borsa* of citizens eligible for civic office, and served for terms of six months. These Ufficiali were paid no salaries from the Commune, however, but rather got a percentage of the registrations and fines collected from those they managed and arrested. There were at least ten other citizens involved in the Onestà; a notary, treasurers, secretary, and six messengers to run errands.[38] This agency had a conveniently central location in the city, inside the church of San Cristofano, where the Piazza Duomo now feeds into Via Calzaiuoli.[39] Of course, over time, it not only dealt with the clothing of prostitutes but with their sexual and social practices as well. Prostitutes had to be licensed, marked by special clothing signs, which changed over time, segregated into specific bordello areas, which also changed over time, and were forbidden certain sexual acts considered too lascivious.[40] As John Brackett has shown, official agencies proliferated in Florence in an attempt to control this potentially dangerous element (even if many of the women involved in prostitution were of foreign origin) and other segments of the city population that were deemed a cause for concern.[41] For example, in 1421, the Commune created the new Conservatori dell'onestà dei monasteri, which was assigned oversight for the morality of convents.[42]

Officiales super ornamentis mulierum | The creation of this magistracy was followed six years later in 1427 with a new sumptuary police board, the

Officiales super ornamentis mulierum. This board, elected from the ranks of Florentine citizens like the Ufficiali dell'onestia, not only was responsible for enforcing existing sumptuary laws but had the power to amend those laws, subject to the approval of communal officials.[43] The enforcement of the laws proved so difficult, however, that the Commune could find few citizens willing to serve, and in the years between 1421 and 1439, the board's duties were often assigned to other official agencies.[44]

The Ufficiali di notte | The communal government seems to have first con-flated control of sumptuary excesses in dress and prostitution in 1439, after the creation of the Ufficiali di notte in 1432. Officially, this new magistracy was assigned the job of controlling prostitution (female *and* male) and other suspicious activities occurring at night, but seven years into its existence, it was also charged with enforcing sumptuary laws relating to women in gen-eral, no matter what their occupation.[45] Many men complained that it was hard to tell honest women from whores, and that clothing was the culprit, as the popular preachers of the time stressed in their sermons to the masses. There is a general consensus among historians that the stance of the Church on sumptuary excesses was distinctly misogynist. The sin of *luxuria* was par-ticularly threatening to the weak nature of women, and the popular Francis-can preachers of the early Quattrocento continually link women, depraved sexuality, and come-hither clothes. Hughes quotes San Bernardino preaching to the women of Siena: "You are not as you used to be. I see a widow today . . . with her forehead bare and her cloak drawn back to show her cheek. And how she shapes it over her brow! That is a prostitute's gesture."[46] Brackett cites the case (undoubtedly one of many) of a Vicenzia Sereni, a Roman woman working in Florence, who was not only charged with living outside one of the areas designated as a bordello district but also with wearing fine clothes of gold and silver, with necklaces of pearls and gemstones, in defiance of sumptuary restrictions on prostitutes.[47] The linkage between overdressed women, prostitutes, and Jews was not accidental in Florence, because communal officials deemed it necessary for each of these groups be clearly marked.[48] It was in the same year that the Ufficiali di notte assumed responsibility for sumptuary enforcement that the city's Jewish population were required to be marked for the first time.[49] The moral state of the city's convent population was also a concern. The role of Franciscan Observant friars in fanning fears of the potential moral depravity of all these groups has been shown by Hughes.[50] In fact, as early as 1433, the Conservatori dell'onestà dei monasteri, which had only been in existence for a dozen years, had been joined to the Ufficiali di notte.[51] By the sixteenth century, these officials (along with the Ufficiali dell'onestà), operated from rooms that were centrally located off the Piazza dei Tre Re between Orsanmichele and Via Calzaiuoli but semi-hidden in the tiny back lane, renamed the Vicolo dell'Onestà, in order better to apprehend anyone out and about at night who was in violation of the sumptuary laws, whether honorable or not.[52]

The larger communal oversight board for sumptuary laws in the Renaissance period would become the Conservatori di leggi.[53] This body's main duty was the prosecution of official corruption, but in 1459, it was also assigned the job of monitoring sumptuary excesses. Now, they took on the responsibility for publicizing the dress restrictions and actively enforcing the ever-changing sumptuary codes, as well as punishing all manner of irregular behavior, including gambling, blasphemy, and crimes committed at night.[54] Again, as with the earlier Officiales super ornamentis mulierum, the additional duties and structure of the office of the Conservatori made it problematic; officials resigned and salaries often were not sufficient, but regulations were periodically adjusted and concerns addressed, and it would stand into the sixteenth century as the primary communal office of sumptuary enforcement.[55]

THE QUATTROCENTO

The first large-scale compilation of sumptuary law in the Quattrocento was included in the Statuta of 1415 and regulated all "ornamenta mulierum."[56] The earliest sumptuary law, in the Trecento, had concerned itself mainly with materials (yardage, fabric type, quality of dye, and ornamentation) and, as we have seen, women had often successfully evaded it by paying a tax on the prohibited feature.[57] By the end of the fourteenth century and certainly into the early years of the Quattrocento, there was little letup in the desire to curb luxury ornamentation on women, but the focus changed to curbing the burgeoning fashion innovations. That there was a runaway problem is eloquently evident in the number of laws and official boards that were created to deal with it. But what began as very harsh in the first decades of the 1400s, seemed to ease at midcentury. Brides proved extraordinary sumptuary cases everywhere, but they seem to have been especially visible in Florence, which was given to less obvious flash in everyday dress than other Italian cities. The families of the ruling oligarchy splendidly dressed these primary players in their marriage alliance strategies, as has been discussed. While fourteenth-century weddings were controlled by sumptuary laws on every front, restrictions specifically concerning the dress of the bride were absent.[58] In the fifteenth century, brides were even less regulated, being free to receive and wear multiple rings at their weddings and for fifteen days thereafter.[59] It was critical for the elite of Florence to allow important weddings to proceed with little sartorial interference. In the Medici family, for example, as Dale Kent has shown, power was consolidated by some twenty-two marriages with families of their "parenti, amici e vicini" between 1400 and 1434 alone.[60]

After the deaths of Cosimo and his son Piero in the 1460s, sumptuary legislation does in fact, seem to have tightened up again, with a flurry of laws attempting to keep up with the fashion of the moment.[61] Rainey has concluded that sumptuary laws do not seem to have been a viable political tool that was easily manipulated by the faction in power, and that overall, "there is no evidence in the legislative documents to suggest that the lawmakers of this period identified sumptuary legislation as either a pro-Medicean or anti-Medicean policy."[62] There was a profound ambivalence toward display among the Florentine elite, even as they all participated to a greater or lesser degree in wearing the products of their own luxury marketplace.

SUMPTUARY "AVOIDANCE" LANGUAGE

The virtual explosion of terms surrounding clothing and ornament is clear testimony to harassment by Florentine sumptuary officials, a phenomenon that did not go unnoticed by Franco Sacchetti (ca. 1330–ca. 1400) and has been noted by scholars of sumptuary law. Names for fashion elements proliferated; neologisms tested the patience of the most determined communal officials.

Lattizi | In one of Sacchetti's short stories, *Novella CXXXVII*, a sumptuary official confronts a woman on the street and begins writing her a citation for wearing what looks like ermine. She protests that it is not ermine but "lattizi," adding vaguely, "E una bestia."[63] The term *lattizi* translates as "milky," but pelts of what creature is unclear. This "mystery fur" of Renaissance documents may have started out as a female strategy to evade late Trecento sumptuary laws, with the name in time becoming a commonly used designation for a pricey fur of indeterminate origin. And in fact, we do not know precisely the type of fur to which *lattizi* referred, for this invented avoidance term became, over time, a commonly used designation. It was still being used by men in their personal family ricordanze some sixty years later, far from the prying eyes of any communal sumptuary official. Marco Parenti among others, records the lining and trimming of his bride Caterina's wedding giornea (of silk velvet dyed with kermes) with such lattizi, which in 1447 cost him 6¾ florins per 100. It took almost 200 of these small furs to complete Caterina's sumptuous sleeveless day gown, undoubtedly luxurious to wear.[64]

Ornaments | The highly ornamented necklines of Renaissance gowns have already been noted. Necklines were the site of some concern to sumptuary officials; their detailed descriptions in legislation undoubtedly signaled an interest in controlling their shape, style, and coverage. The Statutes of 1322–25 had prohibited these neckline ornaments, and goldsmiths and tailors who sold them were to be fined 200 lire. Wearing them carried a 100-lire fine.[65] But apparently officials were not the only ones looking at décolletage, because the variety of ornaments created by craftspeople and bought by the rich to decorate necklines mushroomed in the fifteenth century. Goldsmiths and their often female workers (*lavoratrici*) produced metallic (usually copper) ornaments with many names, including *scaglie*, *tremolanti*, *maspilli*, and *pianette*, which were gilded, silvered or color-enameled into many shapes such as leaves, flowers, or stars.[66] Figure 9.1 shows neckline ornaments on a gown in a detail of a profile portrait by Antonio Pollaiuolo (ca. 1450). Also involved in the creation of these metallic ornaments were the artificers (*armaiuoli*), who fashioned buttons, studs, and other clothing ornaments. In addition, gold beaters, and tinsel makers (*orpellai*), who could be women, contributed to the production of luxury ornaments with their gold leaf, gold wire, and sheets of silver and gold, used both in jewelry and in the weaving of luxury silks. There were at least a dozen names for the glittery ornaments sewn onto the borders or necklines of gowns and into the designs of headgear in Quattrocento Florence, which can be clearly seen in many contemporary profile portraits, and sumptuary officials were apparently either unable or unwilling to cope with this jumble of terminology. As a new clampdown on ornamentation again developed in the late 1460s and 1470s, fashion consumption continually evaded legislation, as especially attested by the rubrics of the laws themselves, such as: "clarification about pearls," October 6, 1472;"clarification about buttons," December 23, 1472; "clarification about wearing chains," June 20, 1483; and "tailors forbidden to make prohibited ornaments," December 20, 1475.[67] It would certainly have proved difficult and awkward for a male official, already staring at a woman's neckline on the street, to identify and write down in his logbook the ornament displayed thereon by its exact technical name.[68] The law of 1472 did contain new restrictions on the clothing of young adults, however, forbidding men and women under the age of thirty extravagant use of gold, silver, furs, and jewels. These clothing prohibitions were unusual in that they made explicit limitations in dress for men.[69] Even Alberti began to rethink his earlier pronouncements regarding the utility of fine garments. Baron noted that in Alberti's *De Iciarchia,* he writes of noticing the decadent dress of the youth while visiting Florence in the late 1460s. In particular, he comments on the moral decline implicit in "the wearing of ever more expensive clothing for men as well as for women."[70]

FASHION INNOVATIONS

Fourteenth-century Florentine fashion called among other things for trains (*code*), horn-shaped head pieces (*corne*), and belts (*cintole*), which were broad, bold and metallic, embroidered and enameled. Communal officials not only grappled with creating laws to control fashion but also sought to demonize it, and trains and stiffly shaped headwear both became fourteenth-century fashion flashpoints. San Bernardino linked trains with bestiality, saying they made a woman look as though she were dragging a tail.[71] The Trecento horned headdresses also occasioned devilish comparisons with women's inner natures, and hairdos were likened to owls.[72] Communal officials approved new

Fig. 9.1. Gown neckline ornaments. Detail from Antonio Pollaiuolo, *Female Portrait* (ca. 1450). Uffizi, Florence.

laws in 1433, noting that it realized "the great desire of these officials to restrain the barbarous and irrepressible bestiality of women."[73] In the Quattrocento, as tailors constructed more closely tailored bodices, sleeves took over in importance, but the intimate contact involved in tailors' fittings came in for its own snide remarks, as we have seen. Over time, the insinuating tailor of women's clothes then became a cultural topos.

Sleeves | In Florence, sumptuary law had to come to terms with sleeves, potentially the most flamboyantly decorative (and foreign-looking) part of an outfit. At least fourteen types of sleeves are mentioned in fifteenth-century documents.[74] In fact, the sleeveless overgown (*giornea*) was initially popular, in part, because the contrasting sleeves from the garment beneath could be shown off to better effect against its different design. Sleeves carried an exotic look, the sine qua non of fashion in a woman's wardrobe, and they were usually listed separately in a clothing inventory after midcentury. The sleeves of the undergowns were probably different from the body of the gown itself, so not two, but three fabrics could be displayed simultaneously.[75] In family records, entry after entry distinguishes one garment from another, not only by color, cut, and fabric, but also by the style of sleeves, or *maniche*. We only have to look to the drawings of Pisanello for flights of imagination in sleeve design. Sleeves could become winglike fantasies in multicolored silks.[76] Figure 9.2 is a drawing by Pisanello (1438–1440) of fanciful sleeves. Tailors, seamstresses, and doublet makers offered a variety of different sleeve styles in Quattrocento Florence. For modesty's sake, sleeves were always full-length. Styles ranged widely from plain, narrow, or gathered (*pullite, strette,* or *agozetti*) to open, often worn folded up at the wrists (*aperto*), trumpet-shaped, covering part of the hand (*atrombe*), flowered with ornament (*fiorite*), or foreign-flavored (*alla bolognese, alla lombarda, spagnolesco,* or simply *alla di là*). Tight sleeves could also be open at the elbow to ease movement (and show the undershirt beneath) or slashed in many different patterns, such as *aburattegli, acotelacio,* and *affettate* (again in order to show the contrasting fabric of the gown or undershirt beneath), with written distinctions now impossible to discern in pictures.[77]

Sleeves *a gozzi.* | By far the most uniquely Florentine sleeve creations were the *maniche a gozzi*, a term the meaning of which many historians of clothing have disagreed upon. In Italian, a *gozzo* is a bird's crop, which has a distinctive baglike shape, and historians of costume believe that these sleeves were named after this shape. These very fashionable fifteenth-century sleeves hung full at the underside of the sleeve, then were gathered up at a wide wristband, creating a volume of fabric that hung with a certain degree of studied nonchalance, especially when the hands were brought up in a posture of praying—beautiful at church. Figure 9.3 is a fifteenth-century profile portrait by Filippo Lippi of a young woman whose ensemble includes sleeves *a gozzi*. However, these sleeves could also be worn in a more casual way. The top

Fig. 9.2. Winglike sleeves. Pisanello (ca. 1438–40). Musée
Condé, Chantilly, France.

seam of the sleeve was slit so that the hand could be pushed through, causing
the sleeve to fall straight down from the shoulder seam, freeing the arm, and
simultaneously displaying the fabric of the gown beneath. The freed sleeve
then hung loosely in back of the arm. If the sleeve was of silk, it became
diaphanous and fluttering, but sleeves of quilted brocade or velvet stiffly
retained the forms of slightly bent arms, hanging down from the shoulder like
an extra appendage, oddly insectlike and giving the wearer the look of an
extra set of arms. This stiff style of sleeve is shown in Figure 9.4, a fifteenth-
century Florentine School manuscript illumination in the Biblioteca riccardiana. Sleeves evolved into elaborately decorative attachments to the shoulder
seam of the bodice, the most visually extreme example being *maniche staccate,*
or detachable sleeves.

Florentine embassies exposed to foreign clothing innovations had brought
the detachable Spanish-style sleeve home in the first decade of the Quattrocento, and by midcentury, fashion dictated that sleeves be made separate from
the gown. Sleeves were attached to the bodice at the arm holes by laces
threaded through singlets. Tailors designed them in colors meant to contrast
with the gown to which they were attached; whereas the gown could be of
plain crimson velvet, the sleeves would be of crimson silk brocaded with
gold, or lined with marten fur. A dark reddish brown overgown (*cioppa
monachina*) might have black slashed sleeves (*nere affettate*); a red wool gown
(*saia rossa*) or style of green gown (*gamurra verde*) might be worn with a pair of
green velvet sleeves.[78] Giuseppe Levantini-Pieroni wrote that Lucrezia Tornabuoni's gowns always had sleeves of contrasting fabric and color.[79] By the
1450s, even priestly vestments could have detachable sleeves of contrasting
fabric—morello or purplish-black sleeves worn with a pure black tunic of rash
(*rascia*), or dark wool jersey.[80]

These sleeves were then listed as separate entries in the family logbooks and
business records of tailors, seamstresses, and doublet makers, interchangeable
between various gowns. This interchangeability, of course, dramatically increased the fashion vocabulary of a woman's wardrobe, and it is no surprise
that sleeves themselves finally began to generate sumptuary restrictions. The
Statuti of 1415 did not allow the sleeves of undergowns (*gamurre*) to be of silk
or velvet, and by January 1456, undoubtedly owing to the development of
more elaborate dress practices, the Commune found it necessary to pass

Fig. 9.3. Sleeve *a gozzi*. Detail from Filippo Lippi, *Profile Portrait of a Young Woman* (fifteenth century). Metropolitan Museum of Art, New York.

Fig. 9.4. Stiff detachable sleeve. Detail from *The Aenead*, Florentine School, fifteenth century manuscript illumination. Biblioteca riccardiana, Florence.

legislation forbidding any woman to have more than one pair of brocaded sleeves (worth more than ten florins) in her wardrobe.[81] Eight years later, by 1464, officials had conceded brocaded sleeves, which could include gold, silver, and be of any fabric or color, but a woman could only have two pairs.[82]

Ornamentation | Sleeves became the most ornamented part of a woman's clothing. This fashion had probably been inadvertently caused by the sumptuary law of 1439 that limited the embroidery and trim of an ensemble to the sleeves.[83] Sleeves could be decorated with any of the tiny metallic ornaments made by Florentine goldsmiths, with made-to-order pearl embroidery or embroidery of gold and silver thread, with silk ribbons (*stringhe*) tipped with points (*aghetti* or *agugielli*) of precious metals, or with lace.[84] Tailors also made striped sleeves of more than one type of fabric, which were embroidered and lavishly lined with fur.

Often, especially in men's ceremonial uniforms and the overgowns women wore to important family occasions, only the left sleeve would carry ornamentation. Polidori-Calamandrei notes the sleeve of an overgown ornamented with metallic studs in the form of a tree, and another with the design of a falcon. Other designs comprise an eclectic inventory of images, from a parrot embroidered in pearls to an arm throwing flowers emerging from a little cloud, to a large cricket.[85] The individual significance of many of these designs undoubtedly went to the grave with their owners, and we see fewer left-arm-only sleeve decorations as the century progresses.

Like the left arm, the left shoulder could be a site of ornamentation, especially of the outermost garment, the mantello. In 1447, for Caterina Parenti's wedding finery, the pièce de résistance was a large brooch, which she was to wear on her shoulder ("da portare in ispalla"). In general, we can identify the left shoulder as the focal point in dress from at least the time of Beatrice and Matilda in Tuscany, as eleventh-century manuscript illuminations clearly show. Figure 9.5 is an image of Matilda of Tuscany from the eleventh-century Domnizo manuscript in the Vatican.[86] It is not surprising that Quattrocento Florence would have inherited this long-lived visual tradition in formal ornamentation.

Fig. 9.5. Left-shoulder clasp. Domnizo manuscript: *Matilda of Tuscany.* Vatican Library, Rome.

Fig. 9.6. Man in *berretto*. Perugino, *Portrait of a Man* (1494). Uffizi, Florence.

THE END OF THE CENTURY

As the fifteenth century drew to a close, the social and political changes of its last decades were reflected both in clothing styles and the way Florentines chose to wear their clothes.[87] With the death of Lorenzo in 1492 and the conversion of Botticelli and Pico to Savonarolan asceticism in the 1490s, clothes seem to be coming apart, as Italy itself did after the French invasion under Charles VIII in 1494. Fashion now dictated that pieces be made separately (sleeves tied on, skirts made separately from bodices.) Even headgear changed. The long strip of fabric on the right side of the cappuccio called the *becchetto* came off, changing the cappuccio from a hood, to a smaller, neat hat. Figure 9.6 is a portrait painting by Perugino (1494) of an unknown man wearing a berretto, the end-of-century choice in headwear in Florence. The becchetto then became a separate piece of cloth carelessly thrown over the shoulder as a sort of stole.[88] This was the final sartorial detaching of the head from the rest of the body. People now wore berets and caps.

In addition, the way in which Florentines and apparently other Europeans wore their clothing changed. A wave of casual unlacing swept the Italic peninsula. Laces on bodices and hose were untied, tunics left at home in trunks or thrown on beds as men went out in *farsetto* and hose.[89] Painting after painting shows this casual clothing collapse as figures heave and swoon under various stresses and strains. Florentine painters emphasize this sartorial stress by highlighting the draperies of stock religious figures in emotional biblical scenes, but not in the depiction of their fellow citizens.[90] In spite of a proliferation of new communal magistracies created in Florence to monitor clothing consumption (beginning with the first sumptuary laws in the late 1200s), Florentines of the upper classes exited the fifteenth century in magnificent display. Even after the fall of Florence to the French, Florentines continued to paint themselves, and be painted by others, in an idealized manner—utterly calm and aristocratic-looking, dignified, unruffled, and above all, impervious to the vicissitudes of life. Chapter 10 examines this type of depiction in the fresco cycles by Domenico Ghirlandaio for both Francesco Sassetti and Giovanni Tornabuoni in their family chapels in Santa Trinita and Santa Maria Novella respectively.[91]

TEN

VISUALIZING THE
REPUBLIC IN ART

An Essay on Painted Clothes

THE PATRONS

Between 1480 and 1490, the Florentine painter Domenico Ghirlandaio received the two commissions that would cap his already illustrious career. In relatively rapid succession, he was hired in separate contracts by the rivals Francesco Sassetti and Giovanni Tornabuoni to decorate their family chapels in Santa Trinita and Santa Maria Novella respectively.[1] For Sassetti, he was to paint scenes from the life of Saint Francis (Sassetti's name saint) in his chapel at Santa Trinita, and for Tornabuoni, stories from the lives of the Virgin Mary and Saint John the Baptist.[2] With the help of his many assistants (his brothers Davide and Benedetto and his brother-in-law Bastiano Mainardi being among the most important),[3] Ghirlandaio's workshop produced three monumental fresco cycles of clarity and grace.[4] Their efforts are relevant to us here, because within the religious scenes of these narrative frescoes appear portraits of members of these two families of the ruling elite of the city, dressed in their best.[5] The Santa Maria Novella frescoes alone contain over forty portraits.[6] Both of these fresco cycles represent a patriarchal point of view and were commissioned and executed to present a dominant, and perhaps personally competitive, vision of the ideal family lineage within an idealized republican state and latter-day city of God.

THE FRESCOES

In this last chapter, I want to very briefly address three aspects of these works: first, the manner in which the men and women of these families are represented in the scenes; secondly, the strategy that may have motivated these gender-specific depictions; and third, and perhaps most important, what these paintings reveal about the way upper-class Florentines dressed in the late fifteenth century. Conversely, I want to ponder what they do not reveal, and in fact, were specifically designed not to reveal. These portraits have often been described as being among the most accurate portrayals of Renaissance clothes produced in the Quattrocento. Ghirlandaio himself has suffered the disdain of many twentieth-century art historians, being called "too specific," a mere "illustrator," not a "genius" with the timelessness of greater Florentine lights. Although his place among late fifteenth-century artists is now more clearly understood, he has been characterized as a rather pedestrian artist whose work offers a "realistic" picture of the material objects of Renaissance life; individual faces and extended family groups, along with the details of their consumption: clothing, jewelry, and domestic interiors.[7] But I would like to ask if these representations are truly realistic.

Many historians' investigations into Renaissance portraits, including the studies of the ancient tradition of profile portraiture by Jean Lipman, Rab Hatfield, Joanna Woods-Marsden, and others, have enhanced our understanding of the larger cultural meanings of painted Renaissance representations.[8] Feminist issues have added to our interpretation of these depictions, with Patricia Simons, Diane Owen Hughes, and others having explored the convention of creating honorably passive female profile portraits for the delectation of the active male gaze within the social context of art patronage.[9] This convention found new currency in Quattrocento Florence. Woods-Marsden has also recently contributed a nuanced understanding of self-portraiture in the Renaissance.[10] Not only the portrait traditions for both male and female individuals have been considered, but also the depictions of complete family groups over time.[11] Simons, Cristelle Baskins, and others have also looked at the interplay between artist and patron in the conceptualization and completion of these important artifacts of family identity, invariably commissioned with a specific agenda in mind.[12] And finally, studies focused on the use of art to represent the virtù and honor of the patron have been produced, especially for the court cities of the north.[13]

In order to read the visual messages in these paintings by Ghirlandaio successfully, it is necessary to look carefully at the pictorial narratives before us, narratives that conveyed a specific intent, using what to contemporary eyes may seem a jarring juxtaposition of images, which have been discussed by many art historians.[14] In the multiple scenes of these two fresco cycles (still in situ in Florence), the artist has created a series of unusually localized and domesticized vignettes by setting traditional stories from the lives of the Virgin Mary and Saints Francis and John within the idealized palazze and piazze of this fifteenth-century city. In these vignettes, we can see the faces of identifiable members of both the Sassetti and Tornabuoni families (along with crucial "parenti, amici e vicini"), who are piously framing (and in some cases, upstaging) the characters of the religious narratives.[15] Much work has already been done by Eve Borsook, Johannes Offerhaus, Simons, and Hatfield, not only on the competition between the two rich patrons of these works and their sociopolitical agendas here, but also on the identities of the various family members portrayed in the paintings, as well as the rationale behind the inclusion (or exclusion) of a given individual in each fresco.[16] Here, however, I want to focus specifically on the way in which these individuals were dressed for their appearance in the paintings, for it is the costume that immediately distinguishes the contemporary actors from the biblical ones for us. Florentines are dressed in the height of late fifteenth-century fashion, religious actors in mantelli loosely draped, all' antica. Simons has noted that the appearance of secular figures in paintings of religious subjects was part of a long development in religious art, however, and so these images should not be read as secular "individualism" encroaching on the sacred.[17] But what *can* we read from these recognizable individuals, dressed in their public best?

OBSERVING AND BEING OBSERVED

In Sassetti's chapel at Santa Trinita, Ghirlandaio's outdoor scene (painted 1483–86) depicting the *Confirmation of the Rule of St. Francis* displays religious figures in the center being solemnly observed on the right-hand side by a very elegant but modestly dressed group of males. Within these frescoes overall, outdoor venues tend to favor males, whereas indoor scenes feature females. In Figure 10.1, we see the patron Francesco Sassetti and his young son Federico, along with his "amici" Lorenzo "Il Magnifico" and Antonio Pucci, standing closely together. Other male family members are grouped on the left side and below on the stairs.[18] The Sassetti male groups calmly frame the religious action, bearing witness to the religious event with an even gaze. By way of contrast, in Ghirlandaio's indoor scenes of the births of both the Virgin and the Baptist from the Tornabuoni Chapel in Santa Maria Novella, painted 1486–90, the events of childbirth are attended by groups of Tornabuoni women, including possibly Lorenzo de' Medici's mother, Lucrezia Torna-buoni, herself. Figure 10.2 shows a detail from the *Birth of John the Baptist*. These women do not frame the religious scene as do the men in the Sassetti fresco, however, but instead almost displace this event, being positioned cen-trally in front of the narrative, which is overwhelmed by the physical presence of a beautifully dressed female. Here, it is most probably the figure of Gio-vanna degli Albizzi, who had married Giovanni's son Lorenzo, that domi-nates the group.[19] The artist has made (or been directed to make) the central secular figure so visually striking that the two biblical mothers in the narra-tives, abed in their chambers following childbirth, are less prominent than their elegant but somehow awkwardly intrusive visitors, who dominate the pictorial space. The viewer looking at the scene has no visual choice but to gaze directly at these Fiorentine, one of whom looks serenely back. Clearly, the action of this fertility narrative is partially usurped by these fifteenth-century women, whose presence across the front of the picture plane is visually arresting.[20]

   The depiction of the males in the frescoes, however, is quite different. No one individual man ever appears alone in any of the many scenes of these three narrative cycles. Rather, men are always grouped together en masse. The women who were born into, or had married into, the Tornabuoni and Sassetti families, on the other hand, are often isolated and segregated from the men.[21] In each scene, either males or females of the family groups are high-lighted, and it is possible to discern distinct differences between the way each gender is presented. In some scenes, a lone female is further singled out by being clothed in a very specific and individualistic manner. The clothing

Fig. 10.1. Upper-class male observers. Ghirlandaio, *The Confirmation of the Rule of Saint Francis* (ca. 1483–86). Sassetti Chapel.

allows the viewer to readily distinguish between actual family members and the generic figures of servant girls and biblical actors, who are juxtaposed in loose, flowing active garments against the Tornabuoni and Sassetti women. It was this type of traditional garment, one that did not require the professional male tailor's precise cut, that disappeared from the formal wardrobes of elite females in Renaissance Florence, and with it, their active participation in making their own clothes. What is displayed here for the rich women are the elaborate, precisely fitted and decorated costumes that were fashioned by the hands of the professional male tailors, hired by the paterfamilias. This customized, tailored look on the back of the females (identified by distinctive family jewels) would have been exactly what the patron wanted and just what Ghirlandaio and his studio were able to deliver. The only part of their ensembles made exclusively by women would have been their undergarments, the camicie, now only tantalizingly hinted at in their new outer clothes, from the interstices of the outfits at neck, shoulders, elbows, and wrists. This

Fig. 10.2. Upper-class females. Detail from Ghirlandaio, *The Birth of John the Baptist* (1486–90). Tornabuoni Chapel.

visual obfuscation in dress emphasizes the tightening of male control in Medicean Florence.

But to address their dress. Is this really what individuals wore, that is, is this a realistic representation of the way fifteenth-century Florentines dressed? Simons has written that these depictions of family members constituted "honor portraits," conceived of as a broad strategy to honorably present and preserve the lineage.[22] While both genders in this city were apparently obsessed with dressing well, it is primarily the image of the upper-class female icon as visually representative of family honor that the art of the Renaissance has left us. And so, first, to the females.

The Women in the Pictures | The only feminine discourse on the type of clothing worn in these frescoes has survived in snippets of protesting prose, providing a verbal female counterpoint to the visual male art. Both Klapisch-Zuber and Hughes have noted that women complained of their clothing being too constrained by sumptuary restrictions, and that their most showy pieces were often withheld from them after a husband's death by his relatives (as we have seen). In other words, the women of Florence lamented being overregulated and regularly robbed of their only expressive outlet—their clothes.[23] And yet here they are, some isolated and much more lavishly dressed than their male kinsmen, who stand off to the sides of the scenes—in homogeneous groups, elegantly understated in dignified robes of plain red wool. Figure 10.3 shows the upper-class male framing groups from Ghirlandaio's *Angel Appearing to Zacharias* in the Tornabuoni Chapel. Significantly enough, some anonymous women can be seen in this display of patrilineage, but only peeking in at the scene, which is set in the outdoor world of male affairs. They are clustered over to the side under a plain arch, through which one sees the only domestic architecture visible, while the men are lined up against a classical frieze.[24] In this idealized scene at least, they are firmly in their place.

We see little visual evidence of overregulation of female dress in these pictures, but we have seen in previous chapters that apart from a woman's

Fig. 10.3. Upper-class male framing groups. Ghirlandaio, *The Angel Appearing to Zacharias* (1486–90). Tornabuoni Chapel.

initial display as a bride, three facts could be said to characterize her wardrobe. First, that wedding finery was often sold or pawned after the festivities and "honeymoon" were over. Secondly, that ongoing indulgence in bedecking a woman past her wedding simply was not usual, even in the case of the supposedly besotted Marco Parenti. Lastly, that a woman's wardrobe, while substantial and even containing a few luxurious items, was generally of no greater worth than her husband's. We can compare the wardrobes of a married couple, Antonio and Maddelena Pucci, from an inventory taken in 1449 upon the death of the paterfamilias, to find how similar they are. Both husband and wife had wardrobes of not only about the same number of garments (twelve and eleven respectively), but of relatively similar value (397 fl. for Antonio, and 327 fl. for Maddelena, including jewelry), Antonio's totals actually exceeding Maddelena's.[25]

And so, it seems that the paintings of women formally outfitted in brocade and pearls, such as those Ghirlandaio has here portrayed, were specific females in particular situations, which allowed them to be elaborately dressed. It has been argued that in some cases, a woman is wearing her wedding ensemble, effectively a bride frozen in time for posterity.[26] It is not that her costume, or the costumes of the other women that are displayed, are not realistic; it is rather that the selective nature of who was portrayed and highlighted to bear the display of honor resulted in an overall visually skewed representation of family members. A few adorned and embellished young females dominate. As we saw in Chapter 9, young women who had not yet reached the age of seventeen were exempt from the sumptuary restrictions that would so limit them as adult married women and were also not yet old enough to assume the wearing of the concealing mantello, demanded of mature females. And so, the nubile females of the Sassetti and Tornabuoni families, whom tailors were paid to dress and artists commissioned to preserve for posterity on the walls of family chapels, became the natural vehicles for the display of familial honor, while still being able to demonstrate the virtù required of an upper-class female from an illustrious *parentado*.

A more realistic portrayal of a Florentine woman in the Renaissance, even a woman of the upper class, would probably have produced the plainly dressed woman that we saw in the Botticelli painting in Chapter 4. The depiction of a slope-shouldered female with hair escaping from her everyday headscarf, wearing an unadorned woolen dress and a bored expression, is an unusual fifteenth-century image of a woman pausing in profile amid a day of house-work. The image of a woman modestly dressed to attend only to concerns in the private realm would never have been valued by a patriarch to visualize family honor, however indispensable the services she performed thus attired actually were. The nubile moment of elegance, promise, and expectation (unsullied by the realities of a woman's later life), on the other hand, was the perfect vehicle for such a message. Older adult women of the lineage, such as the possible figure of Lucrezia Tornabuoni in Figure 10.2, also appear in the narrative scenes of the frescoes, but are *visually* ancillary. While her dual identity as the patron's sister and as mother of Lorenzo de' Medici would certainly have made her valuable to include as a vital link to family power, her position as a married (and widowed) upper-class female rendered her secondary in this depiction.[27] She is clothed in mantello and veil and discreetly positioned with other mature women behind the current female Tornabuoni display vehicle. Simons has argued that her purpose here is to serve as female exemplar to the younger, more dressed-up woman. Both her backgrounded calm, modest posture and her clothing's references to the biblical characters in the scene would reinforce this notion.[28]

READING THE DRESS OF THE "SACRED DOLLS"

Attempting to decipher more specific meanings of the adornment of the "sacred dolls" of the rich families, dressed up and paraded in public, however, proves to be quite challenging. Not only did family insignia and motifs carry meaning but unique jewelry pieces were transmitted through family lines by way of dowry trousseaux, counter-trousseaux, and other wedding gifts. Fabric designs on silk brocades were even apparently shared among prominent patriarchs, if the message could be aptly recycled. Take, for example, the decorative motif on the "sumptuous cioppa" of the young Lena Alamanni that we saw in Chapter 6, which was to be embroidered with an "original design," ostensibly created by none other than her husband-to-be Francesco Castellani. We read there of his invention, characterized by "suns and rays and an eagle flying toward the sun as if to renew itself." In 1448, an embroidery firm had been hired to stitch it on in pearls and silver and gold thread.[29] Some thirty-five years later, in the Tornabuoni Chapel frescoes, the dominant female characters in two of the scenes, the *Birth of the Virgin* and the *Visitation,* are surprisingly wearing gowns with just this design.

Figure 10.4, a detail from the *Birth of the Virgin* scene, shows the young woman now identified by scholars as Lodovica Tornabuoni, Giovanni's only daughter, who is leading a group of women in the foreground visiting Saint Anne (and assumed to be all Tornabuoni females).[30] She is wearing a white-figured brocaded cioppa with fabric of a gold-color ground that shimmers with indications of gold threads throughout (see fig. 6.2 for fabric detail). (This is possibly a depiction of the cloth called *allucciolati* that we saw in Chapter 5, with gold threads woven into little rings above the face of the cloth.) The fabric motif features suns with rays and eagles flying. The cioppa itself laces up the front to show diamond latticework on the gamurra beneath, and has long trumpet-shaped sleeves (*maniche a trombe*) of the same cloth.

Fig. 10.4. Lodovica Tornabuoni. Detail from
Ghirlandaio, *The Birth of the Virgin* (1486–90).
Tornabuoni Chapel.

Although this gown does not appear to have been embroidered in pearls as was Lena Alamanni's, the fabric design is remarkably similar to that described by Castellani.[31]

Moving to a second scene from the frescoes, Figure 10.5 is a detail from the *Visitation,* in which Giovanna degli Albizzi is shown a second time (first seen in *The Birth of John the Baptist,* Fig. 10.2). Here, she wears a garment made of the same fabric as Lodovica's, but fashioned into a sleeveless day gown (giornea), open at the sides. The same patterned fabric has been painted in a slightly different manner by Ghirlandaio and his assistants here, with the eagles solid white, and no indication of the gold threads we saw in Figure 6.2, where the dress was more formal and grand. Obviously, these two gowns were not one and the same. We can see this clearly, for on Lodovica's cioppa, the sun with rays falls across her bodice, while on Giovanna's sleeveless giornea, another part of the fabric design falls on the bodice, that is, a complementary motif of a brace, which gathers two bands together into a bow-shape.

In the *Visitation* panel, there is also more of the diamond latticework design of red and gold visible on the undergown. We only saw a bit of this peeking out of the front lacing in the other gown. The latticework motif corresponds to what some scholars of family coats of arms have identified as one of three Tornabuoni devices, which was a square divided into four quarters transversely, called *inquartato-decussato* in Italian.[32] Both of these Tornabuoni women's outfits display this geometric design on the undergowns and also in the sleeves of the cioppa. What Simons has identified as the Tornabuoni family emblem, a small, triangular device that is part of the brocaded fabric design, is somewhat overwhelmed by the larger suns and rays and eagles flying.[33] In any case, any slavish depiction of a family's escutcheons upon the persons of its women was rare in fifteenth-century Florence.[34]

And so, the question remains. Why are these two highlighted Tornabuoni females wearing an unlikely brocade pattern, ostensibly invented many years before by Castellani? At this point, we can only offer some conjectures. We know that the Castellani were not part of the Medici network of "parenti, amici e vicini," which intimately embraced the Tornabuoni. The Castellani had been aligned with the Albizzi faction in 1433, and Martines asserts that after the rise of Cosimo, they were never again a political force.[35] But webs of marriage alliances ran thick in Florence, and a design worn by a woman that

Fig. 10.5. Giovanna degli Albizzi. Detail from Ghirlandaio, *The Visitation* (1486–90). Tornabuoni Chapel.

was provided as part of her dowry trousseau could have had a complex provenance through not only her father's line but also her mother's family, as we saw in the case of Alessandra Strozzi's daughter Caterina.[36] Here, the Tornabuoni family jewelry acts to readily identify both Ludovica and Giovanna as family members, while the fabric design of their two gowns, even though subtly incorporating a Tornabuoni device, adds another layer of significance, which would undoubtedly have been easily read at the time but now is difficult to assess.[37] Perhaps this motif had no political significance at all.[38] We know that suns and eagles played no part in any of the *imprese* of the families involved.[39] It may be that the large flying eagles and suns that visually dominate the overall decoration of the dresses had a more personal resonance, and that the eagles renewing themselves said more about the husbands' designs in these cases than their families' devices.

THE MALE MESSAGE

The portraits of the rich male oligarchs in these frescoes are exceptional in their dignity and extremely different from those of the females. The men are pictured in solemn groupings, simple and serious in their garb. As we saw in Figure 10.1, one member of the male group from the scene of the *Confirmation of the Rule* in the Sassetti Chapel is Antonio Pucci, on the far left, especially sober in his black garments. Figure 10.6 shows a detail from this same painting. Along with Pucci's black garb, the other three males, Francesco Sassetti, his young son Federico, and Lorenzo de' Medici himself, wear the saturated crimson cloth of the upper-class Florentine male's public costume. Both Pucci and Sassetti were Medici loyalists. Francesco Sassetti was a general manager of the Medici Bank, and Antonio Pucci's son Alessandro had just married Sassetti's daughter Sibilla. Here, Pucci, as a former Gonfaloniere di Giustizia (the highest political office in Florence) and military hero, is represented in the most somber of plain black robes, with fur worn inside his cioppa as lining, not outside as decoration; all in all, a study of the virtuous citizen adorned only by his reputation.[40]

In fact, this cioppa most probably appears in the family inventory of the Pucci family's goods, for a black cioppa with sleeves lined with "pancie," the softest underbelly fur of the vaio, or squirrel, is listed first in his wardrobe, and

Fig. 10.6. Francesco Sassetti and *amici*. Detail from Ghirlandaio, *The Confirmation of the Rule* (ca. 1483–86). Sassetti Chapel.

valued at an impressive fifty florins, almost enough to sustain three people for a year in Florence at midcentury. But this was only one of the many garments that Antonio owned. He had at least a dozen other gowns (that we know of) of various colors, as well as red hats of various types, and six helmets, two of which were pearl-encrusted and valued at some 170 florins. One would never know by looking at this image of the quintessential republican what his actual wardrobe contained. It is also interesting to note that in this group of four members of the oligarchy, each was primarily identified with an essential element of the idealized commune: Sassetti himself was in international business, his son Federico was promised to the Church, Lorenzo "Il Magnifico" was the nominal head of state, and Pucci was a military man. While Charles Hope has reminded us that we have no evidence that Florentines of this time period "looked for contemporary political significance in religious images in ecclesiastical contexts," nothing painted here would have been serendipitous, or at least nothing was not consistent with the patrons' personal goals.[41] Sassetti undoubtedly wanted these images to display an "exaltation of [his] house and family and the enhancement of the said church and chapel," in that order, wording that appeared in Tornabuoni's contract for his own chapel a few years later.[42]

Looking back at Figure 10.3, *The Angel Appearing to Zacharias,* the males of the Tornabuoni family dominate. This family, which included at least six brothers of Giovanni's generation, is presented by the artist in essentially the same egalitarian threads we saw in Sassetti's chapel. They wear the plain woolen lucchi dyed with grana or kermes, without ornamentation, and are only differentiated by their faces, which are accentuated by their various and multiform headwear. This costume of the politically active adult male of Florence displays none of the sartorial dandyism for which both the Milanese and Sienese men were ridiculed by civic humanists such as Alberti and Bracciolini.[43]

In a detail from the same scene, Figure 10.7 contains portraits of three of the best-known humanists associated with the Medici circle, also dressed with restraint, Marsilio Ficino, Cristoforo Landino, and Agnolo Poliziano.[44] It was in the interest of the Commune to portray its men in republican sameness, clustered in groups, away from the pollution of the luxe of their womenfolk's costume, the most luxuriously dressed of whom were pictured somewhat

Fig. 10.7. Humanist group. Detail from Ghirlandaio, *The Angel Appearing to Zacharias* (1486–90). Tornabuoni Chapel.

isolated in the fancy dresses bought for them by the males of their lines, to act as magnificent mannequins. Too much mixing would muddy the sartorial message. In fact, as we have seen from written family records, we know that such visual polarization was not realistic, and that the men of the upper-class families were often in life as richly adorned as the women. In much of the artwork that survives, however, in the paintings and frescoes commissioned by the families of the Florentine oligarchy, the clothes of the nubile women were much more specifically depicted. The men, on the other hand, are grouped and dressed essentially alike, differentiated only by grades of cloth and a subtle hierarchy of dyestuffs, especially red. This subtlety is only faintly perceptible in the paintings that survive, furthering the illusion of cooperative republican egalitarianism.

CONCLUSIONS

Here, in these fresco cycles by Domenico Ghirlandaio, we can see how the families of the Florentine elite carefully crafted their artistic legacy with the help of their artists and tailors, a legacy that represented the ideal of republican Florence. Each gender and age group within the family was assigned a role to play. A conscious attempt was made on the part of the patrons to "freeze-frame" selected young women as objects of honor, while men stood as bearers of the egalitarian ideal. I would argue that what visually constituted honor for the young nubile women was the dazzling sartorial display bought with the power of wealth, while for their husbands and fathers, sameness in costume visualized the family's participation in a more broadly conceived communal authority.

The lesser players here visually were the young males and the mature women. Boys of important family lineage in Florence were clothed as authorities-in-training, essentially functioning in the narrative scenes as visual reinforcements of the dominant male role, being shown of a piece with the men. Their mothers, on the other hand, were dressed in generic, old-fashioned mantelli and stood as exemplars, displaying a visual link to the Christian virtues of modesty, chastity, and obedience being acting out in the backgrounds of the biblical scenes. Here, the role of the males, both young and old, is singular; while the role of the females is split between youth and maturity. Young women embody the virtue of honor; older women, the virtue of modesty.

Viewed all together, however, these values presented the corporeal family ideal: honor, authority, and Christian modesty. As long as the family group remained a strong corporate entity, this divide-and-conquer visual strategy successfully conveyed a complete and powerful message. However, over time, as early modern families became less unified, less group-oriented, and in-creasingly individualized in portraits, this visual message became truncated and confused. Individuals were portrayed separately, but young women still dressed with magnificence, the original meaning of which was now lost. Off canvas, as nubile females married, they attempted to affect the same sartorial splendor whenever they could. But this costume, when unconnected to the family strategy for which it had been originally created, came to be read differently, depending upon the viewer. Men of all ages, on the other hand, continued to dress, on canvas and off, alone or in groups, for cooperative action. They were connected to the world of work and civic involvement, which increasingly was denied to their womenfolk. What had begun as a cooperative venture, namely, the corporate visualization of family honor, piety, and political authority, in time became a divisive practice, in which tailors, among other purveyors of material goods, reaped big rewards. Today, we are the inheritors of this visual display of family members in Renaissance Florence, and its legacy has profoundly influenced the way in which the portrayal of gender is still idealized in our postmodern world.

CONCLUSION

Florence underwent many societal changes in the course of the fourteenth and fifteenth centuries. The early development of a revolutionary form of communal government opened the way to the participation of men from the humbler levels of society, men never before engaged in the formal business of politics. Not only would wealthy merchants now control the Signoria, but lesser guildsmen as well added their voices to produce a truly representative civic government. The egalitarian ideal spread during the first half of the fourteenth century until, at the height of corporatism, perhaps as many as 7,000 or 8,000 guildsmen were included in the ranks of the politically active, making for a government *quod omnes tangit* (in which all participate).

After the shock of the Ciompi revolt in 1378, however, the major guildsmen acted decisively to check the unruly textile *sottoposti*, now perceived as a deadly threat. Broad-based participation in the political process became a thing of the past, and elections, carefully orchestrated by the richest of the major guildsmen, soon guaranteed tighter control over government. By the 1390s, the ruling classes had begun to restrict inclusion in the governing councils to something like one-fourth of the pre-revolt numbers.

After the ascent of the Medici in 1434, the emerging oligarchy continued to shrink the political base by means of a shrewd policy of controlled electoral practices and strategic marriage alliances, particularly among the families of the ruling elite. From then on, every attempt would be made to direct the material resources of this rich merchant city to the creation of a new unassailably aristocratic ruling class. An astonishing amount of energy, attention and money went into this, and the scale of the domestic micromanagement focused on developing this honorable ruling elite has here been revealed for the first time by examining the city's clothing rituals.

Ritual practice marked special occasions, setting these off in opposition to everyday life, but not all Florentines were content to be part of a general appearance of communal honor, "enough to block out the sun." Florentine families of worth schemed and negotiated to carry their individual line to the forefront of communal attention. Clothes in this "clothes town" were powerful tools, skillfully manipulated. Neither being a city with a princely court nor having an aristocracy authorized by the Empire, Florence's rich merchants had to rely on internal civic resources to create their own mandate. Over the span of roughly 100 years, from 1378 (the year the last female tailor appeared on the tax lists of the Estimo) to the 1470s (the decade that saw the richest flurry of sumptuary clarification), the leading groups concentrated on gaining control over the material production of their city. They put scores of local tailors, doublet makers, embroiderers, furriers, jewelers, and hatmakers —all the vast artisanal talent and expertise of this luxury-goods town—to work on the creation of their first aristocracy. In the process, they marginalized the female needleworkers, professionalized the garment trades into a male-dominated enterprise, and made many artisans rich. Some tailors became known as "Il Maestro."

What is new here is obviously not the fact that rich people dressed up for special occasions, but rather the extent to which dress was controlled and manipulated by the males of the merchant elite to attain and retain power. How did the patriarchs of important lineages micromanage dress?

First of all, we know that the male heads of families (or female heads in the absence of a male, as in the case of Alessandra Strozzi) were intimately involved in the decisions regarding female display and the opportunity to visualize the glory of their lines. Patriarchs not only made the major choices concerning an ensemble's cloth, color, motifs, and the pieces of family jewelry to be worn but often also selected the fabric to be used from their own family textile firms, hired the craftspeople who made the garments, and oversaw their making and fitting. They were involved as well in the minutiae of the marketplace, negotiating the many small details that went into assembling a display outfit, from shopping for pearls, feathers, slippers, and hosiery to choosing lining fabrics, lacings, ribbons, and the tiny metallic ornaments that were sewn onto necklines and borders.

Secondly, we can see that the role of the bridal trousseau, which had traditionally provided household and personal linens for the newly married couple, was transformed in the Quattrocento into an extensive inventory of luxury items to specifically bedeck the bride. But even this reorientation from utilitarian to decorative items did not sufficiently satisfy the consolidating aristocracy in its goals for key marriage alliances. A flashier counter-trousseau supplied by the groom (often using the most expensive kermes dye) could usurp the public role of the already-luxurious bridal trousseau. Financed in part by the bride's own dowry funds, the display clothing that made up the counter-trousseau was only a temporary "gift" (or loan) from the groom, and it was often reserved for the most public portion of the wedding process, visually obscuring the bride's own trousseau garments. Even though wedding gowns and counter-trousseaux were nominal gifts to the bride, in the struggle for ultimate control of familial place in society, they turned, in fact, into some of the most contested items in the material culture of the Renaissance.

Thirdly, a surprisingly large percentage of a family's total wealth was tied up in the contents of their wardrobes, clothes being the primary visual sign of honor in Quattrocento Florentine society. Up to 40 percent of a family's resources could be invested in and represented by their clothing. In seeking to provide themselves adequately with the deep crimson garments of understated elegance for communal office or for representing Florence abroad, men came to have just as many clothes as women. Florentine males *appear* routinely to have dressed modestly. But when we look instead at household inventories, family expense books, and the *ricordanze* kept by those of the upper ranks, we can see that what they actually owned was far more sumptuous than the dress in which they had themselves portrayed for posterity. The portraits seem rather to have been a study in modesty: here normal clothing practices were manipulated to convey the image of an idealized egalitarian male citizenry. But we now know, for example, that the seemingly drab getup worn by Antonio Pucci in his portrait in the Sassetti Chapel fresco was listed in an inventory as worth fifty florins.

The making of clothes continued nonstop throughout the year, so as to keep up with the demands of honor, which had to be continually renewed in the streets of the city. However, family clothing budgets responded to allow for maximum display, especially for the marriages of daughters, by a focused scrimping on the clothes of other family members in the years between important ritual events. Domestic records show spikes of potentially ruinous amounts of money spent on clothes, followed by periods when new garments were made of used fabric and worn clothing was mended or taken apart to be remade and relined. A keen business mentality carefully calculated, managed, and recorded the outlay in order to keep the family competitive financially. These records reveal that because of their clothing requirements (whether their father ultimately decided to marry them off or to cloister them), the females of a wealthy Florentine lineage, who could be invaluable assets for the family in forging marriage alliances, were not marginal but central to its long-range financial strategy.

The lavishly dressed young women of the lineage were highlighted in the secular portraits of the upper classes, some in the religious scenes frescoed on the walls of private family chapels, where they were seen as visual symbols of devotion to God. Their nubile or recently married state freed them from the sumptuary restrictions to which mature women were subject. This permitted them to shoulder family honor without transgressing communal laws that governed dress. As the Quattrocento progressed, and especially after 1470, sumptuary laws became increasingly focused on monitoring women's dress. The Commune created a series of new civic magistracies whose function was to control unauthorized sartorial display, thereby seeking to direct visual attention on the rapidly contracting ranks of the ruling elite, recorded in Renaissance art.

When their agendas for specific ritual clothing had been met, however, the heads of these Florentine families gave up the actual garments with dispatch. Pawned, taken apart, sold to a used-clothes dealer or donated to the poor, clothes continued to be worked hard in the service of the elite. The amount of patriarchal control exerted over these ritual garments, from their inception in the *botteghe* of tailors to their final disposition, sometimes generations later, and even in their immortalization in the work of Florentine artists, pays tribute to the power of clothes to manipulate and transform this early modern society.

Currency and Measures in Renaissance Florence

CURRENCY

Money of Account*

—denaro (*a fiorino*) = one-twelfth of a soldo (*a fiorino*); the Florentine penny and, like the penny, a money of account
—denaro (*a oro*) = one-twelfth of a soldo (*a oro*); another penny of account
—denaro (*picciolo*) = one-twelfth of a soldo, the smallest penny of account in Florence
—soldo (*di piccioli*) = twelve denari
—lira (*di piccioli*) = twenty soldi or 240 denari

Base Coins

—biglione, composed of two coins of very base silver: (1) the quattrino = four denari; (2) the denaro, popularly known as the picciolo, the Renaissance equivalent of our penny
—grosso = a silver coin worth approximately ¼₄ of a gold florin (variable). As the silver grosso was progressively devalued during the course of the Quattrocento, its value went from ¼₄ to ¹⁄₄₃ in 1461, and ¹⁄₄₉ by 1481. This had an effect on the money of account. One gold florin was worth roughly 75 soldi and 10 denari in 1402, but by 1481, one gold florin was worth 120 soldi (*di piccioli*).

---

*monetary designations used in bookkeeping

Types of Florins

—fiorini (*d'oro*) = four to seven lire (*di piccioli*) or twenty-nine soldi (*a fiorino*);
worth 3.53 grains of gold in Florence and coined from 1252 until around 1450. In
1447, one fiorino *d'oro* = ninety-two soldi (*di piccioli*) or twenty soldi *d'oro*. The
silver-to-gold ratio constantly fluctuated, and the relative value of the florin in
soldi (the official mint rate and the commercial banking rate) was announced
daily in Florence.

—fiorino *di suggello*: sealed gold florin that had been weighed, tested, and sealed
with others in a *borsa* (purse) in Florence. Originally it was the same as the fiorino
d'oro, except that its weight was tested. It became a money of account for silver
about 1450, when the fiorino *largo* appeared.

—fiorino *largo*: large gold florin that appeared in Florence around 1450 and quickly
rose to become worth 20 percent more than the fiorino *di suggello*

—fiorino *largo di grossi* (abbrev., fiorino *di grossi*): a money of account in silver for a
fiorino *largo*

—fiorino *largo d'oro in oro* (abbrev., fiorino *largo d'oro*, fiorino *d'oro in oro*, or fiorino
di oro): a large gold florin that did not appear until 1482 in Florence and was officially 19 percent higher than the fiorino largo *di grossi*, but in actual transactions
sometimes was not valued that high

—ducato: at the end of the century, even in Florence, the florin, although unchanged in weight, fineness, or design, was often called a ducato and was worth
from seven to ten lire. See *Archivio di stato Firenze*, Mediceo, avanti il principato,
CXXII, the Medici account books of 1515–17.

MEASURES OF LENGTH

—alla = (ell) cloth measurement in England, France, and Flanders which was
around forty-five inches (one and a half Venetian braccia, or half a Genoese
canna).

—braccio (pl. braccia) = (an arm's length) cloth measurement of about a yard, or
one-fourth to one-third of a canna. In Florence, it seems at midcentury to have
been nearer to a third. The braccio was the most frequently used measurement
for cloth sold by the cut.

—canna (pl. canne) = three to four braccia. The most used cloth measurement in
Italy and other countries. Full-length cloths were measured by the canna.

—pezza (pl. pezze) = twelve to fourteen canne. The regulation length of woolen
cloth in Florence, and therefore the measurement found in cloth transactions on
the wholesale market.

MEASURES OF WEIGHT

—libbra (l.) = pound (ca. 300 g)

—oncia (on.) = ounce ($\frac{1}{12}$ of a pound)

—denaro (d.) = $\frac{1}{24}$ of an ounce (used for precious metals, small pearls bought in bulk for embroidery, silver and gold buttons, and other gilded and silvered dress ornaments, and for silver wire)

—carato (ct.) = $\frac{1}{24}$ of an ounce (used for larger gemstones, pearls, etc.)

Categories of Clothiers

Armaiuoli   Literally, "artificers," who made metal buttons, studs, and other metallic ornaments for clothing, working with *orafi*.

Bambagiai   Cotton-wool makers, who were usually females, and provided the material for quilting, doublets, and bed linens.

Battilori   Makers of gold leaf, gold wire, and gold and silver laminates, which were all used in luxury silks, velvets, and in Florentine artwork. This art, which originated in Cyprus and had been brought by Lucchese exiles to the city, fell under the jurisdiction of the Arte della seta.

Bendaiuoli   Independent craftswomen who made *benda* (head cloths).

Berrettai   Beret makers, who were, along with *cappellai*, under the jurisdiction of the Arte della lana, because berets were traditionally made of wool. The craft originated in the wool-manufacturing town of Prato and fell under the jurisdiction of the Arte dei medici, speziali e merciai in Florence.

Borsai   Purse makers, typically female. Under the jurisdiction of the Arte dei medici e degli speziali if the purse was of fabric. Leather purses or pouches fell under the Arte dei correggiai (along with *cinturai*, leather belt makers).

Calzaiuoli   Hosiers, who, along with sarti, were included in the Arte dela seta, and made body hose, stockings, and socks. In addition, many independent female hosiers worked outside of the guild structure.

Calzolai   Shoemakers were united in a guild with slipper makers (*pianellai*) and wooden clog makers (*zoccolai*). Everyone owed them money, and they were the largest occupational group among clothiers in the city. In 1427, there were 264 declared shoemakers in Florence, 7 percent of them female.

Camiciai   Undershirt/blouse makers, typically independent female workers, outside of the guild community and control.

Cappellai   Hatmakers, who worked in straw (*paglia*) and felt (*feltro*) were under the jurisdiction of the Arte dei medici e degli speziali. *Cappellai* and *berrettai* formed a guild together in 1316, but those who worked in wool were later bound to the Arte della lana.

Cinturai   Belt makers, who were traditionally female if they worked in fabric and were known as *zonarii* in the late Duegento and early Trecento. Makers of silk belts were included in the Arte della seta; leather belt makers in the Arte dei correggiai.

Cucitori, Costori (m.), *Cucitrici* (s.)   Literally, "seamsters" or "seamstresses," who simply sewed up clothing from pieces of cloth that had been cut out by tailors. These workers were poorly paid.

Cuffiai   Cap makers, who were traditionally female. *Cuffie* could be made of linen for men, women, or children, used under *cappucci*, as nightcaps, and also for military wear under helmets. They could also be extravagant for women, fashioned of silk or wool, embroidered with pearls.

Farsettai   Doublet makers, who were specialized tailors of this predominantly male garment, which was quilted and waxed to give the upper body shape. A *farsettaio* sometimes went by the title of *sarto/farsettaio*.

Ghirlandai   Women's headdress makers—literally, "garland makers"—who made expensive fashionable "garlands" of precious fabric, which could be adorned with metal ornaments, tinsel, or feathers.

Gioiellieri   Gem dealers, who were retailers of gemstones (diamonds, emeralds, garnets, rubies, sapphires, spinels) and most impressively, in the Quattrocento, of pearls.

Guantai   Glove makers, the sale of whose wares was regulated by the Arte dei medici, speziali e merciai.

Mazzocchiai   Hat foundation makers, who were often women. *Mazzocchi* were the padded rolls worn around the head that formed the foundation for many constructed hats, from *ghirlande* to *cappucci*.

Orafi   Literally, "goldsmiths," but also jewelers and stone setters for brooches, pendants, and rings. The gilded silver filigree work made for headpieces was controlled by the orafi. Female employees made the tiny copper ornaments, which were then silvered or gilded, known as *maspilli, pianette, raperelle, scaglie*, or *tremolanti*, among other names.

Orpellai   Tinsel makers, who worked with *orafi* and *battilori* crafting the gold and silver laminated ornaments used in *ghirlande* for women.

Pellicciai   Furriers, who were either fur dealers or dressers of fur. In the fourteenth century, they dealt especially with fox and wildcat; in the fifteenth, marten was added. The *pellicciai* combined with the *vaiai* in 1317 to form the Arte dei pellicciai e vaiai, one of the *arti maggiori*.

Pianellai   Slipper makers, who worked in cloth and were in the Arte dei calzolai with both shoemakers and makers of clogs (*zoccolai*). Many women exercised this art.

Ricamatori, Ricamatrici   Embroiderers, who worked independently or under the jurisdiction of the Arte della seta. Large embroidery concerns employed both male shop embroiderers and women who did piecework from home. Nuns in convents and uncloistered *pinzocheri* embroidered ecclesiastical vestments, liturgical hangings, purses, sleeves, and bodices.

Rigattieri   Used-clothing and linens retailers, who were often wealthy, as they organized the first retail clothing market in the city of Florence in the early Trecento. There were also poor ambulatory *rigattieri*, many of whom seem to have been female, as there was legislation passed against women pursuing this trade outside of guild controls.

Rimendatori   Menders of woolen cloth, who repaired tiny imperfections in newly woven and sheared cloth, were usually small masters working from home, but sometimes worked from the central workshop of an industrial entrepreneur or *lanaiuolo*. Rimendatori could also be menders of old or torn clothing, these often widows or wives who worked from home for tailors' botteghe.

Sarte or *sartesse*   Female tailors, often cloistered single women (or formerly cloistered married women) who worked making the *biancheria* or *panni lini* for rich families. Female tailors worked outside the guild system informally or sewed at home for the bottega of a *maestro sartore*.

Sarti   Tailors, who were first associated with the Por Santa Maria in early thirteenth century, then subsumed under the dicta of the Arte dei rigattieri, in which they rose in status, becoming a first-rank member in the revised Arte dei rigattieri, linaiuoli e sarti in the late fifteenth century.

Suolai   Shoe sole makers, who sold their leather soles to both shoemakers and stocking makers under the jurisdiction of the Arte dei correggiai.

Ucchiellaiai   Buttonhole makers, traditionally independent craftswomen.

Vaiai   Furriers, who specialized in luxury furs; the gray fur of the *vaio*, (*vair* or *miniver* in English) a squirrel native to Siberia, Russia, and Bulgaria; the fur of a certain species of rabbit, ermine, lynx, sable and wildcat. By 1317, *vaiai* were part of the Arte dei vaiai e pellicellai.

Velettai   Veil makers, usually women, who worked in fine linen, *rensa* from Rheims, and silk and fell under the jurisdiction of the Arte dei medici, speziali e merciai.

Venditrici   Female ambulatory venders, regulated to some extent by the Arte dei rigattiere, who essentially went door-to-door vending a variety of cloth and clothing accessories.

Zoccolai   Wooden clog makers, who were part of the Arte dei calzolai, along with makers of *pianelle* and *chopine*.

Cloth Required for Selected Garments (Florence, 1359–1515)

GARMENT	AMOUNT*	DATE
Berretta (for a man)	1½ braccia	1515
Calzoni (pair for a man)	3¾ braccia	1515
Camiciotto (for a friar)	12 braccia	1469
Capa and *scapulare* (for a friar)	8 braccia	1447
Cappuccio (for a man)	16 braccia	1515
Cioppa (for a woman)	13 braccia	1450
Coperto per uno corsaletto (for a man)	½ braccia	1515
Cotta (for a woman)	18 braccia	1440
Cottardita (for a woman)	5 braccia	1359
Farsetto (for a man)	3¼ braccia	1477
Fodera / saio (for a man)	16 braccia	1515
Fodero / guardacuore (for a friar)	4 braccia	1475
Gamurra (for a woman)	8 braccia	1475
Giornea (for a woman)	26⅓ braccia	1448
Giornea (for a woman)	25¾ braccia	1447
Giubba (for a woman)	1¼ braccia	1359
Giubbone (for a man)	8½ braccia	1515
Giubbone (for a man)	3½ braccia	1515

*A braccio is aprroximately a yard in length.

Guardacuore (for a friar)	6 braccia	1447
Guardacuore (for a friar)	4½ braccia	1447
Maniche (pair for a man)	2½ braccia	1515
Maniche (pair for a woman)	1½ braccia	1448
Maniche (pair for a friar)	1 braccio	1469
Mantellina (for a man)	9 braccia	1477
Mantello/cowl (for mourning woman)	14 braccia	1423
Mantello/cowl (for mourning woman)	26 braccia	1423
Roba (for a woman)	35 braccia	1447
Saio di velluto (for a man)	20 braccia	1515
Saio (for a man)	18 braccia	1515
Saio da chavalchare (for a man)	16 braccia	1515
Scapulare (for a friar)	4 braccia	1452, 1475
Tonachino (for a friar)	4½ braccia	1449
Tonica (for a friar)	14 braccia	1450
Tonica (for a friar)	9 braccia	1449
Tonica (for a friar)	8½ braccia	1469
Tonica (for a friar)	6 braccia	1469
Vesta per l'entrata della città (for Duke Lorenzo)	26 braccia	1515

Two Minerbetti Trousseaux

GHOSTANZA MINERBETTI'S BRIDAL TROUSSEAU (1511)

*A. Trousseau Items Estimated (*stimate*) at 275 Florins, on May 8, 1511*

Important Gowns

An overgown of carnation pink silk trimmed with fur and edged in gray velvet
A day gown of watered blue silk damask with full sleeves, edged with red velvet
A flounced day gown of lemon-colored silk, edged with black velvet
A pair of red violet silk sleeves dyed with kermes
A flounced day gown of white silk, with edging and sleeves of tan silk damask
A silk gown of lilac, with full sleeves, edged with yellow silk
A dress of green woolen cloth, with sleeves, borders and trim of tan silk damask
A pair of red velvet sleeves (lined)

Personal Linens

8 embroidered underblouses (*camicie*)
A pair of embroidered muslin sleeves (lined)
An embroidered cotton apron
Two more aprons of fine embroidered linen
Another apron of embroidered linen

Source: Biblioteca laurenziana, acq. e doni, 229, 2, fols. 80V, 81R, 82V, 77R.

3 towels
3 embroidered headscarves
2 embroidered headdresses
8 embroidered housecaps of very soft fabric
One linen towel, finished along one edge
One linen handkerchief finished along one edge
One very large linen towel
30 little purse-sized handkerchiefs (in one piece)
10 little handkerchiefs (in two pieces)

Special Accessories

One housecap of red silk, with ribbons
2 housecaps woven with gold thread
3 ribbons of gold silk
2 purses with curled golden threads
One small purse banded in gold thread
One purse of red silk decorated with gold
One black velvet cap with a golden ribbon
One black velvet neckband with gold decoration
One belt of golden thread decorated with silver
One gold cord belt, decorated with enameled gold, with two chalcedony insets
One white silk hairnet decorated with swan's-down

Non-Clothing Personal Objects

One printed pocket-sized book decorated with silver
One small printed book decorated with silver
One pair of little knives, decorated with silver
One pair of mother-of-pearl combs
One pair of combs of yellow amber, with jasper
One silver-decorated cup
One silver ring with an aquamarine stone
One copper basin with silver enameled decoration
An ivory comb
A gilded mirror
A Santa Margherita doll dressed in brocade, with pearls (Saint Margaret was the saint invoked as a bridal charm for marital fertility).

*B. Non-*stimate *portion of trousseau. Not included in the total dowry sum. There is no easily discernible order in which items are recorded in this second list. I have therefore grouped items into like objects. Indecipherable words appear as [ ].*

Clothes in General

One housedress with sleeves and trim of green silk
One dress of woolen cloth, with sleeves of tan silk
2 pairs of woolen shoes
2 used underblouses
8 aprons of new linen cloth
2 towels
One large headscarf
11 pairs of socks
14 housecaps of linen cloth
One pair of sleeves

Personal Linens

10 handkerchiefs
11 head veils
10 washable neckbands
9 large veils
2 pieces of fabric (for headscarves)
4 pieces [ ]
7 pieces of cording
6 embroidered stockings [ ]
2 gold-embroidered stockings

Silk Items

6 pieces of silk ribbon [ ]
One [ ]
6 silk underblouses [ ]
One silk underblouse [ ]
One [ ] of many colored silk
One little neckband of violet silk
One little silk purse
One purse of green silk
One silk headcap
4 headcaps of taffeta of many colors
One cap of tan taffeta

Toiletries

One ivory comb
One gilded brush

Sewing Supplies

14 skeins of silk
5 silk pincushions
3 little sacks of [ ] embroidered in gold
6 silk doves (sewing decorations?)
10 silk flowers (sewing decorations?)
6 little skeins of silk, of many colors (for embroidery work)
One seraph (angel), embroidered in gold (for sewing decoration?)

Accessories

One pair of silk gloves
One silk-embroidered [ ]
One pair of small gilded shoes

More Sewing/Spinning Supplies

2 pairs of scissors
One distaff of ivory
3 spindles of ivory
2 [ ]
2 pair of [ ]
One head garland [ ]
2 head garlands of [ ]
One string of [ ]

Writing Supplies

One portfolio w/ivory cover
One ivory inkstand

Chests, Baskets, Small Sewing Supplies, Odds and Ends

One small chest of cypress wood
One little gilded chest
Two small straw baskets
One bread basket

Another basket covered with silk
A pair of scissors
One [ ] with one [ ]
2 big marble basins
One little pail ?
One mirror of [ ]
One tabernacle with painted decorations of saints
One gilded box (embellished)
Two pairs of gloves
Three containers of pins
Two pairs of slippers
Two pairs of shoes
Two green towels
Two pairs of stockings with the family device

MARIA MINERBETTI'S CONVENTUAL TROUSSEAU (1506)

A. Trousseau items valued at 30 lire (ca. 5 ½ florins), on November 7, 1506, when Maria Minerbetti was brought to the convent of Santa Felicita di Firenze.

Clothes

Two dresses (*gamurre*) of gray Flemish wool
One lined shortish dress
One gray wool cloak (*surtane*)

Personal Linens

2 pairs of woolen socks
2 sets of washable personal linens (*panni lini*)
8 underblouses
8 headscarves
8 head caps
4 towels
4 aprons
4 little handkerchiefs
6 bath towels

Miscellaneous

One ivory spoon
One pair of gloves

2 linings
2 pairs of shoes
One pair of slippers

B. About eight months later, on July 3, 1507, Maria's family added:

Yardage

84 yards (*braccia*) of cloth for two pairs of bedsheets
36 yards (*braccia*) of new white cloth for tablecloths

C. Some three months later, on October 30, 1507, they added:

One overgown of gray wool (*cioppa*)
A painting of a crucifixion
A painting of Santo Rocco
These two supplements cost the family 83 lire 12 soldi, added to the initial amount, for a total now of 113 lire 12 soldi, or about 20½ florins.

D. A few years later, in May 1510 and April 1511, the following items were noted in her father's logbook:

Yardage

½ yard (*braccia*) of thin cloth
1½ yards of cloth for aprons
1½ yard of cloth for another [large] apron
Woolen cloth for Maria's habit
14 yards of thin black cloth
One yard of brown cloth for clothing
One yard of thin black cloth

Non-Clothing Items (for Easter?)

2 white candles
Meat
3 pairs of chickens
6 flasks of wine

Yardage

A black cloak for her habit
6½ yards of cloth for a dress
½ yard of cloth (linen / cotton mix) for a dress
33 yards of linen cloth for underblouses (*camicie*)

Shoes and Slippers

For the items paid out in these two years, her father Andrea noted in the margin of his logbook that he had spent 5 additional florins.

E. Last entries in Andrea Minerbetti's ricordanza for Maria, dated December 8, 1512, and July 8, 1514:

Yardage

2 yards of thin black cloth
2¼ yards of additional cloth
40 yards of woolen cloth
18 yards of thin coarse linen cloth(or linen / cotton mix)
In the margin, these last four items were valued at 8 florins. Total Spent on Maria: 33½ florins (over 8 years).

Notes

ABBREVIATIONS

ASF   Archivio di stato Firenze
BL, acq. e doni   Biblioteca laurenziana, acquisiti e doni
Carte strozz.   Carte strozziane
CAT   Catasto
Conv. sopp.   Conventi soppressi
MAP   Mediceo, avanti il principato

INTRODUCTION

1. ASF, Conv. soppr., Santa Verdiana, N. 90, filza 134, dal quaderno di dare e avere e ricordanze di Francesco Castellani dal 1436 al 1458, cc. 35–48, cited by Carlo Carnesecchi, "Suntuosa 'cioppa' di Lena Castellani," *Rivista d'arte* 4, nos. 8–9 (1906): 148–54. See also *The Ricordanza A by Francesco Castellani,* ed. Giovanni Ciappelli (Florence, 1992).

2. Although the document does not specify, this "sontuosa cioppa" may be assumed to have been made of cut silk velvet, because the dyestuff kermes was used only on fabrics of the highest quality.

3. Anne Hollander, *Seeing through Clothes* (New York, 1975), p. 450.

4. Girolamo Gargiolli, *L'Arte della seta in Firenze* (Florence 1868), pp. 149ff. (from dialogue 2, "Tintore del sete"). See also Ronald Rainey, "Sumptuary Legislation in Renaissance Florence" (Ph.D. diss. (Columbia University, 1985), 2:648–56, for the chronology of sumptuary legislation passed from 1281 to 1531, some eighty separate legal entries.

5. "Drappo e colore fa all' uomo onore." Quoted in Rosita Levi-Pisetzky, *Il costume e la moda nella società italiana* (Turin, 1978), p. 58.

6. Vespasiano da Bisticci, *The Vespasiano Memoirs: Lives of Illustrious Men of the XVth Century* (London, 1926), p. 224. Vespasiano writes that the garments consisted of an entire crimson outfit (*cioppa, mantello,* and *cappuccio*), which Cosimo gave him on the morning of a feast day, and that Donatello did wear it, but only a couple of times, thinking it "too fine."

7. Niccolò Machiavelli, *Le istorie fiorentine*, bk. 3 (Florence, 1965), p. 182: "Spogliateci tutti ignudi, voi ci vedrete simili; rivestite noi delle vesti loro ed eglino delle nostre, noi senza dubbio nobili ed eglino ignobili parranno; perché solo la povertà e le ricchezze ci disagguagliano."

8. Jacques Le Goff, "Vestimentary and Alimentary Codes in *Erec et Enide,*" in *The Medieval Imagination* (Chicago, 1985), pp. 132–50, identifies not only vestimentary but also alimentary "codes" of feudal society, pointing out some half dozen vestimentary codes, which he argues communicated everything from societal status to the presence of the miraculous.

9. Diane Owen Hughes, "Earrings for Circumcision: Distinction and Purification in the Italian Renaissance City," in *Persons in Groups,* ed. Richard Trexler (Binghamton, N.Y., 1985), p. 167.

10. See Richard A. Goldthwaite, *The Building of Renaissance Florence* (Baltimore, 1980), and "The Florentine Palace as Domestic Architecture," *American Historical Review* 77 (June–Dec. 1972): 977–1012, which shifted the focus of the family life of the rich (and their women) to a newly removed private realm.

11. Richard A. Goldthwaite, "The Empire of Things: Consumer Demand in Renaissance Italy," in *Patronage, Art, and Society in Renaissance Italy,* ed. F. W. Kent and Patricia Simons (Oxford 1987), and *Wealth and the Demand for Art in Italy 1300–1600* (Baltimore, 1993).

12. Anthony Molho, *Marriage Alliance in Late Medieval Florence* (Cambridge, Mass., 1994), pp. 11–18.

13. Jacob Burckhardt, *The Civilisation of the Renaissance in Italy* (London, 1878).

14. This line of investigation began in 1899 with Niccolò Rodolico, *Il popolo minuto: Note di storia fiorentina (1343–1378)* (1899; reprint, Florence, 1968) and *I Ciompi: Una pagina di storia del proletariato operaio* (1945; reprint, Florence, 1980). Important twentieth-century contributors have included, among others, Gene Brucker, "The Ciompi Revolution," in *Florentine Studies: Politics and Society in Renaissance Florence,* ed. Nicolai Rubinstein (Evanston, Ill., 1968), and "The Florentine Popolo Minuto and Its Political Role, 1340–1450," in *Violence and Civil Disorder in Italian Cities, 1200–1500,* ed. Lauro Martines (Berkeley, Calif., 1972); Victor Rutenburg, *Popolo e movimenti popolari nell'Italia del '300 e '400* (Bologna, 1971); John Najemy, " 'Audiant omnes artes': Corporate Origins of the Ciompi Revolution," in *Il Tumulto dei Ciompi: Un momento di storia fiorentina ed europea*

(Florence, 1981), pp. 78–80; and Richard Trexler, "Neighbours and Comrades: The Revolutionaries of Florence, 1378," *Social Analysis* 4 (Dec. 1983): 53–106.

15. Both carders and dyers (components of the sottoposti) have been identified as at the upper end of the labor force, but by the nature of their occupations, in which each contributed just one step in a long manufacturing process, their work experience, controlled by the wool guild, tended to resemble that of other less elevated sottoposti, such as stretchers, spinners, and burlers. For the Marxist category of "working class" that leaves out the female experience, see Joan Scott, *Gender and the Politics of History* (New York, 1988), esp. pp. 53–67.

16. The "peripheralization" of the *popolo minuto* was first articulated twenty years ago by Samuel Kline Cohn Jr., *The Laboring Classes of Renaissance Florence* (New York, 1980). More recently, both Alessandro Stella, *La révolte des Ciompi: Les hommes, les lieux, le travail* (Paris, 1993), and Franco Franceschi, *Oltre il "Tumulto": I lavoratori fiorentini dell' Arte della Lana fra Tre e Quattrocento* (Florence, 1993), have come to similar conclusions.

17. See Christiane Klapisch-Zuber, preface to Franceschi, *Oltre il "Tumulto,"* p. 14.

18. Goldthwaite, *Building of Renaissance Florence*, p. 44.

19. ASF, MAP, LXXVI, no. 96, dated Mar. 4, 1490 [mod. 1491].

20. Adapting Jacques Heers's wonderful image from *Le clan familial au Moyen Age: Étude sur les structures politiques et sociales des milieux urbains* (Paris, 1974).

21. Most fundamentally, see Christiane Klapisch-Zuber, *Women, Family, and Ritual in Renaissance Italy* (Chicago, 1987).

22. These studies include Stella Mary Newton, *The Dress of the Venetians, 1495–1525* (Aldershot, U.K., 1988); Daniel Roche, *La culture des apparences: Une histoire du vêtement XVIIe–XVIIIe siècle* (Paris, 1989); Philippe Perrot, *Fashioning the Bourgeoisie: A History of Clothing in the Nineteenth Century* (Princeton, N.J.,1994), and John Harvey, *Men in Black* (Chicago, 1995).

23. Cesare Vecellio, *Habiti antichi et moderni* (Venice, 1598).

24. E. Polidori-Calamandrei, *Le vesti delle donne fiorentine nel Quattrocento* (Florence, 1924; reprint, Rome, 1973); Rosita Levi-Pisetzky, *Storia del costume in Italia* (Milan, 1966), and *Costume e la moda nella società italiana*; Rosana Pistolese, *La moda nella storia del costume* (1964; 2d ed., Bologna, 1967); Giorgio Marangoni, *Evoluzione storica e stilistica della moda,* vol. 1: *Dalle antiche civiltà mediterranee al rinascimento* (3d ed., Milan, 1977); Elizabeth Birbari, *Dress in Italian Painting, 1460–1500* (London, 1975).

25. Jacqueline Herald, *Renaissance Dress in Italy, 1400–1500* (London, 1981). See also the wide-ranging *Il costume al tempo di Pico e Lorenzo il Magnifico*, ed. Aurora Fiorentini Capitani, Vittorio Erlino, and Stefania Ricci (Milan, 1994).

26. Caroline Walker Bynum, "Shape and Story: Metamorphosis in the Western Tradition," the 1999 Jefferson Lecture in the Humanities, Kennedy Center for the Performing Arts, Washington, D.C., March 22, 1999.

27. Georg Simmel, *Philosophie der Mode, Moderne Zeitfragen* 11 (1905): 5–41; Frank

Alvah Parsons, *The Psychology of Dress* (New York, 1920); James Laver, *Taste and Fashion* (London, 1937), *Dress* (1950), and *Costume* (New York, 1963); and Quentin Bell, *On Human Finery* (London, 1947). Laver dated the beginning of the phenomenon of fashion to around 1360 and credited it to the influence of court life (*Costume*, pp. 35–36). He also developed an overall theory of fashion periodicity that remains strikingly resonant. Laver's list of fashion adjectives charts the perception of fashionable clothes from ten years before they become accepted, when they are considered "indecent," through acceptance, when they are thought "smart," and up to 150 years after they have gone out of style, by which time they are viewed as "beautiful" (*Taste and Fashion*, p. 7).

28. See J. C. Flugel, *The Psychology of Clothes* (London, 1950), and Lawrence Langner, *The Importance of Wearing Clothes* (New York, 1959).

29. Roland Barthes, *Elements of Semiology* (New York, 1964), *The Fashion System* (New York, 1967), and "The Diseases of Costume," in *Critical Essays,* trans. Richard Howard (Evanston, Ill., 1972), pp. 41–50.

30. Barthes, *Elements of Semiology,* pp. 13–27.

31. Barthes, *Fashion System*, p. 3. Even as he structured his fashion system, however, Barthes was aware that perhaps no pure semiotic system of fashion was possible, apart from language; and, furthermore, that Saussure's basic assertions should perhaps even be inverted, treating semiotics as a subset of linguistics. See his foreword, pp. ix–xii.

32. The epitome of such associative fashion writing in the United States was the J. Peterman mail-order catalogue, where dress styles were linked with such diverse images as Elvira Madigan, Florence Nightingale, or the Orient Express, and a man could become an estate owner tramping over his domain, a Sherlock Holmes, or a Jack London, depending on his choice of trench coat.

33. Thorstein Veblen, *The Theory of the Leisure Class* (1899; Boston, 1973); Hollander, *Seeing through Clothes;* and Alison Lurie, *The Language of Clothes* (New York, 1981).

34. "Dichono che vivono dí per dí chome gli ucielli." Maria Serena Mazzi and Sergio Raveggi, *Gli uomini e le cose nelle campagne fiorentine del quattrocento* (Florence, 1983), p. 365.

35. Florentines made tentative motions toward democratic government in the last decades of the thirteenth century, then turned away from corporatism to develop a more traditional European model of government with increasing oligarchic control. See John M. Najemy, *Corporatism and Consensus in Florentine Electoral Politics, 1280–1400* (Chapel Hill, N.C., 1982), pp. 17–42.

CHAPTER I. TAILORS AND THE GUILD SYSTEM

1. The phrase "gente che nacque ieri" appears in Cohn, *Laboring Classes of Renaissance Florence*, p. 69. Villani characterized the guild community as "uomini grandi di buona fama e opere, e che fossono artefici o mercatanti." See Giovanni Villani, *Cronica* (Florence, 1832), ch. 7, 79.

2. For the population of the guild community at the beginning of the fourteenth century, see John M. Najemy, "Guild Republicanism in Trecento Florence: The Successes and Ultimate Failure of Corporate Politics," *American Historical Review* 84, no. 1 (Feb. 1979): 59.

3. On the contraction of opportunities for artisans in the Arte della lana after the 1378 Revolt of the Ciompi, see Franco Franceschi, *Oltre il "Tumulto": I lavoratori fiorentini dell'Arte della lana fra Tre e Quattrocento* (Florence, 1993), p. 49.

4. Robert Davidsohn, *Forschungen zur Alteren Geschichte von Florenz* (Berlin, 1896), p. 432.

5. Scipione Ammirato noted that as early as 1204, a peace document signed between the Florentines and the Sienese contained the signatures of the consuls of the Arte della lana. See Giovanni Pagnini, ed., *Della decima e di varie altre gravezze imposte dal comune di Firenze*, vol. 2 (Lucca, 1766; reprint, Bologna, 1967), pt. 2, p. 83.

6. One indication that Florentine fabric was esteemed within Italy by 1261 was the fact that after the battle of Montaperti, the victorious Sienese appeared in the Florentine marketplace to buy locally produced cloth to clothe the very ambassadors dispatched to the defeated city on the Arno. Robert Davidsohn, *Storia di Firenze* (Florence, 1956), vol. 4, pt. 2, p. 885.

7. Florence Edler de Roover lists various levels of tailors in her glossary, ranging from a seamster or small master artisan (*cucitore* or *costore*) to a master tailor (*maestro sarto* or the Latinate *sartore*). Florence Edler de Roover, *Glossary of Mediaeval Terms of Business, Italian Series, 1200–1600* (Cambridge, Mass., 1934), pp. 93, 96, 258.

8. See Stella, *Révolte des Ciompi*, p. 293, app. 2.

9. See Alfred Doren's *Le arti fiorentine*, 2 vols. (Florence, 1940), based largely upon the guild statute books. See also Gaetano Salvemini, *Magnati e popolani in Firenze dal 1280 al 1295* (Florence, 1960).

10. The six locations of the stretching grounds (*tiratoi*), were the d'Orbetello, on Via degli Alfani; the Lungarno, near the Palazzo della Borsa; dell'Aquila, in Via dei Servi; del Cavallo at San Pier Gattolino; della Pergola, in Via della Pergola, and dell'Uccello, location now unknown, as it was destroyed early on by fire. See Guido Carocci, *Il mercato vecchio di Firenze* (Florence, 1884), pp. 136–38.

11. Benedetto Dei, *La cronica dall'anno 1400 all'anno 1500,* ed. Roberto Barducci (Florence, 1984), p. 82: "fra 'n via Maggio e 'n Sa' Martino e nella Vignia e nella via del Palagio e fra 'Pillicciai e a San Brocholo e 'n Porta Rossa e a l' artte degli Speziali e fra 'Feravecchi e nel Fondaccio e a San Filicie in Piazza e 'n Borgho Sa' Iachopo."

12. Carocci, *Mercato vecchio*, p. 49; Demetrio Guccerelli, *Stradario storico biografico della Città di Firenze* (Florence, 1929; reprint, Rome, 1985), p. 350.

13. Edgcumbe Staley, *The Guilds of Florence,* 2d ed. (London, 1906), p. 316; Guccerelli, *Stradario*, pp. 49–50.

14. Guccerelli, *Stradario*, pp. 88–89.

15. Carocci, *Mercato vecchio*, p. 151; Guccerelli, *Stradario*, p. 376.

16. Guccerelli, *Stradario*, pp. 78–79.

17. Carocci, *Mercato vecchio*, pp. 143–46. Originally a medieval loggia built of wood, Orsanmichele became the center of guild life in the fourteenth century as a combination shrine, wheat exchange, and granary when it was rebuilt in stone after a fire destroyed it in 1336. The walls of the new loggia were filled in in the 1350s to create the shrine, and guilds and other civic groups in Florence involved in its economy commissioned statues of saints to stand in the newly created niches between the arches on the outside walls. See Frederick Hartt, *History of Italian Renaissance Art,* 3d ed. (New York, 1987), pp. 15–16, 85, 163–70, 320–21; also Goldthwaite, *Building of Renaissance Florence*, pp. 6–7.

18. Carocci, *Mercato vecchio*, p. 31; Guccerelli, *Stradario*, pp. 71–72. See also Davidsohn, *Storia di Firenze*, bk. 4, pt. 2, p. 327.

19. David Herlihy and Christiane Klapisch-Zuber, "Census and Property Survey of Florentine Domains in the Province of Tuscany, 1427–1480," machine-readable data file (Madison: University of Wisconsin, Data and Program Library Service, 1981). Many thanks to Rebecca Emigh for her invaluable assistance with this data base.

20. Doretta Davanzo Poli, "La moda nel *Libro del sarto,*" in *Il libro del sarto* (Ferrara, 1987), p. 57.

21. Étienne Boileau, *Le livre des métiers d'Étienne Boileau,* ed. René de Lespinasse and François Bonnardot as *Les métiers et corporations de la Ville de Paris, XIIIe siècle* (Paris, 1879), pp. 116–17.

22. Enrico Fiumi, "Fioritura e decadenza dell' economia fiorentina," *Archivio storico italiano* 117 (1959): 487–88, n. 274.

23. Davidsohn, *Storia di Firenze*, bk. 4, pt. 2, pp. 97–98.

24. Doren, *Arti fiorentine*, 1:117.

25. The first matriculation lists for the silk guild in Florence do not appear until 1225, some fifty years after the industry was first introduced into Sicily, but it is clear from the 1335 statutes of Por Santa Maria that up until the mid fourteenth century, the silk guild remained actually a federation of diverse "corporazioni," consisting mostly of retailers of foreign-made silk clothing and accessories, and not of locally produced silks. The Arte della seta constituted a "membro" of the Por Santa Maria. See Umberto Dorini, *L'Arte della seta in Toscana* (Florence, 1928), pp. 5–12.

26. ASF, Matricole dell' Arte di Por Santa Maria, dal 1225 al 1532 (unpaginated). Tailors are listed along with other matriculees by *convento*: Bonamicus Sarto f. Uberti, Rusticus Sartor f. Boninsegne, Ugolinus Sartor f. Doni (all from Ultrarno and Burgo S. Jacobi); Azzo f. Bonacti Sartor and Gianni f. Benincasa Sartor (both from S. Cecilia); Bernerus Sartor f. Ildebrandini, from S. Remedio; and Sinibaldus f. Gianni Sartor, from Kalimala.

27. However, there are two doublet makers in the matriculation lists who make a point of listing themselves as working in *garbo*, that is, in foreign woolen cloth (but not in fine

English fleece). *Garbo* probably referred instead to Spanish wool. ASF, Matricole dell' Arte della seta, bk. 2 (unpaginated).

28. Ibid.

29. Doren, *Arti fiorentine,* 1:199. In the Trecento, fees could range anywhere from many florins *d'oro* down to a few lire.

30. Ibid., 199–200. Local service providers such as tailors, bakers, and grocers were only rarely able to make their livings entirely from their trade, the anthropologist John Davis observes. Rather, they engaged in ancillary pursuits as well, such as agriculture. In Sicily, this fragmentation of income is called *combinazioni.* See Davis, *People of the Mediterranean* (London, 1977), p. 55.

31. Polidori-Calamandrei, *Vesti delle donne fiorentine nel Quattrocento,* p. 113.

32. See Edler de Roover, *Glossary,* pp. 96, 258. For gender studies on women in the needle trades in late medieval and early modern Europe, see Merry E. Wiesner, *Working Women in Renaissance Germany* (New Brunswick, N.J., 1986), and "Spinsters and Seamstresses," in *Rewriting the Renaissance,* ed. Margaret Ferguson, Maureen Quilligan, and Nancy Vickers (Chicago, 1986); Martha C. Howell, *Women, Production, and Patriarchy in Late Medieval Cities* (Chicago, 1986); Barbara A. Hanawalt, ed., *Women and Work in Preindustrial Europe* (Bloomington, Ind., 1986); David Herlihy, *Opera muliebria: Women and Work in Medieval Europe* (Philadelphia, 1990); Angela Groppi, ed., *Il lavoro della donne* (Rome, 1996); Pamela Sharpe, ed., *Women's Work: The English Experience, 1650–1914* (London, 1998).

33. Stella, *Révolte des Ciompi,* p. 293.

34. Herlihy and Klapisch-Zuber, "Census and Property Survey."

35. On the marginalization of women within the guild structure, see Roberto Greci, "Donne e corporazioni: La fluidità di un rapporto," in *Il lavoro delle donne,* ed. Angela Groppi (Rome, 1996), pp. 88–91.

36. Istituto degli Innocenti Archive, MS XII, no. 4, fol. 64R. Ricordanze A dello Spedale di Santa Maria degli Innocenti, 1448–1463. I thank my friend Dr. Gino Corti of Florence for this citation.

37. Stella, *Révolte des Ciompi,* p. 293.

38. Goldthwaite, *Building of Renaissance Florence,* p. 43. The Commune began encouraging the planting of mulberry trees to feed silk worms, but Florence would not produce substantial amounts home-grown silk until the sixteenth century. See Luca Molà, *The Silk Industry of Renaissance Venice* (Baltimore, 2000), on the Venetian silk guild.

39. Davidsohn, *Storia di Firenze,* bk. 4, pt. 2, p. 98. Tailors, as sottoposti, paid a deposit of 25 lire to matriculate in this membrum, similar to the goldsmiths. ASF, Arte della Seta, 1, rubric 99, 1334. In 1336, however, this decision was canceled, which took the tailors out of this associate category and demoted them to the status of salaried workers. Rubric 101 said that they must work in general for all silk shops. In 1338, the statutes were again amended to dictate that if tailors or shearers refused any work from guild members, the

consuls of the guild could open those artisans' shops to supply the needs of the guild. ASF, Arte della seta, 1, c. 63, rubric, 99, con approvazione del 1355 e degli anni sequenti, Gli statutari del 1338. See Rodolico, *Popolo minuto,* doc. no. 3, p. 87.

40. Doren, *Arti fiorentine,* 1:198. As an example of the limited rights enjoyed by these *membri minori,* the tailors, dyers, and shearers were all prohibited from having apprentices, which entitled a man to be considered a true master, and therefore a "vero artifice" in the guild. ASF, Arte della seta, 1, statuto [con approvazione degli statutari del 1335 e degli anni seguenti], rubric 128. See Rodolico, *Popolo minuto,* p. 15.

41. Pagnini, *Della decima,* 2:63. There was a third lower stratum of workers (*lavoranti*) associated with the guild as production of silk increased in the Quattrocento, that is, those who sorted cocoons, unwound the silk into skeins, wound it onto reels, twisted it into thread, or sprayed, steamed, or stretched the silk. These sottoposti, predominantly women, did not own their tools or materials, and were subject to strict guild supervision and even threats of corporeal punishment if the work was not properly done. See Raymond de Roover, "Labor Conditions in Florence around 1400: Theory, Policy and Reality," in *Florentine Studies,* ed. Nicolai Rubinstein (Evanston, Ill., 1968), p. 293. There was a similar, multitiered membership system in the Arte della lana, with the owners of wool-producing firms and wool merchants in the first tier and weavers, finishers, dyers, and all the attendant sottoposti in the second and third tiers of membership or association with the guild (ibid.). See also Edler de Roover, *Glossary,* pp. 324–30, for the twenty or more discrete operations involved in the making and packing of woolen cloth.

Different historians have linked tailors to an association with the Arte della lana at this early period. Polidori-Calamandrei, *Vesti delle donne fiorentine nel Quattrocento,* p. 114, cites Rodolico, *Popolo minuto,* p. 14, in grouping the tailors with dyers and shearers in the wool guild. However, a close reading of Rodolico's documents on regulations concerning tailors places them in the Por Santa Maria, not the Arte della lana. See ASF, Arte della seta, 1, c. 63, rubr. 99, cited in Rodolico, *Popolo minuto,* app., p. 87. Brucker, "Ciompi Revolution," and Cohn, *Laboring Classes of Renaissance Florence,* have also placed the tailors among the sottoposti of the Arte della lana. However, along with Rodolico, Doren, *Arti fiorentine,* 1:89, n. 1, and Davidsohn, *Storia di Firenze,* bk. 4, pt. 2, p. 98, n. 1, both note tailors' early connection with the Por Santa Maria and other minor corporazioni instead. Doren gives the occupations listed in the "liber matricularius membrorum suppositorum" of the Arte della lana in 1361. This lists "tintores, affettatores, conciatores, tiratores, manganatores, sensales, cappellarii, gualcherarii, mensuratores, rimendatores" and "tutti i lavoratori più qualificati," with the exception of the "cappellai," who were always associated with the guild, but remained separate. No tailors are listed here. See Doren, *Arti fiorentine,* 1:198, n. 2.

42. Alessandro Stella, " 'La bottega e i lavoranti': Approche des conditions de travail des Ciompi," *Annales: Economies, sociétés, civilisations* 44 (1989): 529–51; see, e.g., table 1 on p. 532 for a sottoposti pay scale.

43. Florence Edler de Roover, "Andrea Banchi, Florentine Silk Manufacturer and Merchant in the Fifteenth Century," in *Studies in Medieval and Renaissance History*, vol. 3, ed. William M. Bowsky (Lincoln, 1966), p. 262. The papacy and the princely courts, not "republican" Florence itself, were the largest markets for luxury fabrics. In 1470, by which time Florentine silk was famous even in northern Europe, and Florence supplied Turkish harems with cloth, Dei counted only eighty-three silk shops in the city, as opposed to 270 wool shops. Dei, *Cronica*, p. 82.

44. Doren, *Arti fiorentine*, 1:60–61, 231. In 1293 and 1295, the Ordinances of Justice organized the new government of Florence on the basis of twenty-one explicitly named guilds. But in what was to be the most far-reaching and important decision for the freedom of the artisan community of Florence, each smaller "societas" or "corporazione" was now gradually subordinated to one of these twenty-one recognized guilds. Doren, *Arti fiorentine*, 1:63–64. See also Najemy, *Corporatism and Consensus*, pp. 22–23, 43–59.

45. Davidsohn, *Storia di Firenze*, bk. 4, pt. 2, p. 328. Luca Landucci, *A Florentine Diary from 1450 to 1516*, ed. Iodoco del Badia (London, 1927), pp. 20, 91, 93, notes two major auctions held in Florence at Orsanmichele in the Quattrocento. The Pazzi family clothes and household effects were auctioned beginning on June 1, 1478. Some seventeen years later, in 1495, Piero de' Medici's clothing and household effects (which Landucci lists as including velvet bedspreads embroidered in gold), were auctioned, beginning on July 9, and the sale was still in progress some four months later, on November 14.

46. Lorenzo Cantini, ed., *Legislazione toscane* (Florence, 1772), 10:66 ("calze, calzini e calzoni e berrette e cappelli"). There would still always remain independent contractors in the Florentine marketplace, working informally outside the guild system, and representing a significant percentage of the total workforce.

47. Evidently, in 1295, the guild of the Rigattieri did not yet have jurisdiction over the tailors, for when a tailor had an altercation with a matriculated guild member, he was referred to the guild consuls for resolution of the dispute not as a guild member, but simply as an individual. Doren, *Arti fiorentine*, 1:200, no. 2. A quick perusal of the records of the Merchants Court (Mercanzia), yields scant evidence of tailors' appeals even in the fifteenth century. ASF, Mercanzia, Reg. 287, fol. 26v, 151v, 152r, 170r.

48. *Statuti dell'Arte dei rigattieri e linaioli di Firenze (1296–1340)*, ed. Ferdinando Sartini (Florence, 1940–48), p. 183.

49. Ibid., p. 29. The fine was 20 soldi.

50. ASF, Rig. et Lin. V, 1367, f. 60.

51. Ibid., f. 60.

52. Ibid., f. 55. Furthermore, in 1350, male and female tailors "who plainly and publicly" practiced their craft had to pay a fee, which increased in 1367, in 1372, and in 1374, etc. (ibid., 1350, f. 34). The socioeconomic position of used-clothing, linens and remnant merchants in Florence rose in the Quattrocento to the extent that among Benedetto Dei's "magiori ricchi di Firenze dell' anno 1472," is a rigattiere whom he lists

as "tTomaso [*sic*] righatiere." This used-clothing dealer appears in about 100th place on a list of around 140 rich men led by Lorenzo de' Medici and ending with Guido Bonciani. Dei, *Cronica,* p. 85.

53. ASF, Rig. et Lin. V, 1372, f. 60; 1376, f. 65.

54. See Stella, *Révolte des Ciompi,* app. 2, pp. 284−88, 293. Those workers who described themselves on their *Estimi* (tax declarations) as shoemakers' helpers ("ista a calzolaio") increased from 0 to 25, as fabric shoemakers' helpers ("lavorante di scarpette") from 2 to 80, as furriers' helpers ("ista a pellicciaio" and "lavorante di pellicciaio") from 1 to about 15, as goldsmiths' helpers ("ista a orafo") from 0 to 23, and as doublet makers' helpers ("lavorante di farsetti") from 3 to 21. To a lesser degree, we can see the same trend for velveteers (*velluti*) and used-clothing dealers as well.

55. On the structure of work in late Trecento Florence, see Victor Rutenburg, *Popolo e movimenti popolari nell' Italia del "300 e "400* (Bologna, 1971), who uses a Marxist model to understand workers' loss of their means of production and increasing proletarianization. Conversely, Federigo Melis, *Aspetti della vita economica medievale* (Siena, 1962), identifies independent artisans in small botteghe as the basic unit of work. Tailors bridge the two models, some working as sottoposti of the arti maggiori, a few as independent master tailors, and still others as lowly lavoranti.

56. The guild statutes for the Por Santa Maria are explicit in their control of tailors in the display and selling of garments. See Statuto 1335, rubric C-CI, in *Statuti dell' Arte di Por Santa Maria del tempo della repubblica,* ed. Umberto Dorini (Florence, 1934−42), pp. 124−26.

57. Cohn, *Laboring Classes of Renaissance Florence,* pp. 71, 66 n. 3. These dowries ranged from 125 to 200 florins. And see also ibid., p. 93 (one notary, one goldsmith).

58. See Chapter 9 for the enforcement of sumptuary laws concerning dress in Florence.

59. Sumptuary laws were passed in 1281, 1290, and 1299. Other laws were added in 1301, 1307, 1318, 1322−25, 1324, 1326, and 1330. Revisions were made continuously throughout the Trecento, and at least thirty-four times in the Quattrocento (beginning in 1402), with a large statute compilation done in 1415. See Ronald Rainey, "Sumptuary Legislation in Renaissance Florence" (Ph.D. diss., Columbia University, 1985), 2, app. 1:648−55.

60. Doren, *Arti fiorentine,* 1:200.

61. Fiumi, "Fioritura e decadenza," p. 471.

62. De Roover, "Labor Conditions," p. 311, writes that he does not understand this demand, but perhaps the surveillance of the Grascia over the sottoposti of the cloth industry was a constant annoyance, or even harassment, of which they were eager to rid themselves.

63. See ASF, Statuto del Podestà, bk. 5, 1325, rubric 41, p. 391, cited in Davidsohn, *Storia di Firenze,* bk. 4, pt. 2, p. 99.

64. Marvin Becker, "Legislazione antimonopolistica fiorentina," *Archivio storico italiano*

117 (1959): 16–18. The occupations under these stringent controls were the tailors, stocking makers (*calzettai*), hosiers (*magliai*), wool finishers (*conciatori*), venders of cloth, rope and grain (*venditori di stoffe, di corde e di grano*), innkeepers and tavern-keepers (*trattori e bettolieri*), and butchers and bakers (*macellari e fornai*).

65. ASF, Statuti, 14, c.10, 25, 29, Statuti del Capitano del Popolo del 1355.

66. ASF, Statuti, 10, c. 15, Statuti del capitano del popolo del 1355, "Quibus sint subdite persone VII maiorum artium et aliis infrascriptis—Rubrica," in Rodolico, *Popolo minuto*, pp. 112–13, doc. no. 24. However, as Rodolico notes, as soon as the minor guilds gained access to the highest communal offices, the rigid statutes on price ceilings fell (ibid., pp. 52–53). In 1415, the Commune moved again to set prices in its revisions of the *Statuta populi et communis florentiae*, with tailors further restricted.

67. Franceschi, *Oltre il "Tumulto,"* pp. 48–49.

68. De Roover, "Labor Conditions," p. 291.

69. Najemy, "Guild Republicanism," p. 66.

70. The identification of those included in the Ciompi has been drawn differently by various sources. Certainly, they were among the sottoposti, whom Cohn, *Laboring Classes of Renaissance Florence*, p. 70, attempts to define as those either in the lowest orders of various guilds or outside of the guild structure altogether. The anonymous opinion of a contemporary chronicler (*Cronaca seconda d' Anonimo*, ed. Gino Scaramella, in *Rerum italicarum scriptores*, vol. 18, pt. 3, p. 121), who voiced the hostility to and fear of "these carders and combers and washers, these men who were born yesterday" was typical among guildsmen of the arti minori. For a detailed look at these workers, see Franceschi, *Oltre il "Tumulto,"* pp. 47–66; for details of their standard of living, ibid., pp. 332–34.

71. Brucker, "Ciompi Revolution," p. 336.

72. Ibid., p. 346, cites the anonymous diarist referred to in n. 70 above, as reporting that the Ciompi not only took salaries but also had "dinners at communal expense."

73. Ibid., pp. 315–31. See also de Roover, "Labor Conditions," pp. 308–9. Much has been written on this revolt of the sottoposti within the textile industry. It has been seen by Marxist historians as a "workers' revolution" and by others as a Ghibelline backlash. See Rutenburg, *Popolo e movimenti popolari*, p. 5 ff.; also, Salvemini, *Magnati e popolani*, pp. 290–91.

74. Doren, *Arti fiorentine*, 1:215–16.

75. Rodolico, *Ciompi*, p. 143, follows the eyewitness to the events, one "lo Squittinatore," in calling the Ciompi guild the 22d guild, with the Farsettai following as the 23d, and the Tintori as the 24th. See also de Roover, "Labor Conditions," p. 308, and Trexler, "Neighbours and Comrades," p. 77, who follow suit. Doren, on the other hand, refers to the Archivio della repubblica (ASF, Reg. delle Provvisioni, no. 67, c. 24 ff.), which lists the Arte dei Farsettai first, and then the Tintori.

76. *Il Tumulto dei Ciompi: cronache e memorie*, ed. Gino Scaramella (Bologna, 1934), p. 77; Najemy, "Guild Republicanism," p. 66.

77. De Roover, "Labor Conditions," p. 308; Trexler, "Neighbours and Comrades," p. 66.

78. Doren, *Arti fiorentine,* 1:215–16. Polidori-Calamandrei also includes cloth weavers and embroiderers in this guild. See Polidori-Calamandrei, *Vesti delle donne fiorentine nel Quattrocento,* p. 114.

79. Rodolico, *Ciompi,* p. 143. The twenty-third guild, the Arte dei tintori, on the other hand, was at least twice as big, with twelve consuls from six *membri,* hierarchically arranged. This arte was made up entirely of artisans who worked directly within the cloth-making industry, led by the dyers, who held four of the consular positions, followed by the wool nappers and soap makers (*cardatori e saponai*) with three, the teasels dealers and wool combers (*cardaiuoli e pettinatori*) with two, and one each for the wool stretchers and menders (*tiratori e rimendatori*), weavers (*tessitori di drappi*), and washers (*lavandai di sudicio*).

80. Trexler, "Neighbours and Comrades," p. 99, n. 45.

81. Doren, *Arti fiorentine,* 1:215–16.

82. Carocci, *Mercato vecchio,* p. 36; see also Giulio Gandi, *Le corporazioni dell'antica Firenze* (Florence, 1928), p. 229.

83. Doren, *Arti fiorentine,* 1:204 (1504 Lin. 8 f. 37 ff.).

84. *Statuta populi et communis florentiae 1415* (Freiburg, 1776–78), pp. 218–23.

85. *Statuta populi et communis,* p. 219.

86. Davidsohn, *Storia di Firenze,* bk. 4, pt. 2, pp. 98–99.

87. Gene Brucker, *Giovanni and Lusanna* (Berkeley, Calif., 1986), p. 101, and *The Society of Renaissance Florence* (New York, 1971), p. 11.

88. *Archivio storico del banco di Napoli,* Banco dello Spirito Santo, "Un sarto napoletano," polizza di pagamento, m. 305, Dec. 15, 1640, p. 524 ("due vestiti di sabbi ondato d'oro, guarnito di pizzilli"). There had been an Italian business presence in Poland since the mid fourteenth century, buying red dyes, furs, and salt and supplying luxury textiles. See A. Sapori, "Gl'italiani in Polonia nel medioevo," *Archivio storico italiano* 83 (1925): 136–42.

89. Alessandra Macinghi negli Strozzi, *Lettere di una gentildonna fiorentina del secolo XV ai figliuoli esuli,* ed. Cesare Guasti (Florence, 1877), pp. 59–60. See her discussion of such finery in her fourth letter.

CHAPTER 2. THE CRAFTSPEOPLE

1. ASF, Matricole del' Arte di Por Santa Maria.

2. Davidsohn, *Storia di Firenze,* bk. 4, pt. 2, p. 104. See also Stella, *Révolte des Ciompi,* app. 3, pp. 297–316, for a glossary of some 875 idiosyncratic occupation descriptions given by the citizens themselves on their tax declarations. These range from *abbrucia porci* (pigskin tanner) to *zoccolaio* (clog maker).

3. See also Guccerelli, *Stradario storico,* pp. 78–79.

4. Carocci, *Il Mercato vecchio,* pp. 31–59.

5. See Herlihy and Klapisch-Zuber, "Census and Property Survey"; Franceschi, *Oltre il "Tumulto,"* p. 143, table 20. The highest concentration for these sottoposti was in Santo Spirito, Drago Verde, and San Giovanni, Chiavi; two of the gonfaloni on the periphery of the city.

6. Herlihy and Klapisch-Zuber, "Census and Property Survey." Only 43½ percent of the families who submitted *portate* listed an occupation. This leaves historians with demographic estimates based on less than half of all urban heads of households, leading us to conclude that the clothier sector of the Florentine marketplace was probably even larger than this. David Herlihy and Christiane Klapisch-Zuber, *Tuscans and Their Families* (New Haven, Conn., 1985), p. 124.

7. Herlihy and Klapisch-Zuber, "Census and Property Survey."

8. For example, Davidsohn, in his *Storia di Firenze,* bk. 4, pt. 2, pp. 85–86, discusses the female venders (*venditrice*) of herbal medicine, especially sought after to lessen the effects of the plague. A large number of religious communities had been established around 1350 in Florence, and by 1540, there were over forty convents for women in the city. See Richard A. Trexler, "Le célibat à la fin du Moyen Age: Les religieuses de Florence," *Annales: Economies, sociétés, civilisations* 27 (1972): 1329–50.

9. Cantini, ed., *Legislazione toscana,* 3:343. The Medici, speziali e merciai (doctors, druggists, and mercers) guild had incorporated the older Arte dei merciai, velettai, profumieri e cartai (mercers, veil makers, perfumers, and stationers) *societas* in the early fourteenth century, making for an eclectic mix under the rubric of this major guild. Many professional artists were also grouped into this guild. Andrea del Sarto matriculated on December 12, 1508, as "Andreas Angioli francisci Luce pintor alla piazza de Grano," with a fee of 6 florins. ASF, *Arte dei Medici e Speziali,* no. 10, c. 93V.

10. Davidsohn, *Storia di Firenze,* bk. 4, pt. 2, pp. 104–5.

11. Giovanni da Uzzano, *La pratica della mercatura,* vol. 4 (1442), pp. 1–8, under "Gabelle di Firenze," in Pagnini, *Della decima,* vol. 2.

12. Pagnini, *Della decima,* vol. 2. *Filugello* was the inferior grade of short thread spun, rather than thrown, from broken silk cocoons and cocoons' outer layers. See Edler de Roover, "Andrea Banchi," p. 239. *Chatarzo* was floss silk, the untwisted silk traditionally used for embroidery. *Stame* referred to long combed wool, as opposed to carded wool (*lana*) and the worsted yarn spun from it, which was also used for the warp threads in almost all woolen cloth, and in addition, for the woof threads in worsted wool. Lana was used for the weft. See Edler de Roover, *Glossary,* pp. 280–81.

13. Najemy spells out the problems of the disparate membership of this composite guild in " 'Audiant Omnes Artes.' "

14. Uzzano, *Pratica della mercatura,* pp. 10–15, in Pagnini, *Della decima,* vol. 2.

15. Miliadusso Baldiccione of Pisa bought "magliette 250 gialle, per la roba e cottardita" from "Piero armaiolo." See "Ricordi di cose familiari di Miliadusso Baldiccione de' Casalberti Pisano (1339–1382)," ed. Francesco Bonaini and Filippo-Luigi Polidori *Archi-*

vio storico italiano 8, app. (1850): 34. Many thanks to Christiane Klapisch-Zuber for pointing out this source.

16. "Era forte innamorato d'una bella giovane, che teneva cuffie, balzi, cordelle, gorgiere, et altri ornamenti da donna da vendere." Matteo Bandello, Le *novelle,* IX, pt. 1 (Florence, 1930), p. 169.

17. Bonaini, "Ricordi di Miliadusso," pp. 34–35, 37: "uno velo grande e uno cigulino bambacigni . . . e uno paio di coppiole bambacigni . . . e una benda migliore per Tedda, e uno orale con la frontiera."

18. Sartini, *Arte dei rigattieri,* p. 170.

19. Doren, *Arti fiorentine,* 1:203, no. 3 (Rig. and Lin. V, f 51).

20. Judith Brown, "A Woman's Place Was in the Home: Women's Work in Renaissance Tuscany," in *Rewriting the Renaissance,* ed. Ferguson, Quilligan, and Vickers, p. 216.

21. See Chapter 9 on sumptuary legislation directed primarily at women's clothes, for example.

22. Christiane Klapisch-Zuber, "Un salario o l'onore: Come valutare le donne fiorentine del XIV–XV secolo," *Quaderni storici* 79, no. 1 (April 1992): 42: "quella gentile tessitore e bettinaglola gretta pidocchiosa rigattiera rubatore di suo primo marito"; "ongne di . . . per tutta Firenze rischotendo i denari di suoi pettini."

23. Personal linens were the *panni lini* or *biancheria.* The most basic piece in the Renaissance was the *camicia,* a blouse of washable fabric worn under every garment.

24. ASF, MAP, CXXXII, fol. 5V. Carlo Cipolla, *Money in Sixteenth-Century Florence* (Berkeley, Calif., 1989), p. 13, writes that "at the end of the fifteenth century, even in Florence, the florin, though unchanged in weight, fineness, or design, was often referred to as a ducato." For currency and measurements, see Appendix 1.

25. ASF, MAP, CXXXII, fols. IV–6R, 17R–21R, detail Lorenzo's wardrobe purchases for the year 1515, including his masks and costumes for "maschere."

26. Herlihy and Klapisch, *Tuscans and Their Families,* pp. 282, 291. A *frérèche* was a joint family household composed of married brothers and their dependents.

27. The letter, dated June 5, 1395, expresses exasperation with her husband Francesco concerning some linen cloth, the provenance of which she gives in detail. See "Le lettere di Margherita Datini," ed. Valeria Rosati *Archivio storico pratese* 52 (1976): 62–64.

28. Strozzi, *Lettere,* Lettera Ottava, Dec. 6, 1450: "In prima, ti mando . . . quattro camice, sei fazzoletti da mano. . . . Le camice tagliate e cucite a modo nostro. . . . Non ho fatte più camice, chè no so se queste ti piaceranno."

29. Strozzi, *Lettere,* p. 100: "vi fornirò si di pannilini la casa, che starete bene. . . . sicché quando ne sarà fuori, non arò attendere ad altro che a fare per tutti a tre voi . . . mi sarò fornita un poco meglio a masserizia."

30. ASF, MAP, LXXX, fol. 67. This letter is dated June 2, 1479.

31. "Lettere di Margherita Datini a Francesco di Marco," ed. Rosati, pp. 27–28.

32. Ibid., pp. 46–48, from a letter dated Oct. 30, 1394: "noi non abiamo auto l'agho da chucire."

33. Ibid., 49–50, letter dated Jan. 21, 1395.

34. See Anthony Molho, " 'Tamquam vere mortua': Le professioni religiose femminili nella Firenze del tardo medioevo," *Società e storia* 43 (Jan.–Mar. 1989): 13–21.

35. Trexler discusses the contribution of prayer by the some 13 percent of all young women of an elevated social standing who were cloistered in the late Quattrocento. See Trexler, "Célibate," pp. 1341–49.

36. Estimates for the extended period from 1368 to 1552 are that some 75 percent of the girls in Florentine convents were from the highest ranks of Florentine society. Ibid., p. 1339.

37. Maria Elena Vasaio, "Il tessuto della virtù: Le zitelle di S. Eufemia e di S. Caterina dei Funari nella Controriforma," *Memoria* 11–12 (nos. 2–3, 1984): 55–56, 59, 63.

38. Vasaio, "Tessuto della virtù," p. 56: "tela grossa di lino tinta del medesimo colore da tessersi parimente in casa."

39. Ibid., p. 63.

40. Herlihy, *Opera muliebria*, p. 64.

41. In the logbook of Miliadusso, he records purchasing thread from a nun at Saint Sylvester ("a una monaca di Santo Salvestro, per boctoni cento di refe"). Bonaini, "Ricordi di Miliadusso," p. 34.

42. Vasaio, "Tessuto della virtù," pp. 59–61.

43. Ibid., pp. 57–59. A scudo was roughly equivalent to the Florentine penny, the soldo, with 20 soldi to the lira. The white gown was to denote *il vestito intrinseco* of the young woman, that is, an interior and external state of *pulizia*, or cleanliness. This is a sixteenth-century example from Rome, which may explain the insistence on white for formerly cloistered girls as a self-conscious reforming feature of the Catholic Reformation.

44. Ibid., p. 59.

45. "Lettere di Margherita Datini a Francesco di Marco," ed. Rosati, pp. 62–63.

46. There were also male practitioners of these crafts who would have most likely specialized in the male customer base for these accessories.

47. Herlihy, *Opera muliebria*, pp. 163–64.

48. Herlihy and Klapisch, "Census and Property Survey." Beside the purse makers, Santa Croce, which had only one-tenth of the city's clothiers, had almost 40 percent of the trimmers (*guarnai*) and 25 percent of the slipper makers.

49. Davidsohn, *Storia di Firenze*, bk. 4, pt. 2, p. 101.

50. Hidetoshi Hoshino, *L'Arte della lana in Firenze nel basso medioevo* (Florence, 1980), p. 133, says that some Florentine products, e.g., *perpignani,* began as imitations of foreign cloth. As early as 1418, Florence initiated a recall of weavers specializing in perpigniano, but in 1458, the Commune was still importing it. In 1470, Florence began producing per-pignan cloth locally, and by 1472, the Commune had prohibited the importation of this cloth. Production then increased. Local weavers produced 800 pieces in 1473; 1,500 pieces in 1474, and a total of 2,000 pieces in 1475. See Hoshino, "Per la storia della lana in

Firenze nel Trecento e nel Quattrocento: Un riesame," *Annuario: Istituto giapponese di cultura* (Rome) 10 (1972–73): 72.

51. ASF, Conv. soppr., N. 97, filza 13, fol. 6R; Carte strozz., 2d ser., 17 bis, fols. 55V, 59V.

52. *Delizie degli eruditi toscani*, ed. Ildefonso di San Luigi, 8:198. Listed under the year MCCXXV are: Benintendi Cintolarius f. Drudoli, Arrigus Cintolarius f .Vernacci, and Ugolinus f. Burnecti Cintolarius.

53. Staley, *Guilds of Florence*, p. 68.

54. Mazzi and Raveggi, *Gli uomini e le cose*, pp. 230–31.

55. Polidori-Calamandrei, *Vesti delle donne fiorentine nel Quattrocento*, p. 86.

56. ASF, Carte strozz., 2d ser., 17 bis, fol. 7R.

57. Polidori-Calamandrei, *Vesti delle donne fiorentine nel Quattrocento*, p. 91.

58. Davidsohn, *Storia di Firenze*, bk. 4, pt. 2, pp. 103–4.

59. Santini, "Studi sull' antica costituzione del comune di Firenze," *Archivio storico italiano*, 5th ser., 25–26 (1900): 3, 10, 28, 518–19.

60. See Robert Delort, *Le commerce des fourrures en occident à la fin du Moyen Age (vers 1300–vers 1450)* (Rome, 1978), for an overview of furs and the European fur trade.

61. Davidsohn, *Storia di Firenze*, bk. 4, pt. 2, pp. 105–7. He also discusses the goat-skin dressers (*cerbolattari*) who dressed these pelts for a more modest clientele in the countryside. Davidsohn says that the *Arte della lana* put economic pressure on this sottoposto craft in 1308, when masters were limited to a maximum of two apprentices, thereby raising the price of the product and essentially putting the cerbolattari, with whom the wool workers were in direct competition, out of business. See ASF, Lana I, Statuto dell' Arte della lana (1317), L. IV.

62. Delort, *Commerce des fourrures*, 1:196.

63. Herlihy and Klapisch-Zuber, "Census and Property Survey."

64. ASF, CAT, Reg. 819, fol. 809R. At about ten florins per lining, this inventory would have represented about twenty-six linings made up and on hand.

65. Ibid., fol. 868R.

66. ASF, Pupilli, Reg. 176, fol. 103.

67. ASF, Carte strozz., 2d ser., 17 bis, fol. 3V.

68. Davidsohn, *Storia di Firenze*, bk. 4, pt. 2, pp. 30–32. ASF, Por Santa Maria, 1, f. 72V, Statuta dell' Arte di Por Santa Maria del 1335: "Capitula artifices tangentia."

69. Herlihy and Klapisch-Zuber, "Census and Property Survey." See also Davidsohn, *Storia di Firenze*, bk. 4, pt. 2, p. 36.

70. Herlihy and Klapisch-Zuber, "Census and Property Survey."

71. Edler de Roover, "Andrea Banchi," pp. 244, 256–57.

72. Davidsohn, *Storia di Firenze*, bk. 4, pt. 2, p. 32.

73. Only one *bambagiaia* is listed in the Catasto of 1427 within the city of Florence. This craft was evidently practiced primarily in the countryside by women from home.

Bambagiai made the cotton wool used in all quilted garments such as doublets, tunics, quilts, processional banners, cushions, and coffin covers. The commerce in these items was carried on by the retailers within the Arte dei Rigattieri. Davidsohn, *Storia di Firenze,* bk. 4, pt. 2, p. 99.

74. Carlo Merkel, "I beni della famiglia di Puccio Pucci," in *Miscellanea nuziale Rossi-Teiss* (Bergamo, 1897), pp. 178, 192. *Farsettini* are also noted in the inventory of children's clothing, and once in a while, in the inventory of a mature woman. Bartolomea, widow of Puccio Pucci, herself owned two farsetti (pp. 186–87).

75. AFS, Matricole dell Arte di Por Santa Maria, dal 1225 al 1532 (unpaginated). The two earliest doublet makers to matriculate, listed by convento are: Mono figuolo Manecti Riedi farsettarius pop S. Cecilia de Conventum Ultraranum and Scottus Ruggerini farsettarius pop S. Pauli.

76. See Chapter 1.

77. Doren, *Arti fiorentine,* 1:219.

78. Herlihy and Klapisch-Zuber, "Census and Property Survey." There were only three doublet makers in all of Santa Croce and eleven in Santa Maria Novella.

79. Doren, *Arti fiorentine,* 1:145, n. 3, 146, nn. 1–4, for the statuta, which varied little from guild to guild. Even these limited rights were curtailed if the woman remarried, or if it was deemed by the guild that she was leading an "immoral life." See Klapisch-Zuber, "Come valutare le donne," pp. 44–47, for the challenge of getting at the participation of the widow of a guild member in maintaining the family business after the death of her husband.

80. Herlihy and Klapisch-Zuber, "Census and Property Survey."

81. ASF, CAT, Reg. 821, fol. 403R.

82. Ibid., Reg. 795, fol. 536R; Reg. 796, fol. 629R; Reg. 821, fols. 128R, 403R, 489R; Reg. 822, fols. 484R, 602R; Reg. 823, fol. 331R.

83. Giorgio Vasari, *The Lives of the Artists* (New York, 1965), p. 230.

84. Herlihy and Klapisch-Zuber, "Census and Property Survey." Unfortunately, although this is an excellent basic index to the occupations of fifteenth-century Florence, the category *ricamatore* has been elided with *rimendatore,* an extremely different type of needlework, so the numbers of embroidery firms in Florence in 1427 can only be very roughly estimated here. A rimendatore was a simple mender, often employed as a wage-laborer for the wool guild.

85. ASF, CAT, Reg. 24, fol. 314.

86. Ibid., Reg. 23, fol. 656.

87. Carnesecchi, "Sontuosa 'cioppa,'" p. 148.

88. ASF, Carte strozz., 2d ser., 17 bis, fols. 17R, 23R, 54R, 55V, 60V.

89. Ibid., fol. 4R, I IV. This is ironic, for as Quentin Bell, *On Human Finery* (London, 1947), p. 31, observes, the merit of the embroidery resides not in the value of the materials, "but in the enormous amount of socially necessary labour time which had been devoted to the making of the product."

90. Davidsohn, *Storia di Firenze,* bk. 4, pt. 2, pp. 101–2. On the struggle for control, see ASF, Lana, 1, Statuto 1317, bk. 3.

91. Doren, *Arti fiorentine,* 1:239.

92. Herlihy and Klapisch-Zuber, "Census and Property Survey." The way in which the occupational categories were inputted also may have contributed to this apparent absence of cappellai and berrettai. Only the first declared occupation was used, and if two brothers living together had entered different occupations, the second occupation would have gone unrecorded. This was the case with Lorenzo di Fede (see p. 53), who did not appear on the occupational tally, his older brother's occupation of barber taking precedence by appearing first on the tax form.

93. Davidsohn, *Storia di Firenze,* bk. 4, pt. 2, p. 104; Herlihy and Klapisch-Zuber, "Census and Property Survey."

94. Slipper makers are separated out as an independent occupation, but only five are recorded as heads of households in 1427.

CHAPTER 3. TAILORS IN FIFTEENTH-CENTURY SOCIETY

1. Goldthwaite, *Building of Renaissance Florence,* pp. 44, 344, 350, notes that the earning power of this "middling" group of artisans (in which he included tailors) "effected a socially downward redistribution of wealth" (p. 44).

2. ASF, CAT, Reg. 790, fols. 385RV–387RV. The Parenti family were moderately wealthy *gente nuova.* Marco's grandfather Giovanni, a merchant and manufacturer of armor (*corazzarius*), had held government office, and Marco's father, Parente, was a member of the Dodici buonuomini (one of the two advisory councils of the nine priors) in 1435 and again in 1448. See Lauro Martines, *The Social World of the Florentine Humanists, 1390–1460* (Princeton, N.J., 1963), p. 346. Marco himself was a silk merchant with humanist interests, who essentially retired from active participation in business some ten years after his marriage. In the Catasto of 1457, he was assessed 9½ florins in tax, which put him just outside the top 3 percent of taxpayers in Florence. See also Mark Phillips, *The Memoir of Marco Parenti* (Princeton, N.J., 1987), p. 30, n. 9.

3. ASF, CAT, Reg. 790, fols. 385RV–87RV. Alessandra Strozzi had been widowed while in exile with her children and husband Matteo at the age of twenty-nine. She returned to Florence and subsequently raised two daughters and three sons, acting as paterfamilias. Her correspondence with her sons, who as Strozzi males were all exiled from the city when they came of age, is collected in Strozzi, *Lettere di una gentildonna fiorentina.* See Ann Morton Crabb, "How Typical Was Alessandra Macinghi Strozzi of Fifteenth-Century Florentine Widows?" in *Upon My Husband's Death,* ed. Louise Mirrer (Ann Arbor, Mich., 1992), pp. 47–52.

4. See Benedetto Dei's listing of Medici faction names in his *Cronica,* p. 66.

5. A staiora was as much land as could be sown with one staio (approximately a bushel) of grain; roughly an acre, which I shall use here.

6. Officials of the Catasto allowed a deduction of 200 florins for each mouth (*bocca*) in the household.

7. See Nicholas A. Eckstein, *The District of the Green Dragon* (Florence, 1995) on the structure of the gonfalone of Drago Verde.

8. Franceschi has located the residences of the sottoposti workers in the wool industry specifically in the two gonfaloni of Chiavi (San Giovanni), and Drago Verde (Santo Spirito). Franceschi, *Oltre il "Tumulto,"* p. 317.

9. Stella, *Révolte des Ciompi,* pp. 263–64.

10. Ibid., p. 213.

11. Primary family residences were left unvalued by the officials of the Catasto, so it is impossible to know the full range of property values represented in this group.

12. ASF, CAT. Antonio d'Agnolo di Martino, worth 100 florins, had about twenty acres (staiora) of land planted with vines (*vignata*) in the popolo of San Martino (Reg. 794, fol. 565R); Filippo di Pagholo, also worth 100 florins, had about five acres of vines in the contado (Reg. 788, fol. 785R); Giuliano di Donato, worth 64 florins, had two pieces of land "due pezi di terre," of about three and twelve acres respectively, and also land in vines at San Miniato (Reg. 819, fol. 409R); and Niccolò di Lucha, worth 54 florins, also had a piece of land in the popolo of San Martino (Reg. 797, fol. 425R).

13. ASF, CAT, Reg. 818, fol. 1063R.

14. See Guidobaldo Guidi, *Il governo della città-repubblica di Firenze del primo Quattrocento,* vol. 2 (Florence, 1981), pp. 323–26, for the establishment of this communal office in 1384. Its role in "protecting the economic interests of children and widows" was enlarged in 1388, and again in 1393. In 1414, the Commune moved to better protect children, passing a law that "no official or minister could sell the goods of children."

15. ASF, Pupilli, Reg. 176, fols. 80RV, 81R: "uno paio di forzeretti dipinti colarme di chasa. . . . una vergine maria di giesso rilevato colarme di chasa. . . . uno tavolo coperto di noccie di braccia 4 . . . colarme."

16. Biblioteca nazionale, MSS Ginori Conti, 30. 22 foli (1498).

17. Stella, *Révolte des Ciompi,* pp. 192–93.

18. Herlihy and Klapisch-Zuber, *Tuscans and Their Families,* p. 129, table 4.8. In Pistoia, tailors ranked eighth, with an average net worth of 232.9 florins. In Arezzo and Pisa, they ranked eleventh, with a net worth 154 florins.

19. ASF, Carte strozz., 2d ser., 17 bis, fol. 3V, 7V.

20. See Goldthwaite, *Building of Renaissance Florence,* p. 346.

21. To put this cost into perspective, a Florentine master weaver of velvet would be doing quite well to make 50 florins annually. See Edler de Roover, "Andrea Banchi," p. 250.

22. By including the six who declared themselves as completely without resources (which includes one retired tailor and the surviving daughter of a deceased tailor and his wife), this average drops to 290 florins.

23. ASF, CAT, Reg. 790, fols. 266R, 316R–319R; Reg. 791, fols. 466R, 869R–870V;

Reg. 796, fol. 662R; Reg. 811, fols. 160R, 212R; Reg. 818, fol. 341R, 1063R; Reg. 819, fols. 897V–899R.

24. John Shearman, *Andrea del Sarto,* vol. 1 (Oxford, 1965), pp. 1–2.

25. ASF, CAT, Reg. 796, fol. 662R.

26. ASF, CAT. Seven of the tailors (or their heirs) were destitute: Miniato e Bartolomeo di Baldo di Miniato (Reg. 791, fol. 460R); Lione di Simone di Francia (Reg. 794, fol. 578R); Giovanni di Antonio (Reg. 795, fol. 648R); Bartolomeo d'Antonio, retired (Reg. 808, fol. 642R), Mona Checha daughter of the late Mona Betta wife of the late Franciescho Fallchucci (Reg. 820, fol. 134R); Domenicho di Rinaldo di Neri (Reg. 821, fol. 341R).

27. ASF, Conv. soppr., N. 102, filza 83, fol. 69V.

28. Ibid., fols. 50V–95V.

29. Many of the tailors' botteghe were in the center of the old city. Out of twelve sarti who listed shops, eight were located in the quarter of San Giovanni. The most common place of residence, however, was on the periphery in Santo Spirito. See Table 3.1.

30. See Franceschi, *Oltre il "Tumulto,"* pp. 43–44, 52–58, for a similar paucity of goods in the shops of shearers, menders, and dyers who worked as sottoposti in the wool industry of Florence.

31. ASF, Pupilli, Reg. 176, fols. 80RV, 81R: "uno chassone grande di braccia 4 . . . una chasse di braccia 3 1/2 et uno serrame . . . uno bancho da tagliare panni grande da sarto . . . due huomini di lengno et chanavaccio da sarti . . . et più altre chosette che non si richordano."

32. For the relatively high price of shearers' and tailors' scissors, see Franceschi, *Oltre il "Tumulto,"* p. 53 n. 101. In 1390, two pairs of scissors were assessed at 12 florins!

33. ASF, Conv. soppr., N. 102, filza 83. I thank Dr. Gino Corti in Florence for pointing me to this source.

34. Ibid., fol. 18V.

35. These garments included "una ghamora azzura . . . senza maniche" and "uno luccho di guarnello biancho," and the 8 florins *grossi* was for the "furnitura delli sopradetti lavorri," acccording to Bartolomeo Natti's ricordanze (ibid., fol. 36V). The florin *largo di grossi* was silver money of account for the florin *largo.*

36. Weavers of wool earned around 43 florins per year. See de Roover, "Labour Conditions," p. 303.

37. The groceries, which cost a total of 67 lire, were a small part of Marco Parenti's shopping list for the feast that was the centerpiece of his wedding to Caterina Strozzi in 1447. The entire celebration, including rented silver plate, candles, and musicians, cost him some 92½ florins. ASF, Carte strozz., 2d ser., 17 bis, fol. 13R.

38. ASF, Conv. soppr., N. 102, filza 83.

39. One contemporary vestigial remain of this personal relationship over time and cultures is the "Lord & Taylor" corporate identity of one prominent American department store.

40. Ronald Weissman, "Taking Patronage Seriously," in *Patronage, Art, and Society in Renaissance Italy*, ed. F. W. Kent and Patricia Simons (Oxford, 1987), pp. 29–30, 42. He argues that "patronage is a recurring pattern of Mediterranean urban organization—the unwritten rules of the game, the way things actually get done."

41. Ibid., p. 44.

42. For the labyrinthine nature of relations among the various strata of society on the streets of the gonfaloni of Renaissance Florence, see Christiane Klapisch-Zuber's "Parenti, amici, vicini," *Quaderni storici* 33 (1976); Anthony Molho, "Cosimo de' Medici: Pater Patriae or Padrino?" *Stanford Italian Review* 1, no. 1 (Spring 1979); Cohn, *Laboring Classes of Renaissance Florence*; D. V. and F. W. Kent, *Neighbours and Neighbourhood in Renaissance Florence: The District of the Red Lion in the Fifteenth Century* (Locust Valley, N.Y., 1982); Trexler, "Neighbours and Comrades"; F. W. Kent, "Ties of Neighbourhood and Patronage in Quattrocento Florence," in *Patronage, Art and Society in Renaissance Italy*, ed. id. and Patricia Simons (Oxford, 1987); Ronald Weissman "The Importance of Being Ambiguous: Social Relations, Individualism, and Identity in Renaissance Florence," in *Urban Life in the Renaissance* (Newark, Del., 1989). Franceschi's *Oltre il "Tumulto"* takes up this thorny issue as well.

43. Kent and Kent, *Neighbours and Neighbourhood*, pp. 53, 49.

44. See, e.g., F. W. Kent's interesting discussion in "Ties of Neighbourhood," p. 95, of "informal" neighborhoods based upon key intersections within the city.

45. Molho, "Cosimo de' Medici," p. 21. See also Weissman, "Importance of Being Ambiguous," pp. 275ff. Eckstein, *District of the Green Dragon*, esp. pp. 39–40, includes an intense example of the rich interconnectedness of neighbors.

46. Sharon Strocchia, *Death and Ritual in Renaissance Florence* (Baltimore, 1992), pp. 195–96.

47. See Molho, *Marriage Alliance*, pp. 298–99.

48. ASF, MAP, filza XXIII, no. 320, dated Feb. 9, 1471 [mod. 1472].

49. For examples of Medici patronage, see Kent and Kent, *Neighbours and Neighbourhood*, pp. 50, 63–64, 93–95.

50. ASF, MAP, filza XXIII, no. 30. A letter from one Anchino di Piero della Magna, sarto in Pisa, written on July 22, 1465, appealed to the seventeen-year-old Lorenzo de' Medici to assist in freeing one of his boys "uno mio gharzone," who was sitting in the Stinche (Florentine prison). Anchino wrote, "I pray that through your kindliness you will help him to be able to leave this place" ("vi preiegho che per vostro benignità vingengnate lui possa uscire di questo luogho"). This tailor, while also drawing a connection between himself and Lorenzo, as does the other tailor, Filippo, pens a conventionally servile close, "I am your servant and slave for eternity . . ." ("sono vostro servo e shiavo in abetterno . . .").

51. ASF, MAP, filza XXIII, no. 320.

52. See Kristen Neuschel, *Word of Honor: Interpreting Noble Culture in Sixteenth-Century France* (Ithaca, N.Y., 1989), p. 96.

53. Molho, "Cosimo de' Medici," p. 17, on the other hand, has stated that neither Cosimo de' Medici's correspondence nor that of any other prominent Florentine of the time contains any requests for help from urban workers, or conversely, any offers of assistance from the rich. This letter was from Viterbo, but the request could as well have come from Florence, where the tailor would not have written it down but instead deferentially waited to see Lorenzo in person. That no patronage correspondence exists from urban workers within the city of Florence itself to the Medici is not surprising and seems not to prove that these lines of patronage did not exist. For examples of Lucrezia Tornabuoni's involvement in her family's patronage network, see also her *Lettere*, ed. Patrizia Salvadori (Florence, 1993) .

54. Karl Polanyi, *Primitive, Archaic and Modern Economies: Essays of Karl Polanyi*, ed. George Dalton (New York, 1968), pp. 66–67, asserts that *all* premodern economic systems were merged in the social, including primitive economies, ancient city-states, and feudalism and urban life between the thirteenth and sixteenth centuries.

55. Molho, "Cosimo de' Medici," p. 19.

56. ASF, MAP, filza LXXX, no. 51, dated June 16, 1477.

57. Ibid.: "la figliuola di Mona Nadda che fu suocera di Messr Giovanni. . . . Io sono sirochia di quella sua prema donna colla quale voi andevate ogni settimane astarvi con esso lei quando fusti qui in questa terra [Volterra] la prima volta."

58. See Klapisch-Zuber, "Parenti, amici, vicini," pp. 953–82, for a full discussion of the group of relatives, friends, and neighbors a Florentine citizen perceived as his or her primary support network.

59. See Dale Kent, *Rise of the Medici: Faction in Florence, 1426–1434* (Oxford, 1978), pp. 84–85.

60. Weissman, "Importance of Being Ambiguous," pp. 275–76.

61. Goldthwaite, *Building of Renaissance Florence*, p. 314, notes the "loose and flexible" system of payment between workers and employer in the fifteenth century, which could not exist in a cash nexus system.

62. Davis, *People of the Mediterranean*, pp. 56–58.

63. Sometimes, the debts were given the routine 50 percent valuation, sometimes less. The debitori list of one Antonio di Ijachopo di Miche detto Barberino, a retired tailor, lists four debts that were between twenty-seven and fifty-two years old. Two of these presumably uncollectable bills were from the Capponi. ASF, CAT, Reg. 791, fols. 869R–70V.

64. ASF, CAT, Reg. 790, fols. 316R–319R.

65. Ibid. The Medici faction in 1458 is given by Dei as the Pitti, Ridolfi, Guicciardini, Martegli, Chorbinegli, Soderini, Tornabuoni, Capponi, Pazzi, Gianfigliazzi, Bartolini, Biliotti, Bartoli, Vespucci, and Salviati. Dei, *Cronica*, p. 66. Other than two sets of brothers, one set whose father possibly was a tailor himself, there is little evidence that tailoring as a profession was handed down from father to son (or daughter) any more than

any other trade in Florence, where occupations in general seemed to be notably market-determinate.

66. ASF, CAT, Reg. 790, fols. 316R–319R.

67. Ibid., Reg. 819, fols. 897RV.

68. Ibid., Reg. 829, fols. 324RV.

69. ASF, Carte strozz., 2d ser., 17 bis, lists three successive tailors who worked for the Parenti from 1447 through 1478: Andrea di Giovanni da Bibbiena (1447–), Agnolo d'Antonio (1447–66), and Bernaba di Francescho (1467–78).

70. ASF, MAP, filza LXXVI, N. 137, letter from one Cicco Simonetta in Milan, to Antonio de' Medici, banker in Florence, dated Dec. 20, 1478. Three Medici tailors are all given the title of master (*maestro*). Filza CL, n. 148, Jan. 27, 1479, also lists three more master tailors and one embroiderer.

71. ASF, MAP, filza CXXXII, fols. 1R–6R, 30R–32V. He apparently had two personal tailors, "Giovanni sarto," and "Lucciola sarto," and two additional foreign tailors, "Maestro Francesco di Girolamo, sarto di Pavia [or Parma]," and "Girolamo da Chalenzano sarto."

72. ASF, MAP, filza 103, n. 91: "la fanciulla che venire affirenze cholamadre. . . . e se venire il sarto e vede la ghamurra in dosso alla fanciulla segniola dove disengino e presele la misura. . . . Loro si chiamano molte chontente."

CHAPTER 4. TAILORING FAMILY HONOR

1. This statement is from a letter to Lorenzo de' Medici dated Aug. 10, 1472 (ASF, MAP, Reg. XXVIII, no. 393), quoted by Julius Kirshner in *Pursuing Honor while Avoiding Sin: The Monte delle Doti of Florence* (Milan, 1978), p. 6.

2. Ibid., pp. 5–6. Davis, *People of the Mediterranean*, p. 99, writes that in Mediterranean honor cultures, men who are "thwarted in their attempts to gain dominance" often settle for second best, "thinking away" the inequalities and inducing cooperative behavior between competitors.

3. Neuschel, *Word of Honor*, pp. 77, 123. As the likelihood of real political power is diminished, "the insistence on honor grows more shrill," she writes (p. 205).

4. Phillips, *Marco Parenti*, pp. 68–69.

5. See Stephen Greenblatt on the Renaissance "gaze" in *Renaissance Self-Fashioning* (Chicago, 1980), p. 49.

6. Leon Battista Alberti, *I libri della famiglia*, ed. Ruggiero Romano and Alberto Tenenti (Turin, 1969), bk. 4, p. 268.

7. Kirshner quotes Paolo Sassetti in *Pursuing Honor*, p. 6.

8. Patricia Simons, "Women in Frames: The Gaze, the Eye, the Profile in Renaissance Portraits," *History Workshop* 25 (Spring 1988): 17.

9. Ian Maclean, *The Renaissance Notion of Woman* (Cambridge, 1980), p. 62, cites the

humanist Torquato Tasso's *Discorso della virtù feminile e donnesca* as saying that a man's greatest virtù is courage and a woman's chastity; conversely, a man's most inexcusable vice is cowardice and a woman's being unchaste.

10. Klapisch-Zuber, "Un salario o l'onore," pp. 45–47, writes that any female inheritance was diminished in honor, for it was perceived as having been taken from some rightful male heir.

11. On the Florentine ricordanza, see F. Pezzarossa, "La tradizione fiorentina della memorialistica," in *La memoria dei mercatores*, ed. G. M. Anselmi, F. P. Pezzarossa and L. Avellini (Bologna, 1980), pp. 39–149.

12. Alberti, *Libri della famiglia*, bk. 3, p. 246: "e per tanto sarebbe non buona masserizia non vestirli bene."

13. Ibid., pp. 316, 274: "voglionsi avere le belle veste, perché ove elle onorano te molto, tu il simile riguardi loro."

14. Ibid., p. 247. See Francesco Barbaro, *De re uxoria*, trans. Alberto Lollio as *Prudentissimi et gravi documenti circa la elettion della moglie* (Venice, 1548), p. 44. Barbaro's humanist treatise on wifely duties was written as a wedding gift to Lorenzo de' Medici "Il Vecchio" and his bride Ginevra Cavalcanti in 1416.

15. Dei, *Cronica*, p. 93, points out eighteen such specifically Florentine "feste."

16. John the Baptist was the patron saint of Florence. See Trexler, *Public Life in Renaissance Florence* (New York, 1980), esp. pp. 215–78, for the definitive discussion of the Florentine festive year.

17. Goro di Stagio Dati, *Storia di Firenze, 1380–1405* as quoted in Cesare Guasti, *Le feste di San Giovanni Batista* (Florence, 1906), p. 4.

18. Dati, *Storia di Firenze*, pp. 4–5.

19. ASF, Conv. soppr., N. 97, filza 13, fols. 3R, 6R.

20. ASF, Carte strozz., 2d ser., 17 bis, fols. 14R, 25V, 39R, 54R, 55V, 60V, 61R, 68V, 72V, 76V.

21. Alberti, *Libri della famiglia*, bk. 3, p. 247: "civili vestimenti, sopratutto puliti, atti e bene fatti; colori lieti, aperti quali più s'afacesse loro; buoni panni."

22. Ibid., pp. 289–90: "Eccoti questa mia cioppa. . . . Qui gia sotto ho io consumato più e più anni, . . . teste per ogni di ancora vedi quanto ella sia non disdicevole. Se io allora non avessi scelto il migliore panno di Firenze, io dipoi n'arei fatte due altre, ne però sarei stato di quelle onorevole come di questa."

23. *Il dizionario tommaseo*, cited in Merkel, "Beni della famiglia di Puccio Pucci," p. 171, n. 1, records that the eight ambassadors in a Florentine embassy to the pope were "vestiti di cremisi" (deep crimson), their clothes being dyed with the highest-quality imported kermes, while the dress of their entourage of seventy-two was "di rosato," more of a rose color, derived from the less expensive grana.

24. Bartolomeo Masi, *Ricordanze di Bartolomeo Masi, calderaio fiorentino dal 1478 al 1526*, ed. Gius. Odoardo Corazzini (Florence, 1906), pp. 19–20: "Andorno a ordine molto

sontuosamente. . . . Ciascuno de' sopradetti inbasciadori aveva seco venti scudieri a cavallo, e quattro istafieri bene a cavallo e meglio vestiti; e Piero de' Medici n'aveva cinquanta, e dimolti stafieri et un numero grande di cariaggi; e non fu mai dí nessuno che in Roma e sopradetti inbasciadori non mutassino vestire, e fu fatto loro dal ponteficie onore grandissimo." They were evidently so well dressed that they shamed all the ambassadors of other powers.

25. ASF, Carte strozz., 2d ser., 17 bis, fol. 75R.

26. Alberti, *Libri della famiglia*, bk. 3, p. 247: "queste frastagli, questi ricami a me piacquono mai vedelli, se non solo a buffoni e trombetti."

27. ASF, Carte strozz., 2d ser., 17 bis, fol. 75R. Dei, *Cronica*, p. 85.

28. ASF, Carte strozz., 2d ser., 17 bis, fol. 75R.

29. Machiavelli, *Le istorie fiorentine*, bk. 7, p. 401: "due canne di panno rosato facevano un uomo da bene."

30. Vespasiano, *Vespasiano Memoirs*. For a description of Cosimo de' Medici, see pp. 213, 223–24, 227; Piero di Neri Acciaiuoli, p. 272; Donato Acciaiuoli, p. 292; Piero de' Pazzi, p. 312; Ser Filippo di Ser Ugolino, pp. 320, 324; Bernardo Giugni, p. 326; Nicolò Nicoli, p. 402; Franco Sacchetti, p. 404.

31. See Martines, *Social World of the Florentine Humanists*, pp. 165–76, on Bruni as Florentine humanist, statesman, gentleman.

32. Vespasiano quoted in Levi-Pisetzky, *Costume e la moda*, p. 196: "Era Messr Lionardo d'un aspetto gravissimo; non era molto grande di persona, ma di mediocre statura. Portava una cappa di cambellotto di grana, lunga appresso la terra, con maniche che si rimboccavano foderate; e in sulla cappa portava un mantello rosato, isparato dallato, lungo insino in terra; in capo un cappuccio rosato, avvolta colla foggia dallato. Andava per la via con grandissima gravità."

33. Trexler, *Public Life in Renaissance Florence*, p. 361.

34. See Cristelle L. Baskins, "Griselda, or the Renaissance Bride Stripped Bare by Her Bachelor in Tuscan *Cassone* Painting," *Stanford Italian Review* 10, no. 2 (1991): 165–66.

35. Alberti, *Libri della famiglia*, bk. 3, p. 291. Even the women of wealthy families had the ultimate responsibility for these never-ending domestic chores. They fill the letters of the women of the Medici family and others. See Margherita Datini's almost daily instructions on her household duties from her ever-absent merchant husband Francesco, which invariably begin "ricorditi bene . . . ," in Iris Origo, *The Merchant of Prato* (London, 1957), pp. 173 ff.

36. San Bernardino of Siena, *Le prediche volgari di San Bernardino da Siena nel 1427*, ed. Orazio Bacci (Siena, 1895), p. 119.

37. Alberti, *Libri della famiglia*, bk. 3, pp. 290–91.

38. Rainey, "Sumptuary Legislation," details restrictions on all aspects of wedding festivities, from numbers of people who could attend, what kinds and quantities of food could be served, and what types of gifts could be distributed, to how many jesters could

entertain. See the Statuti of 1322–25, pt. 1, pp. 56–57; 1356 pragmatica, 1:154–63; laws of 1438–39, 2:438–39.

39. Rainey, "Sumptuary Legislation," 1:60–63.

40. Origo, *Merchant*, p. 275. This letter is dated Sept. 7, 1393.

41. Janet Ross, *Lives of the Early Medici* (London, 1910), pp. 80–81.

42. Rainey, "Sumptuary Legislation," 2:523–26.

43. Strocchia, *Death and Ritual,* pp. 124–26.

44. Ibid., pp. 213–14.

45. Rainey, "Sumptuary Legislation," 2:528–29. A woman could have a cloak, an overgown, a handkerchief, and two veils ("mantello, cioppa, sciugatoio, e due veli").

46. See Isabelle Chabot, " 'La sposa in nero': La ritualizzazione del lutto delle vedove fiorentine (secoli XIV–XV)," *Quaderni storici* 86, no. 2 (Aug. 1994): 421–62.

47. Rainy, "Sumptuary Legislation," 2:529–30.

48. See Lawrence Langner, *The Importance of Wearing Clothes* (New York, 1959), p. 35; also J. C. Flugel, *The Psychology of Clothes* (London, 1950), pp. 46–49.

49. Rainey, "Sumptuary Legislation," 1:55, nn. 49, 50.

50. Alessandro Luzio and Rodolfo Renier, "Il lusso di Isabella d'Este," *Nuova antologia,* 4th ser., 5, no. 147 (June 1896): 459, 468: "quella povera principessa, che fu mandata come una bambola suntuasamente abbligata a recitare la parte d'imperatrice." As Quentin Bell, *On Human Finery,* p. 37, has noted, there are limiting factors to how far clothes can go in extravagance. They may be an encumbrance, as certainly the voluminous skirts of the women were, but they must always be graceful and never overwhelm the body of the wearer.

51. See Greenblatt's sociolinguistic discussion on the interplay between private and communal selves in the Renaissance in his *Renaissance Self-Fashioning,* pp. 49 ff.

52. See Lurie's general comments on ample clothing in *Language of Clothes,* pp. 215–16.

53. Flugel, *Psychology,* pp. 46–49.

54. "In cottardita sta; perch'egli è baldo." The cottardita still figured prominently in the 1415 *Statuta populi et communis florentiae.* Rubric LXXI of this statute limited what a tailor could charge for fashioning garments, and listed nine different types of this garment.

55. ASF, Carte strozz., 2d ser., 17 bis, fol. 11V.

56. ASF, MAP, Reg. CXXXII, fol. 3R.

57. See Strocchia, *Death and Ritual,* p. 125, on clothing sold in 1405 to pay for a funeral, undoubtedly mostly for mourning dress rather than candles.

CHAPTER 5. FAMILY FORTUNES IN CLOTHES

1. Herlihy and Klapisch-Zuber, *Tuscans and Their Families,* p. 124.

2. On sumptuary legislation passed in Florence, see Rainey, "Sumptuary Legislation," 2, app. 1:652–55.

3. See Diane Owen Hughes, "Distinguishing Signs: Ear-Rings, Jews and Franciscan Rhetoric in the Italian Renaissance City," *Past and Present* 112 (Aug. 1986): 28.

4. A braccio equaled 58.4 cm, about 23 inches or ⅔ of a yard, and was the retail measurement into which the longer fabric lengths of the canna (34 braccia) and the pezza (12 to 14 canna) were cut. The large pezza was normally the measurement for wholesale wool transactions. (See Appendix 1 for Florentine measures of cloth.) Taffetas, some silks and other lining fabrics were sold by the pound, with 7½ to 8 braccia of taffeta to a Florentine pound (12 ounces), 5 braccia of satin to a pound, but only 2⅓ to 2½ braccia of "double," or heavy satin, to a pound. See Edler de Roover, "Andrea Banchi," p. 255. The changing width of these fabrics also contributed to their expense. Up until 1450, Italian silks measured 115–120 cm or approximately 46¼ inches selvage to selvage. From 1450 on, however, the width of silk fabric was reduced to only 60–70 cm, or about 25⅔ inches, which allowed for greater control of fabric tension. See Herald, *Renaissance Dress*, p. 77. The stricture on the width could have been caused by the demands of weaving the increasingly complex velvet and brocade designs.

5. This projection is based on Lodovico Ghetti's work on annual food consumption cited by Goldthwaite, also with Brucker's statistics on housing and clothing costs in the 1440s. See Goldthwaite, *Building of Renaissance Florence*, pp. 342–50; Brucker, *Society of Renaissance Florence*, p. 2.

6. Dorini, *Arte della seta in Toscana*, pp. 5–7.

7. Goldthwaite, *Building of Renaissance Florence*, pp. 35, 52.

8. The setaiuolo Andrea Banchi, who specialized in costly fabrics and specialty items such as brocades, brocaded velvets, and orphreys, evidently had difficulty selling his products. His business was largely confined to the Church and northern Italian courts. Local customers would have bought the fanciest silks only for trousseaux and dowries, for special clothing worn for feste, or for the sleeves of elaborate brocade with which outfits were accented. See Edler de Roover, "Andrea Banchi," p. 262.

9. Herald, *Renaissance Dress*, pp. 73–74.

10. This two-soldi figure is based upon the work done by Giuliano Pinto as quoted by Goldthwaite, *Building of Renaissance Florence*, p. 347.

11. Herald, *Renaissance Dress*, p. 77.

12. Italian metallic silks of the period can be identified by the method they used for making these threads. Gold or silver wire was wrapped around a linen or yellow silk core thread, to produce a metallic thread, which was much stronger than pure metal would be. See Anne E. Wardwell, "The Stylistic Development of Fourteenth- and Fifteenth-Century Italian Silk Design," *Aachener Kunstblatter* 47 (1976–77): 180.

13. Herald, *Renaissance Dress*, pp. 78–79.

14. The three-pile velvet, which cost twenty florins per braccio was a brocaded alto-basso *allucciolato*, dyed with kermes, part of the silk merchant Andrea Banchi's inventory, cited by Edler de Roover in "Andrea Banchi," p. 266.

15. The weaver of brocade could make a good living bent over his loom for hours on end, calling instructions to his draw boy—around 168 florins per year. Women were not normally trained to weave the complex figured cloth but instead wove the plain satins and taffeta, for which they could make only 28–30 florins a year in wages. A weaver of damask made about 74 florins a year. Ibid., pp. 246–48.

16. Wardwell, "Stylistic Development," pp. 182–86.

17. Raymond de Roover, "Labor Conditions," pp. 305–6.

18. Edler de Roover, "Andrea Banchi," p. 255, table 5.

19. Dei, *Cronica*, p. 43, tallied the wool botteghe as three times the number of silk shops in 1472. This balance would continue to change into the Cinquecento, as Florence adjusted its woolen production from luxury cloth to lower-quality cloth to meet the changing market. Hoshino's figures in "Per la storia," p. 78, show a high of 283 wool concerns in 1382, to a low of 122 in 1469. By 1500, the wool industry was on the rebound in middling-quality *garbo*, which was sold primarily in the Levant. The Provveditori dell'Arte della lana of 1487 stated that the Turkish empire was "in good part the stomach for our garbo cloth."

20. Hoshino, "Per la storia," pp. 36, 51, 72–73. Incrementally, Florence increased the restriction on the importation of various types of luxury wool (in 1472, *panni perpignani stranieri* was banned), but the lower grades of heavy, coarse cloth, such as the *rasce strette* and *rasce schiave* (slave rash), were still being brought in throughout the fifteenth century. While the city itself did expand into the looming of second-quality cloths at this time, these garbo cloths were, for the most part not sold within the city.

21. Hoshino, *Arte della lana*, p. 290. The prices for panno lucchesino and garbo have been taken from records of Florentine cloths bought by the Camera Apostolica in Rome between 1447 and 1486 and would therefore be slightly higher than this cloth would have been in Florence. See ASF, Conv. soppr., N. 97, filza 13, fol. 6R, for perpignan prices.

22. See Franceschi, *Oltre il "Tumulto,"* pp. 33–38, for a full discussion of these processes.

23. Edler de Roover, "Andrea Banchi," p. 243.

24. Edler de Roover, *Glossary*, pp. 324–29. Edler states that in Florence there were three separate groups of dyers who worked in the silk and wool industries: (1) the *tintori di guado*, who worked with woad and indigo, both of which produced the colors of green, blue, and black; (2) the *tintori d'arte maggiore*, who worked for the major guilds, primarily with madder, and (3) the *tintori d'arte minore o di loto*, who worked for the minor guilds. The first two groups of dyers dyed raw materials and cloth for export, while the third group worked only on the cheaper domestic products, not for the export (luxury) trade. Which group worked with the most costly dyes, kermes, grana, and verzino, is not given, but the second group, the tintori d'arte maggiore, working for both the wool and silk guilds, would be a logical conclusion. Edler de Roover, *Glossary*, pp. 297–98.

25. See Luca Molà's interesting discussion of the politics of red dye between ca. 1450 and 1550 in Venice in *Silk Industry of Renaissance Venice*, pp. 107–12.

26. By way of contrast, Stella Mary Newton, *Dress of the Venetians*, p. 18, writes that in

Venice, kermes was never used for dying woolen cloth, only for silks, and that communal statute decreed that all official state garb was to be made of silk fabric dyed with kermes, known in Venice as *cremesino.* Molà, *Silk Industry of Renaissance Venice,* pp. 109–31, gives the Venetian term as *cremisi.*

27. There is no consensus among dye specialists as to the exact species of insect that was used for the most valuable chermisi dye in fifteenth-century Italy. In addition to *Porphyrophora hameli,* found in the Middle and Near East, there were other insects that had the coloring agent of carminic acid, especially *Coccus polonicus,* found in eastern Europe. See John H. Munro, "The Medieval Scarlet and the Economics of Sartorial Splendour," in *Cloth and Clothing in Medieval Europe,* ed. N. B. Harte and K. G. Ponting (London, 1983), pp. 16–17, and Dominique Cardon, *Les "vers" du rouge* (Paris, 1990), esp. pp. 76–91.

28. Herald, *Renaissance Dress,* pp. 212, 214.

29. Gargiolli, *Arte della Seta,* pp. 78–79. There were twelve ounces to the Florentine pound.

30. Giovanni da Uzzano, *Pratica della mercatura,* vol. 4 (1442), p. 170, in Pagnini, *Della decima,* vol. 2.

31. Munro, "Medieval Scarlet," pp. 15–16.

32. When Marco Parenti's father Parente was called to the priorate, Marco had his tailor Agnolo d'Antonio make him "una cioppa rosata cholle maniche aperte foderata di martore" (*rosata* here refers to grana.) ASF, Carte strozz., 2d ser., 17 bis, fol. 14R.

33. The red dyestuff called *oricello* was associated with the Rucellai family, said originally to have been professional dyers. An Alamanno Rucellai, as tradition has it, perfected the Eastern technique for extracting and fixing the color of the dye using the ammonia in urine. See Levi-Pisetzky, *Costume e la moda,* p. 63.

34. Giovanni da Uzzano, *Pratica della mercatura,* vol. 4 (1442), p. 170, in Pagnini, *Della decima,* vol. 2.

35. Edler de Roover, "Andrea Banchi," p. 243.

36. Gargiolli, *Arte della Seta,* pp. 78–79.

37. Goldthwaite, *Building of Renaissance Florence,* p. 83. One thinks of Lorenzo's pride in how he spent his grandfather's fortune.

38. Philips, *Marco Parenti,* pp. 25–26.

39. Dale Kent, "The Florentine *reggimento* in the Fifteenth Century," *Renaissance Quarterly* 4 (1975): 600–601.

40. ASF, Carte strozz., 2d ser., 17 bis, fol. 14R: "E a di primo di novembre 1450 per fattura di una cioppa rosata cholle maniche aperte foderata di martore per Parente mio padre quando fu de Signori."

41. This fifty-pelt figure is a conservative estimate. The sleeves of a woman's *roba* in 1447 required about ninety-three marten pelts, some of which were possibly used for trim (*orli*). Ibid., fol. 11V.

42. Note that the tailoring of the garment here represented a mere 1 percent of the total cost.

43. ASF, Carte strozz., 2d ser., 17 bis, fol. 75R: "Richordo questo di vii d'agosto di spese fatte per Piero mio quando ando per giovane chogli imbasciadori nostri a Napoli per le noze del Re Ferdinando." The horse was bought in Naples for 25 florins *larghi* (horse furnishings being another ten), and all of this was returned to Marco in Florence at the close of the journey. Marco's brothers-in-law Filippo and Lorenzo Strozzi, who were doing well in business in Naples, undoubtedly provided a line of credit there.

44. Lacca red was also one of the prized bright red colors, second only to chermisi in cost, and more expensive than grana. It was a dyestuff used apparently only to color wool.

45. The actual cost was noted as 92 florins, 38 lire, and 3 denari. Besides Tomaso, the rigattiere, Marco had dealt with two setaiuoli, Agnolo Pandolfini e Chompagni and Piero di Iachopo Guicciardini et Compagni, a linen company run by two brothers, Bartolomeo and Piero di Francesco di Bartolo et Compagni, and the hosier Piero di Nardo calzaiuolo. ASF, Carte strozz., 2d ser., 17 bis, fol. 75R.

46. Vespasiano, *Lives*, pp. 311–13.

47. Pisanello has left us designs for fanciful costumes with elaborate winglike sleeves that could have been worn for these types of activities. See Pistolese, *Moda nella storia del costume*, pp. 78–79, fig. 89, for one of Pisanello's designs. See also Trexler's discussion of the dress of young elite males in the fifteenth-century display ritual of *armeggeria* in his *Public Life in Renaissance Florence*, pp. 225–35.

48. ASF, MAP, CXXXII, fols. 17RV, 18RV. *Il libro del sarto,* first published in 1580 in Venice, provided patterns, designs, and renderings of various fashions and fabrics, including five pages of knights and their mounts draped with matching fabric (fols. 18R, 19R, 22R, 23R, 28R). This created a visual unity between man and beast which is confusing and a bit startling to the modern eye.

49. ASF, MAP, CXXXII, fol. 17R. The two pairs of hose cost 1 lira, 19 soldi, and 3 denari.

50. Ibid., fol. 18V.

51. Diane Owen Hughes, "From Brideprice to Dowry in Mediterranean Europe," *Journal of Family History* 3 (1978): 262–96, is an invaluable overview of the history of marital assigns in the west. See also Manlio Bellomo, *Ricerche sui rapporti i patrimonali tra coniugi* (Varese, 1961).

52. Christiane Klapisch-Zuber, "Le 'zane' della sposa: La fiorentina e il suo corredo nel Rinascimento," *Memoria: Rivista di storia delle donne* 11–12 (1984): 12–13. Trousseaux representing around 11 percent of the total amount of the dowry, which averaged around 1,000 florins for women of the upper classes.

53. BL, acq. e doni, 229, 2, fol. 78V. Chapter 7 discusses her trousseau in detail.

54. See ASF, Carte strozz., 2d ser., 17 bis, fols. 3V, 4RV, 6R, 7RV, 8R, 10R, 11V, 15V, 17R, 18V, 19R.

55. Martines, *Social World of the Florentine Humanists,* pp. 288–94, discusses the relationship between expenditures and the economy.

56. ASF, Carte strozz., 2d ser., 17 bis, fols. 3V, 4RV, 6R, 7R, 8R, 10R, 11V, 14R, 15V, 17R, 19R.

57. Ibid., fol. 14R.
58. Ibid., fol. 39R.
59. Martines, *Social World of the Florentine Humanists*, p. 346.
60. ASF, Carte strozz., 2d ser., 17 bis, fols. 39R, 54R, 55V.
61. Ibid., fol. 68V.
62. Ibid., fol. 14R.
63. Ibid., fol. 39R.
64. Klapisch-Zuber, *Women, Family*, pp. 227–28, emphasizes the seemingly insensitive sale of such wedding gifts by the husband, but Marco Parenti did not sell Caterina's wedding garb until November 1490, after her death, some forty-three years after the wedding. ASF, Carte strozz., 2d ser., 17 bis, fol. 3V.
65. Merkel, "Beni della famiglia di Puccio Pucci," pp. 170–205.
66. Martines, *Social World of the Florentine Humanists*, pp. 73–74. Between 1400 and 1427, the family was not among the upper 10 percent of Florentine families in wealth, and in fact, Puccio's first marriage in 1414 was to a mercer's daughter. It would not be until 1425, with his second marriage to a Spinelli girl, that the family entered the inner Medici circle. Before his death in 1447, Puccio had married his children well, aligning himself with the Biliotti, Spini, Rondinelli, Busini, and Capponi families. His son Antonio became a military commander and recovered Pietrasanta for Florence in 1484. See Eve Borsook and Johannes Offerhaus, *Francesco Sassetti and Ghirlandaio at Santa Trinita, Florence: History and Legend in a Renaissance Chapel* (Doornspijk, Holland, 1981), pp. 37, 67.
67. Merkel, "Beni della famiglia di Puccio Pucci," pp. 145–46.
68. Even though jewelry formed an important part of a family's ritual possessions (especially rings, which passed back and forth between family members on marriage), it cannot be treated here. See Klapisch-Zuber's "The Ring Game," in her *Women, Family*, pp. 231–41. Rab Hatfield has also done much important early work on the Tornabuoni and Sassetti family jewels as depicted in Ghirlandaio's frescoes in their respective family chapels of Santa Maria Novella and Santa Trinita.
69. Merkel, "Beni della famiglia di Puccio Pucci," pp. 199–205. This real estate included one small farm and some thirty-five pieces of land but not the family homes.
70. The one exception to this rather modest range of personal adornment among the Pucci males was Antonio himself, who had a range of helmets, armor, swords, horse covers, banners, flags, and various silver objects, estimated by communal officials to be worth a total of 331 florins. His wife Lena also led wives in decorative potential, her jewel case containing inter alia a diamond, a sapphire, an emerald, and a ruby; her jewelry was appraised at 216 florins. Merkel, "Beni della famiglia di Puccio Pucci," pp. 181–85.
71. Dei, *Cronica*, p. 81. Martines, *Social World of the Florentine Humanists*, pp. 138–39, remarks that Toso di Albizzo di Fortuna owned the bank with which Matteo Palmieri had done business in the 1420s.
72. ASF, Pupilli, Reg. 160, fols. 430R–436R.
73. Ibid., fol. 435R. This wardrobe totaled 18 florins. In addition to a short gown of

slave cloth (*panno schiavio*), a couple of pair of stockings, two hats, a hood, a vest (*di ghuarnello*), and a leather apron, it included an overgown of black damask, possibly a castoff from Albizo's wife Marietta.

74. ASF, Pupilli, Reg. 160, fols. 430R, 432RV.

75. Ibid., fols. 432V,.433R. A few items were identified as being used in childbirth, and of these, the large birthing sheets (*lenzole da parto*) were the most expensive, appraised at 11 florins for the pair.

76. Ibid., fols. 432R, 433V.

77. See Table 5.1.

78. ASF, MAP, CXXXII, fols. 1R–6R, 30R–32V.

79. Ibid., fol. 3V.

80. Ibid., fol. 6R.

81. Ferdinand Gregorovius, *Lucretia Borgia* (New York, 1903), pp. 37–39, 65–66.

82. *La guardaroba di Lucrezia Borgia, dall'archivio di stato di Modena,* ed. Luca Beltrami (Modena, 1903), pp. 49–61, 69–79, 83–85, 100–105.

83. Gregorovius, *Lucretia Borgia,* p. 207, citing a document from the Archivio di stato di Mantua, dated Dec. 13, 1501, from one Giovanni Lucido, family agent in Rome, to the marchese Gonzaga in Mantua. Lucretia was to become sister-in-law to Isabella and Beatrice d'Este when she married their brother, Alfonso I, and assumed the position of duchess of Ferrara.

84. Gregorovius, *Lucretia Borgia,* pp. 217, 223 (letter dated Dec. 28, 1501).

85. According to Pozzi's report, Lucrezia's father, the pope, had also given her 9,000 ducats to clothe herself and her servants, and each of her ladies-in-waiting had a trousseau of her own made especially for the journey to Ferrara. Ibid., pp. 215, 223.

CHAPTER 6. THE MAKING OF WEDDING GOWNS

1. Klapisch-Zuber, "Zacharias, or the Ousted Father," in *Women, Family,* pp. 183–88, 190–93. The *sposalizio* was actually the third event of a four-part marriage process, the nature of marriage being decidedly secular, at least in the Florentine upper class. The first step, after a marriage broker and/or family intermediaries (*mezzani*) completed preliminary negotiations with two prospective families, was a private meeting between the parents of the young man and the young woman to seal the alliance (*fermare il parentado*). They signed a private pledge called a *scritta* and shook hands on the deal; the handshake being called the *impalmamento,* or *toccamano.* After this ceremonial gesture, a parent could say that he or she had *impalmato* his or her daughter. The next step was a solemn public meeting between all the men of both families, at which a notary was present to record the marriage contract, legally binding the two parties. In a sample of 140 fifteenth-century marriages that Klapisch-Zuber surveyed, approximately 10 percent, including all the richest families, were preceded by this formal swearing (*giure).*

2. See Klapisch-Zuber, "The Griselda Complex: Dowry and Marriage Gifts in the Quattrocento," in *Women, Family*, pp. 231–41.

3. Ibid., pp. 218–19.

4. Historians of costume have noted that there seemed to be a female rite of passage enacted with the putting on of the mantello. The age at which a girl turned into a young woman sartorially, however, is contested. In 1388, Florentine sumptuary legislation created a new category between childhood and adulthood dress for girls who were over ten years old but did not yet wear a mantello, independent of their marital status (unmarried, engaged, or married). Rainey, "Sumptuary Legislation," 1:237–39.

5. Klapisch-Zuber, "Zacharias," pp. 56–60, 219–20.

6. See Lauro Martines, "A Way of Looking at Women in Renaissance Florence," *Journal of Medieval and Renaissance Studies* 4 (Spring 1974): 23, where he refers to a female in-law of Alessandra Strozzi from the Adimari family who says that she lacks the clothing and jewelry to attend a wedding.

7. Klapisch-Zuber, "Zacharias," pp. 192–93. She notes that during the tenure of Lorenzo de' Medici, he preferred to "simplify" and privatize the marriage alliances among the Florentine elite. Some have seen the new sumptuary legislation passed in the 1470s as also indicative of Lorenzo's partisan manipulation of urban display. See, e.g., Molho, " 'Tamquam vere mortua,' " 28.

8. Carnesecchi, "Suntuosa 'cioppa.' "

9. ASF, Carte strozz., 2d ser., 17 bis, fols. 3V, 7V. Precisely, it cost 101 florins, 31 lire, 15 soldi, and 7 denari. To put this cost in perspective, a Florentine master weaver of silk velvet made about 50 florins per year. See Edler de Roover, "Andrea Banchi," p. 250. Like the cioppa, a giornea could also be a garment for males, and it had, in fact, originated as military garb. In the Florentine sumptuary laws of both 1456 and 1464, the giornea is assimilated to the cioppa, both being overgowns. Polidori-Calamandrei, *Vesti delle donne fiorentine nel Quattrocento*, p. 44. As for the tailor himself, he was evidently not a resident of Bibbiena by 1427, when he had filed his tax declaration for the Catasto in the quarter of Santa Maria Novella, gonfalone Vipera. ASF, CAT, Reg. 74, fol. 111.

10. The Castellani, who had operated one of the Commune's largest banking firms in the mid 1300s, were traditionally one of the dominant families in the quarter of Santa Croce in Florence from at least the 1350s on (along with the houses of the Alberti, Peruzzi, Antellesi, and Baroncelli). Gene Brucker, *Florentine Politics and Society, 1343–1378* (Princeton, N.J., 1962), pp. 29–35.

11. Caterina Strozzi's gown, *zetani vellutato di chermisi*, was made of figured silk velvet, dyed with kermes. Parenti, a guildsman in the Por Santa Maria, rented a shop in Por Santa Maria for 40 florins a year from the Frati di Certosa. He got the fabric from the stock of his own family silk business, paying his company 3½ florins per braccia for it in 1447, which was extremely expensive at midcentury. ASF, CAT, Reg. 825, fols. 492R–494V; ASF, Carte strozz., 2d ser., 17 bis, fol. 3V.

12. Adornment was traditionally an act of honoring. Martin Wackernagel, *The World of the Florentine Renaissance Artist* (Princeton, N.J., 1981), p. 144, notes that the Bambino of the Madonna of the Impruneta, which regularly received honorific gifts, was given "splendid little cloaks of gold brocade" by the Signoria of Florence and "four other civic bodies" for a procession through the city in 1522.

13. Carnesecchi, "Sontuosa 'cioppa,' " p. 149.

14. Ibid., p. 151: "mi debbe ricamare d'argenteria e perle uno collare grande da levare e porre, e in su ciascuna manicha, su alto al loco della spalla, certa parte di celo con sole e suoi razi d'oro grandi, et acosto e sotto detti razi a meza la manica debbe ricamare una aquila d'oro e perle, grande, volante verso detti razi su al sole, come naturata a rinovarsi. E debbe spandere per tutto detto busto e maniche penne d'oro e perle, a cosi razi picholi con certi sprazi d'oro e perle atorno, e ricamati nel modo e forma de' sopradetti razi grandi."

15. Ibid., p. 148.

16. The first commission was for the pearl embroidery of a pair of sleeves for a "ciopetta pagonaza," on which Francesco requested a complex device incorporating both silver and gold threads ("uno tornio d'oro profilato di perle e fermo in certo mathonato lavorate d'oro, argento e seta, e aombrato come si richiede in su ciascuna di dette maniche, e debbe ricamare certi brevi d'oro in sul busto profilati di perle"). For this job, Francesco gave Maestro Giovanni 17 florins; 9 for the materials and 8 for the *manifattura* of the embroidery. The second commission was for two strips of "zetani allexandrino ricamati d'argenteria," which were to be used for further decorating the sleeves of the cioppa, for which Castellani paid 4 large florins and 45 soldi *da piccioli.* Ibid., p. 152.

17. Ibid., p. 154. The two other embroiderers were Bastiano di Nicolo and Nicholo d'Antonio. The previous year, in 1451, Marco Parenti had patronized the firm of Nicholo d'Antonio e Chompany richamati, buying 4 oz. 3 denari of pearls for 7 florins an ounce. Marco spent well over 28 florins for the pearls in all, and then another 10 for the embroidery work itself, using the pearls to decorate two full sleeves for a *cioppa pagonaza* for his new wife Caterina. ASF, Carte strozz., 2d ser., 17 bis, fols. 7R, 23R.

18. Carnesecchi, "Sontuosa 'cioppa,' " pp. 151–54.

19. Giovanni d'Amerigo del Bene (Florence) and Francesco di Jacopo del Bene (Valdinievole), correspondence, February 1381, ASF, Carte del Bene, vol. 51 (no pagination), cited in Brucker, *Society of Renaissance Florence,* pp. 32–37.

20. Giovanni d'Amerigo del Bene to Francesco di Jacopo del Bene, Feb. 21, 1381, in ibid., p. 34.

21. Giovanni d'Amerigo del Bene to Francesco di Jacopo del Bene, letter of Feb. 24, 1381, in ibid., p. 35.

22. Crabb, "How Typical Was Alessandra," p. 47.

23. Goldthwaite, *Private Wealth,* pp. 51–57. Before his exile, Matteo had been in the wool trade in the quarter of Santa Maria Novella, and in his tax report from the Catasto of

1427, officials set his net worth at 4,400 florins, putting him in the top 2 percent of all Florentine taxpayers. See also Martines, *Social World of the Florentine Humanists,* pp. 334–35.

24. Strozzi, *Lettere,* p. 5. Caterina's wedding dress is identified as a cotta, a gown closer to a gamurra than a cioppa, undoubtedly appropriate for the heat of a summer wedding.

25. ASF, Carte strozz., 2d ser., 17 bis, fol. 3V.

26. Ibid., fol. 7V. Parenti figured 4 lire 16 soldi to 1 large florin for bookkeeping purposes in 1447.

27. See Origo's *Merchant of Prato,* pp. 268–73, for a description of such a domestic reality in the Datini family. The wife was barren and the young woman whose fitting for bridal garments she oversaw was her husband's "natural" daughter by a family slave, whom she raised as her own daughter.

28. "L'arte che adoperiano con questi ta' contrafatti, sempre ma' tondo tagliano i busti che' sien ben fatti: po' bisogna cento patti far con queste strane bestie." From an anonymous poem entitled "Canzona de' Sartori," in *Canti Carnascaleschi del Rinascimento,* ed. Charles Singleton (Bari, 1936), p. 7.

29. At around 9 lire 13 soldi per garment, the tailor was making well over the limit of 4 lire that the Commune had imposed. Parenti paid very slowly, however, and the tailor had to wait three and a half years to get all his money. After the initial payment of a large florin, it was a year and eight months later, on March 7, 1449 [mod], before the tailor received another payment (of only 5 lire). Three more payments, on May 24, 1449, and January 30 and February 9, 1451, finally settled the debt. The Strozzi family lived in the same quarter of Santa Maria Novella as this tailor, where Caterina's deceased father, Matteo di Simone, had been in the wool trade, besides being part of the humanist circle as a collector of manuscripts. See Martines, *Social World of the Florentine Humanists,* pp. 334–35.

30. ASF, Carte strozz., 2d ser., 17 bis, fol. 4R.

31. Ibid., fols. 4V, 6R. The exact price, including the 8 florin 2 lire 11 soldi of a fabrication fee for Nicholo di Bastiano, ghirlandaio, was 59 florins 2 lire 4 soldi 3 denari.

32. Ibid., fol. 7R.

33. Ibid., fol. 8R: "uno fermaglio d'oro entrovi ii zafiri e iii perle da portare in ispalla."

34. Klapisch-Zuber's important early study on the counter-trousseau tends to follow Marcel Mauss's reading of the reciprocal exchange of goods in traditional societies to maintain social equilibrium in fifteenth-century northern Italy; see "Griselda Complex," p. 224.

35. See Molho on Marco Parenti's sense of the importance of some sort of equilibrium in *Marriage Alliance,* p. 235.

36. See Klapisch-Zuber, "Le 'zane' della sposa," pp. 11–12, 15.

37. L. Zdekauer, "Il dono del mattino e lo statuto più antico di Firenze," in *Miscellanea fiorentina di erudizione e storia,* vol. 1 (1886; reprint, Rome, 1978), pp. 33–36, notes that the *donatio propter nuptias* had begun to substitute for the *Morgengabe,* or "bride price," of the

Germanic tribes, with the rebirth of Roman law after the twelfth century. By the thirteenth century, Florentine statute had capped it at the low amount of 50 lire, which prevented it in any way from being an appropriate response to a woman's dowry. On the *donatio propter nuptias*, see also Bellomo, *Ricerche sui rapporti patrimonali,* pp. 223–44.

38. Jane Fair Bestor, "Marriage Transactions in Renaissance Italy and Mauss's Essay on the Gift," *Past and Present* 164 (Aug. 1999): 23–30, discusses the legal character of the groom's counter-trousseau in the "ius commune" law that combined and interpreted late Roman and Lombard law between 1000 and 1600. She notes that the *proper donatio nuptias* of an espoused male was reinterpreted as a loan rather than a gift, because it was constrained by societal mores. Not freely given, it therefore did not pass the legal test of liberality and generosity. Further, the groom's gifts, especially the jewelry and clothing "given" to dress her for optimum display for the leading, or *ductio* to his house, did not pass the further test of irrevocability that a true gift needed to meet, because these "gifts" did not actually become the property of the bride.

39. ASF, Carte strozz., 2d ser., 17 bis, fols. 1R–2R. Caterina's own trousseau totaled 175 florins.

40. Bestor, "Marriage Transactions," pp. 30, 35, 42–44.

41. Diane Owen Hughes, "La moda proibita: La legislazione suntuaria nell' Italia rinascimentale," *Memoria: Rivista di storia delle donne* 11–12 (1984): 99.

42. One justification for the groom's "gifts" of jewelry and clothes for the bride being actually "loans," was to back up the legal beginning of the married state to the *verba de praesenti*, when a couple first took their vows, rather than putting it after the ductio. If a couple were already considered married at the time of a bride's ductio, then the law against husbands and wives exchanging gifts (and thereby transferring property in a manner potentially threatening to the husband's patrilineage), could be cited, *necessitating* that the groom's "gifts" be loans. Bestor, "Marriage Transactions," p. 45.

43. Isabelle Chabot, "Lineage strategies and the control of widows in Renaissance Florence," in *Widowhood in Medieval and Early Modern Europe,* ed. Sandra Cavallo and Lyndan Warner (London, 1999), p. 131.

44. Isabelle Chabot, "Seconde nozze e identità materna nella Firenze del tardo medioevo," in *Tempi e spazi di vita femminile tra medioevo ed età moderna,* ed. Silvana Seidel Menchi, Anne Jacobson Schutte, and Thomas Kuehn (Bologna, 1999), pp. 497–503. Chabot writes that revisions of the communal statutes of 1415 reflected a practice that can be found in family logbooks as early as the late Trecento, whereby a remarried widow's intestate succession could be intercepted by a second husband, with her dowry and one-third of her personal goods going to him (if she died childless), even if she had children from a first marriage. This change severely restricted a woman's right to exercise discretion over her own property and was effected by a legal sleight-of-hand, in which, in negotiations for her second marriage, the dowry was recorded in family ricordanze as if she were being married for the first time, that is, as coming from the original natal family

to which she had returned when she exercised her right of *tornata*. This change essentially cut out any children of her first marriage from inheriting from their mother by denying their legal existence. By employing this fiction, upon her death (should she die childless in her second marriage), her dowry went straight to the second husband. Families of these women consented to this legal fiction because, as they complained, they had trouble finding husbands willing to marry young widows whose dowry succession had to consider any male issue from a previous marriage. See also Julius Kirshner, "Maritus Lucretur Dotem Uxoris Sue Premortue in Late Medieval Florence," *Zeitschrift der Savigny-Stiftung für Rechtsgeschichte, Kanonistische Abteilung* 77 (1991): 111–55.

45. Lauro Martines, *Lawyers and Statecraft in Renaissance Florence* (Princeton, N.J., 1968), p. 94. See also Julius Kirshner, "Wives' Claims Against Insolvent Husbands in Late Medieval Italy," in *Women of the Medieval World,* ed. id. and Suzanne Wemple (New York, 1985), pp. 256–303; Thomas Kuehn, *Law, Family, and Women: Toward a Legal Anthropology of Renaissance Italy* (Chicago, 1991), pp. 238–57.

46. Bestor, "Marriage Transactions," pp. 42–43.

47. Klapisch-Zuber, "Griselda Complex," pp. 224–28.

48. See Giovanni Dominici on women's vanity leading their husbands to penury. Even dressing children too elaborately comes under criticism from the pulpit. Giovanni Dominici, *Regola del governo di cura familiare* (Florence, 1860), pp. 149–51.

49. At the foot of most clothing entries in the logbooks there is a line drawn, then underneath *Venduta* or *Vendei* is written, noting when the item was sold (sometimes years later).

50. Klapisch-Zuber, "Griselda Complex," p. 227, notes that Parenti "was soon to pick apart pitilessly, pearl by pearl, gem by gem, sleeve by sleeve, the various festive garments" which he had made for their wedding in 1447.

51. ASF, Carte strozz., 2d ser., 17 bis, fol. 10V, 1R.

52. Carnesecchi, "Sontuosa 'cioppa,'" p. 153. Francesco sold to one Manuello da Volterra "ebreo e prestatore," "una giornea di dommaschino bigio richamata con argenterie al collare" and also "una cotta di dommaschino bigio con le maniche di detto drappo metesimo e con maglette 80 d'ariento orato."

53. ASF, Carte strozz., 2d ser., 17 bis, fol. 31V: "tutte le sopredette chose fu venderono per Antonio Brancacci in nome delle rede di Giovanni Parenti per mezo del posto veditore degl'uficiali de popilli per poterle vendene ascritte e rimasono a sopradetti Giovanni e Chompagni per pregio di lb. due cento quarantadue p."

CHAPTER 7. TROUSSEAUX FOR MARRIAGE AND CONVENT

1. In 1356, however, if the dowry was over 100 lire, the celebration had to be registered with the Commune (Rainey, "Sumptuary Legislation," 1:156; 2:438–39). I want to express my gratitude to Christiane Klapisch-Zuber for her valuable comments and sug-

gestions on the Minerbetti family ricordanza. I also thank Anthony Molho, who first suggested this source in the Biblioteca laurenziana.

2. Anthony Molho has shown that before 1500, the 6 percent of girls enrolled in the Monte delle doti who decided to take vows were on average 17.6 years old; about 28 percent of this group were between ten and fifteen years old. Molho, " 'Tamquam vere mortua,' " pp. 5, 13.

3. See Richard Trexler, *The Women of Renaissance Florence: Power and Dependence in Renaissance Florence,* vol. 2 (Binghamton, N.Y., 1993), pp. 8-10. Convents required extensive land for their gardens and orchards and therefore originally looked for areas that were cheaper than the center of town. In Florence, convents could be found along the Borgo Pinti, from San Lorenzo up Via San Gallo, around Ognissanti, on Via Ghibellina, and around Porta San Piero Gattolino (present-day Porta Romana).

4. Trexler, "Célibat," pp. 1329, 1331.

5. There were even more than these six sisters in the Minerbetti family, as the pater-familias, Andrea, married three times. Ghostanza was not the only one to be espoused, for her father was also able to arrange "honorable" marriages for two of her half-sisters, Alessandra and Ermellina. The total number of daughters was nine. See Molho, *Marriage Alliance,* pp. 172-78.

6. Molho has written that "typically," a family's aim to was successfully marry all their daughters. However, while Marco Parenti found marriages for his daughters who survived to marriageable age, his son Piero sent one daughter to the convent at age ten. See Molho, *Marriage Alliance,* p. 172. See also Heather Gregory, "Daughters, Dowries and the Family in Fifteenth-Century Florence," *Rinascimento* 27 (1987): 215-37, on the financial burden of dowering daughters, especially large families of girls, who notes, however, that some families took great pleasure in their daughters (Palla di Nofri Strozzi, for example) and were able to dower and secure marriages for many of them.

7. BL, acq. e doni, 229, 2, fol. 2V, 3RV, 9R.

8. Strozzi, *Lettere,* pp. 15-16.

9. See Klapisch-Zuber, "Le 'zane' della sposa," p. 15.

10. Ibid., pp. 16-18.

11. BL, acq. e doni, 229, 2, fols. 81V, 82R.

12. Klapisch-Zuber, "Le 'zane' della sposa," p. 15.

13. See Molho, *Marriage Alliance,* pp. 308-10, on evidence of dowry manipulation in the family logbooks to avoid payment of this 3 percent tax.

14. Not that there were no personal linens in the *stimate* part of the trousseaux, but they are all embellished. In Ghostanza's donora, over 80 percent are listed as embroidered (*lavorati*).

15. See Chapter 2 for location of tertiaries working from their places of residence, clustered primarily in the quarter of Santa Maria Novella in 1457. Trexler, *Women of Renaissance Florence,* p. 12, writes that it was often difficult to distinguish between tertiaries and second-order women who had taken vows, even for contemporary Florentines.

16. Ibid., pp. 11–12, 24. In 1517, the archbishop of Florence limited the number of women from the same family in one convent to two people, as apparently there had been some infighting problems between female family groups within the houses.

17. Gene Brucker, "Monasteries, Friaries, and Nunneries in Quattrocento Florence," in *Christianity and the Renaissance*, ed. Timothy Verdon and John Henderson (Syracuse, N.Y., 1990), p. 46. Trexler, *Women of Renaissance Florence*, pp. 12–13, notes that there were at least six categories of inhabitants in the convents, ranging from consecrated nuns at the top, and novices making their way to this level, to young girls sworn to become nuns but too young to take vows or waiting for an opening in the convent (*fanciulle*). All Florentine convents had a *numerus clausus* limiting how many women could be admitted, based on the convent's economic situation, which created such waiting lists. Then there were the others with varying degrees of spiritual inclinations: the female boarders, often widows (*commesse*), who had committed to live out their days safely behind convent walls, the servants who did the cleaning up, and, lastly, roomers who were being warehoused (*in serbanza*) by their families more or less permanently, and who did not necessarily have any spiritual commitment. For a later demographic survey of the ways in which the convent population had changed by the mid eighteenth century in Florence, see Judith Brown, "Monache a Firenze all' inizio dell' età moderna: un' analisi demografica," *Quaderni storici* 85 (April 1994): 117–52.

18. Trexler, in "Célibat," p. 1332, nn. 13–19, records the names of twenty-five convents. After 1471, the numbers of young girls in Florentine convents as young as the age of six began to rise. Trexler also discusses the contribution of prayer by the some 13 percent of all young women of a certain elevated social standing who were cloistered in the late Quattrocento. Contradicting Trexler's findings for placing kinswomen in pairs, however, each of Minerbetti's daughters went to different convents. Their father did not assign them to orders in pairs. See ibid., pp. 1341–49.

19. Klapisch-Zuber, "Le 'zane' della sposa," pp. 12–13.

20. See Herlihy and Klapisch-Zuber, *Tuscans and Their Families*, pp. 227–28. At the same time, it would on average impoverish her own family's total assets by only 14 percent, a certain percentage of young women of important families marrying down.

21. See Molho on the financial crisis in Florence, precipitated by external conflict and internal population decline, that spurred the Monte delle doti into existence. Molho, *Marriage Alliance*, pp. 27–30.

22. Julius Kirshner and Anthony Molho, "The Dowry Fund and the Marriage Market in Early Quattrocento Florence," *Journal of Modern History* 50 (1978): 403–38. The Monte made critical revisions to its program throughout its long existence, especially in 1433 and 1478, constantly adjusting initial required deposits, interest rates, and length of deposits, among other variables, in order to encourage communal participation.

23. Molho, *Marriage Alliance*, pp. 144–45. The average age for a nubile young woman to marry in the upper classes was around seventeen, younger than for the middling and artisan ranks.

24. Molho, " 'Tamquam vere mortua,' " pp. 32–33.

25. Ibid., pp. 21–22. Deposits had to be left in longer, and upon maturation, the new beneficiary received only from one-half to two-thirds of the sum due from the initial deposit.

26. Ibid., pp. 19–26. The litany of ailments and deformities of a number of these young women who had been set to marry but were later confined to a convent is horrifying.

27. Ibid., pp. 13, 15–17. See also Molho, *Marriage Alliance*, p. 307, where he notes that the decision of whether or not to send a girl to a convent was generally made earlier than whether to enroll her in the Monte.

28. BL, acq. e doni, 229, 2, fols. 2V, 30R, 54R, 76R, 77RV, 78V, 80V, 81RV, 92R, 120R.

29. Each period of residence had lasted about a year and a half. Ibid., 229, 2, fols. 28R, 30R, 32R, 71V, 72R.

30. Christiane Klapisch-Zuber, "Le chiavi fiorentine di barbablù l'apprendimento della lettura a Firenze nel XV secolo," *Quaderni storici* 57 (1984): 777–90, notes that girls housed for varying lengths of time (*in serbanza*) at the discretion of their families would have spiritual and domestic training (sewing, for example) and could receive a basic vernacular education. See also Paul F. Grendler, *Schooling in Renaissance Italy. Literacy and Learning, 1300–1600* (Baltimore, 1989), pp. 44, 93–102.

31. Her father, in fact, married his third wife, Antonia Sassetti, in the same year. The Sassetti were one of the leading ancient families named in the records that grouped around the Cavalcanti during the civil disorders of 1304. By 1469, Francesco Sassetti was the general manager of the Medici Bank. In 1483, his daughter Sibilla had married Alessandro Pucci, son of war hero Antonio Pucci. See Borsook and Offerhaus, *Sassetti and Ghirlandaio at Santa Trinita*, pp. 15–37.

32. BL, acq. e doni, 229, 2, fols. 80V–81R.

33. Santa Margherita, or Saint Margaret, was the patron saint of childless women, which perhaps was the reason this doll had been included in the mother's trousseau as a sort of fertility totem, to be then handed down to the marrying daughter. See Klapisch-Zuber, "Holy Dolls," in *Women, Family*, pp. 311–18.

34. BL, acq. e doni, 229, 2, fols. 81RV, 82R.

35. Brucker's figures on numbers are close to Trexler's, he calculating that by 1500, there were thirty-seven convents in the city and seventeen more within a four-mile radius. Thirteen different orders were represented, including three orders of tertiaries (Franciscan, Dominican, and Servite). See Brucker, "Monasteries," pp. 44, 47–48.

36. Molho, " 'Tamquam vere mortua,' " p. 24.

37. Trexler, *Women of Renaissance Florence*, pp. 12–13.

38. BL, acq. e doni, 229, 2, fols. 77RV.

39. Molho posits that Maria had "health problems" from an early age, for as a baby she was no sooner sent off to a wet nurse than brought back home, and she was then

consigned to Santa Felicita before the age of six. Molho, *Marriage Alliance*, p. 175. However, once there, Maria did survive for at least eight more years, as her father's contributions to the convent on her behalf as late as 1514 attest.

40. As many of these girls of "good" families were infirm and might even be malformed, their being out of sight would be especially important for appearance-conscious Florentines of the upper class.

41. Brucker writes that Santa Felicita was atypical of Florentine houses in the early Quattrocento, being one of the wealthiest of the convents within the city walls of Florence with a population of thirty sisters, and property that had been worth 9,200 florins in the Catasto of 1427. By 1478, the number of nuns had dropped to only twenty-four, part of a convent population that totaled forty-six, counting "ten servants, five priests, three acolytes (*chierici*), . . . a factor . . . [and] three boarders" (Brucker, "Monasteries, Friaries," pp. 53–54). Brucker further notes that the nuns should have been able to live "quite comfortably" in this convent, because they had income and sustenance from fifteen houses, four city shops, and eighteen farms in the surrounding countryside.

42. Vasaio, "Tessuto della virtù," p. 55, writes that the color *grigio* indicates an intermediate state of virginity, between the white of a bride, and the black of widowhood.

43. Ibid., p. 55. The phrase used is "humilità e la mortificazione."

44. See Trexler, *Women of Renaissance Florence*, pp. 13, 18.

45. St. Roch, or San Rocco, was a fourteenth-century healer from Montpellier who nursed the sick (while ill himself), in northern Italy during the Plague of 1348. He was often pictured with his dog.

46. Molho, " 'Tamquam vere mortua,' " p. 25.

47. Trexler, *Public Life in Renaissance Florence*, p. 188, n.2.

48. BL, acq. e doni, 229, 2, fols. 77RV.

49. Klapisch-Zuber, "Le 'zane' della sposa," pp. 14–15.

50. BL, acq. e doni, 229, 2, fol. 11R.

51. Ibid., 229, 2, fols. 2V, 5V for the initial listing of these trousseau items.

52. Ibid., 229, 2, fols. 3V, 81R.

CHAPTER 8. THE CLOTHES THEMSELVES

1. See Introduction for a discussion of Barthes's "Fashion System."

2. The Museo del tessuto in Prato, part of the Istituto tecnico industriale statale Tullio Buzzi, has an important collection of textile fragments from this time period, originating in Loriano Bertini's private collection of 612 pieces, which came from the Florentine antiquarian Giuseppe Salvadori, a late nineteenth-century textile collector. The Guggenheim Collection at the Museo civico Correr in Venice and the Victoria and Albert Museum in London both hold Italian textile examples, mostly silk brocade and cut-and-figured velvet. The British Museum in London, the Ashmolean Museum in Oxford, and

the Museo degli argenti and Palazzo Medici Riccardi in Florence all have jewelry collections. The costume collection at the Palazzo Pitti has a couple of mid sixteenth-century gowns, and the Palazzo Davanzati shows a wooden zoccolo. The Costume Institute of the Metropolitan Museum of Art also has a fourteenth-century *poulaine* (a stylishly narrow shoe of Polish origin).

3. Barthes, *Fashion System,* pp. 12–15.

4. Barthes further notes that language singles out certain elements to stress their importance, which works to divide the garment into discreet mental fragments. By the end of the fifteenth century, the clothes themselves became fragmented; pieces are held casually together by loosening ties and lacings.

5. Useful as visual sources are the Florentines Masolino, Masaccio, Uccello, Fra Angelico and Fra Filippo Lippi, who all included both upper-class and lower-ranking citizens in contemporary dress in their work. Domenico Veneziano, Gozzoli, and Piero della Francesca also inserted well-dressed Florentines into their religious scenes, and others, including Baldovinetti, Pollaiuolo, Botticelli, Ghirlandaio, and Perugino painted individuals garbed in contemporary dress. Holy figures are often depicted wearing fashionable details in their classical garb, such as the exotic silk striped scarves and shawls that originated in Damascus. Predella panels of altarpieces, and the interstices and backgrounds of religious subjects include representations of the general dress of the urban population, with the wretched occasionally included, often receiving charity from the rich.

Another source for local costume is a fifteenth-century illuminated manuscript of the *Aeneid* in the Biblioteca riccardiana in Florence (Scuola fiorentina del Sec. XV, Cod. 492) illustrated by an unknown artist with images of urban women dressed in festive costume. For fashionable attire in this folkloric category see the many wedding chest (*cassone*) and birth tray (*descho da parto*) paintings. A cassone painting by Giovanni di Ser Giovanni, known as "lo Scheggia," portrayed a Florentine marriage ceremony. Marco Parenti himself commissioned this artist for 26 lire in 1451 to paint a wooden tabernacle he had built to house a Virgin Mary. ASF, Carte strozz., 2d ser., 17 bis, fol. 28V. Two cassoni decorated by "lo Scheggia" are displayed in the Palazzo Davanzati in Florence.

6. See, e.g., Najemy, "Audiant omnes artes," p. 91.

7. On the issue of the lack of cinched-in belts on men's exterior mantles and cloaks in Florence, even Alberti, in his *Libri della famiglia,* is clear on how belting ruins good fabric (bk. 3, p. 225). But more compelling than concern for good cloth was the need for fifteenth-century costume to provide an unbroken sweep of line, focusing attention on the head and arms of the upper-rank Florentine male, with no distracting waistline treatment (as seen on the *cioppe* of the Sienese).

8. Polidori-Calamandrei, *Vesti delle donne fiorentine nel Quattrocento,* p. 92.

9. Vasari, *Lives of the Artists,* p. 228.

10. ASF, Conv. soppr., N. 119, filza 857, fols. 6S, 142S. Filze 855 and 857 (1447–92) are

both abundant sources for the vestments and personal clothing of the friars of Santissima Annunziata. I thank Samuel Y. Edgerton Jr. for alerting me to this source.

11. This did not mean that the men did not *own* jewelry, which may have been reserved for display when traveling abroad. In addition to mostly rings and belts, and an occasional gold necklace, chain, or string of coral, many men of the upper class had modest gem collections of unfaceted cabochon stones such as emeralds, garnets, rubies, sapphires, spinels, and a few diamonds and pearls. Other men owned decorative helmets, armor, and swords, some of which were adorned with other precious and semi-precious metals, such as silver, bronze or copper. See Rainey, "Sumptuary Legislation," 1:53, 55, concerning sumptuary restrictions on ornamentation for men. Only knights, judges, and physicians were unrestricted in their wearing of gemstones, pearls, silver threads in belts, and enameled jewelry.

For the extraordinary collections of the Medici (and men of their social circle, such as Niccolò Niccoli), which included antique engraved gemstones, and may, in fact, have sparked an interest in the engraver's art of *niello*, see O. M. Dalton, *Catalogue of the Engraved Gems of the Post-Classical Periods in the British Museum* (London, 1915); Museo Mediceo di Firenze, *Il tesoro di Lorenzo il Magnifico,* vol. 1: *Le gemme* (Florence, 1972); and Antonio Morassi, *Art Treasures of the Medici* (Greenwich, Conn., 1963).

12. " 'Caeteri stulti' inquit 'unica catena se vinciri patiuntur, huius autem insania tanta est, ut non sit una catena contentus.' " Poggio Bracciolini, *Facezie,* ed. Marcello Ciccuto (Milan, 1983), CCLIV, p. 386, under the rubric "Catenis veriis collum cingens stultior aestimatur."

13. Quoted in Kent, *Rise of the Medici,* p. 308. ASF, MAP, filza V, nos. 697, 700, 699.

14. When the important men of the city were not holding office, various colors other than the crimson of the prior's cioppa were worn, but generally these hues were in the same area of the color spectrum: other reds, red browns, red violets, and hues considered to be noncolors, that is, purple and black.

15. There were at least eight basic types of headgear for males, from hoods and cowls to hats, berets, and caps of all sorts, and even turbans—all of which seemed to have been publicly acceptable individual variations here. See Strocchia, *Death and Ritual,* pp. 39–41, on hats and headwear in funerary dress.

16. This, of course, leaves out those who actually worked in the houses of the rich families of Florence or as personal servants to these women.

17. See Goldthwaite, "Florentine Palace," pp. 988–89, 1005, 1011, on the serious ramifications for women's freedom as wealthy families retreated into more privately controlled homes.

18. Barbaro, *De re uxoria,* pp. 44–47.

19. "Lettere di Margherita Datini a Francesco di Marco," ed. Rosati, p. 140. In a letter dated Apr. 14, 1398, Margherita writes in part to her husband, "see if you can find a way that I can have a little [reddish brown cloth] for a hood, because I don't want a new cloak

and an old hood" ("vedi se v'avesi il modo ch'io ne potèsi avere uno pocho [of mona-chino cloth] per uno chapuccio, ch'io non vorei il mantello nuovo e 'l chapuccio vechio").

20. Women of the middling to lower rank, from wives of lesser guildsmen like Brucker's Lusanna ("valde formosa et pulcra") to independent entrepreneurs such as the "pidocchiosa rigattiera" we saw in Chapter 2, would have been much more visually available. See Brucker, *Giovanni and Lusanna*, pp. 15, 25.

21. Diane Owen Hughes, "Sumptuary Law and Social Relations in Renaissance Italy," in *Disputes and Settlements*, ed. John Bossy (Cambridge, 1983), pp. 87–88, has noted that kinswomen did have gowns cut from the same fabric, or decorated with a similar design. See also Robert C. Davis "The Geography of Gender in the Renaissance," in *Gender and Society in Renaissance Italy*, ed. id. and Judith C. Brown (New York, 1998), pp. 31–37, on these imposing female masses in the streets of Venice.

22. Langner, *Importance of Wearing Clothes*, pp. 98–99. In contrast, for women, while necklines were ornamented and headwear decorative, most of the cloth bulk was at waist level (this would include trailing sleeves) or below. Treatises on female decorum advise women to keep their arms down and close to their bodies at all times.

23. E. Polidori-Calamandrei, *Vesti delle donne fiorentine nel Quattrocento*, p. 64. A six-teenth of a braccio would be about three centimeters. See Hughes, "Sumptuary Laws," p. 83.

24. See Glossary for these various ornaments.

25. Flugel, *Psychology*, pp. 46–49. The styling of a sleeve could also create an exotic or "foreign" look to a woman's ensemble.

26. ASF, Carte strozz., 2d ser., 17 bis, fol. 19R. In this record, the one and a half braccia of cloth is a *brocchato d'oro di chermisi*, costing 9 florins per braccio. The separate sleeves were tied on with laces, which were strung through eyelets pierced along the sleeve holes of the dress bodice.

27. Usually particolored hose were worn to distinguish juveniles, such as in the Vene-tian Compagnie delle Calze for young men, rather than adults. In the northern court cities, men's hose were often particolored as part of court livery, with the vestimentary code tagging the members of one group or another. In Mantua, the male members of the Gonzaga court all wore one leg white, the other crimson. For hose of the Compagnie delle Calze, see Newton, *Dress of the Venetians*, p. 104. For Gonzaga court dress, see the frescoes of Mantegna in the Palazzo ducale, Camera degli sposi, in Mantua.

28. Langner, *Importance of Wearing Clothes*, pp. 59–60.

29. Lurie, *Language of Clothes*, p. 17.

30. Women did also make headgear (we have noted a Sandra Mazzochiaia), but most often only cuffie, which were worn in the private sphere, either as nightcaps or under cappucci or helmets.

31. Bell, *On Human Finery*, p. 31.

32. Shoes were not regularly worn in mild weather, however, Florentines instead favoring soled hose. In a letter of October 14, 1438, from Contessina de' Bardi to her son Piero de' Medici (who, along with his brother Giovanni was visiting his uncle Lorenzo), she writes that they should both order shoes while there and notes that Giovanni himself has hose along with him, but that she will send his brother "a pair of his oldest hose, which button onto the shoes" (ASF, MAP, filza XVI, no. 8).

33. In the fifteenth century, the tunic worn under the mantello was often quite short and was worn by *giovane*, who have been pictured in farsetto and hose. The newly briefer tunic would not, however, have been worn by the important adult males of the city's upper class in public. In fact, once the boy of an important family attained puberty, no such figure-hugging outfit would have been proper public attire.

34. In fact, the most expensive garment to make was apparently the villano, for which tailors could get 1 florin 1 lira 15 soldi, if it was of the heaviest silk samite (*sciamito*) and pleated all around.

35. Emma Mellencamp, "A Note on the Costume of Titian's Flora," *Art Bulletin* 51 (June 1969): 174–77, refutes Burckhardt's speculation that these pictures of young women in their camicie were wedding pictures. See also Carole Collier Frick, "Dal giardino dei bei fiori," *Carte Italiane: A Journal of Italian Studies* 8 (1986–87): 37–52.

36. See Ghirlandaio's *Birth of the Virgin*, Tornabuoni Chapel, for this style of bodice on female servants.

37. See Levi-Pisetzky, *Costume e la moda*, p. 184. Polidori-Calamandrei identifies all basic gowns as either a *gamurra* or a *cotta*, all overgowns as either a *cioppa* or a *giornea*, and the cloaks worn over the entire ensemble as *mantelli* (with the exception of one *sopravesta*). The only other clothing term used is *guarnello*, which is identified as a gown with an old-fashioned shape to the skirt, that is, an extra, turned-under flounce between the waist and the knees, *all'antica*. See Polidori-Calamandrei, *Vesti delle donne fiorentine nel Quattrocento*, tables 1–32. Here, I have avoided simplifying the number of garment names because many more terms for pieces of clothing appear in the contemporary Florentine sources.

38. See *Tre lettere di Lucrezia Tornabuoni a Piero de Medici ed altre lettere di vari concernenti al matrimonio di Lorenzo il Magnifico con Clarice Orsini* (Florence, 1859).

39. Lurie, *Language of Clothes*, p. 205.

40. "Le gioie sono cose di che la potrai bene fornire; che so costa arai chi ti servira: si che di queste ne gliene farai carestia. E s'e panni non s'adornano con perle bisogna adornalli con dell' altre frasche che si spende assai ed e gittata via la spesa." Quoted in Polidori-Calamandrei, *Vesti delle donne fiorentine nel Quattrocento*, p. 71.

41. The cost for making a mantello ranged from 5 lire 1 soldo down to 1 lira 2 soldi.

42. The precise age or circumstance of this transition has been a source of scholarly disagreement, but it was definitely after the age of ten and before the first pregnancy, or upon taking vows, if in a convent. See Rainey, "Sumptuary Legislation," 1:284–85, for

references to Dominici, *Regola del governo,* p. 235 and Polidori-Calamandrei, *Vesti delle donne fiorentine nel Quattrocento,* p. 49.

43. ASF, Pupilli, Reg. 160, fols. 430R–36R, a clothing inventory with many names of children's garments.

44. See, e.g., the detail from the Masaccio fresco in the Brancacci Chapel on the cover of Herlihy and Klapisch-Zuber's *Tuscans and Their Families.*

45. Ghirlandaio's well-known mid fifteenth-century *Portrait of an Old Man with a Child* in the Louvre shows a berretto on a male child looking up at his grandfather.

46. A few garments and linens associated with pregnancy carried a *da parto* designation, including mantles (*mantili da parto, mantiletti da parto,* and *mantiluzi da parto*), and large sheets (*lenzuole da parto*). ASF, Pupilli, Reg. 160, fols. 430V, 432V, 433RV, 435V.

47. Linens included not only the washable camicie, of which many individuals seem to have had about five to ten, but also nightgowns, nightcaps, and headscarves, which were also worn at night or when working around the house. Middle-class households often possessed dozens of these caps and scarves, along with the requisite towels, napkins, and bedlinens.

48. Helmets had a unicorn, a leopard, a moor, and two with family crests. Pucci only had about fifteen garments, including hats, stockings and belts, whereas his brother Piero had more than twice that many clothes, with thirty-three garments. See Merkel, "Beni della famiglia di Puccio Pucci," pp. 173–75, 183–85.

49. ASF, MAP, CCCXXII, fols. 1R–6R, 30R–32V.

50. Taking care of these fabrics was critical. Soiled brocades were soaked overnight in warm white wine or vinegar, and grease spots on silk were rubbed with fuller's earth moistened with lye. If all attempts at cleaning failed, stained fabrics were simply "turned," that is, taken apart and resewn inside out. Worn-out gold or silver brocades or tissues were burned to recover the precious metal. Rachel Kemper, *Costume* (New York, 1977), p. 69.

51. See Hidetoshi Hoshino's work on the Florentine wool industry, e.g., *Arte della lana,* p. 289ff., for the wide range of woolen fabrics exported to the papal court. Woolen clothes were cleaned by washing them with homemade lye soap in tepid or cold water. Kemper, *Costume,* p. 69.

52. Alberti, *Libri della famiglia,* bk. 3, pp. 246–47. Care of washables ranged from boiling hardy linen to hand-scrubbing cotton.

53. Pegolotti's *La pratica della mercatura,* ch. 74, lists twenty-one different furs available by the early fourteenth century. Francesco Balducci Pegolotti, *La pratica della mercatura,* ed. Allan Evans (Cambridge, Mass:, 1936; reprint, 1970), p. 298.

54. This squirrel fur could also be found in red.

55. Delort, *Commerce des fourrures,* 1:484.

56. Levi-Pisetzky, *Costume e la moda,* p. 195, cites an overgown of "broccato d'oro foderate de lupi cerveri" mentioned in a 1489 letter to the duke of Ferrara.

57. Herald, *Renaissance Dress,* p. 69.

58. Delort, *Commerce des fourrures,* 1:401, sees the opposite, writing that the development of new types of fabric diminished the market for fur. Care of fur included brushing the pelts with fine oils and then storing them in chests or between presses of cypress wood, with layers of bay leaves or pine needles. In addition, to keep away fleas from one's person at home, a shaggy lounging robe, or "fleacoat," was left draped over a chest to attract the bugs. Out in the street, a "flea fur" could be part of one's ensemble, carried or draped on one's arm to attract fleas off the wearer. See Kemper, *Costume,* pp. 69–70. In other Renaissance cities, upper-class fops even carried about small lap animals for the purpose (see Fig. 8.9). Of course, a Florentine male would never have been pictured with such an ostentation or have been wearing such a fancy, belted-in villano or lucco.

59. Woad alone made sky blue (*cilestrino*), a gray blue (*sbiadato*), clear blue (*azzurrino*), a mossy gray green (*muschino*), and the finest black (*negro finissimo*).

60. Levi-Pizetsky, *Costume e la moda,* pp. 64–65.

61. Vittorio Cian, *Del significato dei colori e dei fiori nel Rinascimento italiano* (Turin, 1894), pp. 8–28.

62. Pellegrino Moretto, late fourteenth–early fifteenth-century Mantua, quoted in Cian, *Del significato,* p. 15. My translation.

63. Anonymous, late fifteenth-century Venice, quoted in Cian, *Del significato,* p. 36. My translation.

64. See Laver's discussion of the "fossilization" of fashion in servants' livery, military or guards' uniforms, and the dress of waiters in restaurants. James Laver, *Dress: How and Why Fashions in Men's and Women's Clothes Have Changed During the Past Two Hundred Years* (London, 1966), p. 24.

65. Ronald F. E. Weissman, *Ritual Brotherhood in Renaissance Florence* (New York, 1982), pp. 51, 82–84.

66. Ibid., p. 45.

67. "Le veste non siano aperte e non troppo corte, ma almeno siano per infino ad mezza ghanba. I capucci foderati di vaio overo di seta non si portino, se non per quegli che per dignità il possono portare. . . . e che non portino anello ne cintole d'oro o d'ariento o di seta se non constituti in dignità sotto pena di lire V e di perdere le dette cose prohibite." Quoted in Rainey, "Sumptuary Legislation," 2:595.

68. ASF, Conv. soppr., N. 119, filze 855 and 857, dating from 1447 to 1492. The friars wore at least sixteen different types of black, gray, and white fabric in their vestments, which consisted of a layered ensemble similar to secular dress. One of the nightshirts (*guardacuore*) of fur was for "uno frater infermo."

69. Langner, *Importance of Wearing Clothes,* p. 132, for his discussion of the implications of uniforms.

70. In Renaissance Rome, prostitutes and Jews were made to wear red gowns; in thirteenth and fourteenth-century Recanati, Jews wore a red circle; in Viterbo in 1450,

Jews again needed a circle of red cloth on their outer clothing. Hughes, "Distinguishing Signs," p. 163. Frederic C. Lane, *Venice: A Maritime Republic* (Baltimore, 1973), p. 300, notes that Jews were required to wear scarlet headwear in Venice, and that this applied even to Jewish physicians, who were highly esteemed by the Venetians.

71. Lurie, *Language of Clothes,* p. 196.

72. Newton, *Dress of Venetians,* p. 21, notes that the *togati* who sat in the deliberative chambers of government in Venice were not allowed to enter clothed in black, unless they were in deep mourning, when they might also wear a beard as a sign of grief.

73. Beltrami, *La guardaroba,* pp. 49–57.

74. Luzio and Renier, "Il lusso," pp. 459–60, noted that when Leonora of Aragon died in 1493, her daughters Beatrice and Isabella d'Este wore sleeved gowns and overgowns of brown wool (*panno bruno*) and covered their heads with veils (*scuffie*) of brown silk. Their one nod to fashion was that their veils were "non gialli ne greggi, ma pur bianchi" (not of unbleached cloth, but pure white), probably of the finest Rheims linen. See also the logbook of Antonio d'Agnolo, sarto, ASF, Conv. soppr., N. 102, filza 83, fol. 28v, on widows' clothing.

75. Records of a court case from the *Mercanzia* for 1456 mention eight "family" garments all alike ("8 giornee di taffetta di grana frangiate et soppannate per famigli") for which a silk dealer is attempting to get paid. ASF, Mercanzia, Reg. 288, fols. 112V, 113R.

76. ASF, Carte strozz., 2d ser., 17 bis, fols. 54R, 55V, 68V.

77. Ibid., fols. 1R, 2R, 14R, 54R, 60V, 68V, 72RV, 76V: "una gamurra di saia biancho di levante maniche di domaschino allexandrino e bianche tragittato" (fol. 68V) and "una cotta di zetani raso allexandrino con maniche raso biancho e fiorito" (fol. 72R).

78. See Klapisch-Zuber, "Le 'zane' della sposa," p. 21.

79. For the Parenti family imprese, see *I blasoni delle famiglie toscane, conservati nella raccolta Ceramelli-Papiani,* ed. Piero Marchi (Florence, 1992), pp. 283, 311, 315. For the Strozzi, see Jacopo Gelli, *Divise-mottie e imprese di famiglie e personaggi italiani* (1916; 2d ed., Milan, 1928), pp. 378–79.

80. The color of dark golden yellow was called *mostanolione* by Florentines, but can also be found as *fulvo, tane, lionato,* and *pelo di lione.* The dark colors of black, brown, and purple could be termed *morello, nero, perssi, monachino, bruschini, pavonazzo,* or *verzino,* among others.

81. See Newton, *Dress of Venetians,* app. C, pp. 178ff. I read *pavonazzo* as dark blue violet, based on the fact that gowns of this hue listed in family logbooks are usually expensive formal overgowns, for which overly bright, dull, or homely hues would not have been appropriate.

82. See Gargiolli, *L'Arte della seta,* p. 159, for these fifteenth-century silk names.

83. Ibid., dialogue 2, "Tintore del sete," pp. 149ff.

84. Here we also find "rotten olive" (*oliva fradicia*), a truly negative color name among the beautiful.

CHAPTER 9. SUMPTUARY LEGISLATION AND THE "FASHION POLICE"

1. Besides Florence, at least fourteen other Italian cities had sumptuary legislation at the end of the fourteenth century. They were Genoa, Rome, Bologna, Milan, Venice, Mantua, Padua, Lucca, Perugia, Gubbio, Pistoia, Siena, Treviso, and Saluzzo. Polidori-Calamandrei, *Vesti delle donne fiorentine nel Quattrocento,* pp. 20–21.

2. The primary area of concern in Filarete's work was, of course, architecture. See discussion of Filarete in John Onians, *Bearers of Meaning: The Classical Orders in Antiquity, the Middle Ages, and the Renaissance* (Princeton, N.J., 1988), chapter 11, p. 165.

3. Getrevi, "Il *Libro del sarto* e i paradigmi del moderno," in *Il libro del sarto,* p. 20. This book of clothing illustrations, patterns, and instructions for men, women, horses, and tents (currently housed in the Biblioteca Querini-Stampalia in Venice), the first printed book devoted to the creation of fashionable attire, was the work of at least three Milanese tailors in the 1570s. Cesare Vecellio's *Habiti antichi et moderni* (Venice, 1598) further diffused fashionable styles, but it is clear that Vecellio was frustrated in his attempts to display definitive regional styles of dress in fashionable attire. By the late Cinquecento, these subtle provincial differences in attire had largely been retired to the realm of folk costume, while the "fashionable" in every region dressed more and more alike.

4. Villani, *Cronica,* bk. 9, ch. 150, pp. 226–29: "ma per gli forti ordini tutte si rimasono degli di traggi; e per non potere avere panni intagliati, vollono panni divisati e istrangi i più ch'esse poteano avere, mandandogli a fare infino in Fiandra e in Brabante, non guardando a costo."

5. Rainey, "Sumptuary Legislation," 2:648.

6. Early communal sumptuary laws inevitably carried the rubric *ornamenta mulierum.*

7. Rainey, "Sumptuary Legislation," 1:45–48. At the outset, this tax was 50 lire, half of what the fine would be for not having paid it. By 1376, the annual tax was from 10 to 50 gold florins (ibid., 201–4).

8. Catherine Kovesi Killerby, "Practical Problems in the Enforcement of Italian Sumptuary Law, 1200–1500," in *Crime, Society and the Law in Renaissance Italy,* ed. Trevor Dean and K. J. P. Lowe (Cambridge, 1994), pp. 112–13. The tagging of offending garments was again attempted in 1356.

9. Hughes, "Sumptuary Law," pp. 73–74, writes that "a popular presence is unmistakable" in these early laws, which were "designed less to keep down the upstart than to fetter the aristocrat."

10. Trexler, *Public Life in Renaissance Florence,* pp. 75–76.

11. Hughes, "Sumptuary Law," pp. 90–91, notes that in Siena and Venice, sumptuary restrictions could actually be lifted for communal occasions.

12. See Ronald Rainey, "Dressing Down the Dressed-Up: Reproving Feminine Attire in Renaissance Florence," in *Renaissance Society and Culture,* ed. John Monfasani and Ronald G. Musto (New York, 1991), p. 219.

13. See Hermann Kantorowicz and N. Denholm-Young, "De Ornatu Mulierum: A Consilium of Antonius de Rosellis with an Introduction on Fifteenth-Century Sumptuary Legislation," in *Rechtshistorische Schriften von Dr. Hermann Kantorowicz,* ed. Helmut Coing and Gerhardt Immel (Karlsruhe, 1970), pp. 357–58. Under the Pragmatica of 1356, if a man refused to pay the fine, he became ineligible to hold communal office (Killerby, "Practical Problems," p. 104).

14. Statuti 1322–25, 1:228, cited in Rainey, "Sumptuary Legislation," 1:105: "et ad apothecas et domos aurificum et sartorum et ipsos condempnare."

15. Rainey, "Dressing Down," p. 226, n. 31.

16. See Hughes, "Sumptuary Law" pp. 84–89, 96–99, for a discussion of sumptuary legislation as an "emblem of republican virtue" among legislators from the ranks of the major guildsmen. She also convincingly shows that throughout the fifteenth century, sumptuary laws increasingly targeted the clothing of women. The laws turned from a more wide-ranging regulation of excessive luxury in funeral, wedding, and general attire to a specific attempt at reining in and controlling specifically female sartorial display.

17. Guido Biagi, *The Private Life of the Renaissance Florentines* (London, 1896), pp. 41–42. The first disruptive influence traditionally has been attributed to Marie de Valois, wife of the duke of Calabria, who in 1326 obtained permission from her husband for Florentine women to wear the yellow and white silk braids in their hair, which sumptuary laws had previously banned. Some sixteen years later in 1342, the duke of Athens's retinue again brought French style to Florence, resulting in another crackdown in the enforcement of existing law (and this time giving more work to the Ufficiali delle donne, created after the first podestà had been sent packing).

18. Strozzi, *Lettere* (letter of June 12, 1450, from Alessandra Strozzi to her son Filippo), p. 100. See also A. Giulini, "Nozze Borromeo nel quattrocento," *Archivio storico lombardo* 37, no. 26 (Milan, 1910), p. 269, and "Drusiana Sforza moglie di Jacopo Piccinino (anno 1464)," in *Miscellanea di studi storici in onore di Antonio Manno* (Turin, 1912), 2:211. And see, too, *Tre lettere di Lucrezia Tornabuoni a Piero de' Medici,* letter of Mar. 28, 1467.

19. In 1356, the Commune passed another extensive Pragmatica of sumptuary legislation, forty-three chapters in length, which Rainey says was to be the model for the rest of the fourteenth century. Rainey, "Sumptuary Legislation," 1:146–47.

20. He had the authority to apprehend and interview the violator and write a citation to appear in court, where the lawbreaker would be fined and brought to justice. Rainey, "Dressing Down," p. 221.

21. Hughes, "Sumptuary Law," p. 76.

22. See Paolo D'Ancona, *Le vesti delle donne fiorentine* (Perugia, 1906); ASF, Prammatica del Vestire (1343).

23. Rainey, "Dressing Down," pp. 221–22.

24. Ibid., pp. 221–22. See also documents from 1343–44, 1347, and 1359 cited on pp. 222–26.

25. Ibid., p. 224.

26. For example, compare the limited language contained in the Statuti of 1415 with the Glossary, which lists the names of garments found in the family ricordanze from the same time period.

27. See Rainey, "Dressing Down," p. 220, for a group of prosecutions for men's foppery in the 1340s; see also p. 227 for his reference to Boccaccio's linkage between men wearing zoccoli and their sexual orientation. Shoe and slipper makers came under communal restraint to keep their footwear under one-sixth of a braccio in height, and could be fined 25 lire by sumptuary officials who found these items in their botteghe. ASF, Capitoli 12, fol. 69v, "De calzolarijs."

28. Killerby, "Practical Problems," p. 115. The boys and girls charged ranged in age from infancy up to the age of nine.

29. Rainey, "Dressing Down," pp. 223–24.

30. Killerby, "Practical Problems," p. 113; Brucker, *Society of Renaissance Florence,* pp. 182–83. In this case, the tailor convinced the authorities that the mantello would not be worn in Florence, the customer being from Foligno, and charges were dropped.

31. Killerby, "Practical Problems," p. 112–13. See also Andrea Zorzi, "The Judicial System in Florence in the Fourteenth and Fifteenth centuries," in *Crime, Society and the Law in Renaissance Italy,* ed. Trevor Dean and K. J. P. Lowe (Cambridge, 1994), p. 42.

32. Zorzi, "Judicial System," pp. 42–43.

33. Ibid., p. 43, n. 25.

34. Hughes, "Distinguishing Signs," pp. 20ff.

35. Isa. 3:16–17, cited in Hughes, "Distinguishing Signs," p. 25. John Brackett also notes, however, that Florence was relatively late in marking prostitutes in comparison with other Italian cities. See John K. Brackett, "The Florentine Onestà and the Control of Prostitution, 1403–1680," *Sixteenth Century Journal* 24, no. 2 (1993): 277, n. 18. He notes that in the first decades of the fifteenth century, in order to persuade more of them to register officially as working prostitutes, these women were no longer required to wear bells on their mantelli. See p. 288, n. 68.

36. See Brackett, "Florentine Onestà," pp. 277–78, in this regard for examples from Boccaccio.

37. Ibid., p. 274. Some scholars believe that the underlying motive behind its establishment, however, was a fear of the spread of homosexual activity among the Florentine males, not to monitor and police its legal female prostitutes. See esp. Michael J. Rocke's *Forbidden Friendships: Homosexuality and Male Culture in Renaissance Florence* (New York, 1996).

38. Brackett, "Florentine Onestà," pp. 284–85.

39. Richard Trexler, "La prostitution florentine au XVe siècle: Patronages et clientèles," *Annales: Economies, sociétés, civilisations* 36 (1981): 989.

40. Brackett, "Florentine Onestà," pp. 286–89.

41. See Trexler, "Prostitution florentine," pp. 985–88, for the origin of the 76 prostitutes who registered with the Onestà in 1436. Only one was a Florentine woman.

42. Brackett, "Florentine Onestà," p. 283.

43. Rainey, "Sumptuary Legislation," 2:456–57.

44. Ibid., pp. 457–59.

45. Ibid., p. 459. The source for this conflation is Guido Morelli, *Deliberazione suntuaria del comune di Firenze del XIII aprile MCCCCXXXIX* (Florence, 1881), p. 15: "Gli uficiali di notte sieno uficiali delle donne per ogni tempo, e alloro s'appartenga e sieno tenuti fare osservare detti ordini; a però possino eleggere uno uficiale o più, chome alloro parrà, senza salario di comune." Michael J. Rocke, "Il controllo dell'omossesualità a Firenze nel XV secolo: Gli ufficiali di notte," *Quaderni storici* 66 (1987): 705, asserts that punishment of the crime of sodomy was a focus of this magistracy, which operated by imposing a system of fines on the offenders. On Florentine prostitution, see also Maria Serena Mazzi, *Toscana bella: Paesaggi, gente, amori nel Medioevo* (Turin, 1999).

46. See Hughes, "Earrings for Circumcision," p. 168. On Bernardino, see also Cynthia L. Polecritti, *Preaching Peace in Renaissance Italy* (Washington, D.C., 2000).

47. Brackett, "Florentine Onestà," p. 279, n. 25. Although this example is from 1607, it is probably not atypical of the general problem of visual confusion.

48. Hughes, "Distinguishing Signs," pp. 17–18, 20–24, details the signs that were to mark the Jewish population of many cities in Italy. In Florence, men were to wear a circle cut out of yellow cloth attached to their clothing. Later in the century, in Tuscany, Jewish women were put behind a yellow veil. However, the real sign of a Jewish male was circumcision, and for many generations, Jewish females were identified by the golden hoops in their ears.

49. Ibid., pp. 20, 34. The year was 1439. The required mark was renewed in 1446.

50. See ibid., pp. 17–29, on the vicious sermonizing of popular preachers who warned of the danger of contamination resulting from the mixing of Jews and Christians. The Observant Franciscans San Bernardino of Siena and Giacomo della Marca took the lead here in the early decades of the fifteenth century and especially demonized Jewish women. Hughes cites shaming laws for prostitutes and Jewish women in other Italian cities; in Viterbo, by 1450, if a person saw a Jewish woman in public without her yellow veil, she could be legally stripped of her clothes. Likewise, a prostitute could be publicly undressed in fourteenth-century Parma for having left the main piazza. In Vigevano, a Jewish man could be ritually disrobed in public by anyone for appearing without his distinguishing sign (pp. 30–31, n. 93).

51. See Rocke, "Controllo dell'omossesualità a Firenze," p. 719, n. 5.

52. Carocci, *Mercato vecchio*, pp. 44, 168.

53. For a description of the Defenders of the Laws, see Martines, *Lawyers and Statecraft*, p. 170.

54. See Andrea Zorzi, "Aspetti e problemi dell'amministrazione della giustizia penale nella repubblica fiorentina," *Archivio storico italiano* 533 (1987): disp. III, 446–53.

55. Ibid., pp. 460–64. This does not mean that other boards and agencies were not still periodically formed. For example, in March 1467, the Council of One Hundred created a five-man group, the "officiali sopra decti vestiri et ornamenti, cosí de' maschi come delle femmine," whose members were to be citizens at least forty-five years of age. But within three weeks, these elected officials had already resigned and had to be replaced by four *new* people. It was obviously not a job anyone took pleasure in doing (pp. 460–62).

56. *Statuta populi*, vol. 11, "De prohibitis ornamentis mulierum," pp. 357–90.

57. Rainey, "Sumptuary Legislation," 2:430.

58. In the Trecento, there were regulations controlling gifts of jewels from the groom to the bride, gifts from the bride to guests, and there were to *no* pearls on this day whatsoever. The number of guests at wedding celebrations was limited, as well as the amount and types of foodstuff consumed and the number of horsemen allowed to accompany the bride to the ceremony. But there is no mention of the bride herself, who would simply fall under the general restrictions of the *Ornamenta mulierum,* that is, no excessively long trains or excessive amounts of precious metals in jewelry, headgear, and dress accessories. Ibid., 1:56–60. In the Quattrocento, limitations were eased. In 1439, a bride could wear as many rings as she pleased at her wedding and for 15 days afterward. A woman could also wear pearls worth up to 160 florins (ibid., 2:438–41).

59. Rainey, "Dressing Down," p. 220.

60. Kent, *Rise of the Medici,* p. 54.

61. Scholars are divided on whether or not Lorenzo attempted to increase sumptuary prohibitions in an attempt to visually dominate his oligarchic competition or to decrease prohibitions in order to demonstrate the splendor of his own circle of adherents. See Trexler, *Public Life in Renaissance Florence,* pp. 409–10; also Rainey, "Sumptuary Legislation," 2:538–43.

62. Rainey, "Sumptuary Legislation," 2:543.

63. Franco Sacchetti, *Il Trecentonovelle,* ed. Antonio Lanza (Florence, 1984), novella 137, p. 276: "Va il notaio all'altra che porta gli ermelline, e dice: 'Che potr'a apporre costei?' Voi portate gli ermellino, e la vuole scrivere': la donna dice: 'Non iscrivete, no che questi non sono ermellini, anzi sono lattizi'; che il notaio: 'Ch'e cosa e questo lattizzo?' e la donna risponde: 'E una bestia. . . . .' " The year given for this exchange is 1384.

64. ASF, Carte strozz., 2d ser., 17 bis, fol. 3V.

65. Rainey, "Sumptuary Legislation," 1:52. Tailors were further prohibted from producing these ornaments in 1475. See ASF, Reg. delle Provv., Reg. 166, fol. 178RV.

66. ASF, Carte strozz., 2d ser., 17 bis, fols. 4V, 11V, 19R, 22R, 23V.

67. Rainey, "Sumptuary Legislation," 2:655.

68. Ornament names included *aghetti, bottoncini, coppelle, coppette, maspilli, pianette, raperelle, scaglie,* and *tremolanti.*

69. Rainey, "Sumptuary Legislation," 2:518–21.

70. Leon Battista Alberti, *De iciarchia,* as quoted by Hans Baron in *In Search of Florentine Civic Humanism,* vol. 2 (Princeton, N.J., 1988), p. 287.

71. Quoted in Polidori-Calamandrei, *Vesti delle donne fiorentine nel Quattrocento,* p. 73.

72. Bernardino da Siena, *Le prediche volgari,* pp. 33–34. For example, from one sermon of many, he preached, "lasciate le frappe, le giornee, le code, le corone, le ghiande, I panni trascinanti, le camicie a reticelle e spinapesce, I dondoli d'ariento, le pettinature a civette." Polidori-Calamandrei, *Vesti delle donne fiorentine nel Quattrocento,* p. 25, noted that in Padua in 1460, a woman wearing an excessively long train would not be accepted at confession.

73. ASF, Deliberazioni dei Signori e Collegi, ordinaria autorità, 42, fols. 5V–6R, cited in Brucker, *Society of Renaissance Florence,* pp. 180–81.

74. See Glossary for sleeve designations from *aburattegli* to *strette.*

75. See Ghirlandaio's rendering of the young Tornabuoni woman in the mural of the *Visitation* from the St. John the Baptist fresco cycle in the Tornabuoni chapel in Santa Maria Novella for an ornately figured overgown (*giornea*) worn over an equally elaborate patterned undergown (*gamurra*). The overgown is sleeveless and open down the side and front, exposing the sleeve and skirt of the undergown to view.

76. Whether or not these extravagant sleeves were ever actually constructed has been the subject of much debate among historians of costume. However, Rosita Levi-Pisetzky, *Storia del costume in Italia* (Milan, 1966), 2:218, points out that San Bernardino and Savonarola both preached against excessive amounts of fabric being used in clothes and that the sumptuary laws made explicit the amount of fabric allowed in each sleeve (in one instance, a sleeve could *only* have a circumference of five braccia).

77. ASF, Conv. soppr., N. 102, filza 83, fols. 8V, 11V, 12V, 13V, 18V, 24V, 25V, 27V, 35V, 37V, 68V, 84V, records many types of sleeves that tailors made for their clientele between 1445 and 1453. Also see ASF, Carte strozz., 2d ser., 17 bis, fols. 14R, 25V, 54R.

78. ASF, Carte strozz., 2d ser., 17 bis, fols. 11V, 14R.

79. Giuseppe Levantini-Pieroni, *Lucrezia Tornabuoni* (Florence, 1888), pp. 28–29.

80. ASF, Conv. soppr., N. 119, filza 857, fol. 11S.

81. ASF, Reg. delle Provv., "Ordinamenta super ornamentis mulierum," Reg. 146, fol. 365R.

82. Rainey, "Sumptuary Legislation," 2:447, 452.

83. Ibid., p. 447.

84. The fifteenth century saw the first lace (*pizzo, merletto,* or *trina*) worked with silk, cotton, or linen thread. Although lace was a specialty of Venice, Florentines did wear it occasionally as the century drew on. The first gold and silver threads, a fifteenth-century innovation, were also used in lacemaking. Women working either at home or in a convent made lace with a needle on a lacemaking pillow (*tomboli*), a process called *lavoro ad ago.* Lace could also be made with the aid of a spindle (*fuselli*), an increasingly important piece of technology for subsequent development of lace design. Levi-Pisetzky, *Costume e la moda,* p. 186.

85. Polidori-Calamandrei, *Vesti delle donne fiorentine nel Quattrocento,* p. 61. The metallic

tree and falcon were recorded in the 1417 inventory of Arrigo di Bandino Falconieri, ASF, Pupilli, Reg. 27, fol. 198V.

86. See James Snyder, *Medieval Art: Painting–Sculpture–Architecture, Fourth–Fourteenth Century* (Englewood Cliffs, N.J., 1989), for a northern European example of the left shoulder as visual site, the Choir statue of Uta in Naumburg Cathedral, Germany (ca. 1245–60). She wears a large brooch on her shoulder, the only ornament in her ensemble save her crown.

87. See Laver's still trenchant remarks about the "decorative unity" of an epoch in this regard. James Laver, *Taste and Fashion* (London, 1937), pp. 92, 248.

88. Landucci, *Diario*, p. 371, notes that Florentines began to give up wearing the cappuccio in 1529, and that by 1532, you no longer saw them: "Nel 1529 si comincio a lasciare la portature de' capucci e nel 1532 non se vedeva puro uno . . . si porta berrette e cappegli."

89. Margaret Scott, *Late Gothic Europe, 1400–1500* (London, 1980), pp. 27, 58–59, notes a similar "untidy" trend in northern European fashion in the 1490s. Seams were not properly sewn, and even King Louis XI of France, was "shabbily dressed."

90. Botticelli's paintings of the last decade of the fifteenth century sweep with emotional rendering of draperies, for example.

91. See the portrait of Maddalena Strozzi Doni by Raphael, ca. 1505 in the Pitti Gallery, for the representation of a stoic early Cinquecento Florentine woman.

CHAPTER 10. VISUALIZING THE REPUBLIC IN ART

1. I want to thank Joanna Woods-Marsden for her insightful comments and suggestions on this chapter. Thank you also to Patricia Simons for her assistance with materials on the Tornabuoni Chapel, Jean Cadogan for allowing me to see the galleys of her new book on Ghirlandaio, and Maria Deprano for making available her work on Giovanna Tornabuoni. My gratitude also to Rab Hatfield for his stimulating graduate seminar at UCLA, based on his research on the Tornabuoni Chapel.

2. See Borsook and Offerhaus, *Francesco Sassetti and Ghirlandaio at Santa Trinita*, on the Sassetti Chapel. For the Tornabuoni Chapel, see Patricia Simons, *Portraiture and Patronage in Quattrocento Florence with Special Reference to the Tornaquinci and Their Chapel in S. Maria Novella* (Ph.D. diss., University of Melbourne, 1985). See also Jean Cadogan, "Domenico Ghirlandaio in Santa Maria Novella: Invention and Execution," in *Florentine Drawing at the Time of Lorenzo the Magnificent*, ed. E. Cropper, Villa Spelman Colloquia, no. 4 (Bologna, 1994): 63–82, and Rab Hatfield, "Giovanni Tornabuoni, i fratelli Ghirlandaio e la cappella maggiore di Santa Maria Novella," in *Domenico Ghirlandaio, 1449–1494: Atti del Convegno internazionale, Firenze, 16–18 ottobre 1994,* ed. Wolfram Prinz and Max Seidel, pp. 112–17 (Florence, 1996).

3. Cadogan notes that Davide was his closest assistant but reminds us that a young

Michelangelo was also working in his workshop by June 1487. See Jean K. Cadogan, *Domenico Ghirlandaio: Artist and Artisan* (New Haven, Conn., 2000), pp. 644–46.

4. Giorgio Vasari, *Le vite de' pittori di Giorgio Vasari* (Bologna, 1648), 1:366, writes that Ghirlandaio "did a chapel in Santa Trinita for Francesco Sassetti with stories of St. Francis, an admirable work, remarkable for its grace, finish and delicacy."

5. See also Cadogan, *Domenico Ghirlandaio: Artist and Artisan*. For a pictorial overview of the work of Ghirlandaio, see Emma Micheletti, *Domenico Ghirlandaio* (Florence, 1990).

6. Simons, *Portraiture and Patronage*, pp. 265–316.

7. Micheletti, *Domenico*, p. 64, writes, for example, "Domenico cannot, and presumably does not want to, renounce his role as narrator and chronicler of surroundings and costumes."

8. Jean Lipman, "The Florentine Profile Portrait in the Quattrocento," *Art Bulletin* 18 (1936): 54–102. Also see Rab Hatfield, "Five Early Renaissance Portraits," ibid. 47 (Sept. 1965): 317–43, and Joanna Woods-Marsden, " 'Ritratto al Naturale': Questions of Realism and Idealism in Early Renaissance Portraits," *Art Journal* 46 (1987): 209–16.

9. See Simons,"Women in Frames," pp. 4–30; Hughes, "Sumptuary Laws."

10. See Joanna Woods-Marsden, *Renaissance Self-Portraiture* (New Haven, Conn., 1998).

11. For example, Diane Owen Hughes, "Representing the Family: Portraits and Purposes in Early Modern Italy," *Journal of Interdisciplinary History* 17 (Summer 1986): 7–38.

12. See *Patronage, Art, and Society,* ed. Kent and Simons, and, inter alia, Patricia Simons, "Alert and Erect: Masculinity in Some Italian Renaissance Portraits of Fathers and Sons," and Cristelle L. Baskins, "Corporeal Authority in the Speaking Picture: The Representation of Lucretia in Tuscan Domestic Painting," both in *Gender Rhetorics,* ed. Richard C. Trexler (Binghamton, N.Y., 1994).

13. On Milan, see, e.g., Evelyn S. Welch, *Art and Authority in Renaissance Milan* (New Haven, Conn., 1995). For Mantua, see Joanna Woods-Marsden, *The Gonzaga of Mantua and Pisanello's Arthurian Frescoes* (Princeton, N.J., 1988); and Randolph Starn, "Seeing Culture in a Room for a Renaissance Prince," in *The New Cultural History,* ed. Lynn Hunt (Berkeley, Calif., 1989), pp. 205–32.

14. See, e.g., Aby Warburg's very early *Gesammelte Schriften* (Berlin, 1932) on these frescoes.

15. See Creighton Gilbert, "The Renaissance Portrait," *Burlington Magazine* 110 (1968): 278–85.

16. Borsook and Offerhaus, *Francesco Sassetti and Ghirlandaio at Santa Trinita;* Simons, *Portraiture and Patronage,* esp. pp. 265–317.

17. Simons, *Portraiture and Patronage,* pp. 69–70.

18. Lorenzo de' Medici was Sassetti's employer at the Medici Bank, where Sassetti had become the general manager of the bank in 1469. Borsook and Offerhaus, *Sassetti and Ghirlandaio at Santa Trinita,* pp. 15, 37.

19. On the depiction of Giovanna degli Albizzi (who became Giovanna Tornabuoni upon marriage) in these frescoes, see Maria Deprano, "Uxor Incomparabilis: The Marriage, Childbirth and Death Portraits of Giovanna Tornabuoni" (M.A. thesis, UCLA, 1997); also see Simons, *Portraiture and Patronage*, pp. 311–14.

20. This "direct gaze" would most closely correspond with Starn's conception of the "glance," one of three ways a Renaissance individual would have "seen," or perceived, a completely decorated interior. For an illuminating analysis of Mantegna's work for Ludovico Gonzaga in his Camera degli Sposi in Mantua, see Starn's article "Seeing Culture," pp. 210–32.

21. See Anthony Molho et al., "Genealogy and Marriage Alliance: Memories of Power in Late Medieval Florence," in *Portraits of Medieval and Renaissance Living*, ed. Samuel Kline Cohn Jr. and Steven A. Epstein, pp. 39–70 (Ann Arbor, Mich., 1996), on the importance that Giovanni Rucellai, for example, attached to the females who married into the Rucellai lineage, creating the thick web of *parentado* (and dowry transmission) that he felt obliged to articulate in detail for his grandsons.

22. Simons, *Portraiture and Patronage*, pp. 70–80.

23. When a widow protests "give me a way to be dressed" to her in-laws, she is asking for her social identity within the family realm. Klapisch-Zuber, "Griselda Complex," in *Women, Family*, pp. 225–27; see also Hughes, "Sumptuary Law," pp. 86–87. Lurie, *Language of Clothes*, p. 22, writes that "the more inarticulate someone is verbally, the more important are the statements made by his or her clothes."

24. My thanks to Lauro Martines for pointing out this gendered subtlety in the narrative scene.

25. Merkel, "Beni della famiglia di Puccio Pucci."

26. Simons, *Portraiture and Patronage*, p. 299.

27. Cadogan, *Domenico Ghirlandaio: Artist and Artisan*, pp. 670–72, argues against identifying this figure as Lucrezia Tornabuoni on precisely these grounds, citing the figure's "inconspicuous position for a person on whose links to the Medici rested the economic and political fortunes of the family." I would counter, however, that her role as a mature woman *visually* here was to embody those feminine virtues of self-abnegation Christians learned from the Church.

28. Simons, *Portraiture and Patronage*, p. 146.

29. Carnesecchi, "Sontuosa 'cioppa,' " p. 154.

30. We have been able to posit the identity of some of the nubile female actors in other panels based upon specific jewelry they are wearing. The central female figure in the *Birth of the Virgin* scene (Fig. 10.4) has been identified by both Simons and Hatfield as Lodovica Tornabuoni because she is wearing a distinctive *crocettina* (cross surrounded by pearls) as part of a necklace, which was mentioned as part of her dowry in her father Giovanni's will of 1490. See Simons, "Women in Frames," pp. 9–10. She is also wearing the triangular Tornabuoni device brocaded into her gown.

31. Carnesecchi, "Sontuosa 'cioppa,'" p. 151.

32. *Blasoni delle famiglie toscane*, ed. Marchi, p. 243. The other two Tornabuoni devices are a lion on a ground, which is *inquartato-decussato* (p. 262), and a cross, or *scudetto del popolo fiorentino* (p. 400). The Tornaquinci line, from which the Tornabuoni branched off in the late fourteenth century, had a similar device, which is simply divided into four quadrants, or *inquartato*. Both the Tornabuoni and the Tornaquinci used the colors of gold and green in their family devices, whereas these two dresses with the inquartato-decussato design are gold and red.

33. Simons, "Women in Frames," pp. 11-13.

34. This was in contrast to the northern dynasties of Ferrara and Milan, where the Este produced brocades with the designs and devices of their arms, and where Beatrice d'Este, who was married to Ludovico "Il Moro" of Milan, appeared in 1493 at a family party in Ferrara wearing a gown of tabi fabric dyed with kermes, the sleeves embroidered with the Sforza device of the two towers at the port of Genoa, and four others on the bodice, front and back ("una camora de tabbi cremexino rachamata al porto del fanale, et supra le maniche teniva due torre per cada una et due altre nel pecto et due de dreto"). Luzio and Renier, "Il lusso," p. 455.

35. Martines, *Social World of the Florentine Humanists*, pp. 201-10.

36. See Chapter 8 under "Family Colors."

37. Giovanna wears this same dress in a separate portrait painted by Ghirlandaio in 1488 (now in the Thyssen-Bornemisza Collection in Lugano), in which she is further identified as Lorenzo Tornabuoni's wife by a capital "L" embroidered onto her left shoulder, the "L" visible in the *Visitation* scene as well. She had recently died, having given birth to a son named Giovanni, his grandfather's namesake. Her replacement, wife number two, Ginevra Gianfigliazzi, appears directly behind her in this picture. See Simons, *Portraiture and Patronage*, pp. 305-6; Simons, "Women in Frames," pp. 9, 13-15. See also Chapter 8 on the left shoulder as a decorative site in costume.

38. On reading narrative frescoes, see Charles Hope, "Religious Narrative in Renaissance Art," *Journal of the Royal Society of Art* 134 (Nov. 1986): 804-18.

39. The key blazons of the families involved were: Castellani, castle; Tornabuoni, lions (on inquartato-decussato ground); Alamanni, doves, at rest or flying; Albizzi, a black dross. See *Blasoni delle famiglie toscane*, ed. Marchi, pp. 123, 145, 243, 262.

40. Borsook and Offerhaus, *Sassetti and Ghirlandaio at Santa Trinita*, p. 37.

41. Hope, "Religious Narrative," p. 807.

42. Cadogan, *Domenico Ghirlandaio: Artist and Artisan*, p. 668.

43. Goldthwaite, "Empire of Things," seems to dismiss the simple garb of the Florentine priors as plain cloaks thrown on in a utilitarian manner by mundanely chosen officials consigned to shuffle papers locked up in the Palazzo Vecchio for an anonymous two-month term of office. If Parenti's personal papers are to be trusted, however, the amount of money he spent in properly outfitting his father Parente in 1450 for just such a term of

office, would revise this rather humdrum assessment of a prior's garb. As we saw in Chapter 6, Marco would have spent just under 100 florins for the fur-lined rich cloak that would identify his father as a prior of the city of Florence. ASF, Carte strozz., 2d ser., 17 bis, fol. 14R.

44. The fourth man is Gentile de' Becchi, who had been Lorenzo de' Medici's tutor and later became the bishop of Arezzo, while maintaining strong ties with the Medici family circle. Simons, *Portraiture and Patronage,* p. 274.

Accessories, Cloth, Clothing, and Linens in

Renaissance Florence

abiti da lutto   Mourning clothes.

abiti di riguardo   Robes of communal dignitaries.

affibiatura   Belt buckle.

aghetti (agugielli)   The tips that finished the laces that attached the sleeves to the shoulders of a gown; made by goldsmiths (and their often female workers) of precious metal. Between the laces, the underblouse (*camicia*), was often pulled out to form showy poufs of white.

alessandrino   An especially prized deep rich blue color for silks, obtained by combining orchil, indigo, and madder dyestuffs. Marietta Parenti's trousseau in 1474 listed "una cotta di zetani raso alexandrino" second, only after a gown of "pagonazo di grana," with "dossi di vai."

aliotti   Decorative facings on a gown or mantle placed around the openings where the sleeves were attached to the bodice with laces. Along with the collar, such "aliotti" could have been designed to direct attention to the face of the wearer.

alla di là   Literally "from beyond," indicating foreign fashions.

appicciolato   A type of striped damask or damask with a flower motif that contrasted with the background.

balasso (balascio)   A red gemstone, either a color variety of the spinel (a crystalline mineral of magnesium and aluminum oxides), or of the ruby (the more precious corundum), which were often collapsed together in early modern Europe. In accounts of gemstones, the elided term *spinello rubino* sometimes appears, evidence of such confusion. The name comes from the Arabic *balakhsh*, Persian *badakhshan*, from a district in Iran. When the color of the stone was vermilion like "the red crest of a rooster," or resembled the color of "rosa incarnate," it was called *balasso* or *balascio* by

Renaissance jewelers. A knowledgeable and unscrupulous jeweler could deliberately confuse a spinel and a ruby in a buyer's mind to pass off the softer, less rare (and less expensive) spinel for the harder, rarer, and more expensive ruby.

baldacchino   A type of brocaded, heavy silk from Baghdad, used in throne and processional canopies known by the same name.

balze   Flounces at the hemlines of gowns, which could be of a contrasting color or type of fabric.

balzo   An extremely bulbous form of turbanlike headdress worn by women in many Italian Renaissance cities, but only rarely seen in Florence; formed of a light willow or wire frame covered with a silk brocaded fabric and sometimes even tiny metallic ornaments.

becca   Laces to which stockings were fastened. *Becche* could be silk or velvet and were worn by both men and women; performed a function similar to our modern-day garter.

becchetto   The hanging fabric on the right side of a hat (*cappuccio*), which was doubled and draped over the shoulder, carried over the arm, or even wound around the head for expediency or style on the streets of Florence. It was fashioned by tailors. In Venice, the becchetto was called a *becho*, and by the late fifteenth century, it had become detached from the hat and was simply a long band of fabric about 25 cm wide worn over the left shoulder by the ruling classes as a badge of office. This becho was of a contrasting color to the gown with which it was worn, in Venice called a *toga*. Later, this became the ceremonial stole, or *stola*.

benda   A simple cloth headcovering for both genders made of linen, cotton, or, for women, silk.

benducci (diminutive of *bende*)   Little head veils, often part of the female *acconciatura*, or hairdo. Trousseaux of the Quattrocento often list benducci "dallato in uno filo," as specialized yardage, to be cut apart and used as the need arose. Gostanza Parenti had thirty-eight such veils in her trousseau of 1470.

berrettino   A dark gray "ashen" color, suitable for mourning clothes. In Venice, permission had to be obtained by males to wear this color to the meetings of the ruling Collegio. Berrettino appears to have been a personal favorite color of Isabella d'Este.

berretto   A type of headgear for both males and females, made by professional male *berrettai*, worn by the *popolo grasso* and friars, but not by the lower guildsmen. Berretti for males were usually of wool felt, but could also be made of silk. Hat brooches (*fermagli*), were often worn on these hats. Women's berretti could be of damask or satin, often decorated with embroidery. Nightcaps (*berrette da notte*) were ordered along with nightshirts (*guardacuore*), and made of the same linen or cotton fabric.

biancho-greggio   Unbleached cloth color, suitable for humble personal linens.

bigello   *A type of thick, coarse woolen cloth with a shaggy, uncut nap on one side, called "frieze" in English. The color term bigio comes from this basic gray cloth.*

bigharri (*bigheri*)   A type of ornamentation made of lace; lace trim. Fancy hose of the kind worn to costume parties were often cut at the knee and trimmed with velvet fringe (*frappate di velluto*), or *bigherino*. In Venice, the Compagnie de Calze wore such decorated legwear.

bigio   Gray color of cloth especially favored in the wardrobes of young girls cloistered at a young age in one of the many Florentine convents.

bisiello   Fine linen cloth made of yellow flax, called "byssus" in English. Traditionally, the best-quality Egyptian linen, which had been used by the ancients for wrapping their dead in mummification; but it could also refer to fine cotton cloth. Used in the Renaissance for personal linens (*pannilini*), such as nightgowns and nightshirts.

boccaccino   A type of fabric of cotton or linen, patterned with little holes sewn around with thread to made an embroidered design. Nightcaps and doublets (*farsetti*) were two garments made of this fabric. *Boccaccini* could also denote the type of garment made from this fabric, usually part of a person's personal linens.

boctoni   Buttons.

bottoncini   Little buttons; studs, often made of copper, then silvered or gilded, for clothing decoration.

borsa   Bag or purse. Since clothes rarely had pockets, bags were used widely, and could be richly worked of many materials (silk, velvet, gold and pearl embroidery, flowered designs). *Borse* were round in shape, and used by both genders. Men's borse were often of leather.

braghetta (*brachetta*)   A codpiece. A "cod" was a bag for male genitalia covering the fork of hose or tights, as doublets became too short for maintaining modesty; the term also could denote that part of a male's pants that covered the fly in front. In the fifteenth and sixteenth centuries, men also carried money and a handkerchief in their codpieces. Braghette became overpadded in some historians' opinions (especially for sovereigns), by the mid sixteenth century.

broccatello   A light brocade. A type of mixed-weave silk fabric which imitated brocade; also called *broccatino*. A garment of broccatello was found in the wardrobe of Duke Lorenzo de' Medici in 1515.

bruschino   A deep red color similar to the gemstone balascio. A *bruschina* overgown lined with *gholpe* (*volpe*, or fox) was part of a man's clothing inventory in 1448.

brusti   Figured silk ornamental borders or bands on some ecclesiastical vestments, richly embroidered, often in gold, called "orphreys" in English. A weaver of brusti could only produce about ten yards per month.

calcetti   Socks; also slippers.

calze   Soled hose for men, made of stretchable woolen jersey fabric called perpigiano cloth, originally imported from the town of Perpignan in southern France. These hose attached to a male's doublet with laces and occupied the attention of many artists, who show wearers in various stages of dishabille. Calze could also button on to shoes. In the later fifteenth-century and into the sixteenth, particolored hose became popular in the northern court cities. The Montefeltro court of Urbino dressed with one leg red, the other white. Particolored hose was also worn at the papal court in Rome and the Compagnie de Calze in Venice, where hose with one leg faded red (*ruosa secha*), and the other white and pale green (*festachina*), was noted in 1508.

calze-brache   As doublets became shorter, for the sake of modesty, and also for durability, these hose were often lined. In the late fifteenth and early sixteenth centuries, they became a decorative feature of clothing, being embroidered, and even beribboned. Eventually, they lost their ornamental nature, and became essentially the forerunner to modern men's plain trousers.

camicia   An undergarment of various soft washable fabrics such as cotton, linen (*rensa*), and occasionally thin silk or wool (*saia*) or cotton. This long shirt with amply cut sleeves was worn next to the skin by everyone and formed the major part of a person's personal linens. In the backgrounds of Masaccio's frescoes in the Brancacci Chapel, camicie can be seen hanging out to dry on wooden rods attached to the sides of Florentine palazze. Camicie *da verno* (for winter) are also listed in clothing inventories for children, made of a heavier fabric for cold weather.

canovaccio   Coarse linen cloth, used for a variety of utilitarian purposes, from tailors' fittings to horse covers.

capeccale (*capezzale*)   A collar.

cappa   A cloak, cape or mantle, for men or women. Also refers to the ecclesiastical tunic, or *tonica*.

cappellina   A small, close-fitting cap for a woman or girl.

cappello   A generic word for hat, which could be made of a variety of materials, and of various shapes. One popular style was a broad-brimmed outdoor traveling hat for men, often of straw lined with silk or velvet. Craftspeople called *cappellai* produced hats for both men and women; those for women often had full-length veils. Rain hats were often made of German wool.

capperone   A large, untailored *cappuccio* in the peasant style.

cappuccio (*cappuzzo*)   A hat composed of three separate parts. First, there was the *mazzocchio*, a padded roll covered with cloth, which circled the head and was closed and lined on the top, providing a headcovering. The second part was the *foggia*, a piece of fabric anchored under the mazzocchio, which hung down to the shoulder, shielding the whole left cheek. The third element was the *becchetto*, a doubled strip of the same cloth that draped to the ground and was folded up again on the right shoulder, often worn surrounding the collar. Those who wished to be more agile and quicker wound it around their head. Cappucci were often fashioned of the same fabric as an overgown, were made by tailors, not by hatmakers, and could be worn by both men and women. The Parenti ricordanze records "uno cappuccio pagonazo della donna" (a blue-violet cappuccio for a woman), for which three ounces of *tremolanti d'ariento dorati* (gilded silver ornaments) were bought for decoration. Further, there were many ways of wearing the foggia and becchetto elements of the cappuccio, according to one's personal sense of style. To salute a person of superior rank, a man pushed the cappuccio slightly up on his forehead with a gesture when passing, without ever raising it. In Milan, among the *sentenze dei podesta* (under the rubric *pro descapuzando*), there was a five-lire fine for pulling someone's cappuccio off his head. By the early sixteenth century, cappucci were out of fashion and had been replaced by berretti and cappelli.

caputeo   A cap or hood.

cassone   Large chests or trunks that held clothing and linens. In the Renaissance, these chests were often ornately decorated and formed an important part of a woman's marriage trousseau.

cascietti   Early fourteenth-century ornamental hairpieces.

cenerito   A medium gray color of pious convent garb, the color of coal cinders, worn by nuns.

cerchiellum (Lat.)   A silver or gilded silver head ornament.

chapia (cappa)   A late fourteenth-century generic word for cloak, cape, mantle, or gown.

chermisi   The highest quality, most brilliant, and longest-lasting crimson dyestuff in the fifteenth century; called "kermes" in English (from Spanish *quermes*, Arabic *qirmizī*, Persian *kirm*, Sanscrit *kr'mih*, all meaning vermin, worm, or insect) because made from the desiccated bodies of the pregnant females of kermes lice (esp. certain Asian species of these insects, probably *Porphyrophora hameli,* found in the Caucasus and Near East). This dye was used in Florence in the fifteenth century for both silk velvets and wool. When a garment was referred to as chermisi, Jacqueline Herald says, fine woolen fabric is meant. This dyestuff was known as *cremisi* or *cremesino* in Venice.

chode (code)   Literally "tails," usually referring to the tailfeathers of the peacock, "occhi di chode di paghone," which were used to decorate very special headdresses, or "ghirlandai" for women. At mid fifteenth century, one such headdress could have 500 of these peacock feather "eyes."

chopine   Very high wooden or cork platform shoes for women slipped on for outside wear over more delicate slippers (*pianelle*). *Chopine* is a foreign term of uncertain provenance that referred to this higher feminine style favored by Florentine women in the Quattrocento. In the Cinquecento, chopine became infamous due to their use by Venetian courtesans (and others), whom Aretino called his "goddesses," perhaps alluding to their elevated height in the streets and plazas, where they were so high (up to 30 cm, if you can believe the sources) that the wearers had to be aided in their city promenades through public piazze by a servant on each elbow. Similar types of shoes were called *zoccoli*, but zoccoli could be worn by men or women, and were not as extremely high or fashionable.

ciambelloto   A generic term for "costly fabric"; could be either woolen cloth or cloth made of camel or goat hair, probably quite hard-wearing. In the fourteenth and

fifteenth centuries, there are also examples of a ciambelloto type of silk, which can refer
to silk the color of camel hair; corresponds to the French *camelot*, and English "camlet."

cintura   Wide belts worn by women, the major decorative piece of clothing through the
Trecento and in the first decades of the Quattrocento. Cinture could be adorned with
embroidery, gold or silver, and/or precious stones. Belts with silver ornaments or
thread were often the only decorative object poor women owned.

cioppa   A Tuscan term for an overgown with sleeves, often made of a type of silk brocade,
velvet, or fine wool, worn by women over the *gamurra* or *cotta*, and also by men over the
doublet. Many inventories and trousseaux begin with *cioppe* at the head of the clothing
lists, probably indicating their importance in a Florentine's public wardrobe. In the
south they were called *pellande*, in Bologna, *veste* or *sacche*. Cioppe were often gathered
(*raccolta*) in flat pleats (*pieghe piatte*) from the neckline; they could also be *a cannoncini*,
that is, long and narrow. High-necked cioppe "*accollato*" were worn by older women.

cioppetta   A short cioppa; could also designate a smaller version of the gown for a child.

clamide   An overdress without sleeves (similar to a *giornea*); riding mantle.

coda (*cauda*)   The train of a dress.

coltre   A counterpane, that is, a bedcover or bedspread, found in family linens inventories.

contigie   Fancy ornaments stamped or tooled into the leather of shoes.

copertoio (*chopertoio*)   A large bed cover, also found in linen inventories.

copoletti   Decorative metallic baubles sewn on gowns. Family records list one *gamurra*
with 152 such copoletti. Made by goldsmiths, many of whom employed women to
make such ornaments.

coppelle (*coppette*)   Metallic dress ornaments like buttons, but that did not need but-
tonholes. This seems to have been a sumptuary legislation avoidance term like *lattizi*.

cordelle   Literally, "small cords." Fine, braided silk used in headpieces, as well as in decorating purses.

cordoni   The smaller and narrower belts that became fashionable as the Quattrocento
progressed, replacing the earlier wide *cinture*. They were usually of silk, also gold
threads, ornamented with pearls.

corne   Literally, "horns." A female style of headdress, part of a woman's *acconciatura*, which
had horn shapes on both sides of the head, then draped with a thin gauze veil. This mid
fifteenth-century fashion imported to Florence from France and Flanders was ridiculed by moralists such as Bernardino da Siena.

corona   A crown; popular head ornament for women in early Trecento. Later outlawed
by sumptuary laws.

corregia   A leather belt for men to which their purse (*scarsella*) could be attached.

corsaletto   Military armor for the upper body. Found in the Medici wardrobe accounts of
1515. Only one and a half yards of gray velvet cloth were needed to fashion a cover for
Duke Lorenzo's corsaletto.

cortine   Curtains, for bed or windows.

cotta   A woman's basic gown, perhaps a lighter summer version of the *gamurra*. The 1466 trousseau that Nannina de' Medici brought to Bernardo Rucellai upon their marriage contained a cotta of white damask brocaded with golden flowers, with sleeves of pearls.

cottardita   An amply cut long gown for men or women, which could be wider or longer, to taste. This garment could be trimmed with fur, and was often magnificent and showy, as its name, *cotta ardita*, that is, "daring or fearless gown," suggests. This style was often associated with older women and can be found in communal statutes codified in the Quattrocento, but not in the fifteenth-century logbooks.

croceus (Lat.)   A golden yellow or saffron color popular in silks.

cuffie (cuffioni)   Name of a headgear that began as a generic term for hoods (*cappucci*) for both men and women. Makers of cuffie, called *cuffiai*, were under the dictates of the Por Santa Maria, as their products could be made of linen, silk, or wool. Cuffie were worn under helmets or as nightcaps, which would often have ties under the chin. They are sometimes also pictured as caps on toddlers and young children. By the Quattrocento, this type of headgear was mostly seen on women, and *cuffia* came to mean a woman's cap or hat, which hid her pulled-back and plucked hair; often ornately embroidered for stiff formal display.

domaschino   A single-color fabric originally from Damascus, "damask" in English. Damask is a firm, shiny, reversible linen, silk, or cotton fabric with woven designs.

dossi   Literally, "backs." Skins of fur from the back of an animal, not as soft and therefore less expensive than *pancie*, cut from the underbelly fur of the animal.

drappo   Originally a generic word for woolen cloth; later any cloth or fabric.

drappi di sete rilevati   Cloth made of figured silk.

dubretto   a type of foreign cloth made of linen and cotton wool, made in both France and Sicily. See the 1359 ricordi of Miliadusso Baldiccione of Pisa, p. 33, where he purchases 44¾ braccia of *dubretto ciciliano* for 9½ soldi a braccio. In England, this term could also signify the garment called a "doublet."

ermellino   The white winter fur of the ermine (a member of the weasel family), used widely in trim on clothing, but generally too costly for an entire lining; imported from Russia through Constantinople until 1453. Ermellino and other furs such as marten were severely restricted by sumptuary legislation in 1439 in Florence. Lorenzo de Medici's Christmas gown, *vestito di natale*, was lined with ermellino in 1515.

farsetto   A man's doublet, quilted with cotton wool stuffing (*bambagia*), which was worn over an undershirt like a form-fitting, hip-length vest, and under a tunic. In the early Quattrocento, the farsetto was always hidden under the longer gown, but after mid-century, clothes became more closely fitted, and men appeared in public in farsetto and hose, with only a loose cloak thrown over them. For sporting events, young men regularly stripped down to farsetto and hose. A few farsetti for women and even *farsettini* for children appear in clothing inventories. In Florence, farsetti were fashioned by clothing specialists called *farsettai*. In Venice, the farsetto was called a *zupon*, and was made by tailors called *zupponieri*.

fermaglia   A decorative badge that could be worn on a cappello or berretto style of hat.

These badges were often personal statements of style. A fermaglia could also be a brooch, which was worn on the left shoulder of a cioppa (for men or women) as the major piece of jewelry in an ensemble.

fibbia   A buckle or clasp for a belt, often gilded or fashioned of silver. This was a basic piece of ornament in a Renaissance ensemble for both genders.

figure de panno   Intaglio decorations or images on cloth.

finestrella   The front seam opening in a sleeve that allowed the wearer to push his or her arm through, leaving the sleeve hanging straight down from the shoulder. Finestrelle also allowed glimpses of the garments of contrasting color, pattern, or fabric worn beneath.

fodero (*frodulo*)   A lining, usually of fur, especially of the gray squirrel (*vaiaio*). Linings could also be of satin, silk, or linen.

foggette   Headwear of the Florentine popolo minuto, as opposed to the berrette worn by the popolo grasso. An insult thrown out to a little man by a magnate would be to call him *una foggettina*.

fogliette   Hemline ornaments shaped like leaves.

frangia (*frappe*)   Fringe, borders, edging.

frastagli   A type of ornament created by cutting the border of a garment into the shape of leaves or tongues, called "dagging" in English. It appeared as a design element in clothing about 1350 and lasted in some places (such as Burgundy) until around 1500. Dagging was not popular in Florence, however. Alberti found it suitable only for "jugglers and trumpeters"; Chaucer's Parson decries it as a sinful extravagance. Nevertheless, some still decorated sleeves with frastagli.

frenello   A head ornament for women worn around the top of the forehead, consisting of a strand of pearls woven with gold or silk "hair," which could form a point at the middle of the forehead. Another style was a woven braid of small pearls set in gold, which was then worked back into the hair, or worn around the border of the cuffia. In 1461, Cino Rinuccini gave his new wife Ginevra a frenello with 271 pearls. A frenello was sometimes also known as a *vespaio* (hornet's nest), perhaps because of the intricacy of the woven pearls.

fustagno   A light- to medium-weight cloth suitable for undergarments, bedding, or summer clothing, called "fustian" in English. It was made of a linen warp and a cotton weft and used for clothing by the urban working classes in Europe throughout the Middle Ages. Fustagno was the same low-priced fabric as *guarnello*, also a cellulose fiber fabric, but of a thinner weave. Into the period of the Renaissance, both fustagno and guarnello displaced coarser homespun peasant wools.

gabbanella   A small knee-length undergown, tunic, or cassock of thin, lining-type fabric. Gabbanelle were worn by assistants and convalescents at the hospitals of Renaissance Florence. They had no collar and were not unlike the simple labcoat worn by doctors and surgeons at hospitals and in practice today.

gamurra (camora, zimarra) A woman's basic gown. In Quattrocento Florence, the gamurra corresponded to our generic word "dress," for it was worn by women of all classes and could be of wildly varying fabrics. The gamurra was usually unlined, being worn over an underblouse, or *camicia.* In late Trecento art, women are often depicted wearing only their gamurre, with neither a cioppa nor a giornea over it. Up until about 1450, the gamurra is usually shown with sleeves, but later, the sleeves were usually detachable, and made of a rich fabric, for contrast. (Duke Lorenzo de' Medici's wardrobe accounts of 1515 also list a *zimarra.*)

garbo In the early Quattrocento referred to woolen cloth that originated in the western Mediterranean region.

gheroni In English "gussets," which were often triangular or diamond-shaped.

ghirlanda (grillanda) Literally means a "garland." In the Renaissance, it was a headdress for women, which could be fashioned of feathers (often peacock "eyes"), pearls, silver ornaments, or of a textile applied over a padded roll that fitted around the head. For extremely festive occasions, even a man could be adorned with a ghirlanda.

ghiro Dormouse. The gray fur of this Old World squirrel-like rodent was used especially for the linings of capes and overgowns.

ghugliata Literally, a "needleful." This was the Renaissance measure of a "little bit" in common parlance.

giannetta Walking stick. Often found listed in inventories of personal household effects.

giornea A long sleeveless overdress worn in public, often elaborately embroidered, lined with fur for winter, silk for summer, which could be bordered and hemmed with fur. The giornea was open both down the front and at the sides to allow for a freer walking stride and also to enable the fabric of the gamurra or cotta beneath could show through. There was much sumptuary discussion about the length of the back hem of a giornea, which was long, and could form a train (*strascico*). The giornea performed a similar role to the cioppa, except that it was sleeveless and open at the sides. The giornea had originated as military dress for day battle in antique times.

giubba From the Arabic, an old-fashioned style of full cloak (two alle, or approximately 90 inches, in back), which opened down the front. It could be worn by men, women, or children. This term appears in the communal legislation but not often in the family ricordanze of the Quattrocento. It could be made of thin, rich silk (called *zendado*) and be decorated with elaborate gold embroidery. For women, a giubba was heel-length. In antique times, the giubba probably also covered the head, similar to a garment called the *cappa,* often worn with an animal skin at the neck for warmth. This generic "cloak" was called an *aljuba* in Spain; in France, a *habit*; in Venice, a *velada*; and in Lombardy, a *marsina.*

golpe (volpe) Fox fur, often used for lining the sleeves of overgowns such as cioppe.

gonnella Predominately a simple shift garment for women, but could also be worn by men as a housegown.

gonnellino   Diminutive of *gonnella*. Often worn by children; could be of embroidered linen cloth.

gorgiere   A gorgette of white cloth wound around the neck up to the chin and around back up under the hair. This fashion is traditionally thought to have been introduced to Italian wear by Lucrezia Borgia when she came in as a new bride into the House of Este at the end of the 1400s, and was quickly adopted as becoming by court watchers in Ferrara.

grana ("grain")   The red dyestuff made from the dried bodies of the Mediterranean shield lice *Kermococcus vermilio* or *Coccus ilicis,* which looked like kernels of grain when dried, thus its name. According to Pliny, Mediterranean kermes came from Portugal, Spain, Tunisia, and Asia Minor. By the fifteenth century, it was considered inferior to the richer red dye imported from the East (*chermisi*) because it was cheaper. This judgment also reflected contemporary taste, which favored a red hue toward the violet end of the spectrum rather than the orange. Grana dye made rose (*rosato*), scarlet (*scarlatto* or *scarlattino*), ruby red (*rubeo*), and deep blue-violet (*pavonazzo*).

grembiali   Utilitarian aprons for housework (*cose casalinghe*); could also be embroidered for wear outside the house, more or less rich. This term also referred to smocks for small children and toddlers. Aprons were called *scossali* in Lombardy.

guado   A dyestuff for fabrics from a plant of the mustard family (genus *Isatis*), called "woad" in English. Guado produced sky blue (*cilestrino*), clear blue (*azzurro*), turquoise blue (*turchino*), and the finest black (*negro finissimo*).

guardacuore   An ample nightshirt or nightgown, worn by men, women and children. Could be made of cotton, linen, or even fur (*pelle*). A *guardacuore pelle* was ordered for a *frater infermo* at SS. Annunziata. They were often lined, and took from 4½ to 6 braccia of cloth to make.

guarnacca (*guarnacchia*)   An amply cut, full-length overgown for men with sleeves, similar to the cottardita, but not as richly made or of such ample proportions. Worn unbelted by city *signori* and *magistrati*.

guarnello   A type of thin, coarse linen or cotton cloth used for linings or undergowns, perhaps akin to *himo*, which is a wool and goat's hair combination, sometimes used now in the interfacing of shoulder pads in men's wool suits (see *fustagno*). This term can also refer to a basic, unadorned gown made from this fabric, of the sort worn by the abandoned children who populated the foundling hospitals.

impiere   To quilt.

inbusto   The bodice of a garment.

increspaturas   Ruffles or pleats (fourteenth-century sumptuary legislation term).

infula   Cloth bonnet.

ingiubare   To decorate or trim a cloak (*giubba*).

intricatorie   Silk hair pieces decorated with precious ornaments or intricately braided with pearls.

ischanpoletti (*scampoletti*)   Little cloth remnants or doffings.

ischugatoi (*schugatoi*)   Towels of all kinds.

lacci   Laces with which sleeves were attached to the bodice of a dress at the shoulders through eyelets (*maglie*).

lana filata (worsted wool)   A firmly twisted thread or yarn made of long-stapled wool, or a cloth made from such thread or yarn. (A long-staple clothstuff has fibers averaging more than 1⅛ inches in length.) This twisted thread was named after Worsted, a town in England where it was originally made.

lattizi   The soft, furred baby skins of indeterminate white animals. Lattizi were tiny and therefore normally too expensive to use for a full lining. They were mostly used for fur borders on special or ceremonial giornee or cioppe. The actual type of fur to which the term *lattizi* referred was left vague in the family ricordanze of the fifteenth century, perhaps to thwart sumptuary restrictions on certain expensive furs such as sable and ermine. Rather than using the words *zibelline* or *ermellino*, the Florentine oligarchy seems to have used the invented "avoidance word" *lattizi*. Women especially were faulted for using this word to identify the fur they were wearing, when trying to deflect the male gaze of the sumptuary police. See Sacchetti, *Il Trecentonovelle,* Novella CXXXVII.

licci   Heddles for the draw-looms used in weaving complex silk brocades and figured velvets in the Renaissance.

licciaruolo   A draw-boy, who sat at the head of the loom and pulled the attached harnesses, which raised or lowered the heddles, at the command of the weaver.

lucco (*ucco*)   A long sleeveless gown, with pleats, fastened at the neck, open in the front, and buckled with a clasp. Worn originally by communal officials and academicians as a generic ceremonial dress. Gradually, it appears in inventories and commissions, usually a garment for men and boys, however, some older women list a lucco in their clothing inventories. In the late fifteenth century, a *lucco catalano* also appears, "in the Spanish style."

lupo ciervieri (*cervieri*)   Fur of the lynx, used for the linings of cloaks, seen listed as "foderata di lupi ciervieri" (lined with lynx), or "fodere di fianchi di lupo ciervieri." Imported from Russia through Constantinople until 1453.

maglia   Literally, a "singlet," of the metal (usually copper) eyelet through which laces or ribbons were threaded to tighten a garment, or to attach sleeves. Sometimes made of silver, or gilded with silver.

malfatto   Literally, "ill-shapen." This appears as a designation in inventories of clothing to denote an old, worn-out garment, usually of undyed bigiello cloth, although the inventory of Albizo del Toso lists one malfatto of *verde foderato di rosato*.

maniche   Literally, "sleeves," which were regularly listed separately from the garments to which they were attached, because they were detachable and laced onto garments with ties (*lacci*). In Renaissance Florence, sleeves could be of many shapes: loose or full, tight or slashed, with a contrasting lining showing through. Modesty, however, dictated that they cover the arm down to the wrist, for women and girls of all classes, except the most wretchedly poor *miserabili*. Often *un paio di maniche ricamata* (a pair of embroidered sleeves) was listed as one of the main items in a young woman's trousseau, directly after the cioppe or giornee. Sleeves were one piece of clothing that reflected the art of the tailor during the course of the Quattrocento, becoming more complex and tailored. Sleeves have been effectively used to date paintings through the Renaissance, as they were the target of repeated sumptuary legislation, which can often be pegged to a specific decade. Types of sleeves:

aburattegli, acotelacio, and *affettate*: three types of cut or slashed sleeves, showing either lining or camicia of a contrasting color underneath

agozetti: probably referred to gathered sleeves

a gozzi: literally, "a bird's crop," after the shape of the sleeve. These unusual full sleeves attached at the shoulder, from which they hung full like a bag, and attached to a tight band at the wrist. Alternately, these sleeves could be worn with the wristband pushed up the forearm, with the sleeves billowing down. A third very elegant, *molto raffinato* manner of wearing this sleeve was to free one's arm from the sleeve by pushing the hand through a long slash (*finestrella*) in the front seam, exposing the sleeve of the undergarment worn beneath. The sleeve would then hang straight down from the shoulder *a gozzi*, often almost to the ground, behind the arm. If the fabric of the sleeve was stiff, this created an odd illusion of having two sets of arms. In Venice, these sleeves were called *maniche a comedo* and were set into the togas of patricians and citizens.

alla bolognese: in the style of the city of Bologna. It is unclear what design features this style of sleeve displayed, but the term does indicate that regional differences could be detected in the sleeve styles, which often were considered the most au courant element of an ensemble.

alla lombarda: in the northern Italian style, probably indicating Milanese style, which could be beribboned with stringhe

aperto: open sleeves, exposing the gamurra underneath; often worn *affaldate* or turned up at the wrists

atrombe: perhaps sleeves shaped like trumpets, falling down over the hand. See the long sleeves partially covering the hands of the kneeling Nera Corsi in Ghirlandaio's fresco in the Sassetti family chapel in Santa Trinita, ca. 1483; also, the Tornabuoni girl's sleeves in the panel entitled the *Birth of the Virgin,* in the Tornabuoni Chapel.

fiorite: sleeves of flower-patterned fabric, often in contrast with a different, solid-color dress bodice

pullite: smooth, close-fitting, neat sleeves

spagnolesco: sleeves in the Spanish style, that is, separate from the dress, attached with laces. The fashion for detachable sleeves, popular from midcentury (1450), may have originated in Spain.

staccate: sleeves attached to the bodice by laces

strette: long, narrow sleeves; traditional for clerical habits. Today in Italian, *di maniche strette* denotes a strict disciplinarian, like the term "straightlaced" in English.

manichini   Cuffs, or the wristbands of sleeves.

mantello   An amply cut, ankle-length overcloak for men or women, often without pleats. Most often made of woolen cloth, but could be of silk. Mantelli had plain lines and were more a garment of necessity against the cold or the intrusive eyes of the street than of elegance. The wearing of the mantello marked a woman's transition from girlhood to womanhood. A short version was worn by youth or children, called predictably a *mantellino*.

Types of mantelli:

alla bramante: possibly, luxurious (see ASF Pupilli, Toso family inventories)

alla catalana: in the Spanish style, seems to have been worn by men

grande: worn especially by mourning women

lungho: worn by mourning men

mantilli   Plain, ordinary tablecloths; "una tavola coperta di netti e onesti mantilli."

martore   The thick brown furred skin of the marten, a large member of the weasel family, available locally in Florence, and regulated by sumptuary legislation. Marten fur was worn as a winter lining in clothing.

maspilli   Gilded silver buttons (*bottoni preziosi*). One gamurra could have twenty-two such decorations, which were often more ornamental than practical, in order to evade sumptuary legislation that targeted too many buttons. Maspilli have also been identified as hat ornaments, often made of silver, with a precious stone inset, or decorated with enameled flowers.

mazzocchio   A padded roll worn around the head as the hat base. For men and women, this hat type would be a cappuccio and would form part of the hood around the crown of the head. Also for women, the mazzocchio could be the base for the more fanciful ghirlanda. Marco Parenti hired a female *mazzocchiaia* to make the headdress for his bride Caterina Strozzi, in 1447 (ASF, Carte strozz., 2d ser., 17 bis, fol. 7R).

merletto   Lacework, done by hand on lace-making pillows called *tomboli*; used for trimming garments.

mochichini   Handkerchiefs, nose wipes.

monachino   A dark, reddish brown color thought suitable for older men and women, nuns, widows, and funeral wear. Eventually was adopted by the Franciscans as the color for their religious vestments.

mormorino (marmorino)   That is, a "mixed" or "marbled" color. The Parenti ricordanza lists a gamurra for a small girl of mormorino.

moscavolieri   Presumed to be a color of gray, with unclear origin. Three cioppe appear in one inventory of this color of fabric, one lined with *puzole*, the dark brown pole cat, valued at eight florins, and two unlined, valued together at twelve florins. See Merkel, "I beni," pp. 173, 186.

mostanolione   A tan color, which denoted a tawny hue popular in the mid Quattrocento for clothing for men, women, and children. Many garments of this color appear in the Parenti ricordanza.

mutande   Men's underwear made of the same washable fabrics (cotton, linen) as the full undershirt (*camicia*) worn by both genders. In the records of SS. Annunziata, the friars order their *camicie e mutande* together in sets. There are no records of similar garments worn gathered between the legs for women, except for long breeches sported by the risqué Venetian prostitutes under their full long skirts.

orale   An old-fashioned ("Trecentesca") term for a bordered veil worn by women to cover the face. In the fifteenth century, the terms *fazzoletto* and *bende* are more often seen. See the ricordi of Miliadusso Baldiccione of Pisa (1359), p. 37, where he buys "uno orale con la frontiera per Tedda" from a "monna Chola venditrice."

oricello   A dyestuff that yields reds and violet colors, obtained from certain lichens (genera *Roccella, Dendrographa, Lecanora*), called "orchil" or "archil" in English. The Rucellai family have been traditionally identified as master tintori, using oricello, from whence it gets its name.

orlo   Border or edging, often of fur; hem.

pancie   The expensive soft, fine, white fur from an animal's underbelly. *Filetti di pancie* are skins of fur which are sewn together to create fur linings for *lucchi, maniche,* and *mantelli.* Fur of a higher grade than *dossi.*

panno   Originally the word for woolen cloth, later a generic term for cloth. See *drappo* above.

panno divisato   Multicolored cloth prohibited by the sumptuary legislation in which this term appears.

panno greggio   Unfinished/unbleached cloth.

pannos curtos   Any short garment that did not cover at least half the thigh when standing.

pannum increspetum (Lat.)   Ruffled or pleated cloth decoration on a garment.

paramento   Ecclesiastical vestment, church tapestry. A tapestry worker was traditionally given the feminine designation of *ricamatrice.*

pavonazzo (*pagonazzo, paonazzo*)   Deep, rich, blue-violet color, similar to the color of the body of the male peacock. This color was popular in the mid Quattrocento for both genders. A color of some confusion, it could be either *pavonazzo scuro* or *pavonazzo morello* and could be associated with mourning or mark an important occasion. Stella Mary Newton notes that in Venice at the death of Leo X in 1520, twenty cardinals came to pay their respect in mantles of pavonazzo, considered a "non-color" appropriate for a solemn occasion there, as were black and ashen gray (Newton, *Dress of the Venetians,* p. 20).

peduli   Rustic rope-soled shoes.

pelo di lione   Literally, "lionskin." This was a tawny, reddish yellow, rust color popular for clothing for both genders at midcentury.

perpigniano   Woolen jersey cloth made in many colors, used mainly for hosiery worn by men, which originated in the town of Perpignan, France. However, in the Parenti *ricordanza*, f. 59V, a gamurra for a girl is also recorded as fashioned of "perpigniano azurro con maniche di velluto verde"; the Dominican friars also occasionally made their *toniche* of *perpigniano cupo*.

pianelli   Slippers that did not cover the heel of the foot, usually made of cloth and worn indoors by both men and women. Outside, high wooden clogs—zoccoli or chopine—were added. Pianelli could, however, be made double-soled, or *assuole doppie*, which increased their durability. Alternately, scarpe, that is, soft shoes with thin leather soles, were substituted for the pianelli.

pianette   Decorative baubles to sew onto gowns as ornaments. One gamurra records 146 such pianette bought as outfit decorations.

piloso (peluzo)   Fine-quality cloth.

pizzo   Fine lacework. Also seen as *pizzilli*.

poulaine   The long, tapering point into which the toe of a shoe or slipper was prolonged. From Old French *poulaine*, "Polish," because the style was said to have originated in Poland.

puzzole   The dark brown fur of the polecat, which had a purplish gloss to it, used to trim cloaks and overgowns. The European polecat is related to the North American skunk and can likewise emit a disagreeable odor; of the weasel and ferret family.

raconciare   To mend a garment; to make new.

raperelle   Small rings, studs or little buttons of copper with pointed bases that were placed on clothing for ornament and to hold whatever was fixed there.

rascia   Originally a type of unrefined woolen cloth, named after the town of its origin, Raska, in Serbia. Called "rash" in English. Often of lower quality than common perpignan cloth. By the sixteenth century, however, the Florentines had developed a special process for shrinking rash and other cloth. Rash became a fine-grade woolen cloth without a nap, used especially for men's clothing. It was, in fact, among the most expensive woolen cloths manufactured in Florence in the 1500s.

raso   A type of silk cloth that was dressed until it had a luster. There are records of *finissimi rasi dommaschi*.

rensa   A type of fine linen used for personal linens and undergarments (*biancheria*) made in Rheims, in northeastern France.

rete   Hair nets (considered stylish on women in the fifteenth century, often worn covering the ears).

rigottos   Hair pieces made of yellow and white silk.

rimboccatura   The "tucking in" of garments or parts of garments, like collars.

robba   Generic term for clothes, clothing, or dress. Also an old-fashioned term for "gown" for men, women or children, from the Duegento and Trecento.

robbia   A red dyestuff from the red root of a vine of the chiefly tropical *dicotyledonous* family (which includes both coffee and gardenia), with prickly leaves and small green-ish yellow flowers. "Madder" in English.

rocchetta   Distaff, that is, the instrument upon which women placed wool or flax or other material to spin.

rovesciatura   The "turning over" of garments or parts of garments, like sleeves.

sabbi   See *tabì*.

sacco   An old-fashioned, generic term for an overgown similar to the fifteenth-century cioppa. A sacco had sleeves, and could be made of velvet, wool, or silk. Also, a sacco could denote a monastic or fraternal habit. Originally, it had been a garment for slaves, made with black and white stripes. Cognates of *sacco* are found in Hebrew (*shaq*), Greek (*sakkos*), and Latin (*saccus*), all signifying linen cloth or coarse cloth (sack cloth).

saia   Thin silk or woolen fabric with a diagonal weave. Also a garment made of such fabric.

sargie   Coarse cloth woven with slanting lines or ridges in it, used especially for men's garments. "Serge" in English. Worsted serge was used for coats; silk serge was used for linings.

sbiadato   "Faded," "whitened," or pale color, popular in the Quattrocento for silk em-broidery and as the color of women's gowns. *Ciambellotto sbiadato* is recorded in the Parenti ricordanza.

scaggiale (scheggiale)   Belts hung with pendants, to which one could attach a purse, horn, or dagger.

scaglie   Spangles for headdresses, made up by goldsmiths. See *tremolanti* for another type of spangle.

scannelli   Engraved decorations or buttons.

scapulare (scapular)   A loose, sleeveless garment hanging from the shoulders, part of the ecclesiastical *vestimento*. It took four braccia of woolen or perpignan cloth to make one.

scarpe   Shoes, often of calf leather (*vitello*), or of cloth, with leather soles. The wardrobe of Duke Lorenzo de' Medici in 1515 lists scarpe of *velluto bianco* and *velluto nero*. Expensive scarpe were often lined and embroidered. The soles of the shoes were made separately by workers called *suolai*, who then sold their product to the *calzolai*, or shoemaker. Scarpe could be made *doppie*, perhaps indicating an extra-thick sole. The calzolai were united in a guild with *pianellai*, or slipper makers, and *zoccolai*, who made wooden clogs. The records of SS. Annunziata reflect this union, for orders for "calze, pianelle e zocholi" are invariably made together.

scarpettine   Little shoes or slippers, for male or female wear.

scarsella   A square or rectangular leather bag, pouch, or purse carried by either gender. A friar wore the scarsella *colla coregia*, that is, on a leather belt.

schiavonetto   A lightweight, cool, silk or linen gown used in the sun, as a woman's sunning dress. Worn when sitting on a loggia, sun-bleaching one's hair, for example. (Originally from *schiave*, slave.)

sciamito   A generic term for silken fabric. "Samite" in English. Originally, this was a type of luxurious silk fabric with a complex weave, more expensive than silk *zendado*. In Latin, this fabric was called *hexamitus*, that is, cloth woven with six heddles on the loom; in Persian, *schiameh* (short gown); in Arabic, *scemuh* (soft gown); in German, *Sammet* or *Sammt*. Ceremonial cloths (*palii*) were often described as being made of sciamito, especially of the color vermilion, sometimes sewn in combination with other rich fabrics of varying colors, or with gold and silver thread. In fabric design, flowers of dark rose color in the form of *pigne* or pinecones, were called *fior di sciamito*.

scollatura A low-cut, décolleté neckline. Popular, based on images, both in Venice (among courtesans) and Ferrara (at court), but never in Florence, even though moralists' concern with the dress of widows may seem to contradict this finding.

sella Literally, a saddle-shaped headdress for women with rounded height on both sides of the face, dipping down in the middle, in the curved shape of a western saddle. The sella was an adaptation of the high French fashion of feminine headgear prohibited by sumptuary legislation in 1456. This fashion was known as *alla di là*, "from outside" or "beyond," which included not only selle but also "corne, "cappucci," and "cappelletti" *alla francese* or *alla fiamminga*.

sertum Head garland (from the Latin).

solana A wide-brimmed, topless hat of fine straw, through which a woman's hair would be pulled, in order to expose it to the bleaching rays of the sun (helped along with the application of lemon juice). The wide brim of the solana would protect her face from tanning.

sopravvesta Long outer garment (overdress) for male or female.

sottana A woman's plainest, most basic shift. The term often designated a poor woman's threadbare only garment (as in Boccaccio's tale of *Poor Griselda*).

sparato An open dress front.

spolverezata Literally, "daubed with dust or powder." "Una cioppetta biancha spolverezata" is recorded, perhaps describing a speckled pattern.

stammae (stamigna) Plain woolen cloth.

stivali Boots, worn by military men, and by men and friars in general for riding. Usually made of calf leather (*vitello*).

strascico The train of a gown or the width of the border around the hemline of a gown, which was regulated by sumptuary laws in Florence.

stringhe The ribbons that can be seen attached to the sleeves of gowns for purely decorative effect. Il Vecellio says that it is a characteristic of Milanese style (p. 164). The left sleeve of young Beatrice d'Este's striped gown in the Pala Sforzesca (as she kneels with son, infant, and husband Ludovico il Moro, ca. 1495) is aflutter with at least twenty sets of these ribbons.

tabarro A cloak or mantle with a large hood.

tabì (sabbi) Silk fabric with a striped, wavy, or watered pattern or marking, such as silk taffeta. From Attabiy, a section of Baghdad, where such cloth was first made.

tela Linen, calico, or canvas cloth.

Types of tela:

di greggia: unbleached linen

di camicie: undershirt fabric

per lenzuola: sheeting

da materassi: ticking

cerata: oil cloth (literally, "waxed cloth")

terzanello   Light silk fabric sometimes used for lining. However, "una giornea di terzanello allexandrino" appears in Marietta Parenti's trousseau in 1474 (ASF, Carte strozz., 2d ser., 17 bis, fol. 72R).

tonica   Literally, "tunic." One of the vestments of the clergy. A long, full-length gown, which could be lined and took six to nine braccia of cloth to fashion. Made of wool or wool jersey (perpignan cloth). A *tonachino* was a shorter, lighter version of this garment, which took only four and one-half braccia of cloth to make. Could be also made of rascia.

torsello   Pincushion. Often found in inventories of personal and household goods.

tovagliole   Table or tray napkins.

tremolanti   Glittering headdress baubles or precious and semiprecious metals, fashioned by jewelers, and sewn into a woman's headdress (*ghirlanda*), the hem of a veil, or on the neckline of a public gown.

tricas (tricenas, triccii)   Hair pieces and inserts made of yellow and white silk, sometimes ornamented.

trina   Lace, point lace, fringe. A *trinaia* is a lacemaker, often associated with convents.

ucchielli   Button holes; also, the fabric known in English as "eyelet." An *ucchielliaia* was a buttonhole maker, an occupation usually associated with older women.

vaio   The generic term for fur, but especially for the gray fur of the large European squirrel, used widely for linings and borders. "Vair" or "miniver" in English.

valescio (gualescio)   A fabric of smooth polished cotton used both for linings and bed coverings (*coltre*). Both *rosso* and *bianco,* among undoubtedly other colors, are recorded.

velluto   Velvet, a silk-based fabric characterized by a surface pile created by the use of an extra warp. During the late medieval period, many types of luxury velvet were developed, and also forbidden by 1346 sumptuary legislation. Velluto allegedly originated with the Velluto family of Florence.

Types of luxury velvet:

velluto allucciolato: velvet with metallic, uncut loops

velluto altobasso: velvet with two different heights of pile

velluto inferriato or *velluto raso:* voided figured velvets with the design created by shaving the pile away to expose the silk ground beneath

verdebruno   Dark green color popular at midcentury for clothing and belts.

verdemirise   A shade of green for English wool.

verzino   A red dyestuff made from the sappanwood tree.

vesta   Generic term for clothing or garment.

vesta da tenere l'acqua   Raincoat. Term in the Medici wardrobe accounts of 1515.

vestimenta dimezzata   Gown made of half one cloth, half another. Forbidden as excessive by sumptuary legislation.

vestimenta scaccata   Checkered cloth gowns. Also forbidden, perhaps as too eye-catching, by sumptuary legislation.

vestitello   Literally, "little dress," diminutive of "vestito." A woman in confinement for childbirth wore a vestitello of silken fabric, without ornamentation.

vestito   To be dressed, variously:

   in borghese: fashionably dressed

   in costume: in an old-fashioned period manner

   in divisa: in uniform, for ritual, occupation, or competition

villano   A longish, simple, rustic, tunic, such as country males would wear, probably mid-calf-length and informally cinched in at the waist with a belt. This Trecentesca term for tunic appears in communal legislative regulation of clothing, but not in the personal ricordanze of the upper-class families of Quattrocento Florence.

virghi   Silk decorations of varying colors woven into woolen dresses.

volanda   Literally, mill dust, or flour sweepings. Volanda perhaps refers to the natural color of fabric used for making the personal linens biancheria. Four "pieces" (approximately 180 braccia) of tela volanda was bought for Duke Lorenzo de' Medici's underblouses in 1515 for 70 ducati, or about 9 soldi a braccio.

zambellotto   Plain woolen cloth (Fr. *camelot*, Eng. *camlet*) which originally could have been made of either camel hair or goat hair. Imported from the Near East.

zampe   Fur pelts with the paws still attached, used for trimming and even lining in the mid Quattrocento. Marco Parenti lined both *una gabbanella pagonaza* and *uno gonnellino di domaschino nero* with zampe for himself in 1478 (ASF, Carte strozz., 2d ser., 17 bis, fol. 76V).

zazzerri   Ornamented hairpieces (early fourteenth century).

zendado   A thin, rich, silk fabric, called "sendal" in English. Also a veil, shawl, or banner made of this silk.

zetani   Satin. In the fifteenth century, all satin was made from silk, although the term "satin" refers to the weave, not to the material from which it is made. Often, a satin weave was used for the ground of figured velvets, such as *zetano vellutato*.

zibellini   Sable fur. Used for luxury trim and strictly controlled by sumptuary legislation. Imported from Russia until the Turks closed Constantinople to free trade with the West in 1453.

zimarra   Long dressing gown, worn by men; later, a priest's cassock. In 1515, Duke Lorenzo de' Medici ordered *una zimarra* of *dommasco bigio* (gray damask) for himself, which was lined with *raso pagonazo* (dark blue-violet silk).

zoccoli   Sandals with a raised wooden sole, often made of white poplar wood, worn over hose or scarpette (thin, slipperlike shoes) in the street to protect more delicate footwear from being soiled. Zoccoli could also be made *chiusi*, or closed, presumably for further protection in cold or rainy weather. Friars at SS. Annunziata routinely ordered zocholi for themselves, along with hose and slippers. Chopine were a fashionable variation of zoccoli.

Select Bibliography

FLORENTINE ARCHIVES AND MANUSCRIPT LIBRARIES

Archivio di stato Firenze (State Archive of Florence)

Carte strozziane
Catasto
Conventi soppressi
Matricole dell' Arte della seta
Matricole dell' Arte di Por Santa Maria.
Mediceo, avanti il principato
Mercanzia
Pupilli, avanti il principato
Registri delle provvisioni
Statuti

Istituto degli Innocenti Archive
Biblioteca laurenziana
Biblioteca nazionale
Biblioteca riccardiana

DATABASE

Herlihy, David, and Christiane Klapisch-Zuber. "Census and Property Survey of Florentine Domains in the Province of Tuscany, 1427–1480." Machine-readable data file. Madison: University of Wisconsin, Data and Program Library Service, 1981.

PRIMARY PRINTED SOURCES

Alberti, Leon Battista [1404–72]. *I libri della famiglia*. Edited by Ruggiero Romano and Alberto Tenenti. Turin, 1969.

Bandello, Matteo [1480–1561]. Le *novelle*. Florence, 1930.

Barbaro, Francesco. *De re uxoria*. Venice, 1427–28. Translated by Alberto Lollio as *Prudentissimi et gravi documenti circa la elettion della moglie* Verona, 1513. Reprint. Venice, 1548.

Bernardino of Siena, Saint. *Le prediche volgari di San Bernardino da Siena nel 1427*. Edited by Orazio Bacci. Siena, 1895.

Berti, Luciano. *Masaccio*. Milan, 1964. University Park, Pa., 1967.

Boccaccio. *The Decameron*. Edited by Mark Musa and Peter D. Bondanella. New York, 1977.

Boileau, Étienne. *Le livre des métiers d'Étienne Boileau*. Transcribed and edited by René de Lespinasse and François Bonnardot as *Les métiers et corporations de la Ville de Paris, XIIIe siècle*. Paris, 1879.

Bracciolini, Poggio. *Facezie*. Edited by Marcello Ciccuto. Milan, 1983.

Canti carnascaleschi del rinascimento. Edited by Charles S. Singleton. Bari, 1936.

Carnesecchi, Carlo. "Sontuosa 'cioppa' di Lena Castellani." *Rivista d'arte* 4, nos. 8–9 (1906): 148–54.

Castellani, Francesco. *The Ricordanza A by Francesco Castellani*. Edited by Giovanni Cappelli. Florence, 1992.

Certaldo, Paolo da. *Libro di buoni costumi*. Edited by Alfredo Schiaffini. Florence, 1945.

Correggio, Niccolo da. *Opere*. Edited by A. T. Benvenuti. Bari, 1969.

Il costume al tempo di Pico e Lorenzo il Magnifico. Edited by Aurora Fiorentini Capitani, Vittorio Erlindo, and Stefania Ricci. Catalogue of an exhibition held in the Palazzo municipale, Mirandola, Italy, Feb. 27–May 1, 1994. Milan, 1994.

Dalton, O. M. *Catalogue of the Engraved Gems of the Post-Classical Periods in the British Museum*. London, 1915.

Datini, Margherita. "Le lettere di Margherita Datini a Francesco di Marco." Edited by Valeria Rosati. *Archivio storico pratese* 52 (1976): 25–152.

Dei, Benedetto. *La cronica dall'anno 1400 all'anno 1500*. Edited by Roberto Barducci. Florence, 1984.

Delizie degli eruditi toscani. Edited by Ildefonso di San Luigi. Vols. 7 and 8. Florence, 1770–78.

Documenti dell' antica costituzione del comune di Firenze. Edited by Emilio Santini. Florence, 1895.

Dominici, Giovanni. *Regola del governo di cura familiare*. Edited by D. Salvi. Florence, 1860.

Fanfani, Pietro. "Notizia della festa fatta in Firenze la notte di carnevale da Bartolommeo Benci in onore della Marietta di Lorenzo Strozzi (Sec. XV)." *Il Borghini: Giornale di filologia e di lettere italiane* (Florence), 1864.

———. "Ricordo d' una giostra fatta a Firenze a di 7 di febbraio 1468 sulla Piazza di Santa Croce." *Il Borghini: Giornale di filologia e di lettere italiane* (Florence), 1864.

Le feste di San Giovanni Battista in Firenze descritte in prosa e in rima da contemporanei. Edited by Cesare Guasti. Florence, 1884.

Filarete, Francesco [ca. 1400–ca. 1469]. *Treatise on Architecture: Being the Treatise by Antonio di Piero Averlino, Known as Filarete.* Translated and edited by John R. Spencer. Yale Publications in the History of Art, no. 16, 2 vols. New Haven, Conn., 1965.

La guardaroba di Lucrezia Borgia, dall'archivio di stato di Modena. Edited by Luca Beltrami. Modena, 1903.

Giulini, A. "Nozze Borromeo nel Quattrocento." *Archivio storico lombardo (Milan)* 37, no. 26. (1910).

———. "Drusiana Sforza moglie di Jacopo Piccinino (anno 1464)" In *Miscellanea di studi storici in onore di Antonio Manno,* vol. 2. Turin, 1912.

Landucci, Luca. *A Florentine Diary from 1450 to 1516.* Notes by Iodoco del Badia. Translated by Alice de Rosen Jervis. London, 1927.

———. *Diario fiorentino dal 1450 al 1516.* Edited by Iodoco del Badia. Florence, 1883. Reprint, 1969.

Legislazione toscana. Edited by Lorenzo Cantini. Florence, 1772.

Il libro del sarto. Venice, 1580. Reprint, Ferrara, 1987.

Machiavelli, Niccolò. *Le istorie fiorentine.* Florence, 1965.

Martineau, Jane, ed. *Andrea Mantegna.* London, 1992.

Masi, Bartolomeo. *Ricordanze di Bartolomeo Masi, calderaio fiorentino dal 1478 al 1526.* Edited by G. Corazzini. Florence, 1906.

Merkel, Carlo. "I beni della famiglia di Puccio Pucci." *Miscellanea nuziale Rossi-Teiss.* Bergamo, 1897.

Micheletti, Emma. *Domenico Ghirlandaio.* Florence, 1990.

Miscellanea fiorentina di erudizione e storia. Edited by Iodoco del Badia. 2 vols. Rome, 1978.

Morassi, Antonio. *Art Treasures of the Medici.* Greenwich, Conn., 1963.

Museo Mediceo di Firenze. *Il tesoro di Lorenzo il Magnifico,* vol. 1: *Le gemme.* Palazzo Medici Riccardi exhibition catalogue. Florence, 1972.

Pagnini, Giovanni F., ed. *Della decima e di varie altre gravezze imposte dal comune di Firenze.* 2 vols. Lisbon and Lucca, 1765–66. Reprint. Bologna, 1967.

Rerum italicarum scriptores. Edited by Lodovico Antonio Muratori. Città di Castello, 1900.

"Ricordi di cose familiari di Miliadusso Baldiccione de' Casalberti Pisano (1339–1382)." Edited by Francesco Bonaini and Filippo-Luigi Polidori. Appendice all'*Archivio storico italiano* 8 (1850): 7–71.

Sacchetti, Franco [ca. 1330–ca. 1400]. *Il Trecentonovelle.* Edited by Antonio Lanza. Florence, 1984.

"Un sarto napoletano." Polizza di pagamento. *Archivio storico del Banco di Napoli,* Banco dello Spirito Santo, m. 305, Dec. 15, 1640.

Sindona, Enio. *Pisanello.* New York, 1963.

Statuta populi et communis florentiae (1415). 2 vols. Freiburg, 1776–78.

Statuti dell'Arte dei rigattieri e linaioli di Firenze (1296–1340). Edited by Ferdinando Sartini. Florence, 1940–48.

Statuti dell'Arte di Por Santa Maria del tempo della repubblica. Edited by Umberto Dorini. Florence, 1934.

Statuto dell'Arte della lana di Firenze (1317–1319). Edited by Anna Maria Agnoletti. Florence, 1940–48.

Strozzi, Alessandra Macinghi negli. *Lettere di una gentildonna fiorentina del secolo XV ai figliuoli esuli.* Edited by Cesare Guasti. Florence, 1877.

Tornabuoni, Lucrezia. *Tre lettere di Lucrezia Tornabuoni a Piero de Medici ed altre lettere di vari concernenti al matrimonio di Lorenzo il Magnifico con Clarice Orsini.* Florence, 1859.

———. *Lettere.* Edited by Patrizia Salvadori. Florence, 1993.

Vasari, Giorgio. *Le vite de' pittori di Giorgio Vasari.* 3 vols. Bologna, 1648.

———. *The Lives of the Artists.* 2 vols. Translated by George Bull. New York, 1965.

Vecellio, Cesare. *Habiti antichi et moderni.* Venice, 1598. Reprint, 2 vols., Paris, 1859–63. See also *Vecellio's Renaissance Costume Book: All 500 Woodcut Illustrations from the Famous Sixteenth-Century Compendium of World Costume* (New York, 1977).

Vespasiano da Bisticci. *The Vespasiano Memoirs: Lives of Illustrious Men of the XVth Century.* Translated by William George and Emily Waters. London, 1926.

———. *Vite di uomini illustri del secolo XV.* Edited by Paolo D'Ancona and E. Aeschlimann. Milan, 1951.

Villani, Giovanni [d. 1348]. *Cronica. Venice, 1537; Florence, 1554.* 8 vols. Florence, 1832.

Wadia, Bettina. *Botticelli.* London, 1968.

SECONDARY SOURCES

Allerston, Patricia. "L'abito come articolo di scambio nella società dell'età moderna: Alcune implicazioni." In *Le trame della moda,* ed. Anna Giulia Cavagna and Grazietta Butazzi. Rome, 1995.

———. "Wedding Finery in Sixteenth-Century Venice." In *Marriage in Italy, 1300–1640,* ed. Trevor Dean and K. J. P. Lowe. Cambridge, 1998.

Baron, Hans. *In Search of Florentine Civic Humanism.* 2 vols. Princeton, N.J., 1988.

Barthes, Roland. *Elements of Semiology.* Translated by Annette Lavers and Colin Smith. New York, 1968.

———. "The Diseases of Costume." In *Critical Essays.* Translated by Richard Howard. Evanston, Ill., 1972.

———. *The Fashion System*. Translated by Matthew Ward and Richard Howard. New York, 1983.

Baskins, Cristelle L. "Griselda, or the Renaissance Bride Stripped Bare by Her Bachelor in Tuscan *Cassone* Painting," *Stanford Italian Review* 10, no. 2 (1991): 153–75.

———. "Corporeal Authority in the Speaking Picture: The Representation of Lucretia in Tuscan Domestic Painting." In *Gender Rhetorics*, ed. Richard C. Trexler. Binghamton, 1994.

Battisti, Carlo and Giovanni Alesso. *Dizionario etimologico italiano*. Florence, 1975.

Becker, Marvin B. "Legislazione antimonopolistica fiorentina." *Archivio storico italiano* 117 (1959): 8–28.

Becker, Marvin B., and Gene Brucker. " 'The Arti Minori' in Florentine Politics, 1342–1378." *Mediaeval Studies* 18 (1956): 93–104.

Bell, Quentin. *On Human Finery*. London, 1947.

Bellomo, Manlio. *Ricerche sui rapporti patrimonali tra coniugi*. Varese, 1961.

Bestor, Jane Fair. "Marriage Transactions in Renaissance Italy and Mauss's Essay on the Gift." *Past and Present* 164 (Aug. 1999): 6–46.

Biagi, Guido. *The Private Life of the Renaissance Florentines*. London, 1896.

Birbari, Elizabeth. *Dress in Italian Painting, 1460–1500*. London, 1975.

Borsook, Eve, and Johannes Offerhaus. *Francesco Sassetti and Ghirlandaio at Santa Trinita, Florence: History and Legend in a Renaissance Chapel*. Doornspijk, Holland, 1981.

Brackett, John K. "The Florentine Onestà and the Control of Prostitution, 1403–1680." *Sixteenth Century Journal* 24 (Summer 1993): 273–300.

Brown, Judith. "A Woman's Place Was in the Home: Women's Work in Renaissance Tuscany." In *Rewriting the Renaissance*, ed. Margaret Ferguson, Maureen Quilligan, and Nancy J. Vickers. Chicago, 1986.

———. "Monache a Firenze all'inizio dell'età moderna. un'analisi demografica." *Quaderni storici* 29 (1994): 117–52.

Brown, Judith, and Jordan Goodman. "Women and Industry in Florence." *Journal of Economic History* 40 (March 1980): 73–80.

Brown, Judith, and Robert C. Davis, eds. *Gender and Society in Renaissance Italy*. New York, 1998.

Brucker, Gene A. *Florentine Politics and Society, 1343–1378*. Princeton, N.J., 1962.

———. "The Ciompi Revolution." In *Florentine Studies. Politics and Society in Renaissance Florence*, ed. Nicolai Rubinstein. Evanston, Ill., 1968.

———. "The Florentine Popolo Minuto and Its Political Role, 1340–1450." In *Violence and Civil Disorder in Italian Cities, 1200–1500*, ed. Lauro Martines. Berkeley, Calif., 1972.

———. *Giovanni and Lusanna: Love and Marriage in Renaissance Florence*. Berkeley, Calif., 1986.

———. "Monasteries, Friaries, and Nunneries in Quattrocento Florence." In *Christianity and the Renaissance*, ed. Timothy Verdon and John Henderson. New York, 1990.

———. ed. *Society of Renaissance Florence: A Documentary Study.* New York, 1971.

Burckhardt, Jacob. *The Civilisation of the Renaissance in Italy.* London, 1878.

Bynum, Caroline Walker. "Shape and Story: Metamorphosis in the Western Tradition." The 1999 Jefferson Lecture in the Humanities, Kennedy Center for the Performing Arts, Washington, D.C., March 22, 1999.

Cadogan, Jeanne K. "Domenico Ghirlandaio in Santa Maria Novella: Invention and Execution." In *Florentine Drawing at the Time of Lorenzo the Magnificent,* ed. Elizabeth Cropper. Villa Spelman Colloquia, no. 4 (1994): 63–82.

———. *Domenico Ghirlandaio: Artist and Artisan.* New Haven, Conn., 2000.

Calvi, Giulia. "Maddalena Neri and Cosimo Tornabuoni: A Couple's Narrative of Family History in Early Modern Florence." *Renaissance Quarterly* 45 (1992): 312–37.

———. "Widows, the State and the Guardianship of Children in Early Modern Tuscany." In *Widowhood in Medieval and Early Modern Europe,* ed. Sandra Cavallo and Lyndan Warner. London, 1999.

Cappi-Bentivegna, Ferraccia, ed. *Abbigliamento e costume nella pittura italiana.* Rome, 1962.

Cardon, Dominique. *Les "vers" du rouge: Insectes tinctoriaux (Homoptera: Coccoidea) utilisés dans l'ancien monde au Moyen-Age.* Paris, 1990.

Carena, Giacinto. *Vocabolario domestico: Pronotuario di vocaboli attenenti a cose domestiche, e altre di uso comune.* 4th ed. Naples, 1859.

Carlyle, Thomas. *Sartor Resartus (1831)* [and] *On Heroes and Hero Worship (1841).* London, 1908.

Carocci, Guido. *Il Mercato vecchio di Firenze.* Florence, 1884.

———. *Il Ghetto di Firenze e i suoi ricordi.* Florence, 1886.

Chabot, Isabelle. "'La sposa in nero': La ritualizzazione del lutto delle vedove fiorentine (secoli XIV–XV)." *Quaderni storici* 86 (Aug. 1994): 421–62.

———. "Risorse e diritti patrimoniali." In *Il lavoro delle donne,* ed. Angela Groppi. Rome, 1996.

———. "Seconde nozze e identità materna nella Firenze del tardo medioevo." In *Tempi e spazi di vita femminile tra medioevo ed età moderna,* ed. Silvana Seidel Menchi, Anne Jacobson Schutte, and Thomas Kuehn. Bologna, 1999.

———. "Lineage Strategies and the Control of Widows in Renaissance Florence." In *Widowhood in Medieval and Early Modern Europe,* ed. Sandra Cavallo and Lyndan Warner. London, 1999.

Chojnacki, Stanley. "Dowries and Kinsmen in Early Renaissance Venice." *Journal of Interdisciplinary History* 5 (Spring 1975): 571–600.

———. "Riprendersi la dote: Venezia, 1360–1530." In *Tempi e spazi di vita femminile tra medioevo ed età moderna,* ed. Silvana Seidel Menchi, Anne Jacobson Schutte, and Thomas Kuehn. Bologna. 1999.

———. "From Trousseau to Groomgift in Late Medieval Venice." In *Medieval and Renaissance Venice,* ed. Ellen E. Kittell and Thomas F. Madden. Urbana, Ill., 1999.

Cian, Vittorio. *Del significato dei colori e dei fiori nel Rinascimento italiano.* Turin, 1894.

Cipolla, Carlo M. *Money, Prices, and Civilization in the Mediterranean World.* Princeton, N.J., 1956.

———. *The Monetary Policy of Fourteenth-Century Florence.* Berkeley, Calif., 1982.

———. *Money in Sixteenth-Century Florence.* Berkeley, Calif., 1989.

Cohn, Samuel Kline, Jr. *The Laboring Classes of Renaissance Florence.* New York, 1980.

Cosenza, Mario Emilio. *Biographical and Bibliographical Dictionary of the Italian Humanists and of the World of Classical Scholarship in Italy, 1300–1800.* Boston, 1962.

Crabb, Ann Morton. "How Typical Was Alessandra Macinghi Strozzi of Fifteenth-Century Florentine Widows?" In *Upon My Husband's Death,* ed. Louise Mirrer. Ann Arbor, Mich., 1992.

———. *The Strozzi of Florence: Widowhood and Family Solidarity in the Renaissance.* Ann Arbor, 2000.

D'Ancona, Paolo. *Le vesti delle donne fiorentine nel secolo XIV.* Perugia, 1906.

Davidsohn, Robert. *Forschungen zur Alteren Geschichte von Florenz.* Berlin, 1896.

———. *Storia di Firenze.* Translated by Giovanni Miccoli. 4 vols. Florence, 1956.

Davis, J. *People of the Mediterranean.* London, 1977.

Delort, Robert. *Le commerce des fourrures en Occident à la fin du Moyen Age (vers 1300–vers 1450).* 2 vols. Rome, 1978.

Deprano, Maria. "Uxor Incomparabilis: The Marriage, Childbirth and Death Portraits of Giovanna Tornabuoni." M.A. thesis, UCLA, 1997.

Doren, Alfred. *Le arti fiorentine.* Translated by G. B. Klein. 2 vols. Florence, 1940–44.

Dorini, Umberto. *L'Arte della seta in Toscana.* Florence, 1928.

Duff, Nora. *Matilda of Tuscany.* London, 1906.

Eckstein, Nicholas A. *The District of the Green Dragon: Neighbourhood Life and Social Change in Renaissance Florence.* Florence, 1995.

Edler de Roover, Florence. *Glossary of Mediaeval Terms of Business, Italian Series, 1200–1600.* Cambridge, Mass., 1934. New York, 1970.

———. "Andrea Banchi, Florentine Silk Manufacturer and Merchant in the Fifteenth Century." In *Studies in Medieval and Renaissance History,* vol. 3, ed. William M. Bowsky. Lincoln, Neb., 1966.

Fabbri, Lorenzo. *Alleanza matrimoniale e patriziato nella Firenze del '400: Studio sulla famiglia Strozzi.* Florence, 1991.

Fanfani, Pietro, ed. *Vocabolario dell 'uso toscano.* 2 vols. Florence, 1863. Reprint, 1976.

Farago, Claire, ed. *Reframing the Renaissance: Visual Culture in Europe and Latin America, 1450–1650.* New Haven, Conn., 1995.

Ferguson, Margaret, Maureen Quilligan, and Nancy J. Vickers, eds. *Rewriting the Renaissance.* Chicago, 1986.

Fiumi, Enrico. "Fioritura e decadenza dell'economia fiorentina." *Archivio storico italiano* 115 (1957): 385–439; 117 (1959): 427–502.

Flugel, J. C. *The Psychology of Clothes.* London, 1950.

Foster, George M. "Peasant Society and the Image of the Limited Good." *American Anthropologist* 67 (1965): 293–315.

Franceschi, Franco. *Oltre il "Tumulto": I lavoratori fiorentini dell'Arte della lana fra Tre e Quattrocento.* Florence, 1993.

Frick, Carole Collier. "Dal giardino dei bei fiori." *Carte italiane: A Journal of Italian Studies* 8 (1986–87): 36–52.

Gandi, Giulio. *Le corporazioni dell' antica Firenze.* Florence, 1928.

Gargiolli, Girolamo. *L'Arte della seta in Firenze.* Florence, 1868.

Garzelli, Annarosa. *Il ricamo nella attività artistica di Pollaiuolo, Botticelli, Bartolomeo di Giovanni.* Florence, 1973.

Gelli, Jacopo. *Divise-mottie e imprese di famiglie e personaggi italiani.* 1916. 2d ed. Milan, 1928.

Gilbert, Creighton. "The Renaissance Portrait." *Burlington Magazine* 110 (1968): 278–85.

Goldthwaite, Richard A. *Private Wealth in Renaissance Florence.* Princeton, N.J., 1968.

———. "The Florentine Palace as Domestic Architecture," *American Historical Review* 77 (June–Dec. 1972): 977–1012.

———. *The Building of Renaissance Florence.* Baltimore, 1980.

———. "The Empire of Things: Consumer Demand in Renaissance Italy." In *Patronage, Art, and Society in Renaissance Italy*, ed. F. W. Kent and Patricia Simons. Oxford, 1987.

———. *Wealth and the Demand for Art in Italy, 1300–1600.* Baltimore, 1993.

Goody, Esther N. *From Craft to Industry: The Ethnography of Proto-industrial Cloth Production.* New York, 1982.

Greci, Roberto. "Donne e corporazioni: La fluidità di un rapporto." In *Il lavoro delle donne*, ed. Angela Groppi. Rome, 1996.

Greenblatt, Stephen. *Renaissance Self-Fashioning.* Chicago, 1980.

Gregorovius, Ferdinand. *Lucretia Borgia.* Translated by John Leslie Garner. New York, 1903.

Gregory, Heather. "Daughters, Dowries and the Family in Fifteenth Century Florence." *Rinascimento* 27 (1987): 215–37.

Grendler, Paul. F. *Schooling in Renaissance Italy. Literacy and Learning, 1300–1600.* Baltimore, 1989.

Groppi, Angela, ed. *Il lavoro delle donne.* Rome, 1996.

Guccerelli, Demetrio. *Stradario storico biografico della città di Firenze.* Florence, 1929. Reprint, Rome, 1985.

Guidi, Guidobaldo. *Il Governo della città-repubblica di Firenze del primo Quattrocento.* Vol. 2. Florence, 1981.

Hanawalt, Barbara A., ed. *Women and Work in Preindustrial Europe.* Bloomington, Ind., 1986.

Hartt, Frederick. *History of Italian Renaissance Art: Painting, Sculpture, Architecture. 1969.* 3d ed. Englewood Cliffs, N.J., 1987.

Harvey, John. *Men in Black*. Chicago, 1995.

Hatfield, Rab. "Five Early Renaissance Portraits." *Art Bulletin* 47 (Sept. 1965): 317–34.

———. "Giovanni Tornabuoni, i fratelli Ghirlandaio e la cappella maggiore di Santa Maria Novella." In *Domenico Ghirlandaio, 1449–1494: Atti del Convegno internazionale, Firenze, 16–18 ottobre 1994*, ed. Wolfram Prinz and Max Seidel, pp. 112–17. Florence, 1996.

Heers, Jacques. *Le clan familial au Moyen Age: Étude sur les structures politiques et sociales des milieux urbains*. Paris, 1974. Translated by Barry Herbert as *Family Clans in the Middle Ages: A Study of Political and Social Structures in Urban Areas* (New York, 1977).

Herald, Jacqueline. *Renaissance Dress in Italy, 1400–1500*. London, 1981.

Herlihy, David. "The Distribution of Wealth in a Renaissance Community: Florence 1427." In *Essays in Economic History and Historical Sociology*, ed. Philip Abrams and E. A. Wrigley. Cambridge, 1978.

———. *Opera Muliebria: Women and Work in Medieval Europe*. Philadelphia, 1990.

Herlihy, David, and Christiane Klapisch-Zuber. *Tuscans and Their Families: A Study of the Florentine catasto of 1427*. Translated by Lydia G. Cochrane. New Haven, Conn., 1985. Originally published as *Les Toscans et leurs familles: Une étude du "catasto" florentin de 1427* (Paris, 1978).

Hollander, Anne. *Seeing through Clothes*. New York, 1975.

Hope, Charles. "Religious Narratives in Renaissance Art." *Journal of the Royal Society of Art* 134 (Nov. 1986): 804–18.

Hoshino, Hidetoshi. "Per la storia dell'arte della lana in Firenze nel Trecento e nel Quattrocento: Un riesame." In Istituto giapponese di cultura, *Annuario*, 10. Rome, 1972–73.

———. *L'industria laniera fiorentina dal basso medievo all' età moderna: Abbozzo storico dei secoli XIII–XVII*. Rome, 1978.

———. *L'Arte della lana in Firenze nel basso medioevo: Il commercio della lana e il mercato dei panni fiorentini nei secoli XIII–XV*. Florence, 1980

Howell, Martha C. *Women, Production, and Patriarchy in Late Medieval Cities*. Chicago, 1986.

Hughes, Diane Owen. "From Brideprice to Dowry in Mediterranean Europe." *Journal of Family History* 3 (Fall 1978): 262–96.

———. "Sumptuary Laws and Social Relations in Renaissance Italy." In *Disputes and Settlements*, ed. John Bossy. Cambridge, 1983.

———. "La moda proibita: La legislazione suntuaria nell'Italia rinascimentale." *Memoria: Rivista di storia delle donne* 11–12 (1984): 82–105.

———. "Earrings for Circumcision: Distinction and Purification in the Italian Renaissance City." In *Persons in Groups*, ed. Richard Trexler. Binghamton, N.Y., 1985.

———. "Distinguishing Signs: Ear-Rings, Jews and Franciscan Rhetoric in the Italian Renaissance City." *Past and Present* 112 (Aug. 1986): 3–59.

——. "Representing the Family: Portraits and Purposes in Early Modern Italy." *Journal of Interdisciplinary History* 17 (1986): 7–38.

Izbicki, Thomas. " 'Ista questio est antiqua': Two *consilia* on Widows' Rights." *Bulletin of Medieval Canon Law* 8 (1978): 47–50.

Kantorowicz, Hermann, and N. Denholm-Young. "De Ornatu Mulierum: A Consilium of Antonius de Rosellis with an Introduction on Fifteenth-Century Sumptuary Legislation." In *Rechtshistorische Schriften von Dr. Hermann Kantorowicz*, ed. Helmut Coing and Gerhhardt Immel, 341–76. Karlsruhe, 1970.

Kemper, Rachel H. *Costume.* New York, 1977.

Kempers, Bram. *Painting, Power and Patronage: The Rise of the Professional Artist in Renaissance Italy.* London, 1992.

Kent, D. V. "The Florentine *reggimento* in the Fifteenth Century." *Renaissance Quarterly* 4 (1975): 575–638.

——. *Rise of the Medici: Faction in Florence, 1426–1434.* Oxford, 1978.

Kent, D. V., and F. W. Kent. *Neighbours and Neighbourhoods in Renaissance Florence: The District of the Red Lion in the Fifteenth Century.* Locust Valley, N.Y., 1982.

Kent, F. W. *Household and Lineage in Renaissance Florence.* Princeton, N.J., 1977.

——. "Ties of Neighbourhood and Patronage in Quattrocento Florence." In *Patronage, Art, and Society in Renaissance Italy*, ed. F. W. Kent and Patricia Simons. Oxford, 1987.

Kent, F. W., and Patricia Simons, eds. *Patronage, Art, and Society in Renaissance Italy.* Oxford, 1987.

Killerby, Catherine Kovesi. "Practical Problems in the Enforcement of Italian Sumptuary Law, 1200–1500." In *Crime, Society and the Law in Renaissance Italy*, ed. Trevor Dean and K. J. P. Lowe. Cambridge, 1994.

Kirshner, Julius. *Pursuing Honor while Avoiding Sin: The Monte delle Doti of Florence.* Milan, 1978.

——. "Maritus Lucretur Dotem Uxoris Sue Premortue in Late Medieval Florence." *Zeitschrift der Savigny-Stiftuny für Rechtsgeschichte, Kanonistische Abteilung* 77 (1991): 111–55.

——. "Wives' Claims Against Insolvent Husbands in Late Medieval Italy." In *Women of the Medieval World*, ed. Julius Kirshner and Suzanne Wemple. New York, 1991.

Kirshner, Julius, and Anthony Molho, "The Dowry Fund and the Marriage Market in Early Quattrocento Florence." *Journal of Modern History* 50 (1978): 403–38.

Kirshner, Julius, and Suzanne Wemple, eds. *Women of the Medieval World.* New York, 1991.

Klapisch-Zuber, Christiane. "Parenti, amici, vicini." *Quaderni storici* 33 (1976): 953–82.

——. "Le 'zane' della sposa: La fiorentina e il suo corredo nel Rinascimento." *Memoria: Rivista di storia delle donne* 11–12 (1984): 12–23.

———. "Le chiavi fiorentine di barbablù: l'apprendimento della lettura a Firenze nel XV secolo." *Quaderni storici* 57 (Dec. 1984): 765–92.

———. *Women, Family, and Ritual in Renaissance Italy.* Translated by Lydia G. Cochrane. Chicago, 1985.

———. "Un salario o l'onore: come valutare le donne Fiorentine del XIV–XV secolo." *Quaderni storici* 79 (April 1992): 41–49.

Koch, Walter A., ed. *Culture and Semiotics.* Bochum-Querenburg, Germany, 1989.

Kreutz, Barbara M. "The Twilight of *Morgengabe.*" In *Portraits of Medieval and Renaissance Living,* ed. Samuel K. Cohn Jr. and Steven A. Epstein. Ann Arbor, Mich., 1996.

Kriedte, Peter, Hans Medick and Jurgen Schlumbohm. *Industrialization before Industrialization.* Translated by Beate Schempp. Cambridge, 1981.

Kuehn, Thomas. " 'Cum Consensu Mundualdi': Legal Guardianship of Women in Quattrocento Florence." *Viator* 13 (1982): 309–31.

———. *Law, Family and Women: Toward a Legal Anthropology of Renaissance Italy.* Chicago, 1991.

Lane, Frederick C. *Venice: A Maritime Republic.* Baltimore, 1973.

Langner, Lawrence. *The Importance of Wearing Clothes.* New York, 1959.

Laver, James. *Taste and Fashion, from the French Revolution until To-day.* London, 1937.

———. *Dress: How and Why Fashions in Men's and Women's Clothes Have Changed during the Past Two Hundred Years.* London, 1950. 2d ed., 1966.

———. *Costume.* New York, 1963.

Le Goff, Jacques. "Vestimentary and Alimentary Codes in *Erec et Enide.*" In *The Medieval Imagination.* Translated by Arthur Goldhammer. Chicago, 1985.

Levantini-Pieroni, Giuseppe. *Lucrezia Tornabuoni.* Florence, 1888.

Levi-Pisetzky, Rosita. *Storia del costume in Italia.* 5 vols. Milan, 1966.

———. *Il costume e la moda nella società italiana.* Turin, 1978.

Limburger, Walther. *Die Gebäude von Florenz: Architekten, Strassen und Plätze in alphabetischen Verzeichnissen.* Leipzig, 1910.

Lipman, Jean. "The Florentine Profile Portrait in the Quattrocento." *Art Bulletin* 18 (1936): 54–102.

Litta, Pompeo. *Famiglie celebri italiane.* Milan, 1820/1856–85.

Lungo, Isidoro del. *La donna fiorentina del buon tempo antico.* Florence, 1906.

Lurie, Alison. *The Language of Clothes.* New York, 1981.

Luzio, Alessandro, and Rodolfo Renier. "Il lusso di Isabella d'Este." *Nuova antologia,* 4th ser., 147 (June 1896): 441–69.

Maclean, Ian. *The Renaissance Notion of Woman.* Cambridge, 1980.

Marangoni, Giorgio. *Evoluzione storica e stilistica della moda,* vol. 1: *Dalle antiche civiltà mediterranee al Rinascimento. 3d ed.* Milan, 1977.

Marchi, Piero, ed. *I Blasoni delle famiglie toscane, conservati nella raccolta Ceramelli-Papiani.* Florence, 1992.

Marshall, Richard K. *The Local Merchants of Prato.* Baltimore, 1999.

Martines, Lauro. *The Social World of the Florentine Humanists, 1390–1460.* Princeton, N.J., 1963.

————. *Lawyers and Statecraft in Renaissance Florence.* Princeton, N.J., 1968.

————. "A Way of Looking at Women in Renaissance Florence." *Journal of Medieval and Renaissance Studies* 4, no. 1 (Spring 1974): 15–28.

————. *An Italian Renaissance Sextet: Six Tales in Historical Context.* New York, 1994.

————. ed. *Violence and Civil Disorder in Italian Cities, 1200–1500.* Berkeley, Calif., 1972.

Mauss, Marcel. *The Gift.* Translated by Ian Cunnison. London, 1966.

Mazzi, Maria Serena. *Gli uomini e le cose nelle campagne fiorentine del Quattrocento.* Florence, 1983.

————. *Toscana bella: paesaggi, gente, amori nel medioevo.* Turin, 1999.

Mazzi, Maria Serena, and Sergio Raveggi. "Ai margini del lavoro: I mestieri per 'campare la vita.'" *Studi storici* 2 (1986): 359–69.

Melani, Alfredo. *Svaghi artistici femminili.* Milan, 1892.

Melis, Federigo. *Aspetti della vita economica medievale.* Siena, 1962.

Mellencamp, Emma. "A Note on the Costume of Titian's Flora." *Art Bulletin* 51 (June 1969): 174–77.

Molà, Luca. *The Silk Industry of Renaissance Venice.* Baltimore, 2000.

Molho, Anthony. "Visions of the Florentine Family in the Renaissance." *Journal of Modern History* 50 (June 1978): 304–11.

————. "Cosimo de' Medici: Pater Patriae or Padrino?" *Stanford Italian Review* 1 (Spring 1979): 5–33.

————. " 'Tamquam vere mortua': Le professioni religiose femminili nella Firenze del tardo medioevo." *Società e storia* 43 (Jan.–Mar. 1989): 1–44.

————. *Marriage Alliance in Late Medieval Florence.* Cambridge, 1994.

————, ed. *Social and Economic Foundations of the Italian Renaissance.* New York, 1969.

Molho, Anthony, and Julius Kirshner. "The Dowry Fund and the Marriage Market in Early Quattrocento Florence." *Journal of Modern History* 50 (1978): 403–38.

Molho, Anthony, Roberto Barducci, Gabriella Battista, and Francesco Donnini. "Genealogy and Marriage Alliance: Memories of Power in Late Medieval Florence." In *Portraits of Medieval and Renaissance Living,* ed. Samuel Kline Cohn Jr. and Steven A. Epstein, pp. 39–70. Ann Arbor, Mich., 1996.

Munro, John H. "The Medieval Scarlet and the Economics of Sartorial Splendour." In *Cloth and Clothing in Medieval Europe: Essays in Memory of Professor E. M. Carus-Wilson,* ed. by N. B. Harte and K. G. Ponting. London, 1983.

Najemy, John M. "Guild Republicanism in Trecento Florence: The Successes and Ultimate Failure of Corporate Politics." *American Historical Review* 84 (Feb. 1979): 53–71.

————. " 'Audiant omnes artes': Corporate Origins of the Ciompi Revolution." In *Il Tumulto dei Ciompi: Un momento di storia fiorentina ed europea.* Florence, 1981.

———. *Corporatism and Consensus in Florentine Electoral Politics, 1280–1400.* Chapel Hill, N.C., 1982.

———. *Between Friends: Discourses of Power and Desire in the Machiavelli-Vettori Letters of 1513–1515.* Princeton, N.J., 1993.

Neuschel, Kristen. *Word of Honor: Interpreting Noble Culture in Sixteenth-Century France.* Ithaca, N.Y., 1989.

Newton, Stella Mary. *The Dress of the Venetians, 1495–1525.* Aldershot, U.K., 1988.

Onians, John. *Bearers of Meaning. The Classical Orders in Antiquity, the Middle Ages, and the Renaissance.* Princeton, N.J., 1988.

Origo, Iris. *The Merchant of Prato.* London, 1957.

Parsons, Frank Alvah. *The Psychology of Dress.* New York, 1920.

Perrot, Philippe. *Fashioning the Bourgeoisie: A History of Clothing in the Nineteenth Century.* Translated by Richard Bienvenu. Princeton, N.J., 1994

Pezzarossa, F. "La tradizione fiorentina della memoralistica." In *La memoria dei mercatores,* ed. G. M. Anselmi, F. P. Pezzarossa, and L. Avellini. Bologna, 1980.

Phillips, Mark. *The Memoir of Marco Parenti: A Life in Medici Florence.* Princeton, N.J., 1987.

Pieri, Piero. *Intorno alla storia dell'Arte della Seta in Firenze.* Bologna, 1927. Reprint, 1966.

Pistolese, Rosana. *La moda nella storia del costume.* 1964. 2d ed., Bologna, 1967.

Polanyi, Karl. *Primitive, Archaic and Modern Economies: Essays of Karl Polanyi,* ed. George Dalton. New York, 1968.

Polecritti, Cynthia L. *Preaching Peace in Renaissance Italy.* New York, 2000.

Polidori-Calamandrei, E. *Le vesti delle donne fiorentine nel Quattrocento.* Florence, 1924. Reprint, Rome, 1973.

Pope-Hennessy, John, and Keith Christiansen. "Secular Painting in Fifteenth-Century Tuscany: Birth Trays, Cassone Panels, and Portraits." *Metropolitan Museum of Art Bulletin* 38 (Summer 1980): 1–66.

Queller, Donald E., and Thomas F. Madden. "Father of the Bride: Fathers, Daughters, and Dowries in Late Medieval and Early Renaissance Venice." *Renaissance Quarterly* 46 (Winter 1993): 685–711.

Rabb, Theodore, and Jonathan Brown. "The Evidence of Art: Images and Meaning in History." *Journal of Interdisciplinary History* 17 (1986): 1–6.

Rainey, Ronald. "Sumptuary Legislation in Renaissance Florence." 2 vols. Ph.D. diss., Columbia University, 1985.

———. "Dressing Down the Dressed-Up: Reproving Feminine Attire in Renaissance Florence." In *Renaissance Society and Culture,* ed. John Monfasani and Ronald G. Musto. New York, 1991.

Repetti, Emanuele. *Dizionario geografico fisico storico della Toscana.* 6 vols. Florence, 1833.

Roach, Mary Ellen, and Joanne Bubolz Eicher, eds. *Dress, Adornment, and the Social Order.* New York, 1965.

Roche, Daniel. *La culture des apparences: Une histoire du vêtement XVIIe–XVIIIe siècle.* Paris, 1989.

Rocke, Michael J. "Il controllo dell'omossesualità a Firenze nel XV secolo: Gli ufficiali di notte." *Quaderni storici* 66 (1987): 701–23.

———. *Forbidden Friendships: Homosexuality and Male Culture in Renaissance Florence.* New York, 1996.

Rodolico, Niccolò. *I Ciompi: Una pagina di storia del proletariato operaio.* Florence, 1945. Reprint, Florence 1980.

———. *Il popolo minuto: Note di storia fiorentina (1343–1378).* Bologna, 1899. Reprint, Florence, 1968.

Roover, Raymond de. *The Rise and Decline of the Medici Bank 1397–1494.* Cambridge, 1963.

———. *San Bernardino of Siena and Saint Antonio of Florence: The Two Great Economic Thinkers of the Middle Ages.* Boston, 1967.

———. "Labor Conditions in Florence around 1400: Theory, Policy and Reality." In *Florentine Studies,* ed. Nicolai Rubinstein. Evanston, Ill., 1968.

Rosenthal, Elaine. "The Position of Women in Renaissance Florence: Neither Autonomy nor Subjection." In *Florence and Italy: Renaissance Studies in Honor of Nicolai Rubinstein,* ed. Peter Denley and Caroline Elam. London, 1988

Ross, Janet. *Lives of the Early Medici.* London, 1910.

Rubinstein, Nicolai, ed. *Florentine Studies: Politics and Society in Renaissance Florence.* Evanston, Ill., 1968.

Rutenburg, Victor. *Popolo e movimenti popolari nell' Italia del '300 e '400.* Translated by Gianpiero Borghini. Bologna, 1971.

Salvemini, Gaetano. *Magnati e popolani in Firenze dal 1280 al 1295.* Florence, 1899. Reprint, 1960.

Santini, Emilio. "Studi sull' antica costituzione del comune de Firenze." *Archivio storico italiano,* 5th ser., 25–26 (1900).

Sapori, A. "Gl'italiani in Polonia nel medioevo." *Archivio storico italiano,* 7th ser., 83 (1925): 125–55.

Scaramella, Gino, ed. *Il tumulto dei Ciompi, cronache e memorie.* Bologna, 1934.

Schevill, Ferdinand. *History of Florence.* New York, 1936.

Schneider, Jane. "Rumpelstiltskin's Bargain: Folklore and the Merchant Capitalist Intensification of Linen Manufacture in Early Modern Europe." In *Cloth and Human Experience,* ed. Annette B. Weiner and Jane Schneider. Washington, D.C., 1989.

Scott, Joan Wallach. "Gender: A Useful Category of Historical Analysis." *American Historical Review* 91 (1986): 1053–75.

———. *Gender and the Politics of History.* New York, 1988.

———. "Experience." In *Feminists Theorize the Political,* ed. Judith Butler and Joan W. Scott. New York, 1992.

Scott, Margaret. *Late Gothic Europe, 1400–1500.* London, 1980.

Sharpe, Pamela, ed. *Women's Work: The English Experience, 1650–1914.* London, 1998.

Shearman, John. *Andrea del Sarto.* 2 vols. Oxford, 1965.

Simmel, Georg. *Philosophie der Mode. Moderne Zeitfragen* 11 (1905): 5–41.

Simons, Pat. "Portraiture and Patronage in Quattrocento Florence with Special Reference to the Tornaquinci and Their Chapel in S. Maria Novella." Ph.D. thesis, University of Melbourne, 1985.

———. "Women in Frames: The Gaze, the Eye, the Profile in Renaissance Portraiture." *History Workshop* 25 (Spring 1988): 4–30.

———. "Alert and Erect: Masculinity in Some Italian Renaissance Portraits of Fathers and Sons." In *Gender Rhetorics,* ed. Richard C. Trexler. Binghamton, N.Y., 1994.

———. "Portraiture, Portrayal, and Idealization: Ambiguous Individualism in Representations of Renaissance Women." In *Language and Images of Renaissance Italy,* ed. Alison Brown. Oxford, 1995.

Simons, Pat, and F. W. Kent, eds. *Patronage, Art, and Society in Renaissance Italy.* Oxford, 1987.

Skinner, Patricia. "The Widow's Options in Medieval Southern Italy." In *Widowhood in Medieval and Early Modern Europe,* ed. Sandra Cavallo and Lyndan Warner. London, 1999.

Snyder, James. *Medieval Art: Painting–Sculpture–Architecture, Fourth–Fourteenth Century.* Englewood Cliffs, N.J., 1989.

Staley, Edgcumbe. *The Guilds of Florence.* 2d ed. London, 1906. Reprint, New York, 1967.

Starn, Randolph. "Seeing Culture in a Room for a Renaissance Prince." In *The New Cultural History,* ed. Lynn Hunt. Berkeley, Calif., 1989.

Stella, Alessandro. "La bottega e i lavoranti: approche des conditions de travail des Ciompi." *Annales: Economies, sociétés, civilisations* 44 (1989): 529–51.

———. *La Révolte des Ciompi: Les hommes, les lieux, le travail.* Paris, 1993.

Strocchia, Sharon. *Death and Ritual in Renaissance Florence.* Baltimore, 1992.

Travaglini, Carlo M. "Rigattieri e società romana nel Settecento." *Quaderni storici* 80 (Aug. 1992): 415–48.

Trexler, Richard C. "Le célibat à la fin du Moyen Ages: les religieuses de Florence." *Annales: Economies, sociétés, civilisations* 27 (1972): 1329–50.

———. *Public Life in Renaissance Florence.* New York, 1980. Reprint. Ithaca, N.Y., 1991.

———. "La prostitution florentine au XVe siècle: Patronages et clientèles," *Annales: Economies, sociétés, civilisations* 36 (1981): 983–1015.

———. "Neighbours and Comrades: The Revolutionaries of Florence, 1378." *Social Analysis* 4 (Dec. 1983): 53–106.

———. *The Women of Renaissance Florence.* Vol. 2 of *Power and Dependence in Renaissance Florence.* Binghamton, N.Y., 1993.

———. ed. *Persons in Groups: Social Behavior as Identity Formation in Medieval and Renaissance Europe.* Medieval and Renaissance Texts and Studies, vol. 36. Binghamton, N.Y., 1985.

———. ed. *Gender Rhetorics: Postures of Dominance and Submission in History.* Medieval and Renaissance Texts and Studies, vol. 113. Binghamton, N.Y., 1994.

[Il] Tumulto dei Ciompi. Convegno Internazionale di Studi (Firenze, 16–19 settembre 1979). Florence, 1981.

Vasaio, Maria Elena. "Il tessuto della virtù: Le zitelle di S. Eufemia e di S. Caterina dei Funari nella Controriforma." *Memoria: Rivista di storia delle donne* 11–12 (1984): 53–64.

Veblen, Thorstein. *The Theory of the Leisure Class.* 1899. Boston, 1973.

Wackernagel, Martin. *The World of the Florentine Renaissance Artist.* Translated by Alison Luchs. Princeton, N.J., 1981.

Warburg, Aby. *Gesammelte Schriften.* Leipzig, 1932.

Wardwell, Anne E. "The Stylistic Development of Fourteenth- and Fifteenth-Century Italian Silk Design." *Aachener Kunstblatter* 47 (1976–77): 177–226.

Weissman, Ronald F. E. *Ritual Brotherhood in Renaissance Florence.* New York, 1982.

———. "Taking Patronage Seriously." In *Patronage, Art, and Society in Renaissance Italy,* ed. F. W. Kent and Patricia Simons. Oxford, 1987.

———. "The Importance of Being Ambiguous: Social Relations, Individualism and Identity in Renaissance Florence." In *Urban Life in the Renaissance,* ed. Susan Zimmerman and Ronald F. E. Weissman. Newark, Del., 1989.

Weissman, Ronald F. E., and Susan Zimmerman, eds. *Urban Life in the Renaissance.* Newark, Del., 1989.

Welch, Evelyn S. *Art and Authority in Renaissance Milan.* New Haven, Conn., 1995.

Wiesner, Merry E. "Spinsters and Seamstressses." In *Rewriting the Renaissance,* ed. Margaret Ferguson, Maureen Quilligan, and Nancy Vickers. Chicago, 1986.

———. *Working Women in Renaissance Germany.* New Brunswick, N.J., 1986.

Woods-Marsden, Joanna. " 'Ritratto al Naturale': Questions of Realism and Idealism in Early Renaissance Portraits." *Art Journal* 46 (1987): 209–16.

———. *The Gonzaga of Mantua and Pisanello's Arthurian Frescoes.* Princeton, N.J., 1988.

———. *Renaissance Self-Portraiture.* New Haven, Conn., 1998.

Zdekauer, L. "Il dono del mattino e lo statuto più antico di Firenze." In *Miscellanea fiorentine di erudizione e storia.* 1886. Vol. 1. Reprint, Rome, 1978.

Zorzi, Andrea. "Aspetti e problemi dell'amministrazione della giustizia penale nella repubblica fiorentine." *Archivio storico italiano* 533 (1987): 446–64.

———. "The Judicial System in Florence in the Fourteenth and Fifteenth Centuries." In *Crime, Society and the Law in Renaissance Italy,* ed. Trevor Dean and K. J. P. Lowe. Cambridge, 1994.

Index

References to illustrations are printed in boldface type.

accessories (see also belts; decoration; footwear; headwear), 31, 36–38
Alamanni, Lena, 1–2, 117–19, 210
Alberti, Leon Battista, 78–80, 81–83, 85–86, 88, 131, 168, 190, 216, 282n. 7
Albizzi family, 73, 212; Giovanna degli (Tornabuoni), **iv**, 204, **213**, 297n. 19, 298n. 37
alessandrino. See colors
alla di là. See clothing: foreign
Andrea del Sarto, 36, 63, 253n. 9
Antoninus, Archbishop, 173–74
appraisers, 21, 135–36
"aristocratization," 4, 68, 137, 181
arti (see also guilds): Calimala, 15; Calzolai, 15, 17, 36, 55–56; Lana, 14–15, 20, 26, 28, 34, 36, 55, 243n. 15, 245n. 3; Medici, speziali e merciai, 17, 28, 36–37, 45, 48; Por Santa Maria, 18–19, 20, 28, 45, 51, 55, 246nn. 25, 26, 250n. 56, 257n. 75; Rigattieri e linaiuoli, 15, 17, 21–22, 23, 28–29, 36, 249nn. 47, 52; Seta, 15, 19–

21, 34, 37, 247n. 39, 248nn. 40, 41; Vaiai e pellicciai, 15, 34, 48–50
arti maggiori, 15, 18, 34, 35 (table 2.1)
arti mediani ("middling guilds"), 21
arti minori, 21–23, 25, 35–36 (table 2.1)
auctions, 21–22, 131, 249n. 45

bambagiai. See cotton-wool makers
Banchi, Andrea (see also silk: merchants), 20, 50, 267n. 8
Bandello, Matteo, 38
Barbaro, Francesco, 80, 264n. 14
Barberino, Francesco da, 45
Baron, Hans, 190
Barthes, Roland, 7–8, 147–49, 177, 244n. 31
Baskins, Cristelle, 86, 202
Bell, Quentin, 7, 159, 257n. 89, 266n. 50
belt-makers, 18, 44–46
belts, 46, 127, 190, 282n. 7
Bernardino of Siena (see also Franciscans; luxuria), 86, 186, 190, 292n. 50, 294nn. 72, 76
berrettai. See cap-makers
berretto, 152, **199**, 200

337